A CENTURY OF CRIMINAL JUSTICE

Perspectives on the Development of Canadian Law

by

MARTIN L. FRIEDLAND
Q.C., F.R.S.C.
Faculty of Law, University of Toronto

1984
CARSWELL LEGAL PUBLICATIONS
TORONTO, CANADA

Canadian Cataloguing in Publication Data

Friedland, M.L. (Martin Lawrence), 1932-
    A century of criminal justice

ISBN 0-459-36580-0

1. Criminal law — Canada — Addresses, essays, lectures.
2. Criminal justice, Administration of — Canada —
Addresses, essays, lectures. I. Title.

KE8809.F75 1984   345.71   C84-098764-1

PREFACE

The central theme of this collection of essays is the analysis of the development of the law. As stated in the first chapter on codification in the nineteenth century, "law reform is affected by a great number of factors apart from the merits of the proposals." Often, a "combination of politics, personalities and pressure groups" can affect the outcome. Canada has now embarked on a "comprehensive and accelerated review" of the criminal law, designed to lead to a new Criminal Code, and, no doubt, similar considerations will affect its progress.

All of the chapters deal with areas of law currently the subject of discussion and controversy. Most look at the law from an historical and comparative viewpoint. The chapters range from a discussion of codification, gun control, entrapment and national security to the constitutional division of power and the new Canadian Charter of Rights and Freedoms. The final chapter, "A Century of Criminal Justice", from which the title of this book has been taken, examines changes in criminal justice over the past 100 years and observes that because rights are now included in the Charter and thus entrenched in the Constitution it is not likely that there will be radical changes in criminal justice over the next 100 years.

Except for chapter 2, all the papers have been published separately elsewhere. I am grateful to the editors of those journals and collections for permission to use the material in this volume. In all cases the original material has been brought up to date.

I am indebted to the Donner Canadian Foundation for generously supporting my work on the process of change. Assistance was also given by the Solicitor-General's Department, Ottawa, for research relating to gun control and the constitutional division of power and by the McDonald Royal Commission on the R.C.M.P. for research on national security and entrapment. I was fortunate to have had the very able assistance at various times over the past few summers of three excellent research assistants, Gordon Cameron, Stephen Rosenhek and Paul Schabas, now all recent graduates of the University of Toronto Faculty of Law. Expert secretarial assistance was given by Julia Hall, Joyce Kawano, Gerry Naunheimer and Kathy O'Rourke.

I would like to thank Frank Iacobucci, now the Provost of the University of Toronto, but who was the Dean of Law when most of these papers were prepared, for his encouragement and support. A number of colleagues gave generously of their time and ideas in discussing the process of change. I would particularly like to thank John Ll.J. Edwards, J.R.S. Prichard, R.C.B. Risk, R.J. Sharpe and Stephen Waddams of the Faculty of Law, Peter Russell and Peter Solomon of the Department of Political Science and John Beattie of the Department of History, for their help and encouragement.

Librarians and archivists in Canada and England willingly assisted me in my research and I am indebted to the following libraries and archives: the Faculty of Law Library, the Robarts Library and the Centre of Criminology Library, all at the University of Toronto; the Institute of Criminolgy Library, the Squire Law Library and the University Library, all at Cambridge University; the Public Record Office and the British Library, London; and the Public Archives of Canada, Ottawa.

To all the above persons and institutions I am sincerely grateful.

May, 1984

M.L. Friedland
Faculty of Law
University of Toronto

CONTENTS

TABLE OF CASES

R. S. WRIGHT'S MODEL CRIMINAL CODE: A FORGOTTEN CHAPTER IN THE HISTORY OF THE CRIMINAL LAW*

1. INTRODUCTION

In 1870 Mr R. S. Wright, a thirty-one-year-old barrister, and fellow of Oriel College, Oxford, was asked by the Colonial Office to draft a criminal code for Jamaica which could serve as a model for all of the colonies.[1]

The Code of Criminal Law and Procedure which the future Mr Justice Wright subsequently produced has now been almost forgotten.[2] This is unfortunate because in many, if not most, respects it is a much better Code than either James Fitzjames Stephen's Draft Code of 1878[3] or the Royal Commissioners' Draft Code of 1879,[4] both of which are well known. The Commissioners' Code, which was primarily the work of Stephen,[5] was subsequently adopted (with various changes) by a large number of British colonies, including, of course, Canada.

---

* This paper was written while the author was a Visiting Fellow at the Institute of Criminology and Clare Hall, Cambridge, 1980, and was originally published in (1981) 1 Oxford Jour. of Legal Studies 307. I am grateful to Peter Glazebrook, Glanville Williams and the late Rupert Cross for reading an earlier version of this paper and making a number of very helpful comments.

1 Letter to R. S. Wright from the Colonial Office, dated 22 June, 1870: Public Record Office, Jamaica files, C.O. 137/454/6764.

2 Wright is not mentioned, for example, in Kadish's excellent article "Codifiers of the Criminal Law: Wechsler's Predecessors" (1978) 78 Col. L. Rev. at p. 1098; nor in M. E. Lang, *Codification in the British Empire and America* (Amsterdam 1924); J. Michael and H. Wechsler, "Historical Note" in *Criminal Law and its Administration* (Chicago 1940), at pp. 1284-6; Manchester, "Simplifying the Sources of the Law: James Fitzjames Stephen and the Codification of the Criminal Law of England and Wales" (1973) 2 Anglo-American L. Rev. at p. 527; L. Radzinowicz, *Sir James Fitzjames Stephen* (London 1957); nor in the valuable book based on the Irish University Press' British Parliamentary Papers Series, W. R. Cornish *et al, Crime and Law in Nineteenth Century Britain* (Dublin 1978). *Cf.* Glanville Williams, *Criminal Law,* 2nd ed (London 1961) who cites Wright's Code at p. 584, note 11; and Rupert Cross, "The Making of English Criminal Law: Macaulay" [1978] Crim. L. Rev. who refer to Wright's Code on p. 519.

3 Bill 178, Criminal Code (Indictable Offences) Bill, 1878.

4 *Report of the Royal Commission appointed to consider the law Relating to Indictable Offences* 1879, C 2345. The Commission consisted of Lord Blackburn (Chairman), Lush and Barry JJ. and J. F. Stephen, who became a judge during its deliberations.

5 J. F. Stephen, *A History of the Criminal Law of England* (London 1883), Vol. III, at p. 349: "By far the greater part of the Code and of the Report was my own composition."

During the 1880s and 90s, though, Wright's Code was the Model Code for the colonies — although, as we shall see, it was not adopted by any of the important ones — not even by Jamaica. The Code was, however, highly regarded by the Colonial Office, by the parliamentary draftsmen and by others[6] in England. In 1900 Sir Courtenay Ilbert,[7] the leading parliamentary draftsman, in a confidential memorandum to the Colonial Office,[8] compared Wright's Code with the Commissioners' Draft Code of 1879: "The two draft Codes are framed on different principles and different lines, and in the opinion of many, perhaps of most, competent authorities, the Jamaica draft is the better work of the two".

This article outlines the background to Wright's Code, discusses some of its features, and recounts its fate. The story tells us something about Wright, one of England's finest criminal lawyers, and about the Stephens: James Fitzjames, who worked with Wright on the Jamaica Code and later had his own rival code, and James Fitzjames' son, H. L. Stephen, who revised Wright's Code in 1900. Moreover, an understanding of Wright's Code will place Stephen's more authoritarian Code in its proper perspective. It will also tell us something about the nature of Canadian Society that accepted Stephen's Code in 1892. The whole story — one more sad tale in the politics of legislation — will have a familiar ring to those who have been or are now engaged in producing a new criminal code.

2. BACKGROUND TO THE CODE

The idea of producing a criminal code for the colonies came from Sir Henry Taylor, a then well-known literary figure who had been a powerful force in the Colonial Office for the previous half century.[9] Sir Henry, who was not a lawyer, had originally hoped to stimulate change in England itself. In 1868 he published a letter to the Prime Minister, Mr Gladstone, entitled "Crime Considered", in which he proposed a number of changes in the criminal law.[10] The Government was not interested in the proposals and so Sir Henry turned to a captive audience, the Crown Colonies.

6 *E.g.* Professor C. S. Kenny's *Outlines of Criminal Law*, first published in 1902 (Cambridge), had a large number of references to Wright's Code (see pp. 33, 130, 145, 148, 238, 263 and 306). The 19th and last edition published in 1966 and edited by J. W. C. Turner still had a solitary reference to the Code in the bigamy section (at p. 230).

7 1841-1924: see *DNB* 1922-1930.

8 Memo dated 27 April, 1900: Colonies General files, C.O. 323/460/8180.

9 *DNB;* J. W. Cell, *British Colonial Administration in the Mid-Nineteenth Century: The Policy-Making Process* (New Haven 1970) at p. 23. See also Taylor's 2 volume *Autobiography* 1800-1875 (London 1885). He is now known for his autobiography and his study, *The Statesman,* reprinted in 1927 with an introduction by Harold Laski, which used James Stephen, James Fitzjames' father, as the model. After his retirement in 1872 he maintained his involvement with the Code: *Autobiography*, at pp. 292 *et seq.*

10 See his *Autobiography*, at pp. 280-2. An article by Sir Henry, "The Habitual Criminals'

In 1870, in a somewhat naive document entitled "Some Considerations preliminary to the Preparation of a Penal Code for the Crown Colonies",[11] Sir Henry set out a number of the innovative measures he had earlier advocated. These were primarily concerned with punishment, and included a form of habitual criminal legislation (which he called 'protective imprisonment') and provisions for punishing drunkenness. He also proposed that evidence of previous convictions should be admitted *before* the verdict.

Mr R. S. Wright was asked to undertake the task, starting with the draft of a Code for Jamaica, "as Sir John Grant, the Governor of Jamaica, is now in this Country, and is ready to afford any assistance in his power".[12] In particular, the Governor was willing to provide the draftsman with five hundred pounds from Jamaica funds. This was for a Penal Code; the drafting of a Code of Procedure and the adaptation of both Codes for use in other colonies was left to subsequent and separate arrangements.

The Colonial Office then sent a circular[13] to all the colonies informing them that

> Her Majesty's Government have directed the preparation of a draft Penal Code for the Colony of Jamaica, with the intention that it should be subsequently adapted to the circumstances of each of the other Crown Colonies respectively, and of such Colonies, not being Crown Colonies, as may desire to avail themselves of it, and that it should be submitted to their respective Legislatures for consideration, with a view to its enactment.

The circular from the Colonial Secretary then set out the financial arrangements that had been made and went on to state:

> I am desirous to be informed whether you have any reason to doubt that the Legislature of the Colony under your Government will appreciate the assistance intended to be afforded them, and be willing to incur a moderate expenditure on account of it.

The replies from the colonies were not encouraging.[14] Lord Carnarvon, the Colonial Secretary, was not surprised, stating in a note to

---

Bill", based on the letter was published in (1869) 79 Fraser's Magazine 661. The actual letter dated 10 Dec., 1868 can be found in the Gladstone Papers, British Library, Add. MSS 44417, ff 29 and 252.

11 Dated 20 May, 1870, appended to Drafts of a Criminal Code and Code of Criminal Procedure for the Island of Jamaica, presented to Parliament by Command of Her Majesty, 9 Aug., 1877, C 1893. The Code is not included in the Irish University Press' British Parliamentary Papers Series.

12 Letter to R. S. Wright from the Colonial Office dated 22 June, 1870: C.O. 137/454/6764.

13 Circular from Lord Kimberley, the Colonial Secretary, dated 20 Feb., 1871: C.O. 137/478/7990.

14 Memo to Lord Carnarvon from H. T. Holland, later the Colonial Secretary (Lord Knutsford), dated 9 July, 1874: C.O. 137/478/7990. The actual replies have not been located.

the file: "I would doubt whether many Colonies will be inclined to subscribe. They will I apprehend get nearly all they want for nothing."[15]

How is it that the Colonial Office chose Wright to undertake this important work? Wright was not well known as a lawyer in 1870. He had published a book of ancient Greek poetry[16] as well as a book of Greek prose,[17] but his book on conspiracy was not published until 1873[18] and his book on possession, which he produced with Sir Frederick Pollock, did not appear until 1888.[19] He was, however, already well known to the Colonial Office, having produced for them in 1867 a significant and lengthy Report on Colonial Prisons.[20] This Report, which like his Criminal Code has been forgotten, analyzed replies from the colonies concerning their prisons and also summarized "for the benefit of Colonial Authorities, the chief results of the experience of this country in the management of Criminals".[21] Although he did not visit any of the colonies, he inspected a number of prisons in England and France.[22] Moreover, he had obtained the assistance of Florence Nightingale on questions relating not only to health matters, but also to prison construction. "I send you," he wrote to her (in a light-hearted way) on 23 October 1865,[23] "a specimen of the materials sent home by colonial prison authorities, with the endorsement of a colonial governor: Question: What is the mode of treating lunatic or maniacal prisoners? Answer: Maniacles is not nor ever has been in use in this prison."

The Prison Report contains a valuable description of the state of

---

15 Dated 10 July, 1874: C.O. 137/478/7990.

16 *Golden Treasury of Ancient Greek Poetry* (Oxford 1866), subsequently revised by Evelyn Abbott (1889).

17 *Golden Treasury of Greek Prose* (Oxford 1870), in collaboration with J. E. L. Shadwell.

18 *Law of Conspiracies and Agreements* (London 1873); reprinted 1980 by Wildy & Sons, with a preface by J. M. B. Crawford.

19 *An Essay on Possession in the Common Law* (Oxford 1888). It was "a composite, not a joint work" (preface). Wright did the part, nearly half of the whole, relating to possession in respect of criminal offences against property. In addition to the above books, Wright published in 1884, together with Henry Hobhouse, *An Outline of Local Government and Local Taxation in England and Wales* (London), which was based on two elaborate memoranda on local government written by Wright for two M.P.'s, W. Rathbone and S. Whitbread in 1877 and privately circulated.

20 Digest and Summary of Information Respecting Prisons in the Colonies, supplied by the Governors of Her Majesty's Colonial Possessions, in answer to Mr Secretary Cardwell's Circular Dispatches of 16 and 17 Jan., 1865, C 3961, 1867, hereafter cited as "Prison Report".

21 Prison Report, extract from letter from R. S. Wright dated 3 Jan., 1867.

22 Colonies General files, C.O. 323/276/7314.

23 Sir Edward Cook, *The Life of Florence Nightingale* (London 1913), vol 2, at p. 60. The letter can be found in the Nightingale papers, British Library, Add. MSS 45799, f 156.

colonial prisons at the time.[24] Health conditions at Kingston Penitentiary in Canada, to take one example, are strongly criticized (no doubt influenced by Miss Nightingale). After outlining some of the sanitary conditions, he writes[25]: "It is not strange under these conditions that typhoid fever has prevailed uninterruptedly since the beginning of 1862, producing sixteen deaths in 1863 and twenty-one in 1864 (out of 352 cases), while diarrhoea has been so prevalent that 206 cases were admitted to hospital in 1864. ..."

His emphasis in the Report on deterrence as the primary function of punishment for those sentenced to penal servitude is reflected in his later Code.[26] Within the limitations of this philosophy, which was current at the time[27] and called for separation of prisoners from each other, silence, and particular types of hard labour such as the treadwheel, crank or shot drill,[28] the Report contains many sound recommendations. It recommends, for example, the segregation of classes of prisoners (juveniles from adults, untried from convicted, civil from criminal, first offenders from repeaters, crimes of violence from crimes of fraud)[29] and that fines be

---

24 Including the Imperial Convict Establishments in the colonies. It is surprising that the Irish University Press' British Parliamentary Papers Series does not include this Report in one of its 39 volumes on Prisons, Transportation, and Penal Servitude.

25 Prison Report, at p. 56.

26 But in his Code he allowed the "widest discretion" in sentencing first offenders: Jamaica Code, at p. 102. And as a judge he was well-known for his leniency: see The Times, 15 Aug., 1904 ("mercy was largely mingled with justice in his sentences"); C. Chapman, From the Bench (London 1932) at pp. 46-7 ('apostle of mercy'); C. Biron, Without Prejudice (London 1936) at p. 160.

27 See the Report from the Select Committee of the House of Lords on the Present State of Discipline in Gaols and Houses of Correction, 1863, vol IX. The chairman was Lord Carnarvon who became Colonial Secretary on 6 July 1866, while Wright was preparing his Prison Report. See also the view of Chief Justice Cockburn appended to the Report of the Commission appointed to inquire into the operation of the Acts relating to Transportation and Penal Servitude, 1863, vol XXI, C 6457. The Royal Commission Report itself is less severe in the punishment imposed, but would impose it for a longer period. By implementing both reports England therefore had harsh punishments for lengthy periods. See generally S. & B. Webb, English Prisons Under Local Government (London 1922, reprinted with an introduction by Leon Radzinowicz, 1963); M. Ignatieff, A Just Measure of Pain: the Penitentiary in the Industrial Revolution 1750-1850 (London 1978); A. G. L. Shaw, Convicts and the Colonies: A Study of Penal Transportation from Great Britain and Ireland to Australia and other parts of the British Empire (London 1966).

28 Wright justified this form of labour (at p. 88) on the basis that "labour at the wheel, the crank, or shot drill is capable of adaptation to varieties of strength, is compatible with health, and is known to be keenly felt and ill spoken of, more than any form of industrial labour. ..."

29 Prison Report, at p. 67. See the Report of the Commissioners appointed to Inquire into the Workings of the Penal Servitude Acts, C 2368, 1879.

"made payable by instalments according to the rate of earnings of the offender".[30]

Wright concluded his Prison Report with a comment on the necessity of a review of the criminal law:

> The criminal laws of different colonies are very various. Apart from the fact of the existence in several colonies of some dangerous if not wholly objectionable laws,[31] it would seem that a revision of ordinances affecting the length and nature of sentences is a necessary preliminary to the establishment of a good penal system.[32]

Wright's views were thus consistent with, and perhaps influenced, Sir Henry Taylor's proposals a few years later.

Henry Taylor's private correspondence with Wright[33] shows that Taylor had assumed that Wright would be too busy to undertake the task. Taylor wrote to Wright in 1870 asking for names of young barristers who might undertake the work. Wright gave some suggestions and then added, "Failing all the other men, I should like to be added, if you think I could do the work, and if it can wait for two months to be commenced." Wright had already thought about the subject stating, "I have notions as to the manner in which a criminal code should be drawn, and I should be glad to test them by an experiment at large." Taylor quickly said "yes".

One can understand, then, why Wright was asked to draft the Criminal Code. But how did it come about that he did the Prison Report? Once again, it was because of excellent work that he had previously done for the Colonial Office. The Permanent Under-Secretary of State, Frederic Rogers, wrote on 30 July 1864[34] asking the then twenty-five year-old Wright, not yet a member of the Bar, to undertake the Prison Report because of "the valuable assistance which you have rendered to this Department in conducting an inquiry into the state of the Colonial Hospitals and Lunatic Asylums and suggesting the reforms required in those institutions. . . ."

The Colonial Office records do not show how it was that they had heard of Wright in the first place, but it is likely that three of the key figures in the Colonial Office at the time would have known him. Wright had been a brilliant classical scholar at Balliol College, winning a number of important prizes, and had been elected a Fellow of Oriel in 1861. Rogers, the Permanent Under-Secretary,[35] had had a similar career: he too had been a Craven scholar and a Fellow of Oriel. Edward Cardwell,[36] the

---

30 Prison Report, at p. 89.

31 Citing the whipping laws in some parts of the West Indies and Australia.

32 Prison Report, at pp. 88-9.

33 Henry Taylor correspondence, Bodleian Library, Oxford.

34 Colonies General file, C.O. 323/276/7314.

35 1811-1889. Later Baron Blachford. See *DNB*.

36 1813-1886. See *DNB*.

Colonial Secretary, had been a Fellow of Balliol and was the MP for Oxford. Finally, Sir Henry Taylor had become friendly a few years earlier[37] with Benjamin Jowett, then a Fellow and Tutor, and later the Master, of Balliol, and Wright had been a favourite pupil of Jowett's.[38]

3. PREPARATION OF THE CODE

Wright wrote to the Colonial Office in June 1871, a year after he had been asked to undertake the task, that "considerable progress has been made in the work . . . and that another twelve months will probably suffice for its completion".[39] Like most law reformers he underestimated the time that would be required to complete the task. He submitted his Code in January 1874 stating that "The work proved to be more onerous than I anticipated".[40]

It is surprising that Wright had made much progress on the Code in the first year because during that year he was the Secretary to the Royal Commission on the Truck System[41] (i.e. payment to workers in kind or requiring purchases, often at excessive prices, at the "company store"). The Commission's lengthy Report, which has been described as "one of the most comprehensive and intelligent social inquiries of the Victorian period",[42] and for which over 500 persons were interviewed, owed a great deal to Wright. The Commission under the chairmanship of Charles (later Lord) Bowen[43] (a lifelong friend of Wright's) acknowledged "the remarkable assistance afforded . . . by its secretary, Mr Wright . . . The . . . labour of the Commission has been more than shared with him . . ."[44] Wright thus came to the task of preparing a Code with considerable experience in conducting major social inquiries.[45]

The Colonial Office had attempted to collect documents and statistics for Wright to use in preparing the Jamaica Code. According to Sir

---

37 *Autobiography of Henry Taylor 1800-1875* (London 1885) vol II, at p. 195.

38 *DNB* for Wright. See also G. Faber, *Jowett: a portrait with background* (London 1957). Jowett died in Wright's home in 1893.

39 Letter dated 15 June, 1871: C.O. 137/461/5942.

40 Letter dated 12 Jan., 1874: C.O. 137/478/395.

41 Report of the Commissioners appointed to Inquire into The Truck System, 1871, C 326, appointed by the Truck Commission Act, 1870.

42 G. W. Hilton, *The Truck System, including a History of the British Truck Acts, 1465-1960* (Cambridge 1960), at p. 132. See also p. 24 describing the night Wright spent at a colliery observing people line up at the company store.

43 See H. S. Cunningham, *Lord Bowen* (London 1897), at pp. 118-121, describing the Commission.

44 At p. XLVIII of the Report.

45 A further inquiry that Wright had earlier undertaken was in 1866 as an Assistant Commissioner for the Schools Inquiry Commission: see the General Reports by Assistant Commissioners for the Schools Inquiry Commission, at pp. 1867-68.

Henry Taylor, "what should be endeavoured is to ascertain the results of *changes* in Penal Law; that is, the effect of one punishment for a particular offence compared with the effect of another".[46] Sir Henry drafted lengthy requests for such information to the India Office and, through the Foreign Office, to various European countries, as well as to the United States.[47] Not surprisingly, the replies were not as helpful as the Colonial Office would have liked. Lord Merrivale of the India Office simply stated: "No special report on the working of the Penal Code has been received in this office, but no complaint having been made of its provisions it is believed to have been successful in its operation".[48] The reply from Washington was more discouraging[49]:

> I conceive that the only way of giving a satisfactory answer to the questions propounded by the Colonial Office would be by sending a special agent to the capitals of the different States, where he could himself go through the Statute Book and extract the substance of the Penal Law.

The writer adds, unnecessarily, "but this would be a work of great labour and duration and would involve considerable expense".

Wright eventually received a copy of Livingston's Code[50] produced for Louisiana in 1828, but never adopted there, of Field's New York Code,[51] and a number of European Codes. The European Code that appears to have been of the greatest interest to Wright was the North German Penal Code which had just recently been published. This is consistent with the growing interest in England in German scholarship at the time.[52] The Code was translated into English[53] for Wright and was cited by him on a number of occasions, particularly in his discussion of insanity. Wright's Code, in his own words,[54] "attempts to reproduce with amendments the English Criminal Law", but he spread his net widely in order to reproduce what he considered the best possible Code.

James Fitzjames Stephen played a role in revising the completed Code. The Colonial Office took the view that it would not be "satisfactory to send it out to the Colony for adoption without some revision".[55] Neither the officials of the Colonial Office nor the Law Officers of the

---

46 Appendix to Wright's Jamaica Code, at p. 117.

47 C.O. 137/454/6764.

48 C.O. 137/453/8439.

49 C.O. 137/453/10732.

50 See Kadish, "Codifiers of the Criminal Law: Wechsler's Predecessors" (1978) 78 Col. L. Rev. at pp. 1098, 1099 *et seq.*

51 *Ibid,* at pp. 1130 *et seq.*

52 See C. H. S. Fifoot, *Judge and Jurist in the Reign of Victoria* (London 1959), at p. 11.

53 C.O. 137/461/2203 and 2885.

54 Jamaica Criminal Code, at p. 96.

55 Memo from Henry Holland dated 17 Jan., 1874: C.O. 137/478/572.

Crown had the time to undertake the task. "The best man to do this work", the Colonial Office memorandum went on to say,[56] "would be Mr Fitzjames Stephen. He would, I have reason to believe, take a fee of Five Hundred Guineas, but not less".[57] Five hundred pounds would have been a large sum for Stephen considering that around 1876 his income from his profession was only £3,000 or £4,000 a year.[58] (Stephen, it should be noted, was married and at that time had eight children;[59] Wright was a bachelor and remained so until after he became a judge.) The Colonial Office, however, was prepared to pay only two hundred pounds. They wanted Stephen to "assume the accuracy of the Draft in so far forth as it professes to do no more than Digest",[60] and to direct his attention to those provisions "not conforming to the English criminal law, but designed to introduce improvements".[61]

Stephen accepted the arrangement and submitted his Report on the Code nine months later.[62] Unfortunately this Report is no longer in the file, but from Stephen's letters, Wright's replies[63] and other documents, it is possible to piece together what Stephen's views were. He made a number of objections to particular sections of Wright's draft, for example, the sections on insanity and attempts, and also four general criticisms. In the first place Stephen wanted illustrations to be used in the Code, as they were in the Indian Codes. Wright was willing to concede this point:[64] "While retaining my own opinion, I do not contend against Mr Stephen's authority." It should be noted, however, that Stephen did not use illustrations when he drafted his own Code a few years later.[65]

Stephen also objected to what he considered to be the over-elaboration of parts of the draft. Wright firmly defended his approach; he

---

56   *Ibid.* Wright had been informed in Nov., 1873 that they were considering Stephen for this task: letter from Henry Taylor, C.O. 137/478/572. Wright had sent a copy of part of a "rough draft" of his Code to Stephen in Aug., 1873: C.O. 137/475/8170.

57   Letter dated 16 Jan., 1874 from Henry Holland to Henry Taylor: C.O. 137/478/572.

58   See John Roach, "Sir James Fitzjames Stephen, A Study of his Thought and Life" (1953, unpublished Cambridge Ph.D. thesis), at p. 260.

59   See Table of the Stephen Family appended to Radzinowicz, *Sir James Fitzjames Stephen,* at p. 67.

60   Letter to J. F. Stephen from R. G. W. Herbert dated 19 Jan., 1874: C.O. 137/478/395.

61   *Ibid.*

62   Letter from Stephen dated 26 Oct., 1874: C.O. 137/478/12358.

63   Particularly Wright's lengthy letter dated 4 Nov., 1874 in reply to Stephen's letter of 26 Oct., 1874: C.O. 137/478/12758.

64   *Ibid.*

65   See J. F. Stephen, *History of the Criminal Law of England* (London 1883), vol 3, at p. 304: "A criminal code drawn in the style of the India Penal Code could never be passed through Parliament, and even if it could I do not think English judges and lawyers would accept and carry out so novel a method of legislating".

wanted to supply the judges with more concrete answers than Stephen, who was willing to leave greater scope to the judges. Wright stated in his reply to Stephen's memorandum[66]:

> the great bulk of those special provisions to which Mr Stephen's objection is applied in his remarks on particular passages of the Draft are in my judgment essential to the safe working of such a code. Things cannot be made simpler than they are, and law is not and never can be simple in all its parts. If a particular provision will be necessary to meet a case when it arises, it is in my judgment no justification for omitting such a provision that the case is extraordinary or unusual, so long as it cannot be called unnatural or very extreme; as a section would be (e.g.) which should provide for such a case as that of the Siamese twins. If a particular provision, although not absolutely necessary, is yet right and not such as to be obvious, so that a judge who has to supply it without much time for consideration is likely to be puzzled in its absence, it ought to be supplied for him.

In particular, Wright's Code supplied detailed rules on when one person was under a duty to supply another with necessaries of life, and on when justifiable force may be used. In the latter case, Wright argued:[67] "There is no civil code in existence from which a man can learn when he may or may not strike a blow. Failing such a code it seems to me essential that the Criminal Code should tell him."

Stephen's third objection was with respect to Wright's "very general propositions about the mental elements of crime".[68] Wright had adopted the technique, which one now finds in the American Model Penal Code and the codes based upon it, of carefully defining the mental elements required for the various provisions:[69]

> A code without general definitions of general elements would miss the greatest advantage of codification. I cannot suppose that Mr Stephen means what some of his expressions . . . seem to imply, that definitions of intention, negligence etc. should be repeated at length in the definition of each particular crime.

What Stephen really meant, as we can see from his own Code of 1878,[70] was that these terms should be left undefined.

Finally, Stephen complained of the overall arrangement of Wright's draft. Wright's plan, "the result", as he says, "of many trials"[71] was to have

---

66 C.O. 137/478/12758.

67 *Ibid.*

68 *Ibid.* Wright here is quoting from Stephen's memo.

69 *Ibid.* Wright was critical of Field's New York Code because "it seldom defines the elements of a crime": see the Jamaica Code at p. 98.

70 Bill 178, Criminal Code (Indictable Offences) Bill, 1878. The same lack of definition is found in his 1874 Homicide Bill (No. 315). Perhaps Stephen was referring to Wright when, in giving evidence before the House of Commons Select Committee on the Bill (at p. 14) he stated in reply to the chairman, Lowe: "I was not at Oxford; I have noticed that some members of your distinguished university have some notion about definitions which I could not follow".

71 Wright's letter, 4 Nov., 1874: C.O. 137/478/12758.

"general provisions common to all or many kinds of crimes . . . collected in Part I", then in Part II to divide the crimes into "groups, each of which forms a title". "Each group commences with the names and punishments of all the crimes forming the group, proceeds to define those crimes severally, and lastly prescribes any special limitations subject to which the general provisions of Part I are to be understood for the purposes of this group."[72] The arrangement was a clever one and flowed from Wright's decision to define his terms in Part I: "it constantly refers every subject to the general principles, thereby conducing to consistency, and, in my judgment, to ultimate clearness, though at the cost of some turning over of pages". There was an indication in the text every time a word which had been specially defined was used.

Wright's Code may well have provoked Stephen into attempting to draft his own. It was precisely at the time he was completing his memorandum on Wright's Code that, according to his letters, he resolved to draft a penal code and a code of criminal procedure.[73] His letters show that in October 1874 he decided to convert the second edition of his book, *A General View of the Criminal Law of England,* first published 1863, into a code or digest, a task which was completed several years later and published in the spring of 1877.[74] Stephen was, of course, already strongly in favour of codification;[75] he had drafted a number of important codes for India and, at the time he was working on Wright's Code, was hoping to be appointed the legal member of an English Codification Commission, which, however, was never set up.[76]

How were the differences between Stephen and Wright to be resolved? Stephen had suggested a conference and the Colonial Office requested Stephen and Wright "to confer and state jointly how far they are agreed and on what points they agree to differ".[77] When we have this statement", a Colonial Office memorandum states,[78] "we must decide in some rough way between these two great lawyers whose views are to prevail".

---

72 *Ibid.*

73 Leslie Stephen, *The Life of Sir James Fitzjames Stephen* (London 1895), at pp. 376-7.

74 *A Digest of the Criminal Law (Crimes and Punishment)* (London 1877). The second edition of his General View was published in 1890.

75 See J. F. Stephen, "Codification in India and England", *Fortnightly Review,* Dec., 1872, at pp. 644-672.

76 See Leslie Stephen's biography of his brother; L. Radzinowicz, Selden Society Lecture, *Sir James Fitzjames Stephen* (London 1957); and the unpublished 1953 Ph.D. thesis by John Roach, "Sir James Fitzjames Stephen". Stephen's papers are in the University Library, Cambridge, Add. MSS 7349.

77 Memo from E. Fairfield dated 31 Oct., 1874: C.O. 137/478/12358.

78 *Ibid.*

A few months later Stephen wrote to the Colonial Office:[79] "I am happy to say that we speedily arrived at an agreement upon most of [the points of difference]". But there were still a number of significant disagreements[80] which they agreed to "submit to the judgment of the Secretary of State as being matters of policy". The differences were put to Lord Carnarvon in a lengthy memorandum prepared by an Assistant Under-Secretary of State,[81] which included the permanent official's own observations. Not surprisingly, the Minister, for the most part, accepted the views of his permanent official.

The points in dispute boiled down to two questions as to the form of the Code and nine questions relating to specific provisions.[82] Some of the differences in specific sections will be discussed later in this chapter. The two general points were with respect to illustrations and the arrangement of the Code. It will be recalled that on the question of illustrations Wright had given way to "Mr Stephen's authority". In this round Wright reverted to his original position that illustrations were unnecessary. But Lord Carnarvon agreed with Stephen and was "prepared to accept the innovation" because of "the circumstances of Jamaica and of the other Colonies in which I hope the Code will be applied".[83] As to the arrangement of the Code, Lord Carnarvon was prepared to accept Wright's approach but noted that "on general grounds I incline to agree with Mr F. Stephen".

Lord Carnarvon did not decide the points in dispute until about two years after Wright and Stephen had agreed to disagree. In the meantime, Wright had been asked to undertake a Code of Procedure, and it is likely that the Colonial Office wanted to see that draft before finally deciding on the Code of Criminal Law.

The Code of Procedure for Jamaica was drafted by Wright and submitted to the Colonial Office in November 1876,[84] this time within one year after he was officially asked to do it.[85] (He was paid five hundred pounds for this task because his earlier labour had been "much

---

79 Letter dated Jan., 1875: C.O. 137/480/613.

80 Letter from Wright dated 31 May, 1875: C.O. 137/480/6005.

81 Undated memo from J. Bramston: C.O. 137/480/613.

82 In addition there were 15 questions as to particular parts of the Code in which Sir Henry Taylor dissented from Wright and Stephen.

83 Memo from Lord Carnarvon dated 16 April, 1877: C.O. 137/480/613.

84 Letter dated 6 Nov., 1876: C.O. 137/482/13418, reproduced at the end of Wright's Jamaica Code.

85 Letter dated 24 Nov., 1875: C.O. 137/480/11978. Wright replied (Nov. 25) that "more than a year ago Sir Henry Taylor informed me that such a proposal was in contemplation, and I have already made considerable progress with the work. . . .": C.O. 137/480/12946.

undervalued"[86].) No outside expert was asked to review the Code, which dealt not only with offences under the Criminal Code, but also with what was referred to as "police" procedure. To a considerable extent the Code of Procedure was based on the Indian Procedure Code which Wright felt contained "most of the elements necessary for a completely satisfactory system of procedure."[87]

A number of innovations are contained in the Code of Procedure including the appointment of a public prosecutor, a provision for examining accused persons, and rights of appeal. Wright simply noted in his letter to the Colonial Office[88] that "Substantially similar provisions have been adopted in most other countries, including India". The provision for full-time public prosecutors caused some concern in Jamaica and so in Wright's final draft he permitted "temporary" appointments.[89]

The accused was not to be allowed to give evidence under oath, but there was a mandatory provision with respect to his examination by the court. The accused's answers were not to be subject to a charge of perjury, nor was there to be a penalty for failure to answer, but the accused's answers or his failure to answer were to be admissible in evidence.[90]

Wright's Code provided for a wide right of appeal by the accused — and even a right of appeal by the prosecutor against sentence, or against an acquittal "by way of an application for a new trial, whenever the judge certifies that, in his opinion, the jury have perversely acquitted the accused person".[91] In addition, there were sections providing for less than unanimous verdicts[92] (eleven out of twelve in murder and other serious cases; six out of seven in other cases), giving the court extensive powers of amendment and of correcting errors,[93] giving the court the "power of its own motion to call or recall any competent person as a witness, and to examine him in such manner as it thinks fit",[94] and requiring the prosecutor to provide the accused prior to the trial with a copy of the depositions taken at the preliminary inquiry and also notice of any

---

86 Dispatch to the Governor of Jamaica, 13 July, 1874 asking for approval: C.O. 137/478/ 7990. One year later a second dispatch was sent out because no reply had yet been received from Jamaica.

87 Letter dated 6 Nov., 1876.

88 *Ibid.*

89 S. 76 of the Code. See letter dated 26 July, 1877: C.O. 137/485/9651, set out at the back of Wright's Jamaica Code.

90 Ss. 101-102 of the Code.

91 S. 47.

92 S. 24.

93 See *e.g.,* ss. 17 and 23.

94 S. 100.

additional evidence proposed to be adduced at the trial.[95] Further, the Code required the Supreme Court judges to meet at least once a year to consider the operation of the Code and to regulate "so far as appears to them practicable and expedient, the standard and kind of punishments to be inflicted for crimes within the limits prescribed by the Criminal Code or this Code, with especial reference to any crime or class of crimes appearing to be more than ordinarily prevalent for the time being."[96]

There was another provision relating to the admissibility of previous convictions that had the tell-tale number 103A, showing that it was a late addition to the Code. Wright had not included in his Code the suggestion found in Sir Henry Taylor's 1870 Memorandum that evidence of previous convictions should be admitted *before* the verdict. Sir Henry scrutinized Wright's draft and wrote to him about the omission.[97] Wright replied:[98] "I confess that I cannot at present see the way to going the whole length with you, but I will carefully reconsider the question". Wright then set out a draft clause "supposing your view to be adopted". Henry Taylor continued to press for its inclusion: "I attach a good deal of importance to it", he wrote to the Permanent Under-Secretary.[99] The Colonial Office documents do not indicate whether the decision to include it, which did considerable harm to the acceptability of the Codes, was taken with or without Wright's concurrence. However it came about, Wright supported the provision when Jamaica later rejected that particular section.[100]

Both the Code of Criminal Law and the Code of Procedure were finalized in July, 1877[101] with the "alterations desired by the Secretary of State". Sir Henry then suggested to the Colonial Office[102] that "if, instead of printing it as hitherto for the office, it were to be presented for Parliament a great addition would be made to its opportunities of usefulness. It would become acceptable to British and other Jurists and Writers and Legislators. . . ." Sir Henry still wanted the Code he fathered to influence the law in England. The Codes were presented to Parliament in early 1878, with a note on the inside page stating: "The first of the Draft Codes in-

---

95 S. 21.

96 S. 75.

97 Letter dated 7 Nov., 1876: C.O. 137/482/13418.

98 Letter dated 9 Nov., 1876: C.O. 137/482/13418.

99 Letter from Taylor to R. G. W. Herbert, dated 21 Nov., 1876: C.O. 137/482/13418.

100 Letter from Wright dated 8 Jan., 1880: C.O. 137/498/350: "I regret the omission of clause 103A (relating to giving evidence of former convictions); but probably it ought not to be pressed in view of the strong and general feeling against it which the late Attorney General's report shows to exist in Jamaica."

101 Letter from Wright dated 3 July, 1877 and 26 July, 1877: C.O. 137/485/8235 and 9651, set out at the back of Wright's Jamaica Code.

102 Letter dated 5 July, 1877: C.O. 137/485/8235.

cluded in this Paper (the Draft Criminal Code) was revised by Sir James Fitzjames Stephen, QC, KCSI, 1874-5".

4. CODIFICATION IN ENGLAND

Wright's Code appeared, therefore, just prior to the first reading of the bill to give effect to Stephen's Code in May 1878.[103] Wright's Code does not appear to have been mentioned, however, in the Parliamentary debates on Stephen's Code nor in the Royal Commissioners' Report of 1879 or the debates on it, but it is likely that Wright's Code was used as a standard by the permanent government officials to judge Stephen's Code. We have already seen that Ilbert, who was, it should be said, a good friend of Wright's, thought more highly of Wright's Code than of Stephen's or the Commissioners' Codes. Ilbert revealed in a memorandum in 1900:[104]

> The Commissioners' Code, notwithstanding the high authority of its framers, especially of the late Sir James Fitzjames Stephen, was found on examination to require material alterations both in form and in substance, and this is probably the reason why it was not carried further in Parliament.

Then in a footnote Ilbert states, "I can speak with knowledge on this point, because the draft was referred confidentially to the late Sir Francis Reilly,[105] with whom I worked upon it. Sir James Fitzjames Stephen was a great writer on law, but he was not a great draftsman, and he was not very tolerant of criticism". Ilbert expressed a similar, but somewhat more tactful, view[106] shortly after Stephen died, when he reviewed Stephen's work as a legislator in an article in the *Law Quarterly Review:*[107]

> Fitzjames Stephen was a Cyclopean builder. He hurled together huge blocks of rough hewn law. . . . Whenever the work of codifying the English criminal law is again taken seriously in hand, it is doubtful whether the admirable Penal Code which Mr Justice

---

103 See Cross, "The Making of English Criminal Law: Sir James Fitzjames Stephen" [1978] Crim. L. Rev. at pp. 652, 657.

104 Memo dated 27 April, 1900: C.O. 323/460/8180.

105 Reilly's negative views on Stephen's own Bill of 1878 can be found in a confidential memo to the Lord Chancellor dated 6 Dec., 1877: Lord Chancellor's Office files: L.C.O. 1/42. Whether Stephen ever knew of the role Reilly and Ilbert played is not known. But Stephen later had some harsh things to say about Ilbert in a letter to Lady Grant Duff dated 20 Feb., 1882 after Ilbert was appointed to the position Stephen had occupied in India: "I do not feel specially flattered by Ilbert's appointment. He is not a man of any particular eminence, and practically I know little or nothing about him." Cambridge University Library, Add. MSS 7349.

106 For a similar view of Stephen's qualities as a draftsman see James Bryce, *Studies in History and Jurisprudence* (Oxford 1901), Vol. 1 at p. 129. Bryce was a contemporary of Wright's at Oxford and won the Arnold Prize the year after Wright won it. See also Leslie Stephen, *The Life of Sir James Fitzjames Stephen* (London 1895) at pp. 281-2.

107 'Sir James Stephen as a Legislator' (1894) 10 L.Q. Rev. at pp. 222, 224-5.

Wright drew for Jamaica would not afford a better foundation to build upon than either the Indian Penal Code or the Judges' Bill of 1879.

Not only was there doubt about the quality of Stephen's work in the minds of a number of influential persons within the civil service, but there were those who thought that a more gradual approach to codification was to be preferred.

During the period when the Government was trying to decide whether to ask Stephen to draft a code, the Statute Law Committee,[108] a committee of experts set up by the Lord Chancellor in 1868, which included such distinguished lawyers as Sir Henry Maine, then Professor of Jurisprudence at Oxford, Sir Erskine May, the Clerk of the House of Commons, and Sir Henry Thring, the Parliamentary Counsel, was working on the consolidation of the criminal law.[109]

The person that the Committee asked to report on the subject was none other than Mr R. S. Wright. Once again we find in his detailed eighty page report the same careful scholarship characteristic of all of Wright's work. And once again we find that his work is later forgotten. No mention of this Report — nor indeed of any of his other Reports so far mentioned in this article — is contained in any of the later biographical sketches of Wright. Wright's Report was commissioned before Stephen was asked to draft his Code,[110] and was completed by him in late 1877 before Stephen's Code was completed.[111]

Wright analyzed all the statutes relating to criminal law and set out a detailed plan for distributing the material into sixteen chapters. He estimated that the bulk of the new Consolidation Acts "would not exceed a sixth part of the bulk of the existing Statutes relating to the same matter, and it may be much less."[112] The Committee praised Wright's efforts and felt that his work was "capable of being applied in various ways to purposes of great public importance".[113]

---

108 See C. Ilbert, *Legislative Methods and Forms* (Oxford 1901) at pp. 65 *et seq.* The Committee was established by Lord Cairns L.C. in 1868 with Erksine May as chairman. Lord Cairns was the Lord Chancellor again between 1874 and 1880.

109 See Papers relative to the Proceedings of the Statute Law Committee respecting Consolidation, and Reports preliminary to Consolidation submitted by the Committee to the Lord Chancellor, ordered to be printed 30 July, 1878, Paper No. 178. In answer to a parliamentary question on 16 Feb., 1877 (Hansard, col. 462) the Attorney-General, Sir John Holker, stated that the question of codification and consolidation was "now undergoing very careful consideration by the Lord Chancellor and the Law Officers of the Crown, in conjunction with the Statute Law Revision Committee".

110 *I.e.,* sometime before the Committee's memo of 6 June, 1877: see Paper No. 178.

111 Wright's Introduction is dated 3 Dec., 1877: see Paper No. 178.

112 *Ibid.* at p. 5. Wright also included sample draft bills relating to treason and piracy.

113 *Ibid.* at p. A2. Ilbert refers to Wright's "valuable" proposals for codification in his

Having already chosen Wright to do this work, the Committee was understandably not keen on Stephen being asked to draft a code. Sir Francis Reilly wrote to the Lord Chancellor on 20 July, 1877:[114] "Some members of our Statute Law Committee . . . concur in thinking it would be inexpedient to give Stephen 'a large order' for consolidation, or still more, for codification, and that his powers and authority might well be applied to emendation of the substance of the Law." Reilly added an interesting footnote to his letter. "I find Wright is of 12 years standing". There is no copy of a letter from the Lord Chancellor prompting this information, but it suggests that Lord Cairns had expressed concern about Wright's position in the legal profession.

The Statute Law Committee was worried about the idea of combining significant changes in the law with an accurate statement of the law. "The danger", the Committee told the Lord Chancellor,[115] "is that the two kinds of improvements may clash, and obstruct one another". The Committee[116] — and, no doubt, Wright himself[117] — favoured law reform in three categories: amendment of the law; consolidation of the law; and, finally, codification of the law.

Contrary to the advice of the Statute Law Committee, the Government in August, 1877 asked Stephen to prepare a Criminal Code.[118] Stephen had built up considerable momentum. Early in 1877 he had written to the Attorney-General, Sir John Holker, saying that he thought that his *Digest of Criminal Law*, to be published before Easter, would form a

---

Legislative Methods and Forms (Oxford 1901) at p. 69: "further progress on the lines thus suggested was stopped by the introduction of the Criminal Code Bill prepared about the same time by Sir James Stephen."

114 L.C.O. 1/42.

115 Memo from the Committee dated 2 Jan., 1878 adopting the comment of Francis Reilly dated 6 Dec., 1877: L.C.O. 1/42.

116 *Ibid.* See also Henry Thring, *Simplification of the Law* (London 1875).

117 See Wright's comments (in the Papers relative to the Proceedings of the Statute Law Committee (Paper No. 178 at p. 37) on the 1861 Consolidation of the Offences against the Person Act: "It could no doubt be very greatly improved and shortened if the criminal statutes were to be re-made and embodied in a code with declarations and amendments of the common law." Similarly, with respect to the Larceny Act he stated (at p. 37): "Such a departure and reconstruction are probably desirable, but they seem to belong rather to codification than to consolidation."

118 See Radzinowicz, *Sir James Fitzjames Stephen,* 20; Cross, "The Making of English Criminal Law: Sir James Fitzjames Stephen" [1978] Crim. L. Rev. pp 652, 656-7. Cross points out: 'The original idea had been to have three Bills, the first to contain the amendments and be brought before Parliament in advance of the others. The decision to proceed by means of a single bill may have been the undoing of the entire project."

useful basis for a criminal code.[119] This was followed by a speech to the Trades Union Congress[120] (reported in *The Times*[121] and *The Law Times*[122] and later printed in the *Fortnightly Review*)[123] that got organized labour behind his efforts.[124] Wright, who had had a very close involvement with the Trades Union Congress since 1872 and had played a key role on behalf of the TUC in drafting legislation affecting labour,[125] attended that lecture and spoke in favour of the TUC resolution, unanimously carried by the meeting:[126]

119 20 Jan., 1877: Cross, at pp. 656-7. He also wrote to the Lord Chancellor, 10 and 26 May, 1877: L.C.O. 1/42. See also Stephen's letter to Lord Lytton, 19 July, 1877: "I have also been pressing the Lord Chancellor to let me draw an English Penal Code for him." Cambridge University Library, Add. MSS 7349. The Home Secretary, R. A. Cross' involvement is documented in H.O. 45/9551/63062.

120 "A Penal Code", 6 Feb., 1877.

121 8 Feb., 1877.

122 10 Feb., 1877.

123 March 1877, 362-375. See also Stephen, "Improvement of the Law by Private Enterprise", The Nineteenth Century, Sept., 1877 at p. 198; Stephen, "Suggestions as to the reform of the Criminal Law", The Nineteenth Century, Dec., 1877 at p. 737.

124 See Hansard of 15 Aug., 1878, col 2039: "It was due to the working men of the country that the Bill had first been drawn up."

125 See S. & B. Webb, *The History of Trade Unionism* (London 1902), at p. 348 ("frequently . . . rendered invaluable service as a draughtsman"); S. Maccoby, *English Radicalism 1853-1886* (London 1938), 324-5; R. Harrison, *Before the Socialists: Studies in Labour and Politics 1861-1881* (London 1965); F. M. Leventhal, *Respectable Radical: George Howell and Victorian Working Class Politics* (London 1971); and G. Howell, *Labour Legislation: Labour Movements and Labour Leaders* (London 1902). The Bishopsgate Library, London, contains dozens of letters from Howell, the Secretary from 1872 of the TUC's Parliamentary Committee, to Wright. Wright was involved in Bills relating to Merchant Shipping, Arbitration, Liability of Employers to Workmen, the Truck System, Master and Servant legislation and the criminal liability of workmen. In 1874 the Conservatives introduced and Parliament passed two important pieces of legislation (Conspiracy and Protection of Property Act, and Employers and Workmen Act) for which Wright had drafted some crucial provisions. Wright's own version of the Conspiracy Act had passed the Commons in 1873, but was amended by the Lords and so abandoned. Wright's version did *not* contain the words "in furtherance of a trade dispute" which the 1875 Act did, and which have caused considerable controversy since then. Wright attended a number of Annual Meetings of the TUC. After an address on "The Land Question" at the Sept., 1879 meeting in Edinburgh he was thanked with the words: 'there was no man in England to whom they were more indebted for the improved labour laws under which they lived." Wright's involvement with the labour movement and his later landmark opinion in *Allen v. Flood*, [1898] A.C. 1 would provide the subject for another study.

126 *The Law Times*, 10 Feb., 1877, at pp. 265-6. Wright's comments are not reported. In introducing his lecture Stephen indicated how the lecture came about. According to *The Law Times*, Stephen stated, "At the meeting of the Trades Union Congress, held last summer at Newcastle, his friend, Mr. Crompton read a paper on the codification of the criminal law, in the course of which he was good enough to make a flattering reference to himself (the speaker). Subsequently a correspondence ensued, and in the result he was asked to address them that evening."

That this meeting is of opinion that the time has now arrived when it is incumbent upon the government to codify the criminal laws of the country, and earnestly prays her Majesty's Government not to let this Session of Parliament pass away without steps having been taken to secure this object.

It is not surprising, therefore, to find the Attorney-General writing to the Lord Chancellor on 5 March, 1877:[127] "There is a feeling in the country which is rapidly gaining strength that something ought to be done in this direction".

Stephen's Code was completed in early 1878 (this time he received 1,500 guineas for his work[128]) and debated in Parliament that summer. It was then referred to a Royal Commission under the chairmanship of Lord Blackburn with Stephen as a member. The Commission reported, with an accompanying Draft Bill, in 1879.

Labour's role in promoting the issue of codification and then putting brakes on the movement is an important one. Henry Crompton, a good friend of labour, had argued at the Annual Meeting of the TUC in 1876[129] that criminal law codification was a desirable goal, pointing out in his address that "A large amount of the preliminary work has been accomplished. A penal code has already been drawn up for our Crown Colonies, and a code of criminal procedure is in the course of construction." The TUC passed a resolution[130] that it is "the duty of the Government to undertake the consideration of a new penal code which will simplify the law and improve the administration of criminal justice". Stephen's Code was not, however, what labour had hoped for, although it was what it should have expected. Stephen's involvement with labour was anomalous, as he himself acknowledged in a letter to his friend Lord Lytton:[131] "One does certainly meet with very strange bed fellows indeed in this exceedingly unaccountable state of life." A paper read to the TUC in September, 1878[132] pointed out, amongst other criticisms, that Stephen's Code[133] provided that three armed persons in pursuit of game at night were liable to fourteen years penal servitude. But it was the Code's treat-

---

127 L.C.O. 1/42.

128 L.C.O. 1/42. The original arrangement was for 1200 guineas, but Stephen later suggested that it should be more. He also received 1500 guineas for his later work as a Commissioner.

129 Report of the 9th TUC, Sept., 1876, Newcastle-on-Tyne.

130 Ibid.

131 3 May, 1878. Cambridge University Library, Add. MSS 7349. Stephen's lack of sympathy for organized labour is mentioned in Leslie Stephen, at p. 348.

132 See E. D. Lewis, A Paper on the Codification of the Criminal Law (London 1878). Lewis produced his own Code, A Draft Code of Criminal Law and Procedure (London 1879).

133 S. 50. The same provision was in the Commissioners' Code, s. 94.

ment of organized labour that caused the greatest concern.[134] The TUC therefore urged that the Bill be referred to a Royal Commission.[135] Labour tried to have a representative on the Royal Commission, but without success. Sir Charles Dilke accurately predicted in the House[136] that "the Government would never succeed in carrying the Bill next Session, unless they considerably modified the Commission. . . ." When the Commissioners' Code appeared, Henry Crompton wrote to the Home Secretary about the anti-labour aspects of the Code[137] and prepared a paper[138] strongly criticizing a great many sections of the Code, as did others, including George Howell, the former secretary of the TUC's Parliamentary Committee.[139] Crompton wrote:

> There are parts of the Code of such a nature as to constitute a danger of the most serious description. These may all be removed or substantially altered, and we most earnestly hope that this will be done. If not, if they are maintained, then the Bill should be stoutly resisted and fought, clause by clause, at every stage, so as to insure postponement, and prevent such clauses becoming the law of the land.

The TUC thereafter continued to support codification, but with serious reservations. In 1881, the TUC passed a unanimous resolution[140] that the Government complete the work of codification but added a rider that "no code will be satisfactory which does not repeal the law of conspiracy and secure the right of public meeting".

There are a number of reasons often advanced[141] why the Commissioners' Code was never enacted: the extensive changes it made in the law; criticism by Chief Justice Cockburn that it was only "partial codification";[142] lack of parliamentary time; and the change of Government in

---

134 The Home Secretary, Cross, must have anticipated trouble. The Attorney-General, Holker wrote to Stephen on 16 May, 1878: "Cross wishes the clauses relating to trade offences to be split up and inserted under some other heads. He does not wish it to be recognized that breaches of contract of service etc. is a trade offence." Cambridge University Library, Add. MSS 7349.

135 11th Annual TUC Parliamentary Committee's Report, Sept., 1878.

136 Hansard, 15 Aug., 1878. See also the speech the same day by Sir William Harcourt.

137 3 July, 1879: H.O. 45/9551/63062.

138 "A Paper on The Criminal Code Bill" (June, 1879, London).

139 12th Annual TUC, Edinburgh, Sept., 1879.

140 *The Law Times,* 17 Sept., 1881, at pp. 341-2.

141 See *e.g.,* Radzinowicz, *Sir James Fitzjames Stephen,* at pp. 20-1; Leslie Stephen, *The Life of Sir James Fitzjames Stephen,* at pp. 380-1; Cross, at pp. 657-8; Manchester, "James Fitzjames Stephen and the Codification of the Criminal Law of England and Wales" (1973) 2 Anglo-American L. Rev. 527.

142 See copy of letter from the Lord Chief Justice of England, dated 12 June, 1879, containing Comments and Suggestions in relation to the Criminal Code (Indictable Offences) Bill, Paper No. 232, 1879, Parl Papers, Accounts and Papers (1878-9). The

1880.[143] We can now add three more: organized labour's reservations about the Code; concern about the quality of Stephen's work shared by a number of influential people; and the detailed programme of gradual reform put forward by the Statute Law Committee.

The unstated alternative to Stephen's Code was Wright's plan for consolidation and a Code based on his Jamaican model. Indeed, there is a fair likelihood that if Stephen's Code had not made its appearance when it did, and thus monopolized the stage, Wright's scheme for consolidation leading to codification would have been accepted and England might now have a criminal code.

The Statute Law Committee did not return to the subject until 1887. Lord Thring, the Chairman of the Committee, sent a memorandum to Lord Halsbury, the Lord Chancellor, stating:[144]

> In the year 1877 Mr R. S. Wright prepared a series of papers for the Statute Law Committee showing in great detail how the enactments relating to this subject might be consolidated, but his suggestions were laid aside owing to the more ambitious projects of framing criminal codes of procedure, and no action has been taken upon them. As there seems to be no immediate probability of either of these codes becoming law, effect might perhaps be given to Mr Wright's suggestions, or at least to some of them.
>
> Pending the completion of a criminal code it would be of advantage to have the existing enactments relating to criminal procedure, or at least those prior to 1861, thrown into an intelligible form and reduced to reasonable dimensions.

But it was too late. Lord Halsbury was not keen on the issue of codification,[145] and wind had for the time being gone out of the sails of the movement for consolidation.

5. WRIGHT'S CODE

Wright's Code differed from Stephen's and the Commissioners' in a number of ways. Some of these have already been mentioned, in particular Wright's technique of carefully defining the meaning of *mens rea*

---

letter criticized the Code on a number of grounds apart from partial codification. This was to be the first of three letters. There is no indication whether the other two were sent; likely, they were not. Stephen made his reply in "The Criminal Code (1879)", The Nineteenth Century, Jan., 1880, at p. 136. Stephen wrote to Lord Lytton on 29 Dec., 1879 that he was going on circuit with Cockburn and was going to try "judicious flattery". On 20 Jan., 1880 he wrote that they now "get on like houses on fire". Stephen Papers, Cambridge University Library, Add. MSS 7349.

143 See J. F. Stephen, *History of the Criminal Law* (London 1883), vol 1, vii. Both James and Herschell, the Attorney-General and Solicitor-General in the new government, had attacked the Bill because it combined important changes along with statements of the existing law: Hansard, 3 April, 1879.

144 "Consolidation of Statutes", dated 24 Nov., 1887.

145 L.C.O. 1/42.

terms, as well as his scheme of arrangement of the Code.[146] A few others deserve specific mention.

(a) Classification

Wright kept the distinction between felonies and misdemeanours[147] — as did the Model Penal Code almost 100 years later.[148] "It seems inexpedient", he wrote[149] with respect to felonies, "to throw away a term which already carries associations of grave reprobation". Of course, he removed some of the procedural difficulties then associated with the distinction between felonies and misdemeanours, such as the rule that prevented their joinder.[150] Felonies and misdemeanours were to be determined according to the potential punishment ("death or penal servitude" for a felony)[151] and not according to the procedure for trying the case. In contrast, Stephen and the Commissioners eliminated the distinction between felonies and misdemeanours and classified offences into indictable and non-indictable.[152] This classification is not a good one, however, when, as in Canada, many indictable offences can be tried either summarily or by indictment.[153]

(b) Extent of Codification

Wright's Code was more exhaustive than either Stephen's or the Commissioners'. Wright, like the earlier Benthamite drafters, Macaulay in India[154] and Livingston in the United States,[155] specifically eliminated all common law crimes and attempted to be exhaustive as to defences.[156] Stephen did not exclude common law offences — except to the extent that the matter was covered by legislation,[157] but he attempted to be exhaustive

---

146 Note also that Wright followed Bentham's suggestion that crimes affecting the individual come before crimes affecting the state, the reverse of the usual arrangement. See Wright's Jamaica Code, at p. 97: "the more simple should come before the more complex, the ordinary and every-day crimes before those which are rare."

147 Jamaica Criminal Code, s. 21.

148 Model Penal Code, Proposed Official Draft, s. 1.04.

149 Jamaica Criminal Code, at p. 100.

150 See s. 18 of the Jamaica Code of Procedure.

151 Jamaica Criminal Code, s. 21.

152 Neither Code, however, dealt with non-indictable offences, as Wright's did.

153 The classification makes no sense for a number of indictable offences in Canada, such as theft under $200, which *cannot* be tried on indictment.

154 See Kadish, "Codifiers of the Criminal Law: Wechsler's Predecessors" (1978) 78 Col. L. Rev. 1098, at p. 1106.

155 *Ibid.,* at p. 1099.

156 Jamaica Criminal Code, at p. 96.

157 S. 5. S. 28 specifically refers to offences "against the common law".

with respect to defences (such as necessity), although not actually excluding the possibility of judges recognizing new ones. The Commissioners reversed Stephen's approach: they eliminated common law offences but specifically left many defences to the development of the common law.[158]

In particular, Wright eliminated the offence of common law conspiracy,[159] restricting conspiracy to the commission of a "crime", that is, an offence punishable on indictment.[160] He had expressed that view in his book on criminal conspiracies which was published in 1873[161] and was undoubtedly inspired by his sympathy for the labour movement: "There appear to be great theoretical objections to any general rule that agreement may make punishable that which ought not to be punished in the absence of agreement." And with respect to using conspiracy to prosecute breaches of minor offences, he wrote the oft-quoted words.[162] "To permit two persons to be indicted for a conspiracy to make a slide in the street of a town, or to catch hedge-sparrows in April, would be to destroy that distinction between crimes and minor offences which in every country it is held important to preserve".

Stephen's Code is not clear on the subject. Conspiracy was certainly to apply to offences punishable on summary conviction,[163] and most probably to conduct which was not itself subject to a criminal penalty. The Commissioners' draft restricted conspiracy to conspiring to commit an indictable offence, but they were careful to provide that the law as to trade conspiracies was not to be affected,[164] presumably to allow the law of conspiracy to continue to be used against labour unions. Moreover, Wright's Code did not contain vague general offences of mischief or nuisance,[165] such as were contained in Stephen's[166] and the Commissioners'[167] Codes. Nor does it contain the vague phrase "duty imposed by law" relating to omissions that one finds in the later Codes.[168]

Not only did Wright want to exclude any major judicial development of offences or defences, he wanted to eliminate reliance on earlier cases.

---

158 Commissioners' Report, at pp. 10 and 16. See Code, ss. 5 and 19.

159 Ss. 35 and 36.

160 S. 19.

161 *The Law Relating to Criminal Conspiracies and Agreements* (London 1873), at p. 86. Unfortunately, only Lord Reid adopted Wright's view in *Shaw v. D.P.P.,* [1962] A.C. 220 (H.L.).

162 *Ibid.,* at p. 83.

163 S. 33(c).

164 Ss. 420-1. See p. 16 of their Report.

165 See Wright's Jamaica Code, at p. 112.

166 Ss. 108 and 273.

167 Ss. 151 and 406.

168 Stephen's Code, ss. 127 and 128; Commissioners' Code, s. 167.

He provided that "In the interpretation of this Code, a court shall not be bound by any judicial decision or opinion on the construction of any other statute or of the common law as to the definition of any crime or of any element of any crime".[169]

(c) Law and Morality

John Stuart Mill's view expressed in his essay *On Liberty*[170] that "the only purpose for which power can be rightfully exercised over any member of a civilized community, against his will, is to prevent harm to others" is, to a great extent, reflected in Wright's Criminal Code. Stephen, as is well known, opposed Mill's view in his own book, *Liberty, Equality, Fraternity,*[171] and so we find a sharp cleavage between Wright's Code and the later Codes on the issue of law and morality.

Attempted suicide, for example, is an offence in Stephen's Code[172] and the Commissioners' Code,[173] but is not punishable in Wright's Code. Wright followed Mill, stating,[174] "it may be added to the usual arguments based on the absence of injury to any other person, that to impose a punishment for the attempt would be merely to supply an additional motive for taking care to ensure the success of the attempt." He did not, however, permit a person to assist another to take his own life.[175]

Sodomy is also treated differently in the Codes. Stephen's[176] and the Commissioners' Codes[177] provide for penal servitude for life (with a

---

169 S. 8 (iii). Wright was not eliminating *stare decisis* for future interpretations of the Code; he proposed a court of appeal (Code of Procedure, s. 47) to make sure that trial judges did not go astray.

170 (Pelican edition, London 1974), at p. 68.

171 2nd ed, 1874, reproduced with an introduction and notes by R. J. White (Cambridge 1967). Stephen's views on opium expressed in 1891 in The Nineteenth Century after he retired from the Bench ("The Opium 'Resolution' ", vol. 29, June 1891, at p. 851) are more tolerant than his earlier writings would suggest: "Thousands consume it without any pernicious results, as thousands do wine or spirits without any evil consequences . . . When it is used in excess it produces dreadful results, but in moderation it is highly beneficial. . ." Stephen's correspondence with Lord Lytton in India shows that Stephen himself smoked opium. "I do still now and then smoke an opium pipe", he writes on 15 Sept., 1889, "as my nose requires one occasionally and is comforted by it. I wonder your doctors don't suggest it but no doubt they know best." Cambridge University Library Add. MSS 7349. Could his opium smoking explain the lapse of concentration in the notorious Maybrick murder case several months earlier?

172 S. 145.

173 S. 184.

174 Jamaica Criminal Code, at p. 108.

175 *Ibid.*

176 S. 101.

177 S. 144.

minimum penalty of ten years in Stephen's Code) for buggery or bestiality. Wright's Code placed buggery (with consent) and bestiality in the section headed "Public Nuisances"[178] and had originally provided for a maximum two year penalty. This was one of the provisions from which Stephen "strongly" dissented.[179] Lord Carnarvon raised the penalty in the Jamaica Code from two to ten years.[180] When Wright became a judge he took a somewhat harder line on sodomy with consent than he did as a draftsman. He thought that the "normal" sentence of three years for sodomy between consenting adult males as suggested in 1901 by his fellow King's Bench judges was "too low".[181] On the other hand, he thought that the proposal of up to a year for bestiality was "unnecessarily high".[182]

Wright also had a much more liberal abortion section than Stephen, stating[183] that "any act which is done in good faith and without negligence for the purposes of medical or surgical treatment of a pregnant woman is justifiable, although it cause or be intended to cause miscarriage or abortion, or premature delivery, or the death of the child". (Wright's view on abortion is also consistent with what we know of his interest in other "women's rights" issues, such as female education. For example, he gave three hundred pounds in 1876, '77, '78 and '79 — his total Oriel Fellowship money — to the newly founded Girton College, Cambridge for scholarships and was a member of the College from 1878-1900.[184]) Stephen, on the other hand, limited justifiable abortion to cases where it was "reasonably necessary . . . for the preservation of the life of the mother"[185] and the Commissioners seemed to limit it even further to the preservation of the life of the mother at the time of the birth of the child.[186]

(d) Political Offences

Wright and Stephen's political philosophies are reflected in their

---

178 S. 345. Buggery without consent (s. 65) was, like rape, punishable by penal servitude for life.

179 Memo from Bramston: C.O. 137/480/613.

180 C.O. 137/480/630.

181 The Judges Memorandum of 1901 on Normal Punishments, reprinted in R. M. Jackson, *Enforcing the Law* (London 1967), at p. 255.

182 *Ibid.,* at p. 256.

183 S. 132 (ii).

184 See Barbara Stephen, *Emily Davies and Girton College* (London 1927), at p. 372. See also the Girton College Reports, 1876-1880.

185 S. 168.

186 S. 212. No such defence is provided in s. 213. The "surgical operations" defence in s. 67 was probably not meant to apply to abortion. See *Morgentaler v. R.* (1975), 53 D.L.R. (3d) 161 (S.C.C.).

Codes. Although each stood unsuccessfully for Parliament on two
occasions as Liberals (Stephen in 1865 and 1873, Wright in 1885 and
1886), their political views were fundamentally different. Stephen was a
conservative.[187] Indeed, Disraeli once said that Stephen would have made
an excellent leader of the Conservative Party.[188] Many of Stephen's law
reforming ventures, such as his amendments to the Indian Penal Code,
could, in fact, be considered reactionary.

Wright, in contrast, held radical views.[189] For example, he favoured
land nationalization and was, it would seem, a member of the Land
Nationalization Society which had as its object: "To restore the Land to
the People and the People to the Land".[190] He was further to the left than
many of those who were called radicals during the last quarter of the
nineteenth century, although he was not, of course, a revolutionary, nor,
as far as I can see, a socialist, except on the land issue. His letter[191] to the
Citizens and the Electors of the City of Norwich in his unsuccessful bid for
a parliamentary seat in 1885[192] is instructive:

> My views on all these subjects [e.g., the land question, free education, the House of
> Lords, reform of local government] have often been laid before you. If on all of them I
> hold advanced opinions, believing that great and radical changes are called for and
> may be safely made, I have always been careful to make it plain that I will be no party to
> taking away any man's private property or rights for the public good without
> compensation.

Wright's close involvement with the Trades Union Congress,

---

187 See J. F. Stephen, *Liberty, Equality, Fraternity,* 2nd ed. (London 1874), reprinted with an
introduction by R. J. White (Cambridge 1967); J. Roach, "Sir James Fitzjames Stephen," unpublished 1953 Ph.D. dissertation; J. Roach, "Liberalism and the Victorian
Intelligentsia" (1957) 13 Camb Hist. J. at p. 58; Kadish, "Codifiers of the Criminal Law:
Wechsler's Predecessors" (1978) 78 Col. L. Rev. at pp. 1098, 1124.

188 Letter from Disraeli to Lord Lytton in 1881, cited in L. Stephen, *The Life of Sir James
Fitzjames Stephen* (London 1895), at p. 349.

189 See *e.g.,* the *DNB* ("radical opinions"); *The Times,* 15 Aug., 1904 ("Radicalism in
politics"); *Vanity Fair,* 27 June, 1891 ("a good Radical").

190 For a description of the Land Nationalization Society see E. E. Barry, *Nationalization in
British Politics* (London 1965); David Martin, "Land Reform" in P. Hollis (ed), *Pressure
from Without in Early Victorian England* (London 1974), at pp. 131 *et seq;* A. R. Wallace, *Land
Nationalization* (London 1892); "Essential Principles of Land Nationalization", National
Reformer, 24 May, 1885, at pp. 394-5. The founder of the Society gave up his seat in
Stepney to let Wright run there in 1886.

191 See *The Norwich Mercury,* 18 Nov., 1885.

192 He came very close to winning this election as well as the one the following year in
Stepney. Norwich was a two-seat constituency and the Conservatives ran only one
candidate, who attacked Wright as a "stranger" to Norwich. The other Liberal
candidate, Colman, the mustard manufacturer, employed over 2,600 in Norwich at
decent wages. The result was Bullard (C) 7,279, Colman (L) 6,666 and Wright (L) 6,251.
For a discussion of these two contests see H. Pelling, *Social Geography of British Elections
1885-1910* (London 1967), at pp. 45 and 91.

stemming, no doubt, from his earlier work on the Truck System, has already been mentioned. But further, he urged the TUC to become more involved in politics. At the conclusion of an address he delivered on the land question at the Annual Meeting of the Trades Union Congress in Edinburgh in 1879[193] he stated: "I think I shall not be infringing on your rule which prohibits the introduction of party politics, if I venture to suggest to you that you have, in times past, carried political indifference too far".

His political views are reflected in his views on the criminal law. For example, he viewed offences against the person more seriously than offences against property.[194] His support for labour is reflected in his desire to limit the offence of conspiracy (and in his later landmark opinion in 1897 in *Allen v. Flood*[195]). Stephen, as we have seen, wanted to maintain common law conspiracy, no doubt to be available as a weapon against unions.

In defining the offence of sedition, to pick one of the more conspicuous political offences, Wright allowed the citizen very wide scope to criticize government policy (although not Her Majesty), limiting a seditious purpose[196] to "a purpose to excite any of Her Majesty's subjects to the obtaining by force or other unlawful means of an alteration in the laws or in the form of government, or to the commission of any crime punishable" under the laws relating to treason. Stephen and the Commissioners, on the other hand, allowed far less scope for free speech. They included[197] in the definition of sedition an intention to bring "the Government and Constitution of the United Kingdom or any part of it" into "hatred or contempt", or "to raise discontent or disaffection amongst Her Majesty's subjects". There were, it is true, provisos limiting the scope

---

193 12 Annual TUC Meeting, Sept., 1879.

194 "No one can either deny or justify the comparative severity with which offences against property are punished, or rather perhaps the comparative lenience with which offences against the person are punished": Letter from Wright to Mrs Ponsonby, dated 26 April, 1878, in the Gladstone Papers, British Library, Add. MSS 44456, f 269. She was the wife of the Queen's Private Secretary and a friend of Wright's (probably through their association with Girton College), and may have passed the letter on to Gladstone because Wright had, in reply to a letter from her on the administration of justice, said: "You could not do greater than by interesting the public men who are your friends in these issues." The Gladstone papers do not contain any correspondence with Wright, although they knew each other through the Liberal party. Henry Ponsonby records a note of a dinner on 18 Nov., 1893: 'Dined with Mr Gladstone. Mrs Gladstone the only woman, Lord Elgin, Judge Wright, Acton, Mr Milner . . .': A Ponsonby, *Henry Ponsonby* (London 1942), at p. 263.

195 [1898] A.C. 1.

196 S. 243.

197 S. 55 of Stephen's Code; s. 102 of the Commissioners' Code.

of the definition, but the general intent of the section was to restrict speech to a greater extent than in Wright's Code.

(e) Insanity

Wright's clause on insanity is of interest:[198] a person was to be acquitted if he was prevented by reason of, *inter alia*, "any mental derangement or disease affecting the mind, from knowing the nature or consequences of the act in respect of which he is accused". A further subsection would acquit if "he did the act . . . under the influence of a delusion of such a nature as to render him, in the opinion of the jury, an unfit subject for punishment of any kind in respect of such act". Wright was influenced by the North German Code which had adopted the philosophy that "fewer difficulties would occur and fewer mistakes would be made if the law attempted no explanation of insanity".[199] "Nature or consequences" would seem to combine both branches of the *M'Naughten* rule, that is "nature and quality" of the act as well as knowledge of whether the act is wrong.

The test had been worked out by Wright and Stephen in their conference. Stephen wrote to the Colonial Office[200] that he and Wright had "settled a clause which I think deals with the subject as satisfactorily as the great difficulties of the subject and the state of medical knowledge about it permit". Nevertheless, when Stephen came to draft his own Code he reverted to the *M'Naughten*-style test[201] (although broader because he included "morally wrong" coupled with an irresistible impulse subsection) that he had included in his 1874 Homicide Bill.[202] The Commissioners' Code[203] rejected irresistible impulse and adopted the definition now found in many Codes: "incapable of appreciating the nature and quality of the act or that the act was wrong". Remnants of the concept "nature and consequences" agreed upon by Wright and Stephen can still, however, be found in the section dealing with children in many colonial codes, including the Canadian Code,[204] the Commissioners[205] having adopted those specific words in that section.

---

198   S. 38. Wright's earlier draft was much more complex than this and included a form of irresistible impulse.

199   Jamaica Criminal Code, at p. 104.

200   Letter dated Jan., 1875: C.O. 137/480/613.

201   S. 20.

202   Homicide Law Amendment Bill (No. 315) 1874, s. 24.

203   S. 22.

204   Canadian Criminal Code, R.S.C. 1970, c. C-34, s. 13.

205   S. 21: "sufficient intelligence to know the nature and consequences of his conduct, and to appreciate that it was wrong." Stephen (s. 19) had used the test: "sufficient capacity to know that the act was forbidden by law".

(f) Attempt

The attempt section [206] contains a number of interesting aspects. Attempt is not defined, "but relies on the ordinary understanding of the word, with special provisions intended to meet cases which the English law has failed to reach".[207]

The Commissioners' Code, which left the issue to the judge as "a question of law", inferentially defined attempt and thereby created needless confusion by suggesting that "preparation" would be "too remote".[208] Wright, on the other hand, specifically included as attempts a number of cases of preparation, such as possession of instruments or materials for use in certain crimes.[209]

With respect to the punishment of attempts, Wright followed the French Code and punished the attempt in the same manner as the completed crime.[210] Most other codes,[211] following Livingston's Louisiana Code, made the punishment for an attempt half that for the completed crime. Wright's Code was built on the concept of deterrence and thus there was no reason for him to mitigate the punishment, except in the case where the accused voluntarily desists from completion.[212] Wright stopped short, however, of providing that attempted murder be punishable by death, although he did so in the case of attempts to murder by convicts,[213] stating that "no other generally adequate deterrent can be found for the protection of prison officers".[214] Stephen, on the other hand, taking the view that one of the purposes of punishment was to permit vengeance by society ("vengeance affects, and ought to affect, the amount of punishment"[215]) considered that a lesser punishment would be needed if the crime was not completed. So we find Stephen's Code and the Commissioners' Code punishing attempts far less harshly than the completed crime.[216]

Wright's desire to deter persons from engaging in criminal conduct

---

206 S. 30.
207 At p. 102. A similar approach was taken with respect to causation (s. 12 (V)) on which Wright commented (at p. 99): 'The vagueness of this enactment . . . appears preferable to an attempt to lay down rules of casuistry.'
208 S. 74.
209 S. 31.
210 S. 30 (ii).
211 See p. 103.
212 S. 30 (ii).
213 S. 118.
214 See p. 107.
215 J. F. Stephen, *Liberty, Equality, Fraternity,* 2nd ed. (London 1874), at p. 152, reprinted with an introduction by R. J. White (Cambridge 1967).
216 S. 33 of Stephen's Code; ss. 422-4 of Commissioners' Code.

also led him to provide for conviction in cases of impossibility, including cases where the crime was not possible "by reason of the absence of [the] person or thing".[217] Not surprisingly, Stephen took the opposite view and provided[218] that "an act done with intent to commit an offence, the commission of which in the manner proposed was, in fact, impossible, is not an attempt to commit that offence". Stephen thus agreed with the earlier Court for Crown Cases Reserved decision in *Regina v. Collins*[219] and would have been delighted to learn that the House of Lords had a century later expressed the same view in *Haughton v. Smith*.[220] The Commissioners, however, did not take the same approach as Stephen and would, like Wright, convict in the "empty pocket" case.[221]

(g) Murder

The murder provisions in Wright's Code[222] are not as wide as in Stephen's or the Commissioners'. Wright does not include intent to cause grievous bodily harm, as the other Codes do. Nor does he include any constructive felony-murder provisions as the Commissioners',[223] but not Stephen's Code, does. Murder, for Wright, is defined simply as "intentionally caus[ing] the death of another person by any unlawful harm";[224] and, as we have seen, "intent" is carefully defined in the Code. The definition of intent does not contain the "ought to have known" test found in the Commissioners'[225] — and therefore many Colonial Codes'[226] — definition of murder.

It is difficult to say, though, whether Wright's Code would have cut down the number of convictions for murder compared with the other Codes because of Wright's surprisingly harsh treatment of drunkenness.

---

217 S. 30 (i). Wright J was a member of the Court in *R. v. Ring* (1892), 17 Cox C.C. 491 (C.C.R.) which did not follow *R. v. Collins* (1864), 9 Cox C.C. 497 (C.C.R.).

218 S. 32.

219 (1864), 9 Cox C.C. 497 (C.C.R.).

220 [1975] A.C. 476.

221 S. 74.

222 Title X. Although the heading is "Criminal Homicide", the word "homicide" is not used in any of the sections. Thus murder and manslaughter are defined directly, and not as in Stephen's Bill or the Commissioners' Code indirectly by first defining homicide. Wright's technique causes less confusion to the reader and, of course, to a jury. Wright also, wisely, separates manslaughter from "manslaughter by negligence".

223 S. 175.

224 S. 120.

225 S. 174 (d). Wright's definition of intent (s. 10) does, however, contain a rebuttable presumption of intent in such a case "until it is shown that he believed that the act would probably not cause or contribute to cause the event".

226 Canadian Criminal Code, s. 212 (c) ("ought to know").

Wright's Code provided that "a person who does an act while in a state of intoxication shall be deemed to have intended to cause the natural and probable consequences of his act".[227] He was concerned about an excuse "easily feigned or fabricated".[228] Stephen, on the other hand, had a more tolerant section which stated that drunkenness "may be taken into account by the jury in deciding whether he had" the requisite intent.[229] The Commissioners' Code omitted any mention of drunkenness, leaving the matter to the development of the common law.[230] Wright's definition of provocation (which would reduce murder to manslaughter) was also less liberal to the accused than the Commissioners' section because Wright did not, as the Commissioners did,[231] include an "insult" as possible provocation. "Such cases" he wrote,[232] "may be dealt with by leaving a discretion . . . to recommend the exercise of the prerogative of mercy. But it cannot be laid down in a Criminal Code that jealousy is a sufficient extenuation of intentional homicide". In this situation, as with drunkenness, he was probably concerned with fabricated excuses as well as desiring to maintain the law of murder as a deterrent against persons giving way to provocation.

In one respect, however, Wright's definition of provocation was better than that in the later Codes. They required that provocation must not only provoke the accused but "be sufficient to deprive an ordinary person of the power of self-control",[233] a question which has caused considerable difficulty in later cases.[234] Wright handled the issue directly by providing[235] that the provocation must "be likely to deprive a person, being of ordinary character, and being in the circumstances in which the accused person was, of the power of self-control".

This discussion of some of the provisions of Wright's Jamaica Code shows that most of them are sound, many of them imaginative, and all of them interesting.[236]

---

227 S. 39.

228 Jamaica Code, at p. 105.

229 S. 21.

230 Report, 18: "Reference to the matter might suggest misunderstandings of a dangerous kind".

231 S. 176.

232 At p. 109.

233 S. 136 of Stephen's Code; s. 176 of Commissioners' Code.

234 See *Mancini v. D.P.P.*, [1942] A.C. 1 (H.L.); *Bedder v. D.P.P.*, [1954] 1 W.L.R. 1119 (H.L.); *R. v. Camplin*, [1978] A.C. 705 (H.L.).

235 S. 122.

236 In addition to the above provisions, see also his sections on theft (ss. 165 *et seq*) about which Professor Glanville Williams states in a note to the author in June, 1980: "We on the CLRC did not know the details of Wright's code, but the section . . . is an almost uncanny prevision of s. 1 of the Theft Act which we drafted."

6. WHAT HAPPENED TO THE CODE?

(a) Jamaica

The Jamaica Legislative Council passed both the Code of Criminal Law and the Code of Procedure (without any opposition), as requested by the Colonial Office.[237] Jamaica telegraphed the Colonial Office on 21 January, 1879: "two codes through Committee."[238] But they were never brought into force in Jamaica. This required the approval of the Colonial Office and the Colonial Office was starting to get cold feet. Wright thought that the changes in the Codes made in Jamaica were not major[239] and that the Codes should be implemented, but the Colonial Office thought that it would be wise to wait until after the Commissioners' Code was debated in Parliament: "during its consideration points may be raised with respect to which it may be found desirable to reconsider parts of this legislation."[240] Moreover, the Under-Secretary went on to point out to the Colonial Secretary that,[241] "as there are many novelties in these Laws for which the public are no doubt imperfectly prepared, it may perhaps be well on the whole to lay a further paper before Parliament containing the Codes of Laws as proposed. . . . On the other hand some trouble no doubt may be saved by launching these novelties at once: but I incline to a waiting period." The Colonial Secretary, Hicks-Beach, agreed:[242] "I think the 'waiting policy' is the safest. We shall not lose many months."

There was then (April, 1880) a change of government in England and, as we know, the Commissioners' Code was not enacted. The new Colonial Secretary, Lord Kimberley, wanted to bring the Codes into force, stating, "I think there is much to be said in favour of bringing the Code into force, as the discussion even, much less the passing of the English Criminal Code cannot be counted on within any reasonable time, but I would ask

---

237 Memo from Edward Wingfield, later the Permanent Under-Secretary, dated 16 Feb., 1888, outlining the earlier history: C.O. 137/534/2457. The Colonial Office dispatch was dated 29 April, 1878. Stephen's Bill was given its first reading in May, 1878.

238 Jamaica Correspondence Register No. 11, 922.

239 Letter from Wright dated 8 Jan., 1880: C.O. 137/498/350. Wright thought the changes made in the Criminal Code were "not numerous, and they are for the most part introduced for the purpose of better adapting the Code to the local requirements of the Colony." With respect to the Code of Procedure, as pointed out above, he regretted the omission of the clause relating to evidence of former convictions (s. 103A). The Jamaica Legislative Council had also altered the clause relating to giving the accused a copy of the depositions but this omission, Wright felt, could be remedied by a Rule of Court.

240 Memo from R. G. W. Herbert, the Permanent Under-Secretary, dated 14 Jan., 1880: C.O. 137/498/350.

241 *Ibid.*

242 *Ibid,* 19 Jan., 1880.

first Sir Lucie Smith's opinion."[243] Sir Lucie, the Chief Justice of Jamaica, who was then in England, reported[244] that his "brother judges of the Supreme Court would like to see the Code brought into force" but he was worried, as was Kimberley, about the extension of corporal punishment to various offences[245] and he also had doubts about the provision concerning the examination of the accused, although he acknowledged he had not felt strongly enough about the issue to object before. This latter reservation struck a sympathetic chord in Kimberley. He not only wanted the corporal punishment sections changed, but he wanted the provision with respect to the examination of the accused amended to permit the accused to be a witness at his own trial, an innovation not introduced in England until 1898. Kimberley wrote to the Governor of Jamaica:[246]

> I think it is desirable to admit an accused person to give evidence for himself upon his trial and in that case to subject him to cross examination like any other witness for the defence and I enclose a copy of a clause to that effect taken from the Criminal Code Bill which was introduced into Parliament by Her Majesty's late Government which with the necessary variations might be substituted for s. 101 of the Criminal Procedure Code.

In 1882 Jamaica complied with the request to change the sections on corporal punishment and the examination of the accused.[247] In the meantime, opposition was building up in Jamaica to the Code of Procedure. The Attorney-General and the Chief Justice raised various objections to it and the Attorney-General recommended that the Criminal Code alone should be put in force and that the Procedure Code should be repealed.[248] Wright objected to this proposal:[249] "In my opinion," he wrote, "the Criminal Code cannot be brought into operation alone . . . I should even be disposed to go farther and to submit that the Procedure Code is the more important of the two." He argued that the two Codes could be brought into operation at once and amended, to the extent that amendments were necessary, afterwards.

Would half a loaf have been a wiser choice? If Wright had agreed to the division there is a fair likelihood that his Criminal Code and not the

---

243 Memo dated 25 June, 1881: C.O. 137/502/13560. A story in the *Pall Mall Gazette* of 20 June, 1881 about judges in Jamaica sentencing "pilferers to be publicly flogged in the market place" highlighted the inadequacy of the existing Jamaica law.

244 *Ibid.* See memo from Wingfield dated 28 June, 1881.

245 *Ibid.* Wright was asked about this extension and wrote back on 25 July, 1881 that "The extension of the application of corporal punishment was no part of my suggestions. It was part of the instructions by which I was bound. It then appeared and it still appears to me in a high degree inexpedient."

246 *Ibid.* Dispatch dated 30 July, 1881.

247 See C.O. 137/512/10070.

248 See C.O. 137/534/2457.

249 Letter dated 19 Oct., 1882: C.O. 137/507/18279.

Commissioners' Code would have been the one adopted by other colonies.

The Colonial Office decided, however, that it would be better to amend the Code of Procedure first and to bring the two Codes into force at the same time.[250] The Attorney-General of Jamaica was therefore asked to prepare an amended Code of Procedure. This amended Code was strongly criticized in Jamaica by the Press, the Bar and by the elected members of the Legislative Council.[251] In 1888 when the Codes were to come once more before the Legislative Council the Governor recommended to the Colonial Office that the Codes, passed almost ten years earlier, but never brought into force, should be repealed. A Colonial Office memorandum[252] records that both the Attorney-General and the Governor "think that there would be no chance of the Council passing the Criminal Procedure Code which the elected members view with intense dislike for which it is difficult to assign an intelligible reason. It appears also that the Criminal Code is also viewed with intense dislike. . . ." The hostility to the Procedure Code had now spilled over to the Criminal Code itself. The principal objection to the Codes seemed to be that Jamaica was the "victim to an experiment, which certain members of the legal profession at home desired to try and which the public here conceived was to be forced on them, as being subjects in a Crown Colony, when such a code would never be carried at home. . . ."[253]

The Colonial Secretary, Henry Holland, who had been an Assistant Under-Secretary in the Colonial Office in the early 1870s and was thus very familiar with Wright's Codes did not want to repeal them.[254] He wanted the Governor, with respect to the Code of Procedure "to consider carefully the question whether it would not be better to introduce the measure . . . and to leave to the Council the responsibility of declining to assent to it," but not to do so if he was "of the opinion that such an attempt would be hopeless and perhaps lead to hostility and distrust extending

---

250 C.O. 137/534/2457.

251 C.O. 137/534/2457; C.O. 137/536/23088.

252 Memo from Wingfield dated 16 Feb., 1888: C.O. 137/534/2457.

253 Governor's dispatch dated 1 Nov., 1888: C.O. 137/536/23088. It is interesting to note that about 50 years earlier Fitzjames Stephen's father, James Stephen, the Colonial Under-Secretary had, unlike his good friend Henry Taylor, warned against getting too far ahead of the mother country: "For however weighty may be the arguments of the great Jurist to whom I have referred [Bentham, on the law of evidence], I think it desirable that on such subjects the Legislatures of the Colonies should rather follow than attempt to precede the course of public opinion and of legal reform in the parent state." See J. Knaplund, *James Stephen and the British Colonial System 1813-1847* (Madison 1953), at pp. 230-1. Stephen senior was, however, in favour of criminal law reform: *ibid*, ch 9; see also J. L. Robson, *New Zealand: the Development of its Laws and Constitution* (London 1967), at p. 362.

254 Memo dated 20 Feb., 1888: C.O. 137/534/2457.

beyond the measure itself". With respect to the Criminal Code the Colonial Secretary took a somewhat firmer stand: "I am not prepared to advise its repeal. . . . I should still hope that with further explanation and possibly further amendments, the Code might still be accepted by the Council. . . . The Act is one of great importance, and should not be lightly given up."

The Governor attempted to pass the Codes through the Council, but the opposition, following his opening address, was so intense and the chances of passage so hopeless that he took the decision to drop the Codes.[255] Added to the earlier opposition were the judges of the Supreme Court, who wrote with respect to criminal procedure in Jamaica that[256] "the present system works smoothly and satisfactorily". They objected particularly to the elimination of peremptory challenges and to allowing the accused to give evidence, the latter, as we have seen, being an innovation introduced by the Colonial Secretary. The final straw for the Governor and the Colonial Office was the fact that the Attorney-General dissociated himself from the Code, stating:[257] "The Code as a whole is not my work and I feel myself quite at liberty to say that I join in deprecating its introduction." The Governor therefore asked[258] again whether "it may not be expedient to repeal the two Codes of 1879". This time the Colonial Office concurred[259] and in 1889, ten years after their passage, both were repealed.[260]

(b) West Indies

The Colonial Office had greater success in other West Indian colonies. The Code was brought into force in British Honduras, and later in Tobago.[261] Then St. Lucia's Chief Justice prepared a Code for that island based partly on Wright's and partly on the Commissioners' Code, apparently taking the view, perhaps influenced by events in Jamaica, that "it may be better to follow rather than to lead 'the Mother Country' ".[262] But the Colonial Office took a firm line, Lord Kimberley sending a dispatch stating:[263] "I request therefore that, unless you see any strong

---

255 Dispatch from Governor, dated 1 Nov., 1888: C.O. 137/536/23088.

256 Letter from the Judges to the Governor dated 3 Oct., 1888: C.O. 137/536/23088.

257 Undated memo from the Attorney-General to the Colonial Secretary: C.O. 137/536/23088.

258 Dispatch dated 1 Nov., 1888: C.O. 137/536/23088.

259 Dispatch to Governor dated 12 Dec., 1888: C.O. 137/536/23088.

260 Jamaica Correspondence Register No. 15.

261 See memo from Wingfield dated 21 May, 1888, Windward Islands files: C.O. 321/106/9423.

262 *Ibid.*

263 Dated 28 May, 1888: C.O. 321/106/9423.

objection, you will cause a draft Ordinance [to be drawn] in the form of the British Honduras Criminal Code." St. Lucia complied with this request[264] and, when the Chief Justice was later transferred to British Guiana,[265] Wright's Code was adopted there as well.

(c) Africa

The Jamaica Code was adopted in the Gold Coast in 1892 but, as it turned out, nowhere else in Africa.[266] Again, one sees the effect of personalities and local concern on the issue of codification.

A Colonial Office memorandum in 1889 had stated:[267] "We have now got Mr. Wright's Jamaica Criminal Code, which the Jamaicans rejected, enacted in St. Lucia and British Honduras and I think we might have it introduced in the West African Colonies." So a request was made to the Governors of Lagos, the Gold Coast, Sierra Leone and the Gambia to adopt legislation modelled on that of St. Lucia. But only the Gold Coast responded and took half a loaf: *i.e.,* the Code of Criminal Law but not the Code of Procedure.[268] Ten years later Lagos wished to adopt the Gold Coast Code which was thought to have "worked well",[269] but the Bill was politically mismanaged and local opposition caused the matter to be dropped. Then in 1903 the Chief Justice of Northern Nigeria, H. C. Gollan, tried his hand at drafting a Code and rejected the Gold Coast Code in favour of the Queensland Code of 1899, the work of its Chief Justice, S. W. Griffith.[270] That Code, which in general followed the

---

264 See C.O. 321/107/14789.

265 Windward Island Register No. 16: C.O. 376/16.

266 I have relied primarily on H. F. Morris' excellent writing for the description of events in Africa. See Morris, "How Nigeria Got Its Criminal Code" [1970] J.A.L. at p. 137; Morris, 'A History of the Adoption of Codes of Criminal Law and Procedure in British Colonial Africa, 1876-1935' [1974] J.A.L. at p. 6. See also H. F. Morris and J. S. Read, *Indirect Rule and the Search for Justice* (Oxford 1972), at pp. 109 *et seq.*

267 Memo from Wingfield in 1889: see [1970] J.A.L. at pp. 137, 138-9.

268 The Code of Procedure enacted in 1876 was kept: [1974] J.A.L. at pp. 6, 7-8. J. F. Stephen had been asked for his advice when the Colony was established in 1874 and, in the words of an official in the Colonial Office (Stephen's letter is not in the file), had advised that the Gold Coast judges should administer "such principles of natural justice as thought applicable to the circumstances of the cases coming before them. ..." The official noted that Wright's Jamaica Code, then in the process of preparation, might be adopted "if that Code can be made intelligible to ordinary minds." The word "minds" replaced the word "mortals" which had been crossed out. See memo from Fairfield dated 6 Nov., 1874: C.O. 96/112/12406. Not all divisions of the Colonial Office were as enthusiastic as the West Indies Division.

269 Dispatch from Governor of Lagos to the Colonial Secretary, Joseph Chamberlain dated 29 Jan., 1898: see [1970] J.A.L. at pp. 137, 140.

270 Later the first Chief Justice of the High Court of Australia. See Pannam, 'The Radical Chief Justice' (1964) 37 Aust. L.J. at p. 275; Pannam, "Dante and the Chief Justice" (1959) 33 Aust. L.J. at p. 290. J. F. Stephen was also a Dante scholar (see Leslie Stephen, 464-5), but I do not know whether anything can be drawn from this fact!

Commissioners' draft, Gollan reported,[271] "avoided what seems to me to be the fault in particular of the Gold Coast Code, the relegation to definition sections of practically all the essential features of the offences constituted under its provisions". That was the crucial turning point. The Queensland Code with various modifications then slowly swept across Africa.[272] The first stage was for the Colonial Office to make sure that Southern Nigeria adopted the same Code as Northern Nigeria. (Southern Nigeria, in fact, wanted a Code based on the Indian model with which its Governor was familiar.) Then the Nigerian Code replaced the Indian Codes in East Africa. Why the Colonial Office was so keen on eliminating the Indian Codes is not entirely clear. It seemed to stem from a bias by the white population, shared by the Colonial Office, in favour of an "English" Code. The choice of "English" Code was of less importance to the Colonial Office than the objection to the Indian or yet another new Code. A Colonial official noted in 1925:[273] "The work has already been admirably done in Nigeria and the Gold Coast. I sincerely hope that Kenya is not proposing to produce a newfangled Code of its own." Other writers[274] have traced the migration of the East African "Queensland" Codes into British administered Cyprus and then into British mandated Palestine.

Bits and pieces of Wright's Jamaica Code still remain in all these Codes. So, for example, in the present Israeli Penal Law, approved in 1977,[275] which replaced the British Criminal Code Ordinance of 1936, there is a provision[276] reading as follows:

> A person who, knowing that a person designs to commit a felony, fails to use all reasonable means to prevent the commission or completion thereof is liable to imprisonment for two years.

Wright's Jamaica Code had a provision[277] which read:

> Whoever, knowing that a person designs to commit or is committing a felony, fails to

---

271 'Report on (Draft) Criminal Code Proclamation', 6 Oct., 1903: [1970] J.A.L. at pp. 137, 143-4.

272 See Morris, "A History of the Adoption of Codes of Criminal Law and Procedure in British Colonial Africa, 1876-1935" [1974] J.A.L. at p. 6.

273 See [1974] J.A.L. at pp. 6, 14.

274 See Shachar, "The Sources of the Criminal Code Ordinance 1936" (1979) 7 *Iyunei Mishpat* 75 (in Hebrew, with a resume in English); Abrams, "Interpreting the Criminal Code Ordinance, 1936 — the Untapped Well" (1971) 7 Is. L. Rev. at p. 25. I am indebted to Dr Yoram Shachar, Faculty of Law, Tel Aviv University, for his assistance in helping me understand the origins of the Israeli Penal Code as well as for stimulating discussions on the subject of codification.

275 The new Integrated Version was approved by the Constitution, Legislation and Juridical Committee of the Knesset on 7 June, 1977.

276 S. 262. Authorized translation prepared by the Ministry of Justice, Jerusalem.

277 S. 34.

use all reasonable means to prevent the commission or completion thereof, is guilty of a misdemeanor.

If Chief Justice Gollan had not decided to adopt the Queensland Code, Israel might now have a Criminal Code based on Wright's Code. One ironical twist is that Northern Nigeria, having started the adoption of the Queensland Code, changed back to an Indian-style code in 1960.[278]

(d) Other Colonies

A full discussion of the adoption of Codes in other parts of the Commonwealth is outside the scope of this article. It should be mentioned, however, that the Commissioners', and not Wright's, Code formed the basis of the new Code in Canada in 1892,[279] in New Zealand in 1893, [280] and later in Australia, the first being the Queensland Code of 1899.[281] Whether Wright's Code was considered and rejected by the drafters is not apparent. Wright's Code is not mentioned in the Canadian Parliamentary Debates. The Working Papers for the Canadian Code unfortunately cannot be consulted, having, it seems, been destroyed by a fire in the Parliament Buildings in 1897.[282] Chief Justice Griffith's

---

278 See [1974] J.A.L. at pp. 6, 23. The new Penal Code was based on the Sudan Penal Code of 1899, which was derived from the Indian Codes.

279 S.C. 1892, c. 29, which came into force on 1 July, 1893. See G. Parker, "The Origins of the Canadian Criminal Code" in D. H. Flaherty (ed.), Essays in the History of Canadian Law, vol. 1 (Toronto 1981) at pp. 249 *et seq.*; Note, (1982) 60 Can. B. Rev. 502. See also R. C. Macleod, "The Shaping of Canadian Criminal Law: 1892 to 1902" [1978] *Historical Papers* at p. 64.

280 See F. B. Adams, *Criminal Law and Practice in New Zealand*, 2nd ed. (Wellington 1971), referring to the Report of a Commission in 1883 which prepared a draft based on the 1880 English Bill but advised that enactment should be deferred until the English Parliament had finally dealt with the subject: see Public Acts of New Zealand (Reprint) 1908-1931, vol II at p. 176.

281 Colin Howard, *Criminal Law,* 3rd ed. (Sydney 1977), at p. 3; E.J. Edwards, R.A. Hayes and R.S. O'Reagan, *Cases on the Criminal Code* (Sydney 1969) at p. vii. The Western Australian Code was adopted in 1902, and the Tasmanian in 1924.

282 At least one influential Canadian was familiar with Wright's Code. Sir James Robert Gowan, a Senator who played an important role in promoting codification of the Criminal Law and in supporting the Canadian Code in the Senate, had met Wright in England in 1872 when Gowan was a judge and active in law reform. The Public Archives of Canada contains a number of letters between Gowan and Wright in 1891 and 1892. Gowan wrote congratulating Wright on his appointment to the Bench and reminded him of "the long talk we had about codification and the criminal law", adding that "a printed copy of your Criminal Code for Jamaica was afterwards sent to me in Canada". Gowan later sent Wright a copy of the Canadian Criminal Code, stating that they took as their model "the abundant labour of the great Jurist at home . . . and built on and around that good solid English foundation". Wright's reply (27 Oct., 1892) did not comment on the Canadian Code except to say: "I am a little alarmed at the tendency to

Report[283] on the Queensland Code does not mention Wright's Code. It may be that the copy which no doubt had been received twenty years earlier was lost in a Government file. Or it may be that he did not want to use as a model a code which had been rejected by the colony for which it was drafted.

(e) H. L. Stephen's Draft Code

The final episode in the history of Wright's Code is its unfortunate redrafting by J. F. Stephen's son, H. L. Stephen.

In March, 1900, Henry Lushington Stephen, the forty-year-old son of the late James Fitzjames Stephen, approached the Colonial Office with a proposal that he redraft Wright's Jamaica Code which he suggested was "obsolete".[284] H. L. Stephen had a few months earlier attempted to interest the Society of Comparative Legislation[285] in the idea. The Society, of which Mr Justice Wright was a member of Council, did not (probably to its great relief) have to pass a resolution on the issue because Mr H. B. Cox, an Assistant Under-Secretary in the Colonial Office, stated at the meeting that anything submitted to the Colonial Office by Mr Stephen would be "most carefully considered".[286]

Cox was not enthusiastic about Stephen's proposal. He sent a memorandum to Joseph Chamberlain, the Colonial Secretary, stating,[287] "Mr Stephen is a very able lawyer and a good draftsman, but my fear is that his natural respect for his father's work and great legal attainments may lead him to regard the work from one point of view only." Sir Courtenay Ilbert, whose favourable view of Wright's Code has already been mentioned, advised[288] that although the Jamaica Code "would doubtless be the better for being revised and brought up to date . . . it is a complete mistake to suppose that the Jamaica draft is obsolete, or is superseded by the Commissioners' draft". He warned that "it would be unadvisable to

---

detail which modern legislation shows and from which your code is not exempt. I should favour great abbreviation."

283   Griffith's letter to the Attorney-General of Queensland is dated 29 October 1897: Journal of the Queensland Legislative Council, vol 49.

284   Letter from H. L. Stephen to the Colonial Secretary dated March, 1900: General files, C.O. 323/460/8180.

285   The Society grew out of a Conference organized by the Lord Chancellor, Lord Herschell, in 1894, following suggestions by Sir C. Ilbert. See H. L. Stephen, "A Model Code for the Colonies" (1899) 1 Journal of the Society of Comparative Legislation 439.

286   See memo from Cox dated 27 April, 1900: C.O. 323/460/8180.

287   *Ibid.*

288   Memo dated 27 April, 1900: C.O. 323/460/8180.

select as a draftsman any person who proceeds on the assumption that the Commissioners' Code of 1879 is the proper model to be followed."[289]

In spite of these views Chamberlain, for almost inexplicable reasons, instructed Cox to ask Stephen to prepare a draft Model Criminal Code.[290] I say *almost* inexplicable because it may just be that the financial retrenchment that was being faced by the Department[291] and the fact that Stephen would charge very little explained why he was chosen. Moreover, J. F. Stephen had been a good friend of Chamberlain's from the 1860s.[292] Cox reported[293] back to Chamberlain the financial terms. Stephen, he wrote, "said that if he had been asked by the Department to undertake the work he should have mentioned 100 guineas as a fair sum but that as he had put forward the proposal himself he would accept 50 guineas." They decided to give him 100 guineas, a paltry sum compared to the 1,500 his father had received for his Code over twenty years earlier. But H. L. Stephen had very little legal business. In one remarkably frank note to Cox early in 1901 he stated:[294] "If business continues as slack as it is at present, which it probably will, I hope to have that Criminal Code ready to go to the printers [within a few months]." (It is not surprising therefore that Stephen accepted an appointment as a judge in Calcutta later that year.)

H. L. Stephen's Code was a second-rate piece of work. As Cox and Ilbert had suspected, he transformed Wright's Code into his father's Code. In doing so he got rid of the *mens rea* definitions, one of the strengths of Wright's Code, as well as most of the Code's other good features. "The general arrangement of my draft", Stephen wrote in the introduction,[295] "follows that of the English Code, with only a few unimportant exceptions." This transformation may well have been Stephen's intention from the beginning. Indeed, this may have been Chamberlain's intention too; for, as pointed out above, he had been a good friend of J. F. Stephen[296] and would have been out of sympathy with Wright's form of radicalism.

A bitter dispute then arose between Cox and Stephen over Stephen's

---

289 Ilbert noted that the Lord Chancellor, Lord Halsbury, had been privately consulted, but was "not himself in favour of a Criminal Code". Halsbury had not been keen on codification in 1886-7 in correspondence with J. F. Stephen: L.C.O. 1/42.

290 Memo dated 2 May, 1900: C.O. 323/460/8180.

291 See R. C. Snelling and T. J. Barron, "The Colonial Office and its permanent officials 1801-1914" in G. Sutherland (ed), *Studies in the Growth of Nineteenth-Century Government* (London 1972), at pp. 139, 159.

292 Leslie Stephen, at p. 232.

293 Memo dated 4 May, 1900: C.O. 323/460/8180.

294 Letter dated 6 Feb., 1901: C.O. 323/472/4881.

295 C.O. 885/7/136.

296 See Leslie Stephen, at p. 232.

right to send the Code to the newspapers. It is summed up in Cox's memorandum to Chamberlain:[297]

> Please see the correspondence which I have had with Mr Stephen. He came to see me this morning and evidently did not like my letter at all. He said he had in part been led to undertake the work as a 'legitimate advertisement' and that he wanted to send his code to people like the judges, to *The Times* and to other newspapers for criticism. I said that as he had been appointed to a judgeship in India I hardly thought advertisement was necessary for him to which he replied that he desired to be known as a draftsman, that some day he would return from India[298] and that he was particularly anxious to show that his father's criminal code was not dead but was workable and working.

Chamberlain noted[299] that 'it is not unnatural that Mr Stephen should desire the advertisement' but agreed with Cox that "at this stage" it should be kept confidential.

In the end the Code was sent, marked "Confidential", to about twenty persons selected by Stephen, including Mr Justice Wright, whose reaction to it is nowhere noted in the Colonial Office records. The Code was entitled simply "Draft Criminal Code" and not "Model Criminal Code" and was sent out to the Crown Colonies. It was never made public. The permanent officials in the Colonial Office no doubt felt they had been used, and wanted to minimize the damage. But the damage had been done. Wright's Code was now one of several competing Colonial Office codes. Its primacy was gone. The Colonial Office would no longer attempt to encourage colonies to adopt it. It is not surprising, therefore, that Gollan was free to choose the Queensland Code for Northern Nigeria in 1903.

7. CONCLUSION

It remains now to give a thumb-nail sketch of Wright's later career and to attempt to draw some conclusions from the story. Wright was appointed a judge of the High Court in 1890 after spending seven years as junior counsel to the Treasury[300] (i.e. senior counsel to the Attorney-General, or, as it was popularly known, "Attorney-General's devil") where

---

297 Memo dated 5 Oct., 1901: C.O. 323/472/34694.

298 He, in fact, returned from Calcutta in 1914, and was an Alderman of the London County Council from 1916-28. In 1904 he married a relative of Florence Nightingale and succeeded to his father's baronetcy when his older brother died in 1932. He died in 1945. See *Who Was Who 1929-1940* (London 1967); Radzinowicz, *Sir James Fitzjames Stephen* (London 1957), at p. 68.

299 Memo dated 8 Oct., 1901: C.O. 323/472/34694.

300 During this period he was, *inter alia*, appointed by the Colonial Office as a Commissioner to decide on the delicate issue of German Land Claims in Fiji, a task which he accomplished in 1885 with great success: see C.O. 881/6/107. The file mentions that he had earlier been employed by the Foreign Office, but I have not been able to discover what he was engaged to do for it.

he prosecuted in a number of major cases including the Fenian trials of 1883.[301] He also acted for the complainant in the notorious Dilke divorce cases in 1886.[302] Before then he had prepared a number of Reports presented to Parliament on explosions in mines.[303] A future Prime Minister, H. H. Asquith, was Wright's junior from 1883-1885 and acknowledged in his memoirs his "heavy debt of gratitude to Wright".[304] He noted Wright's eccentricities, including the fact that he sat in his chambers "with a tall hat on his head and a briar pipe in his mouth". But he also noted that Wright "was one of the best-hearted and most generous of men, though abrupt in speech and angular and peppery in manner".[305]

The Lord Chancellor, Lord Halsbury, appointed Wright following a strong request to do so by Lord Chief Justice Coleridge (with the concurrence of Mr Justice Bowen):[306]

> We want a strong man in the Queen's Bench very badly, not only a lawyer but a man of force of mind and character and one who can do the duties and functions of a judge with vigour and ability. If you have made up your mind of course there is no more to be said. If you have not, we both wish to put before you for consideration the name of R. S. Wright, he is a very able, probably the ablest, man at the Bar, except four or five men at the very head who don't practically count for this place, a scholar, a man of distinction and for seven and a half years Treasury devil which used formerly to be thought to give a man a claim. ... [T]he Chief Justice need not apologise for writing to the Lord Chancellor as to a vacancy in his Division, but I am sure you will believe that I write simply and solely on public grounds.

Wright replied to the Lord Chancellor's offer:[307]

> Dear Lord Chancellor,
>   Gratefully, but with many misgivings, I accept the offer. There were so many

---

301 See, e.g., *R. v. Gallagher and others* (1883), 15 Cox C.C. 291; *R. v. Deasy and others* (1883), 15 Cox C.C. 334. The final volume of the Queen's Bench Reports ([1890] 1 Q.B.) gives some indication of Wright's practice before his appointment to the Bench. There are, for example, six reported Divisional Court cases in which he took part in the month of Nov., 1890.

302 See R. Jenkins, *Sir Charles Dilke* (London 1958). He acted as junior counsel for Crawford, a Scottish lawyer, who had been a fellow of Lincoln College, Oxford, and against Wright's fellow radical Dilke.

303 See the Report on the Risca Colliery Explosion, 1880 C 2743, in which 120 persons died; Report on the Seaham Colliery Explosion, 1880 C 2924, in which 160 persons died; and Report on the Whitfield Colliery Explosion. 1881 C 2965, in which 21 persons died.

304 Asquith, *Memories and Reflections 1852-1927* (London 1928) at p. 82 *et seq.*

305 *Ibid.* For other, not dissimilar assessments, see the *DNB*; Earl Russell, *My Life and Adventures* (London 1923), at p. 54 ("the kindest soul that ever breathed").

306 Letter dated 2 Feb., 1890, reprinted in R. F. V. Heuston, *Lives of the Lord Chancellors 1885-1940* (Oxford 1964), at p. 44. The appointment did not directly follow after the letter, but was made when a further vacancy arose.

307 Letter dated 9 Dec. 1890, reprinted in Heuston, at p. 44.

grounds on which I might have been passed over without injustice that I had no expectation of being made a Judge for a long time to come.

Very faithfully yours,

R. S. Wright.

Coleridge later told Jowett that he thought Wright would become a "great judge".[308] Wright did distinguish himself in his fourteen years as a Queen's Bench judge, although the opportunities to do so at that level were somewhat limited. His reasons for judgment in *Sherras v. De Rutzen (mens rea)*[309] *R. v. Pittwood* (omission)[310] *R. v. Button* (attempt)[311] and *R. v. Ollis* (estoppel)[312] are well known to criminal lawyers. His opinion in *Allen v. Flood,*[313] which was supported by the House of Lords, and his reasons for judgment in the *Moçambique*[314] case, upheld by the House of Lords,[315] are perhaps his best known in civil cases. C. H. S. Fifoot[316] places him in a class with Blackburn and Lindley, and R. F. V. Heuston[317] concludes that he was in the very first rank of High Court judges. Wright died in 1904 at the comparatively young age of sixty-five[318] without being elevated to a higher court.

It seems likely that his political background and ideas blocked his advancement. Lord Halsbury, a Conservative, was the Lord Chancellor at the time of Wright's appointment in 1890 and then from 1895 until after Wright's death in 1904. Lord Salisbury, the Prime Minister, in whose hands lay nomination to the higher courts, wanted political considerations to play a role in appointments.[319] It is to Halsbury's credit that he

308   See letter from B. Jowett to Coleridge dated 1 Dec., 1891, printed in E. H. Coleridge, *Life and Correspondence of John Duke Coleridge, Lord Chief Justice of England,* vol 2 (London 1904) at p. 372.

309   [1895] 1 Q.B. 918 (Div. Ct.).

310   (1902), 19 T.L.R. 37 (Assizes).

311   [1900] 2 Q.B. 597 (C.C.R.). He was a member of the Court but did not give a separate judgment in *R. v. Ring* (1892), 17 Cox C.C. 491 (C.C.R.).

312   [1900] 2 Q.B. 758 (C.C.R.).

313   [1898] A.C. 1 (H.L.).

314   *Companhia de Moçambique v. Br. South Africa Co.,* [1892] 2 Q.B. 358.

315   *The Br. South Africa Co. v. Companhia de Moçambique,*[1893] A.C. 603.

316   *Judge and Jurist in the Reign of Victoria* (London 1959), at p. 91.

317   *Lives of the Lord Chancellors, 1885-1940* (Oxford 1964), at pp. 40 and 65. See also E. Bowen-Rowlands, *Seventy-Two Years at the Bar* (London 1924), at p. 376 where he is ranked with Coke and Selden and others.

318   He had an operation in May, 1904 and never recovered, dying on 13 Aug., 1904: see *DNB.* His funeral was reported in *The Times,* 18 Aug., 1904: 'By his own wish, it was of the simplest possible character . . . a simple oak casket, without brass fittings.' His will stated: 'It is my wish that no monument or memorial of any description shall be provided in reference to me.' His son, who was born in 1901 and died in 1976, was in the Foreign Office and was, at one time, the Ambassador to Norway.

319   See R. F. V. Heuston, at p. 37.

appointed Wright in the first place, because as the Solicitors' Journal[320] pointed out at the time, Wright "has been well known as an opponent of the present Government". Moreover, his refusal, on egalitarian grounds, to accept a knighthood at the time of appointment can hardly have pleased the Conservatives. He eventually received the knighthood after being persuaded to do so by his friend Bowen.[321] *Vanity Fair*[322] caricatured Wright with the caption "He declined Knighthood, but thought better of it" and observed: "He is now a Judge of six months' standing, unpolished in manner, abrupt in speech and full of superciliousness, as a good Radical should be".

What conclusions can be drawn from the story of Wright's Jamaica Code? Perhaps it is simply the obvious one that law reform is affected by a great number of factors apart from the merits of the proposals. Then, as now, a combination of politics, personalities and pressure groups affected the outcome. The crucial events seem, in retrospect, largely unplotted and accidental: Labour's backing in 1877 of J. F. Stephen's efforts at codification; Kimberley's decision in 1881 to permit the accused to give evidence on his own behalf; Wright's view in 1882 that the Criminal Law Code should not be introduced without the Code of Procedure; Chamberlain's decision in 1900 to appoint H. L. Stephen to revise Wright's Code; the Northern Nigerian Chief Justice's preference for the Queensland Code; and many more.

Moreover, the available records will tell only part of the story. We cannot, for example, now reconstruct the interrelationship between Wright and Stephen, the two principal rivals in codifying the criminal law in the British Empire in the second half of the nineteenth century. The Stephen papers in the University Library, Cambridge, contain no correspondence with Wright (or, as far as I could see, any mention of him), nor does his three-volume *History of the Criminal Law* refer to Wright's Code; and Wright's papers are apparently no longer in existence.[323]

---

320   (1890), 35 Sol. Jo. 100.

321   *The Times,* 15 Aug., 1904.

322   27 June, 1891.

323   I have not discovered any evidence of hostility between the two, but a few double-edged references to each other's works leave one wondering what they actually thought of each other. In 1878 Wright commented on Stephen in a letter to Mrs Ponsonby: "Sir J. F. Stephen's books are all sensible and philosophical, if not perhaps always accurate or thorough". See the Gladstone Papers, British Library, Add. MSS 44456, f269. Stephen's History (vol 2, at p. 229) after referring in the text to an early treatise on the Star Chamber by Hudson, cites Wright's Conspiracy book in a footnote: "Mr Wright has gone into this subject at great length and with much learning in his work on the law of criminal conspiracies. He does not happen to quote Hudson." Elsewhere (vol. 3, at p. 217) he states: "Mr Wright has laboriously collected every case. . . ." In another place (vol 3, at p. 209), however, Stephen is very complimentary to Wright's book: "a work of remarkable learning and ability."

One matter that is clear, however, is the way the Stephen family affected Wright's reputation. James Fitzjames Stephen worked with Wright on the Jamaica Code, produced his own competing Code, and, it would seem, studiously avoided mentioning Wright's Code or his efforts at consolidation in any of his extensive writings[324] or his voluminous correspondence. James Fitzjames' son, H. L. Stephen, redrafted and emasculated Wright's Code. Further, James Fitzjames' brother, Leslie Stephen, as the editor of the *Dictionary of National Biography*, probably chose another of James Fitzjames' sons, Herbert, to be the author of the less than enthusiastic biographical note on Wright, which again does not mention either Wright's Code or his plan for statutory consolidation. Nor is there any mention of Wright in Leslie Stephen's biography of his brother. It almost seems as if the Stephen family tried to eliminate Wright from the history of the codification of the criminal law.

---

324 The one reference I have been able to find to Wright's work on codification or consolidation is in "The Criminal Code (1879)", The Nineteenth Century, 1880, Jan. p. 136 at 151 where Stephen states that the Royal Commission checked the contents of his Bill "by reference to a variety of indexes to the statute book, and to catalogues of indictable offences of more or less authority, amongst which I may particularly mention lists prepared by Mr R. S. Wright for the Statute Law Revision Committee".

2

CRIMINAL JUSTICE AND
THE CONSTITUTIONAL DIVISION
OF POWER IN CANADA*

1. INTRODUCTION

There have been numerous major clashes in recent years between the federal and provincial governments on the division of power over criminal justice. Issues have arisen, for example, on the control of prostitution, the treatment of drug addicts, the creation of unified criminal courts and the power to control prosecutions. This paper explores the historical background to the division of powers and analyses some of the recent court decisions. Let us first look at the origins of section 91(27) of the British North America Act, now called the Constitution Act, 1867,[1] which gives the federal government exclusive legislative authority over "the criminal law . . . including the procedure in criminal matters."

2. CONFEDERATION

The discussion and legislative debates leading to Confederation show that there was no controversy over whether legislative power over criminal law and procedure should be given to the federal government. Centralizing the criminal law power was in deliberate contrast to the American Constitution which left control over the criminal law power to the individual states.

Why was the criminal law power given to the federal government? Sir John A. Macdonald, then the Attorney-General, expressed what must have been the consensus at the time when, in the parliamentary debates in 1865, he stated:[2]

---

* This essay has, in part, drawn on a talk, "The Constitution and the Criminal Law", given by the author in January, 1981 at a University College Symposium, *Towards Nationhood: Canada in the Second Half of the Nineteenth Century.* I am grateful to Steven Rosenhek, a recent graduate of the Faculty of Law, for his very helpful assistance. I am also indebted to Peter Hogg, John Laskin, Peter Russell and Kathy Swinton for a number of helpful comments on an earlier draft of this essay.

1 30 & 31 Vict., c. 3 (U.K.); R.S.C. 1970, App. II, No. 5; now the Constitution Act, 1867.

2 See M. A. Lapin and J. S. Patrick (eds.), *Index to Parliamentary Debates on Confederation of the British North American Provinces* (Ottawa, 1951) at pp. 40-1. See generally, Sterling, "The Criminal Law Power and Confederation" (1957) 15 U.T. Fac. of Law Rev. 1.

> The criminal law too — the determination of what is a crime and what is not and how crime shall be punished — is left to the General Government. This is a matter almost of necessity. It is of great importance that we should have the same criminal law throughout these provinces — that what is a crime in one part of British America, should be a crime in every part — that there should be the same protection of life and property in one as in another.[3]

He then commented on the American division of authority:[4]

> It is one of the defects in the United States system, that each separate state has or may have a criminal code of its own, — that what may be a capital offence in one state, may be a venial offence, punishable slightly, in another. But under our Constitution we shall have one body of criminal law, based on the criminal law of England, and operating equally throughout British America, so that a British American, belonging to what province he may, or going to any other part of the Confederation, knows what his rights are in that respect, and what his punishment will be if an offender against the criminal laws of the land. I think this is one of the most marked instances in which we take advantage of the experience derived from our observations of the defects in the Constitution of the neighboring Republic.

There is no doubt that the Civil War in the United States was a major factor in the desire of many to place some of the more important powers and symbols of nationhood within the legislative authority of the federal government. The criminal law plays an important role in society in stating fundamental values. This can be seen today in the discussions taking place on such criminal law issues as the law of abortion, the law relating to homosexual conduct, the question of the reintroduction of capital punishment, and the activities of the police and the security service. At the Quebec Conference in 1864, Oliver Mowat had commented on the advantages of a uniform system of law, stating:[5] "It would weld us into a nation." The Colonial Secretary, Lord Carnarvon, expressly gave his approval of the arrangement in his speech on the British North America Act in the House of Lords:[6]

> To the Central Parliament will also be assigned the enactment of criminal law. The administration of it, indeed, is vested in the local authorities; but the power of general legislation is very properly reserved for the Central Parliament. And in this I cannot but note a wise departure from the system pursued in the United States, where each State is competent to deal as it may please with its criminal code, and where an offence may be visited with one penalty in the State of New York, and with another in the State of Virginia. The system here proposed is, I believe, a better and safer one; and I trust that before very long the criminal law of the four Provinces may be assimilated — and assimilated, I will add, on the basis of English procedure.

---

3 See also *R. v. Lawrence* (1878), 43 U.C.Q.B. 164 at 174 (C.A.) *per* Harrison C.J.

4 Lapin and Patrick, *supra* note 2 at p. 41.

5 See G. P. Browne (ed.), *Documents on the Confederation of British North America* (Toronto 1969) at p. 120.

6 See R. Herbert (ed.), *Speeches on Canadian Affairs by the Fourth Earl of Carnarvon* (London 1902) at p. 103.

That assimilation did in fact happen. Shortly after Confederation, Sir John A. Macdonald introduced a series of consolidation statutes,[7] prepared by James Gowan,[8] then a county court judge in Barrie, Ontario, later a Senator, who drew on provincial as well as English legislation. The drafters would also have been interested in having the criminal law power in federal hands because of the importance of the criminal law in controlling political dissent and revolutionary conduct through the laws of treason and sedition. The British had recently introduced a uniform criminal code in India that had been drafted by Macaulay[9] twenty years earlier — its adoption no doubt hastened by the Indian Mutiny.[10]

3. QUEBEC AND ENGLISH CRIMINAL LAW

A further reason for making the criminal law federal was to ensure that Quebec maintained English criminal law, first introduced into Canada in 1763 following the victory of the English over the French. Governor Murray was given full power in 1763 to make laws "not to be repugnant, but as near as may be agreeable to the laws and statutes of this our Kingdom of Great Britain."[11] As is well known, the French civil law was reintroduced by the Quebec Act of 1774,[12] but not French criminal law. Clause 11 of the Quebec Act stated:

> And whereas the certainty and lenity of the Criminal Laws of England, and the benefit and advantages resulting from the use of it, have been sensibly felt by the inhabitants, from an experience of more than nine years, during which it has been uniformly administered; be it therefore further enacted by the authority aforesaid, that the same shall continue to be administered, and shall be observed as Law in the Province of Quebec, as well in the description and quality of the offence, as in the method of prosecution and trial; and the punishments and forfeitures thereby inflicted, to the exclusion of every other rule of Criminal Law, or mode of proceeding thereof, which did or might prevail in the said Province, before the year of our Lord 1764 . . .

It was not a foregone conclusion, however, that English criminal law

---

7 See S.C. 1869, cc. 18-36.

8 See H. H. Ardagh, *The Life of Hon. Sir James Robert Gowan* (Toronto 1911) at pp. 66 *et seq.;* A. H. U. Colquhoun, *The Hon. James R. Gowan: A Memoir* (Toronto 1894) at pp. 59-61. See the Gowan correspondence set out in Professor Graham Parker's Newsletter (1981), 2 Now and Then 17.

9 See Cross, "The Making of English Criminal Law: Macaulay" [1978] Crim. L. Rev. 519; Kadish, "Codifiers of the Criminal Law: Wechsler's Predecessors" (1978) 78 Col. L. Rev. 1098.

10 See M. Edwardes, *British India 1772-1947* (New York 1968) at pp. 176 *et seq.*

11 A. Shortt and A. G. Doughty (eds.), *Documents Relating to the Constitutional History of Canada 1759-1791* (2nd ed., Ottawa 1918) at p. 126.

12 14 Geo. 3, c. 83 (U.K.). See generally, H. M. Neatby, *The Administration of Justice under the Quebec Act* (Minneapolis 1937); A. L. Burt, *The Old Province of Quebec* (Carleton Library edition 1968).

would be applied in Quebec. Some had suggested the reintroduction of French law,[13] and some an amalgamation of English and French law.[14] The differences between English and French criminal law at the time were substantial. Perhaps the most significant difference was the potential use of judicial torture in France[15] and in New France.[16] England had not officially used torture to extract a confession for well over 100 years,[17] but continental criminal law virtually required it because of the rigidity of its formal laws of proof. The English rules of evidence allowed a conviction based on circumstantial evidence; French rules did not. Judicial torture was not eliminated from French procedure until it was suppressed by Louis XVI in 1780,[18] six years *after* the Quebec Act. Had judicial torture been eliminated before the Conquest we might well find that French criminal law would still be applicable in Quebec today. But the climate of opinion in both France and England at the time was against the French system. Becarria wrote his famous book[19] criticizing the criminal process of the old regime in 1764, and Voltaire published his work[20] on the same subject in 1766. In contrast, Blackstone's work,[21] published around the same time in England, showed a much more humane system of criminal law, a system which not only prevented torture, but prevented any compulsory self-incrimination. Moreover, both Becarria and Voltaire cited with approval English criminal law.[22]

There were other differences between the French and English criminal laws. French law, for example, permitted somewhat different

---

13   See Sterling, "The Criminal Law Power and Confederation" (1957) 15 U.T. Fac. of Law Rev. 1 at pp. 2-3.

14   *Ibid.* at p. 2. See also W. P. M. Kennedy (ed.), *Statutes, Treaties and Documents of the Canadian Constitution 1713-1929* (2nd ed., Oxford U.P. 1930) at p. 80.

15   See generally J. H. Langbein, *Torture and the Law of Proof* (Chicago 1977).

16   Hay, "The Meanings of the Criminal Law in Quebec, 1764-1774" in L. A. Knafla (ed.), *Crime and Criminal Justice in Europe and Canada* (W.L.U. Press 1981) 77 at p. 81; A. Lachance, *La Justice Criminelle Du Roi Au Canada Au XVIIIe Siècle* (Québec 1978) at pp. 79 *et seq.;* H. M. Neatby, *The Administration of Justice under the Quebec Act* (Minneapolis 1937) at p. 298; and W. J. Eccles, *Canada Under Louis XIV; 1663-1701* (Toronto 1964) at p. 34. See generally J. Boucher and A. Morel, *De L'Ordonnance Criminelle au Code Penal* (U. of Montreal 1975-76), part II, Le Proces; Morel, "La Reception du Droit Criminel Anglais au Québec (1760-1892)" (1978) 13 Rev. J. Thémis 449.

17   Langbein, *supra* note 15, chapter 6.

18   *Ibid.* at p. 66.

19   C. B. Beccaria, *An Essay on Crimes and Punishments,* first translated into English in 1767.

20   F.-M. Voltaire, *Commentaire sur le Livre des Délits et des Peinés.*

21   W. Blackstone, *Commentaries on the Laws of England* (the fourth book was published in 1769, Oxford).

22   See Langbein, *supra* note 15 at p. 68.

punishments[23] than the English law, but it is hard to say that English law was less severe considering the punishment imposed on Maclane, convicted of treason in Quebec in 1797:[24]

> It remains that I should discharge the painful duty of pronouncing the sentence of the law, which is, That you, David Maclane, be taken to the place from whence you came, and from thence you are to be drawn to the place of execution, where you must be hanged by the neck, but not till you are dead; for, you must be cut down alive and your bowels taken out and burnt before your face; then your head must be severed from your body, which must be divided into four parts, and your head and quarters be at the King's disposal; and the Lord have mercy on your soul.

Other differences concerned the certainty of the charge and the elimination of evidence of other conduct in English procedure. And, of course, the right to a jury trial was absent from the French system. The French Canadians were not, however, enthusiastic about the jury.[25] They did not like the idea of the unanimity rule, some preferring a verdict by two-thirds of the jury.[26] Moreover, the upper levels of French society did not favour being tried by ordinary citizens. It was, however, the potential use of judicial torture and the dark cloud it cast on French criminal law that was probably the key factor in bringing about the use of the English criminal law.

Quebec therefore lived with and came to accept English criminal law, procedure, and rules of evidence for the 100 years before Confederation. Indeed, Quebec lawyers had been using English rules of evidence even in their civil cases.[27] The Honourable Mr. Cauchon from Montmorency stated during the Confederation Debates:[28]

> For my own part, I infinitely prefer the criminal law of England to that of any other country. It affords more protection to the party accused, than, for instance the criminal code of France does. . . . If the English criminal law gives the criminal too great a chance of escaping, it at least saves society the stigma of condemning the innocent. The accused is tried for the single act for which he is indicted, and is not questioned concerning his whole past life and conversation.

One effective way of insuring that English criminal law would continue to apply in Quebec was to give power over criminal law and procedure to the federal government.

Federal jurisdiction over the criminal law has been a very positive force in the development of the country. Occasionally one hears

---

23   See generally Hay, *supra* note 16.

24   *R. v. Maclane* (1797), 26 State Trials 721 at 826.

25   Hay, *supra* note 16 at pp. 94 *et seq.;* Evidence of Chief Justice Hay set out in W. P. M. Kennedy (ed.), *Statutes, Treaties and Documents of the Canadian Constitution 1713-1929* (2nd ed., Oxford U.P. 1930) at pp. 123 *et seq.*

26   *Ibid.*

27   Neatby, *supra* note 16 at p. 45.

28   Confederation Debates, *supra* note 2 at p. 74.

suggestions that criminal law should be given to the provinces;[29] this would be a serious mistake. The United States could only achieve through the activism of the Supreme Court some of the uniformity that is taken for granted in Canada. One of the key reasons why the Warren court was so active in the 1960's and 70's was because it sought to impose on the States minimum standards in areas of criminal law and procedure, such as confessions, search and seizure, double jeopardy, and capital punishment. The technique employed was to apply the Bill of Rights to the States by using the "due process" clause of the 14th Amendment.[30] Uniform rules can be achieved in Canada through the federal Criminal Code.

4. SCOPE OF THE CRIMINAL LAW POWER

There have, of course, been numerous disputes between the federal government and the provinces over the scope of the criminal law power. Let us first look at challenges to federal legislation.

A hundred years ago, the courts gave the criminal law power a very wide meaning. In 1882, in *Russell v. The Queen,*[31] the Privy Council seemed to uphold the validity of the Canada Temperance Act of 1878 under the criminal law power. The Court stated:[32]

> Laws . . . designed for the promotion of public order, safety, or morals, and which subject those who contravene them to criminal procedure and punishment, belong to the subject of public wrongs rather than to that of civil rights. They are of a nature which fall within the general authority of Parliament to make laws for the order and good government of Canada, and have direct relation to criminal law, which is one of the enumerated classes of subjects assigned exclusively to the Parliament of Canada.

But doubt was thrown on *Russell* by Lord Watson in 1896 in the *Local Prohibition* case.[33] He explained *Russell* as based on the "peace, order and good government" clause,[34] and went so far as to say, in one example,[35] that "an Act restricting the right to carry weapons of offence, or their sale to young persons, within the province would be within the authority of the provincial legislature" and not of the federal parliament. Lord Watson's enhancement of provincial power over "property and civil rights" at the expense of federal powers such as the criminal law power was also found in Lord Haldane's judgments in the 20th century.

---

29 See, *e.g.,* A.S.A. Abel, *Towards a Constitutional Charter for Canada* (Toronto 1980) at p. 5; Abel, "A Chart for a Charter" (1976) 25 U.N.B.L.J. 20 at pp. 50-52.

30 The first case was *Mapp v. Ohio* (1961), 367 U.S. 643.

31 (1882), 7 App. Cas. 829 (P.C.).

32 *Ibid.* at 839.

33 *A. G. Ont. v. A. G. Can.,* [1896] A.C. 348 (P.C.).

34 *Ibid.* at 361-2.

35 *Ibid.*

In 1922, in the *Board of Commerce* case,[36] Lord Haldane severely restricted the criminal law power to cases "where the subject matter is one which by its very nature belongs to the domain of criminal jurisprudence".[37] But later decisions have broadened that definition. Lord Atkin in the *P.A.T.A.*[38] case in 1931 gave the following definition: "The criminal quality of an act cannot be discerned by intuition; nor can it be discovered by reference to any standard but one: Is the act prohibited with penal consequences?" But just as Haldane's definition was too narrow, Lord Atkin's has proven to be too wide. The federal government cannot take jurisdiction simply by imposing a criminal penalty. The *Margarine Reference*[39] case in 1951 demonstrated this limitation on the criminal law power. The Supreme Court held that to forbid manufacture and sale of margarine for economic purposes is "to deal directly with the civil rights of individuals in relation to particular trade within the Provinces."[40] A similar approach was taken by the Supreme Court in 1979 with respect to the marketing of apples under the Canada Agricultural Products Standards Act in *Dominion Stores Ltd. v. The Queen*[41] and with respect to the marketing of "light beer" under the federal Food and Drugs Acts in the *Labatt Breweries*[42] case. In both cases the majority of the Supreme Court held that the criminal law power could not justify the legislation and so declared parts of the federal legislation *ultra vires*.[43]

Subsequently, the Ontario Court of Appeal upheld a provision of the federal Consumer Packaging and Labelling Act[44] because it is designed to prevent the deception of the consumer and therefore comes within the criminal law power. The recently enacted federal gun control provisions

---

36 *Re The Board of Commerce Act, 1919, and The Combines and Fair Prices Act, 1919,* [1922] 1 A.C. 191 (P.C.).

37 *Ibid.* at 198-9.

38 *Proprietary Articles Trade Assn. v. A. G. Can.,* [1931] A.C. 310 at 324 (P.C.).

39 *Reference Re Section 5(a) of the Dairy Industry Act,* [1949] 1 D.L.R. 433 (S.C.C.). Affirmed [1951] A.C. 179 (P.C.).

40 *Ibid.* at pp. 473-4.

41 (1979), 50 C.C.C. (2d) 277 (S.C.C.).

42 *Labatt Breweries of Can. Ltd. v. A. G. Can.* (1979), 52 C.C.C. (2d) 433 (S.C.C.). See also *Boggs v. R.* (1981), 58 C.C.C. (2d) 7 (S.C.C.).

43 See also *Regional Municipality of Peel v. MacKenzie* (1982), 139 D.L.R. (3d) 14 (S.C.C.), holding that it is not necessarily incidental to the criminal law power and therefore *ultra vires* for Parliament to impose a financial burden on a municipality to support the care of a young offender.

44 *R. v. Steinberg's Ltd.* (1982), 66 C.C.C. (2d) 484 (Ont. C.A.), upholding Van Camp J. in (1982), 65 C.C.C. (2d) 434 (Ont. H.C.). See also *R. v. Zelensky* (1978), 41 C.C.C. (2d) 97 (S.C.C.), upholding the validity of the Criminal Code's compensation provisions.

have been challenged — unsuccessfully — in a number of cases.[45] The Supreme Court of Canada has not yet dealt with the issue. When it does, no doubt it will disregard Lord Watson's statement, quoted earlier, and uphold the federal legislation. Controlling firearms is directly related to the criminal law. One of the reasons why the United States has a gun problem is because of the absence of strong federal legislation which would effectively prevent guns being sent from lax gun control states to other states.

5. PROVINCIAL LEGISLATION

The provinces were given the legislative power under section 92(15) of the B.N.A. Act to impose "punishment by fine, penalty, or imprisonment for enforcing any law of the Province . . ." An accused recently challenged a seven day minimum penalty under a provincial statute for driving while the accused's licence was suspended, but the British Columbia Court of Appeal held[46] that such a minimum mandatory jail term could be imposed by a province. There have been a large number of other cases challenging the validity of provincial legislation, on the basis that such legislation is invalid because it can only be enacted by the federal government.

In the early years after Confederation, the federal power of disallowance,[47] or to be more accurate, the threat of its use, was employed to prevent the provinces from passing laws within the ambit of what the federal government considered the proper domain of the criminal law. All provincial Acts were scrutinized by the federal Minister of Justice who would advise the Governor General whether the Act should be disallowed. For example, five Acts passed by the Ontario legislature in its first session after Confederation were objected to by the Minister of Justice, Sir John A. Macdonald, as encroachments on the criminal law power.[48] However, the

---

45 *R. v. Northcott*, [1980] 5 W.W.R. 38 (B.C. Prov. Ct.), upholding the licensing provisions; *A. G. Can. v. Pattison* (1981), 59 C.C.C. (2d) 138 (Alta. C.A.), upholding the search and seizure provisions; *R. v. Anderson* (1981), 59 C.C.C. (2d) 439 (Ont. Co. Ct.) and *Re Motiuk and R.* (1981), 60 C.C.C. (2d) 161 (B.C.S.C.), upholding the prohibition provisions in the legislation.

46 *Re Skelley and R.* (1982), 69 C.C.C. (2d) 282 (B.C. C.A.).

47 There is also the power of reservation whereby the Lieutenant-Governor of a province may reserve his assent to a provincial Act for the signification of the pleasure of the Governor-General in Council. For a discussion of the power of reservation and disallowance, see generally G. V. La Forest, *Disallowance and Reservation of Provincial Legislation* (Dept. of Justice, Ottawa 1955); D. A. Schmeiser, *Civil Liberties in Canada* (Toronto 1964) at pp. 17-20; W. P. M. Kennedy, *The Constitution of Canada* (2nd ed., Toronto 1938) at pp. 415 *et seq.*

48 W. E. Hodgins, *Dominion and Provincial Legislation, 1867-1895* (Ottawa 1896) at pp. 79 *et seq.*

disallowance power gradually became more sparingly used and the courts were left to wrestle with the problem of overlapping laws.

Provincial laws can be struck down either for lack of constitutional power under section 92 or for conflict with federal legislation. Under both heads the Supreme Court of Canada has tended to uphold provincial law. A trio of cases in 1960 showed the reluctance of the Supreme Court of Canada to declare provincial legislation inoperative because of existing federal legislation. Of course it will do so if it *conflicts* with federal legislation. But what is meant by conflicts? In *O'Grady v. Sparling*[49] the Supreme Court upheld provincial careless driving legislation, although the federal Criminal Code makes it an offence to operate a motor vehicle in a criminally negligent manner. In *Stephens v. The Queen*[50] the Supreme Court upheld provincial competence to require a driver involved in an accident to stop, provide particulars, and offer assistance, in spite of a provision in the Criminal Code making the same conduct an offence, though with the added element of "intent to escape civil or criminal liability". Finally, in *Smith v. The Queen*[51] the Supreme Court upheld a section of the Ontario Securities Act making it an offence to furnish false information in any document required to be filed or furnished under the Act, although the Criminal Code makes it an offence for a person to publish a prospectus which he knows is false in a material particular with intent to induce persons to become shareholders in a company. In none of these cases was there held to be a conflict. In order to *conflict,* these cases say, the laws must require the accused to act in an inconsistent manner. In the Securities Act case, Martland J. stated:[52]

> The fact that both provisions prohibit certain acts with penal consequences does not constitute a conflict. It may happen that some acts might be punishable under both provisions and in this sense that these provisions overlap. However, even in such cases, there is no conflict in the sense that compliance with one law involves breach of the other. It would appear, therefore, that they can operate concurrently.

In the nineteenth century the courts solved the double jeopardy problem by being careful not to permit concurrent jurisdiction. Today, the Courts are, to a considerable extent, prepared to permit both the federal and provincial governments to legislate on the same matter. This tendency to uphold concurrent jurisdiction[53] means, of course, that the

49 (1960), 128 C.C.C. 1 (S.C.C.). See also *R. v. Chiasson* (1982), 66 C.C.C. (2d) 195 (N.B.C.A.) (provincial offence of careless handling of a firearm valid).

50 (1960), 128 C.C.C. 21 (S.C.C.).

51 (1960), 128 C.C.C. 145 (S.C.C.).

52 *Ibid.* at 168.

53 See Leigh, "The Criminal Law Power: A Move Towards Functional Concurrency?" (1967) 5 Alta. L. Rev. 237; Lederman, "The Concurrent Operation of Federal and Provincial Laws in Canada" (1962-3) 9 McGill L.J. 185. See also *Multiple Access Ltd. v. McCutcheon* (1982), 138 D.L.R. (3d) 1 at 23-24 (S.C.C.) *per* Dickson J.: "In principle, there

courts should be careful not to permit double jeopardy in these cases.[54] The Supreme Court has not yet heard such a case. When it does, it will no doubt distinguish or overrule an earlier lower court case[55] holding that multiple convictions are possible in these circumstances.

The tendency to uphold provincial legislation can also be seen in a number of recent Supreme Court of Canada cases in which provincial legislation was challenged as not falling within section 92. In 1978 in *Dupond*[56] the majority of the Supreme Court of Canada upheld a Montreal by-law designed to prevent assemblies and passed to cope with occurrences such as the F.L.Q. rallies. The same year the Supreme Court in the *McNeil* case[57] upheld Nova Scotia legislation which permitted the banning of the movie, "Last Tango in Paris", even though there was also federal obscenity legislation in the Criminal Code. In 1982, in the *Schneider* case,[58] the Supreme Court upheld provincial legislation providing for the compulsory treatment of heroin addicts. In the most recent Supreme Court case, *Westendorp v. The Queen*,[59] however, the Court struck down a Calgary

would seem to be no good reason to speak of paramountcy and preclusion except where there is actual conflict in operation as where one enactment says 'yes' and the other says 'no'; the same citizens are being told to do inconsistent things; compliance with one is defiance of the other." And see *R. v. Robar* (1982), 68 C.C.C. (2d) 448 (S.C.C.); *R. v. Grusko* (1981), 62 C.C.C. (2d) 431 (Man. C.A.).

54   See M. L. Friedland, *Double Jeopardy* (Oxford 1969), chapter 13.

55   *R. v. Kissick* (1942), 78 C.C.C. 34 (Man. C.A.). *Cf.* Jones J.A., dissenting, in *R. v. Logan* (1981), 64 C.C.C. (2d) 238 at pp. 251-2 (N.S.C.A.); *R. v. Chiasson* (1982), 66 C.C.C. (2d) 195 at p. 204 (N.B.C.A.) *per* La Forest J.A.

56   *A.-G. Can. and Dupond v. Montreal,* [1978] 2 S.C.R. 770. See also *R. v. Jarvis, Warrington and Verge* (1980), 57 C.C.C. (2d) 65 (N.S.C.A.), upholding provincial legislation making it an offence "to loiter on the street or highways or in the doorways . . ."

57   *Re N.S. Bd. of Censors and McNeil* (1978), 44 C.C.C. (2d) 316 (S.C.C.).

58   *Schneider v. R.* (1982), 139 D.L.R. (3d) 417 (S.C.C.). See generally, Laskin, "Constitutional Authority in Relation to Drugs and Drug Use" (1980) 18 Osgoode Hall L.J. 554. See also *Reference Re Intoxicated Persons Detention Act* (1980), 55 C.C.C. (2d) 130 (Man. C.A.), upholding provincial legislation providing for detention of an intoxicated person for up to 24 hours in a detoxification centre.

59   (1983), 2 C.C.C. (3d) 330 (S.C.C.). Leave to appeal to the Supreme Court of Canada was granted on Feb. 21, 1983 from the Quebec Court of Appeal case of *Goldwax v. City of Montreal* (1983), 3 C.C.C. (3d) 542, holding a comparable Montreal by-law to be valid. *Cf. Re Sharlmark Hotels Ltd. and Municipality of Metro. Toronto* (1981), 32 O.R. (2d) 129 (Div. Ct.), upholding provincial legislation authorizing municipalities to pass by-laws licensing, regulating and inspecting adult entertainment parlours. In June, 1983, the Minister of Justice, Mark MacGuigan, appointed a Committee chaired by Vancouver lawyer, Paul Fraser, to inquire into the question of prostitution and obscenity. The Committee commenced public hearings in early 1984. One solution that will no doubt be considered is to transfer responsibility to the provinces. Note that the *Final Report of the Special Committee of the Senate and House on the Constitution of Canada* (Molgat/MacGuigan Report) (Ottawa 1972) at p. 74 favoured "greater freedom for the Provinces to control the behaviour of their people, and to experiment on a province-wide scale" and so recommended "in this one area, a power of delegation from the Federal to the Provincial Legislatures."

by-law which had attempted to deal with prostitution by prohibiting a person from remaining on the street for the purpose of prostitution or approaching another person on the street for the purpose of prostitution. Laskin C.J., for a unanimous Supreme Court, held[60] that the by-law was "a colourable attempt to deal, not with a public nuisance but with the evil of prostitution . . . If a province or municipality may translate a direct attack on prostitution into street control through reliance on public nuisance, it may do the same with respect to trafficking in drugs, and, may it not, on the same view, seek to punish assaults that take place on city streets as an aspect of street control!" Thus, just as there are limits on federal legislation, there are limits[61] on the creation of provincial offences.

6. ADMINISTERING THE CRIMINAL LAW

Section 92 (14) of the B.N.A. Act gives the provinces authority over "the administration of justice in the province, including the constitution, maintenance, and organization of provincial courts, both of civil and of criminal jurisdiction, and including procedure in civil matters in those courts." Does this give the provinces or the federal government the primary power to prosecute federal offences enacted under the criminal law power? In 1979 in the *Hauser*[62] case the Supreme Court was called on to decide whether the federal government could control prosecutions under the Narcotic Control Act. The Court held that the federal government had this power, although, to the surprise of many, not on the basis that the Narcotic Control Act was criminal law, but rather because it was enacted under the "peace, order and good government" clause. The Court, therefore, left open the question of what would happen when the issue related directly to enforcing the criminal law.

Two important cases decided by the Supreme Court in 1983 dealt with that question. In *A. G. Canada v. Canadian National Transportation Ltd. et al.*[63] the issue was whether the federal government has the power to control prosecutions under the Combines Investigation Act. Section 2 of the

---

60 *Ibid.* at pp. 338-9.

61 See also *R. v. Zellers Ltd.* (1982), 66 C.C.C. (2d) 236 (Man. C.A.).

62 *R. v. Hauser,* [1979] 1 S.C.R. 984. See J. B. Laskin, "Constitutional Authority in Relation to Drugs and Drug Use" (1980), 18 Osgoode Hall L.J. 554; Hovius, "*Hauser:* Narcotic Drugs, Criminal Law, and Peace, Order and Good Government" (1980) 18 U. West. Ont. L. Rev. 505; Stanley, Note (1981) 59 Can. Bar Rev. 153; Elliot, Note (1979-80) 14 U.B.C. L. Rev. 163.

63 [1984] 1 W.W.R. 193 (S.C.C.). The carefully crafted judgment of Mr Justice Martin in *R. v. Hoffman-La Roche Ltd.* (1981), 62 C.C.C. (2d) 118 (Ont. C.A.) is heavily relied on by the majority of the Supreme Court. Laskin C.J. concludes his judgment by stating: "I would add that the reasons of Mr Justice Martin in *Hoffman-La Roche* are in my view unassailable and, in themselves, would justify responding affirmatively to the federal claim of prosecutorial authority."

Criminal Code gives the power to prosecute federal offences not under the Criminal Code to the Attorney-General of Canada. Chief Justice Laskin gave the judgment for the majority of the seven-member court, holding that the Combines Act is valid under section 91(27), the criminal law power, and that the federal government has exclusive authority to control prosecutions. The majority judgment did not deal with the validity of the legislation under any other head of federal power. Dickson J. upheld federal prosecutorial authority for violations of the Combines Investigation Act under the federal "trade and commerce" power. With respect to the criminal law power, Dickson J. maintained the position he had taken in his dissent in *Hauser* that only the provincial Attorney-General can validly prosecute criminal enactments. Beetz and Lamer JJ. agreed with Dickson J. that the Act did not depend on section 91(27) and so did not find it necessary to consider the question of what would happen if it did.

In *The Queen v. Wetmore and Kripp*,[64] released the same day as the *Canadian National Transportation* case, the issue was the power to prosecute under the federal Food and Drugs Act. Again, Laskin C.J. held that because the Act fell under the criminal law power the federal government could control who had the power to prosecute. Dickson J., dissenting and characterizing the view of the majority as "blind centralism", held that the legislation was only valid under the criminal law power and thus it was the provincial, not the federal Attorney General who had the power to prosecute. Beetz and Lamer JJ. did not join in the dissent, feeling bound by the majority decision in the *Canadian National Transportation* case.

The result of the cases, then, appears to be that the federal government has exclusive power to prosecute federal offences. This power can, however, be delegated to the provincial Attorney General as is done directly in section 2 of the Criminal Code for Criminal Code offences and implicitly for non Criminal Code federal offences where the federal government has not instituted the proceedings.[65]

Thus far the courts have not dealt directly with the question whether the federal government could, if it wished, control prosecutions under the Criminal Code itself. The issue is not likely to arise because section 2 of the Code now gives this power to the provincial Attorneys General. But it could arise on a reference or possibly in a contest on who is to pay for prosecutions, or the federal legislation could change.

The logic and most of the language of Laskin C.J.'s judgments would lead to the conclusion that the federal government could, if it wished, control prosecutions under the Code. But there is one intriguing part of Laskin C.J.'s judgment which could be relied on in a later case to limit the

---

64 (1983), 49 N.R. 286 (S.C.C.).

65 See *R. v. Sacobie and Paul* (1983), 1 C.C.C. (3d) 446 (S.C.C.).

holding to non Criminal Code cases. Laskin C.J. refers to the assumption that the Combines Investigation Act rests only on the criminal law power and then adds in parenthesis "as distinguished from a Criminal Code offence, an important distinction in my opinion." Was this inserted by Laskin C.J. as an innocent statement of the existing legislative distinction, or deliberately in anticipation of such a constitutional distinction, or possibly as the price of gaining the support of the majority of the Court?

Such a distinction between Criminal Code offences and criminal law offences under other statutes would be a sensible distinction. The ultimate control of prosecutions of offences set out in the Code would then be a provincial responsibility, not as a matter of federal delegation, but as a constitutional right. The federal government could not obtain ultimate control by artificially dismantling the Criminal Code. Similarly, if an offence was in the Criminal Code and could, however, be justified under some other head of power apart from the criminal law, such as "peace, order and good government" in the case of offences involving national security,[66] then the ultimate control of prosecutions would constitutionally be federal. Moreover, if there was a serious breakdown in the will or the ability of a province to prosecute, then the federal government could assume power to do so under the "peace, order and good government" emergency power. In all cases, in the absence of a clear conflict, the power to prosecute would be concurrent.

The distinction would also be in accord with the probable intention of the framers of the B.N.A. Act. Laskin C.J., of course concludes otherwise, stating that the words "administration of justice" in section 92(14) refer only to civil justice. "By no stretch of language", he states, "can these words be construed to include jurisdiction over the conduct of criminal prosecutions . . . neither logic nor grammar support this construction." Nor does Laskin C.J. find any support for this position in the pre-Confederation debates. Yet when one rereads the quote, set out earlier, by Lord Carnarvon, the Colonial Secretary, discussing the British North America Act in the House of Lords, it is clear that the British Government thought that the administration of criminal justice was to be a provincial responsibility:

> To the Central Parliament will also be assigned the enactment of criminal law. The administration of it, indeed, is vested in the local authorities; but the power of general legislation is very properly reserved for the Central Parliament.

Lord Carnarvon, as we will see in a later section, was very knowledgeable about criminal law matters and so these words cannot be lightly dismissed. No doubt, the Canadian Fathers of Confederation shared

---

66 See the *Report of the Special Committee of the Senate on the Canadian Security Intelligence Service* (the Pitfield Report), November 1983 at pp. 33-34.

Carnarvon's view. As Dickson J. stated "it was not within the contemplation of the Fathers of Confederation that ultimate constitutional authority for the conduct and prosecution of all criminal offences — the multitude of cases arising daily in the hundreds of communities in what was then Canada — would centre in Ottawa." The Canadian delegates, as we will see in later sections, even wanted the pardoning power and penitentiaries to be in the hands of the provinces, which is a strong indication that they assumed that other aspects of the administration of criminal justice would be in provincial hands.

Thus, the administration of justice in section 92(14) would generally refer to Criminal Code offences, although criminal law under section 91(27) would have a much wider meaning. We have not heard the last of section 92(14). It is safe to predict that the subsection will continue to be the subject of judicial scrutiny in other areas involving the administration of justice, such as policing and investigation,[67] and may continue to be litigated within the seemingly settled area of prosecutorial authority.

7. APPOINTING POWER

Section 96 of the British North America Act gives the federal government the power to appoint judges to the Superior, District and County Courts established by the provinces under section 92(14). Nothing was said in the Act about justices of the peace and magistrates. The federal government took the position in the early years after Confederation that the appointment of all judges, without distinction, rested solely with the federal government as a matter of prerogative right, but the Privy Council established in 1892[68] that this was not correct. So their appointment is a provincial responsibility under the heading "the administration of justice in the province".

Although the hierarchy in the criminal courts that exists today was understandable at the time of Confederation, there have been a number of suggestions[69] that we should abandon the earlier structure and set up

---

67 See, e.g., DiIorio v. Montreal Jail Warden (1976), 33 C.C.C. (2d) 289 (S.C.C.); A. G. Que. and Keable v. A. G. Can. (1978), 43 C.C.C. (2d) 49 (S.C.C.); A. G. Alta. v. Putnam (1981), 62 C.C.C. (2d) 51 (S.C.C.).

68 Liquidators of Maritime Bank v. Receiver General of N.B., [1892] A.C. 437; see also Reference Re Adoption Act, [1938] S.C.R. 398 at pp. 410 et seq. per Duff C.J. The Ontario Queen's Bench division in R. v. Bush (1888), 15 O.R. 398 had earlier upheld the power of the provinces to appoint magistrates and justices of the peace; see also R. v. Reno and Anderson (1868) 4 P.R. 281 (Ont. Chambers). The Supreme Court held in Re Vancini (No. 2) (1904), 8 C.C.C. 228 that it was not ultra vires for the federal government to impose duties on provincially appointed officers.

69 See Marc Lalonde, "The Future of a Unified Criminal Court" (1980) 4 Prov. Judges J. 3; see also Friedland, "Magistrates' Courts: Functioning and Facilities" (1968), 11 Crim. L.Q. 52.

unified criminal courts, just as there has been a strong movement for unified family courts. There are, however, serious constitutional problems involved. The Supreme Court of Canada has recently held in the *McEvoy* case[70] that the federal government cannot legislatively transfer jurisdiction over all criminal offences to a tribunal the judges of which are appointed by the Province. "What is being contemplated here", the Court stated,[71] "is not one or a few transfers of criminal law power, such as has already been accomplished under the Criminal Code, but a complete obliteration of superior court criminal law jurisdiction." The proposal is not helped, said the Court, by providing for concurrent superior court jurisdiction. Parliament could probably establish a unified criminal court under section 101 of the B.N.A. Act, which permits the federal government to establish "any additional courts for the better administration of the laws of Canada", but this may not permit the by-passing of the necessity for having federally appointed section 96 judges. The federal government could, perhaps, add a federal appointment to the provincially appointed judges, but might be unwilling to do so. A constitutional amendment may well be the only solution.

8. PENAL INSTITUTIONS

There are a number of other sections in the British North America Act which are relevant to the subject of criminal law. One of these is section 91(28): "The establishment, maintenance, and management of penitentiaries."[72] This was transferred from the provincial to the federal list at a very late stage. The Quebec Resolutions of 1864 had given to the *provinces* "the establishment, maintenance and management of penitentiaries, and of public and reformatory prisons," and this had been approved at the 1866 London Conference.[73] In the final draft, however, "Public and Reformatory Prisons in and for the Province" were given to the provinces and "Penitentiaries" to the federal government. Why was this change made? The public record does not supply an answer. The change has been labelled "inexplicable".[74] It may well have been that the Colonial Secretary himself, Lord Carnarvon, requested the change. In 1863 he had chaired a very important Select Committee of the House of

---

70 *McEvoy v. A. G. N.B. and A. G. Can.* (1983), 148 D.L.R. (3d) 25 (S.C.C.).

71 *Ibid.* at 37.

72 Penitentiaries became the property of the federal government by virtue of s. 108 and the Third Schedule.

73 The earlier Charlottetown Conference had taken the same position: see Appendix 4, "A Brief Legislative History of Penitentiaries Prior to Confederation" in the government document dated April 29, 1976, *Bi-Lateral Discussions on the Division of Correctional Responsibilities Between the Federal Government and the Government of British Columbia.*

74 *Ibid.* See also p. 7 of the Report.

Lords on "the State of Discipline in Gaols and Houses of Correction".[75] The Committee was of the view that discipline in prisons throughout England was not strict enough. It wanted the system known as the "separate system" to be rigorously enforced. Prisoners should be kept isolated from one another and subjected to hard labour at the treadwheel, crank or shot drill. Discipline, according to the Report, was an integral part of the criminal process and the Committee wanted to "establish without delay a system approaching as nearly as may be practicable to an uniformity of labour, diet, and treatment".[76] Placing penitentiaries under federal jurisdiction was, therefore, a step towards achieving that objective in Canada.[77] The desire to achieve uniformity in prison discipline is a better explanation of the change respecting penitentiaries than some of the others that have been offered, such as economic considerations,[78] politics,[79] giving the provinces responsibility over treatment,[80] and providing a means "through which the federal government could exercise its monopoly of coercive force."[81]

The dividing line later established by federal legislation[82] between federal penitentiaries and provincial institutions was a two-year penalty. Two years less a day would be served in a provincial institution; two years or more in a federal institution.[83] It reflected the practice with respect to penitentiaries before Confederation,[84] and is still the law today.[85] Note that the specific two-year dividing line is not mentioned in the Constitution. Over the years there have been many suggestions that the

---

75 See their Report, 1863, vol. IX.

76 *Ibid.* at p. iv.

77 See Senate Debates, May 12, 1868 at pp. 282-3. See also the 1867 Prison Report prepared by R. S. Wright, *Digest and Summary of Information Respecting Prisons in the Colonies,* supplied by the Governors of Her Majesty's Colonial Possessions, in answer to Mr. Secretary Cardwell's Circular Dispatches of 16 and 17 Jan., 1865, C. 3961, 1867.

78 R. M. Zubrycki, *The Establishment of Canada's Penitentiary System: Federal Correctional Policy 1867-1900* (Publication Series, Faculty of Social Work, U. of T. 1980) at pp. 22 *et seq.*; Jaffary, "Correctional Federalism" (1965) 7 Can. J. of Corr. 362 at p. 365.

79 See *Bi-Lateral Discussions on the Division of Correctional Responsibilities, supra* note 73 at p. 7.

80 *Report of the Canadian Committee on Corrections* (Ottawa, 1969) (the Ouimet Report) at p. 279.

81 Zubrycki, *supra* note 78 at p. 36.

82 See the Procedure in Criminal Cases Act, S.C. 1869, c. 29, s. 96.

83 There were exceptions. Until the law was changed in 1978, it was, in fact, possible to spend almost four years in a provincial institution because in Ontario and British Columbia there could be a 2-year indefinite term added to a 2-year-less-a-day sentence: see the Prisons and Reformatories Act, R.S.C. 1970, c. P-21, ss. 44 and 150.

84 See the Procedure in Criminal Cases Act, S.C. 1859, s. 100, initially introduced in 1842: see the Archambault Report, *infra* note 87 at p. 339.

85 See the Criminal Code, s. 659.

specific division be changed. In 1887 an Interprovincial Conference called at the request of the Premier of Quebec recommended that a six-month dividing line be substituted for the two-year division.[86] The 1938 Archambault Report similarly wanted to centralize corrections,[87] as did the 1956 Fauteux Report.[88] A swing back to the provinces is reflected in the 1969 Ouimet Report[89] and a Report by the Law Reform Commission of Canada.[90] The debate continues.

In 1978 the federal government brought into force a new Prisons and Reformatories Act[91] which gives the provinces control over provincial penal institutions, subject to federal law with respect to matters such as temporary absence and parole. This legislation has not been tested. Some take the view [92] that there are no constitutional limits on federal legislative authority over provincial institutions and if there is a conflict, federal legislation prevails; but surely the courts would give the historical division between reformatories and penitentiaries some substance and not allow complete federal control of provincial institutions, even though they may not freeze the division at the 1867 solution. So, for example, it appears reasonable for the federal government to have legislative authority over parole of those in provincial institutions convicted of federal offences,[93] but not to have authority over, say, the qualifications or pay of prison guards. Similarly, the federal government could probably unilaterally set the dividing line between federal and provincial institutions at, say, six months, but could not abolish provincial institutions.

9. PARDONING POWER

Another change between the Quebec Resolutions and the British

---

86 See Needham, "Historical Perspectives on the Federal-Provincial Split in Jurisdiction in Corrections" (1980) 22 Can. J. Criminology 298 at p. 299.

87 *Report of the Royal Commission to Investigate the Penal System of Canada* (Ottawa, 1938) at pp. 339 *et seq.*

88 *Report of a Committee Appointed to Inquire into the Principles and Procedures followed in the Remission Service of the Department of Justice of Canada.* (Ottawa 1956) at p. 50.

89 *Supra* note 80 at pp. 279 *et seq.*

90 *A Report on Dispositions and Sentences in the Criminal Process: Guidelines* (Ottawa 1976).

91 Criminal Law Amendment Act, S.C. 1976-77, c. 53, ss. 45-6, amending the Prisons and Reformatories Act, R.S.C. 1970, c. P-21.

92 See Needham, *supra* note 86, at p. 298. See also *R. v. Casserley* (1982), 69 C.C.C. (2d) 126 (Ont. C.A.), holding *ultra vires* a provincial regulation requiring an accused serving an intermittent sentence in a provincial institution for a federal offence to pay a certain amount for each day of service of sentence.

93 *Cf.* Hogg, "Administration of Justice" in S. M. Beck and I. Bernier (eds.), *Canada and the New Constitution: The Unfinished Agenda* (Inst. for Research on Public Policy, 1983) 91 at pp. 111-2; see also "The Parole System in Canada" (1973) 15 Can. J. of Crim. and Corrections 144 (a policy statement by the Can. Crim. and Corr. Assoc.).

North America Act was with respect to the Pardoning Power.[94] The Quebec Resolutions had given this power to the Lieutenant-Governor in Council, that is, the provincial cabinet, "subject to any instructions he may, from time to time, receive from the general Government, and subject to any provisions that may be made in this behalf by the general Parliament". But the Colonial Secretary, Cardwell, objected to this provision. Indeed it was only one of two provisions arising out of the Conference that the British government formally took objection to.[95] "It appears to her Majesty's Government", Cardwell stated,[96] "that this duty belongs to the representative of the Sovereign, — and could not with propriety be devolved upon the Lieutenant-Governors, who will, under the present scheme, be appointed not directly by the Crown, but by the Central Government of the United Provinces." In spite of the Colonial Office objections, the delegates at the 1866 London Conference reaffirmed the view that the pardoning power belonged to the provinces, but conceded that the federal government should have the sole responsibility in capital cases.[97] The Colonial Office, however, would not accept this version and as a result nothing was stated in the British North America Act with respect to the pardoning power.

After Confederation there was a continuing controversy over the issue. The Colonial Office[98] and the federal government[99] took the position that the pardoning power for federal and provincial offences rested solely with the federal government.[100] The provinces took the

---

94 See generally, the excellent Carlton University Master's thesis, M. K. Evans, The Prerogative of Pardon in Canada: Its Development 1864-1894 (1971).

95 The other provision objected to related to the life appointment of senators: see the letter from the Colonial Secretary, Edward Cardwell, to Viscount Monck, Dec. 3, 1864, set out in W. P. M. Kennedy (ed.), *Statutes, Treaties and Documents of the Canadian Constitution 1713-1929*, (2nd ed., Oxford U.P. 1930) at pp. 547 *et seq.* The Colonial Office eventually gave in on this matter, but not on the pardoning power.

96 *Ibid.* at p. 548.

97 See Evans, The Prerogative of Pardon at p. 8.

98 See the views of the Colonial Secretaries: Lord Granville, set out in Canadian Sessional Papers, 1869, No. 16, p. 5, and Lord Carnarvon, set out in Canadian Sessional Papers, No. 11, 1875, p. 38.

99 See the views of Sir John A. Macdonald in 1869 (Canadian Sessional Papers, 1869, No. 16, p. 1) and of Sir John Thompson in 1889 (see the correspondence between Thompson and Mowat set out in J. M. Beck (ed.), *The Shaping of Canadian Federalism: Central Authority or Provincial Right?* (Toronto 1971), at pp. 92-3.)

100 Another controversy — this time between the Colonial Office and the federal government — involved the question whether the Governor-General could act on his own without the advice of the federal government. This was resolved in 1877, whereby the Governor-General could not act without the approval of the Cabinet in capital cases and of a cabinet minister in other cases, although he could act on his own in extra-Canadian matters: see the thorough discussion of this issue in Evans, *supra* note 94 at pp. 62 *et seq.*

position that they could pardon those convicted of provincial offences and the 1887 Interprovincial Conference called by the premier of Quebec passed a resolution to this effect.[101] Matters were brought to a head in 1888 when Ontario passed An Act Respecting the Executive Administration of Laws of this Province.[102] The ensuing litigation, known as the *Executive Power Case,* settled the issue in favour of the provinces.[103] Chancellor Boyd stated:[104] "The power to pass laws implies necessarily the power to execute or to suspend the execution of those laws, else the concession of self-government in domestic affairs is a delusion." Thus, today, the pardoning power over offences under federal jurisdiction belongs to the federal government and for offences under provincial jurisdiction belongs to the provinces.

10. A CHARTER OF RIGHTS

A Charter or Bill of Rights was not considered for Canada at the time of Confederation. Legislative power was to be divided. The total of the power of Parliament and the legislatures was, with a few exceptions, equal to the power of the Sovereign in England. The preamble to the British North America Act recited that our Constitution was to be "similar in Principle to that of the United Kingdom". The Benthamite and the Austinian view of English government did not envisage any limitation on the power of Parliament. It will be recalled that Bentham referred to natural rights as "nonsense upon stilts".[105] As Donald Creighton has written,[106] the Fathers of Confederation "would have been sceptical about both the utility and validity of abstract notions such as the social contract and the natural and inalienable rights of man. The magic formulae of the American and French Revolutions — 'life, liberty, and the pursuit of happiness' and 'liberty, property, security, and resistance to oppression' — would have sounded in their ears like irrelevant and questionable rhetoric."

This is not the place to discuss the history of the enactment of the

---

101 Set out in Beck, *supra* note 99 at p. 91.

102 S.O. 1888, c. 5.

103 *A. G. Can. v. A. G. Ont.* (1890) 20 O.R. 222 (Chancery Div.), affirmed (1892), 19 O.A.R. 31 (C.A.), which was affirmed without a decision on the substantive issue, (1894), 23 S.C.R. 458. Before the Supreme Court case, the Privy Council had decided the important *Maritime Bank Case (Liquidators of Maritime Bank v. Receiver General of N.B.)* [1892] A.C. 437, establishing the status of the Lieutenant-Governors. This put the question beyond dispute.

104 (1890), 20 O.R. 222 at 249.

105 *The Works of Jeremy Bentham* (J. Bowring ed.) (New York 1962), Vol. II, at p. 501.

106 D. G. Creighton, *The Road to Confederation* (Toronto 1964) at p. 142.

Canadian Charter of Rights and Freedoms[107] or its interpretation (see Chapter 7) except to point out that one of the reasons for enacting the Charter was to provide a central symbol ultimately administered by the Supreme Court of Canada — another central symbol — to help unify the nation,[108] the same type of unifying function that the criminal law itself was meant to have. The Charter may, in fact, prove more effective in this regard than the criminal law, which over the years has been more and more decentralized by the courts upholding concurrent provincial authority in many areas of penal law, and by the federal government giving the provinces considerable responsibility in areas such as abortion and gambling. It may be, however, that the criminal law will again play a greater unifying role through the enactment of a new Criminal Code.

11. CONCLUSION

Many of the fundamental issues in Canadian society have been fought out in the constitutional arena — and many of these have involved the allocation of power over the criminal law. The criminal law represents the ultimate power of the state and so one can expect many more clashes in the future between the federal and provincial governments on the question of legislative authority over criminal justice.

---

107 Canadian Charter of Rights and Freedoms, set out in Part I of the Constitution Act, 1982, as enacted by the Canada Act, 1982 (U.K.), c. 11.

108 See Russell, "The Effect of a Charter of Rights on the Policy-making Role of Canadian Courts" (1982), 25 Can. P. Admin. 1 at p. 18; "The Political Purposes of the Canadian Charter of Rights and Freedoms" (1983), 61 Can. Bar Rev. 30.

3

PRESSURE GROUPS AND THE
DEVELOPMENT OF THE CRIMINAL LAW*

1. INTRODUCTION

There is nothing new about pressure groups influencing the development of the law. Thomas à Becket and the Church in the twelfth century dispute with Henry II, and the Barons who forced King John to grant Magna Carta in 1215, are early, if extreme, examples. Over the centuries groups have continued to shape the law. In the criminal law field one finds, for example, in the seventeenth century the pamphleteers (such as the Levellers and the Diggers)[1]; in the eighteenth, Societies for the Reformation of Manners[2], and in the nineteenth the groups of Moral Reformers.[3]

In spite of their importance in the legal system and the growing number of studies of pressure groups,[4] the subject continues to be one

---

* This paper was originally published in P. R. Glazebrook (ed.), *Reshaping the Criminal Law: Essays in Honour of Glanville Williams* (London, Stevens and Sons 1978). I am indebted to John Unger, a former student in the Faculty of Law, for his assistance.

1 Veall, D. *The Popular Movement for Law Reform 1640-1660* (Oxford 1970), especially Chapter 4.

2 Radzinowicz, L., *A History of English Criminal Law* (London 1957) Vol. 3, at pp. 141 *et seq.*

3 Harrison, "State Intervention and Moral Reform in Nineteenth-Century England" in *Pressure from Without in Early Victorian England* (ed. P. Hollis) (London 1974) Chapter 12.

4 For Canada, studies include *Pressure Group Behaviour in Canadian Politics* (ed. A. P. Pross) (Toronto 1975); Presthus, R., *Elite Accommodation in Canadian Politics* (Toronto 1973); Presthus, R., *Elites in the Policy Process* (Toronto 1974); Engelmann, F. C. and Schwartz, M. A., *Canadian Political Parties: Origin, Character, Impact* (Toronto 1975) Chapter 7; and Van Loon, R. J. and Whittington, M. S., *The Canadian Political System* (2nd ed.) (Toronto 1976) Chapter 12; and studies of specific groups (in addition to those found in Pross) include Clark, S. D., *The Canadian Manufacturers' Association* (Toronto 1939); Kwavnick, D., *Organised Labour and Pressure Politics* (Montreal 1972); Lang, R. W., *The Politics of Drugs* (Lexington, Mass. 1974); and Stanbury, W. T., *Business Interests and the Reform of Canadian Competition Policy, 1971-1975* (Toronto 1977). A full bibliography on Canadian pressure groups can be found in Pross.

For Britain, studies include, Wootton, G., *Pressure Groups in Britain 1720-1970* (London 1975); Stewart, J. D., *British Pressure Groups* (Oxford 1958); Finer, S. E., *Anonymous Empire* (2nd ed.) (London 1966); Roberts, J. K., *Political Parties and Pressure-Groups in Britain* (London 1970); *Pressure from Without in Early Victorian England* (ed. P. Hollis) (London 1974); and Moodie, G. C. and Studdert-Kennedy, G., *Opinions, Publics and Pressure Groups* (London

that is "wrapped in a haze of common knowledge,"[5] and lawyers have, for the most part,[6] left it to political scientists, sociologists and economists to attempt to penetrate the haze.

Whether one uses the term "pressure group," "lobby" or "interest group" is unimportant: they are all more or less interchangeable. "Interest" is probably the most ancient term, followed by the American word "lobby" (literally, influencing legislators in the lobby of the House).[7] For convenience, the modern term will be used in this paper. A Canadian writer, Pross,[8] provides as good a definition of the concept as any: "Pressure groups are organizations whose members act together to influence public policy in order to promote their common interest."

Bodies that are part of the structure of government, such as judges, grand juries, inquests, ombudsmen, other levels of government, and political parties are not normally included in studies of pressure groups, although they exert considerable pressure on other governmental organizations. However, when they act outside their special area of activity, such as judges seeking higher salaries, they would be considered as pressure groups.

Some American writers have taken the position that groups are all-important in society. Bentley, whose influential work was published in the United States in 1908 stated that "society itself is nothing other than the complex of the groups that compose it. ... When the groups are adequately stated, everything is stated. When I say everything I mean everything."[9] This is an obvious overstatement.[10] Yet the individuals who

---

1970). A bibliography can be found in Roberts. For a bibliography on the U.S. and other jurisdictions see Wootton, G., *Interest-Groups* (Englewood Cliffs, N.J. 1970); see also Zeigler, L. H. and Peak, C. W., *Interest Groups in American Society* (2nd ed.) (Englewood Cliffs, N.J. 1972).

5   MacKenzie, "Pressure Groups in British Government," (1955) Br. J. of Soc. 133 at p. 134. This was the first British study of the subject.

6   Some of the exceptions are Heinz, Gettleman and Seeskin, "Legislative Politics and the Criminal Law," (1969) 64 Northwestern U.L. Rev. 277; Landers and Posner. "The Independent Judiciary in an Interest-Group Perspective," (1975) 18 J. of Law and Economics 875; Sherry, "The Politics of Criminal Law Reform," (1973) 21 Am. J. of Comparative Law 201; and Trebilcock, "Winners and Losers in the Modern Regulatory System: Must the Consumer Always Lose?" (1975) 13 Osgoode Hall L.J. 619.

7   Wootten, *Pressure Groups, supra* note 4 at pp. 1-8. Some writers draw distinctions between the terms; *e.g.* Roberts, *supra* note 4 at p. 78 states that "a lobby is organized and operates solely for purposes of political influence on a particular matter"; "a pressure-group has political functions alongside its other functions."

8   *Supra* note 4 at p. 2.

9   Bentley, A. F., *The Process of Government* (Cambridge, Mass. 1908) at pp. 222, 208-209. Criminologists who view the creation of criminal law from a "conflict" rather than a "consensus" perspective will also stress the importance of groups: see *e.g.* Quinney, R., *The Social Reality of Crime* (Boston 1970) at p. 35.

10   Heinz *et al.*, (1969) 64 Northwestern U.L. Rev. 277 at 335 *et seq.*

have played key roles in law reform have in many cases worked closely with pressure groups. John Stuart Mill, for example, like many reformers in the nineteenth century, was very involved with pressure groups and Glanville Williams, the leading criminal law reformer of the twentieth century, has been closely identified with a number of them: for example, the Abortion Law Reform Association,[11] the Euthanasia Society,[12] and the Haldane Society.[13]

If groups are not "everything," they are, however, more a part of our political and legal system than is usually acknowledged. One of the principal conclusions of this chapter is that Canadian and British governments have fostered and encouraged pressure groups and have brought them openly into the decision-making process. Some describe this as a form of "corporatism," that is, "a conception of society in which government delegates many of its functions to private groups, which in turn provide guidance regarding the social and economic legislation required in the modern national state."[14]

This chapter concentrates on Canadian pressure groups. Are these typical of the operation of pressure groups in other jurisdictions? One has to be cautious because pressure group activity is a reflection of the political system in which it operates and therefore necessarily varies from country to country. To take an obvious example, pressure groups are relatively unimportant in the Soviet Union since "the Communist Party . . . frowns on the creation of specialized structures for the formulation of special interests. . . . In Soviet theory and practice, all interest groups are subject to Party control, and all group interests must be reconciled with the Party's interests if they are to be considered legitimate."[15] Nevertheless, even in the Soviet Union some pressure group activity takes place.[16]

Even comparisons with other common-law jurisdictions require caution. The Canadian and United Kingdom parliamentary system gives the civil service and the Cabinet more control over legislation than is the case in the American Congressional system. As a result, on most issues the individual member of parliament in Canada and the United Kingdom is not as important a target of pressure group activity as the congressman in the United States. The backbencher in Canada can nonetheless play a key

---

11 Hindell, K. and Simms, M., *Abortion Law Reformed* (London 1971) at p. 119.

12 See *inter alia*, Williams, "Voluntary Euthansia — the next step" (An address to the Society's annual general meeting) (London 1955).

13 See *The Reform of the Law* (London 1951), edited by Glanville Williams for the Haldane Society.

14 Presthus, R., *Elite Accommodation in Canadian Politics* (Toronto 1973) at p. 25.

15 Barry and Berman, "The Soviet Legal Profession," (1968) 82 Harv. L. R. 1 at pp. 2-3. See also Roberts, J. K., *Political Parties and Pressure-Groups in Britain* (London 1970) at p. 86.

16 *Interest Groups in Soviet Politics* (eds. H. G. Skilling and F. Griffiths) (Princeton 1971).

role in affecting government policy through the government caucus, by direct access to the appropriate minister and his advisors, in parliamentary committees, in opposition attacks on government measures, and, of course, in cases where the government allows a free vote.

In the criminal law, as in other areas of the law, pressure group activity ranges from quiet diplomacy to strident confrontation: from the Law Society of Upper Canada making discreet representations to the provincial Attorney-General on the provision of legal aid, to riots by groups of inmates. But there appears to be a greater tendency than in other areas to use confrontation tactics. In most other circumstances, to quote Pross again,[17] "The Canadian policy system . . . tends to favour élite groups, making functional, accommodative, consensus-seeking techniques of political communication, rather than conflict-oriented techniques that are directed towards the achievement of objectives through arousing public opinion."

In the criminal law field, however, conflict-oriented techniques are often employed. The nineteenth century moral reformers adopted these techniques: "the petition, the subscription-list, the procession, the public meeting, the local branch, the reforming periodical, and the letter to the M.P. Publicity of discussion was their means, influence with parliament and with religious groups their objective."[18] Canada, in common with many other jurisdictions, has recently experienced this in such fields as capital punishment, abortion, homosexual offences, and gun-control. Why are these techniques used more frequently in the criminal law area?

One explanation is that the battle has to be fought out at the legislative level. Regulations are seldom used in criminal law and the administrative agency enforcing the law — the police — is split into a large number of separate forces. If pressure were not directed at legislation, groups would have to deal with each police force separately, always assuming that the police would discuss the enforcement of the law with them.

Not only must the battle usually be at the legislative level, but also it often concerns a matter on which the political parties have not taken firm positions, so that pressure groups can have considerable effect on the outcome. In England many of these issues have been dealt with by free votes on private members' bills, for example, the Acts dealing with the temporary abolition of the death penalty in 1965, homosexuality and abortion in 1967, and divorce in 1969. In Canada there were free votes on capital punishment in 1967 and 1976. On other controversial issues the

---

17 *Pressure Group Behaviour in Canadian Politics* (ed. A. P. Pross) at p. 19.

18 Harrison, "State Intervention and Moral Reform in Nineteenth-Century England" in *Pressure from Without in Early Victorian England* (ed. P. Hollis) (London 1974) at p. 292.

government has not allowed a free vote, although sometimes parties have not rigidly enforced party discipline.[19]

A further reason for the greater use of publicity and confrontation in the criminal law area is that many of the groups are ad hoc issue-oriented groups without the contacts or finances to engage in the more usual tactics. The photocopier has meant that any group can distribute a press release at a very low cost and television has given any group with a little imagination the opportunity to appeal to a wide audience.[20]

Finally, in these sensitive areas legislators are concerned about public opinion and use pressure groups as one method of gauging opinion.

2. PUBLIC OPINION

Pressure groups constitute some evidence of public opinion. Indeed, on some topics they may provide the only evidence.[21] Individuals usually do not have the resources or the incentive to become sufficiently knowledgeable about proposed legislation to comment intelligently on it.[22] When Dicey in his *Law and Public Opinion in England During the Nineteenth Century*[23] claimed that it is possible to ascertain public opinion because there is a "body of beliefs, convictions, sentiments, accepted principles, or firmly-rooted prejudices, which, taken together, make up the public opinion of a particular era," he was as Hermann Mannheim has shown,[24] not talking about mass public opinion, but rather élite opinion, equating "the people of England" with "those citizens who have at a given moment taken an effective part in public life."[25]

---

19 H.C. Deb. (25 Feb., 1969) 5919.

20 Pross, "Canadian Pressure Groups in the 1970s: their Role and their Relations with the Public Service," [1975] Can. Pub. Admin. 121 at p. 127, for a discussion of the effect of technology on the rise of pressure groups.

21 *E.g.* it is unlikely that there is or was any general public opinion on a proposed amendment to the Criminal Code (s. 406) requiring fake coins to be specially marked. The government received letters from the Canadian Association of Numismatic Dealers, the Canadian Paper Money Society and the Canadian Numismatic Association: H.C. Debs. (11 Feb., 1977) 2993. At the Justice and Legal Affairs Committee, evidence was given on 23 June, 1977 by the Canadian Association of Numismatic Dealers, the Canadian Numismatic Association and the Royal Canadian Mounted Police.

22 See Beckman, "The Problem of Communicating Public Policy Effectively: Bill C-256 and Winnipeg Businessmen," (1975) 8 C.J.P.S. 138, showing the lack of knowledge by Winnipeg businessmen of proposed anti-combines legislation.

23 (2nd ed.) (London 1914), at pp. 19-20.

24 "Criminal Law and Penology" in *Law and Opinion in England in the 20th Century* (ed. M. Ginsberg) (London 1959) at pp. 264 *et seq.*

25 *Supra* note 23 at p. 10. Of course, in the nineteenth century the "social similarities that existed between members of the government, Members of Parliament, local leaders, leaders of industry, landowners, the cultural figures of the period, and the smaller electorate were much stronger than exist today": Roberts, J. K., *Political Parties and*

Politicians are concerned about the state of public opinion because, being politicians, they would like to be re-elected at the next election and, being human, they want their policies to meet the wishes of the citizenry. Public opinion is, however, hard to gauge. Opinion polls may indicate the public's mood at a certain time but they do not usually indicate the strength of the views held.[26] Pressure groups, on the other hand, usually manifest an intensity of feeling not held by those who keep silent.[27]

Moreover, the public's mood is easily changed by specific events, and particularly by the manner in which they are covered by the media. So, for example, a Gallup Poll conducted in Canada in the first week of July, 1975 showed 83 per cent of Canadians in favour of the registration of all firearms. There is little doubt that this very high percentage was strongly influenced by the well-publicized shooting (and subsequent inquest) in which three persons died in a high school in Brampton, Ontario, at the end of May, 1975, when a teenager brought a rifle to school intending to kill two of his teachers.[28] Early in 1976, the federal government brought in legislation, but partly because of the attack waged by the "gun lobby," it had not been enacted when the parliamentary session ended in October. Another well-publicized shooting by a mentally disturbed sniper, and the inquest,[29] gave public support to the reintroduction of a gun control bill on 20 April 1977. Its eventual approval by the Commons in July was assisted by the shooting of a police officer in Ottawa by another mentally ill gunman. This occurred while the house was debating the gun control bill[30] and the Minister of Justice appeared at the scene of the shooting shortly afterwards and stated[31]: "Maybe this is the kind of incident we

Pressure-Groups in Britain (London 1970) at p. 5. The percentage of the population over 21 eligible to vote was only 3% in 1800, 13% in 1867 and not 100% until women received the vote in 1928: ibid. at p. 4.

26 Although good surveys should: see Lane, R. E. and Sears, D. O., Public Opinion (Englewood Cliffs, N.J. 1964) Chapter 9, on the problem of "intensity."

27 Downs, A., An Economic Theory of Democracy (New York 1957) at p. 92; see also Bartlett, R., Economic Foundations of Political Power (New York 1973).

28 Friedland, M.L., "Gun Control: The options," (1975) 18 Crim. L.Q. 29 at pp. 30 and 32. See also p. 42 showing that the Winnipeg General Strike was responsible for the gun control legislation introduced just after the First World War.

29 The Toronto Globe and Mail, 18 Nov., 1976. Inquests are often used to mobilize public opinion. As the Ontario Law Reform Commission's Report on the Coroner System in Ontario (1971) stated, one of the primary functions of the inquest is to serve "as a means for formally focusing community attention on and initiating community response to preventable deaths" (p. 29). A widely reported coroner's inquest in Toronto lasting for 22 days which reported on 22 July, 1977 heard extensive evidence and made recommendations on a case of child abuse. This has made the public aware of the nature of the problem and will undoubtedly serve as a catalyst for further action in the future. See The Toronto Globe and Mail, 23 July, 1977.

30 Bill C-51, Criminal Law Amendment Act 1977.

31 The Toronto Globe and Mail, 12 July, 1977.

need . . . to get Parliament and the opposition moving to pass a bill we've been trying to get through for 18 months." This use of public opinion, mobilized by focussing on specified dramatic events, was necessary since there were very few effective pressure groups seeking gun control compared to the well-organized anti-gun control organizations.[32]

Similarly, the passage of gun control legislation in the United States has been aided by the effect of specific events on public opinion. The shootings of Robert Kennedy and Martin Luther King were major factors in the passage of the 1968 Gun Control Act, while the escape of John Dillinger from jail had expedited the passage of the National Firearms Act of 1934.[33]

Public opinion on the issue of capital punishment, to take another example, also changes with the specific event. Well-publicized cold-blooded murders will, of course, influence public opinion in favour of capital punishment. There was a significant shift in Canadian public opinion in favour of capital punishment after the 1970 Quebec crisis in which a minister of the Crown was murdered and an English diplomat came close to meeting the same fate.[34] On the other hand, publicity concerning alleged miscarriages of justice, such as, in England, the murder cases of Bentley, Evans-Christie, and Ellis[35] will influence public opinion the other way.

Not only is public opinion often transient, it is also often ill-informed, and it has been shown how, for instance, "an informed public opinion about the death penalty may differ substantially from one that is uninformed."[36] Members of Parliament in both England and Canada no doubt took this into account in voting against capital punishment in spite of the public opinion in favour of its retention.[37]

Pressure groups attempt, of course, not only to mobilize public

32 Public opinion polls were cited by the Minister of Justice in his second reading speech on Bill C-51, see H.C. Debs. (11 May, 1977) 5527. See generally, Hodder-Williams, R., *Public Opinion Polls and British Politics* (London 1970) at pp. 78 *et seq.*

33 Friedland, M. L., (1975) 18 Crim. L.Q. 29 at pp. 45-46. See also Sherrill, R., *The Saturday Night Special* (New York 1973) at p. 291, and Zimring, "Firearms and Federal Law: The Gun Control Act of 1968," (1975) 4 J. of Legal Studies 133 at pp. 147-148.

34 The Solicitor General of Canada, *Capital Punishment, New Material: 1965-1972* (Ottawa 1972) at pp. 69-71.

35 Christoph, J. B., *Capital Punishment and British Politics* (London 1962) at pp. 174-175.

36 Sarat and Vidmar, "Public Opinion, The Death Penalty, and the Eighth Amendment: Testing the Marshall Hypothesis," [1976] Wisconsin L. Rev. 171 at p. 195.

37 Fattah, E. A., *The Canadian Public and the Death Penalty* (Burnaby, B.C. 1976). See also Vidmar, "Retributive and Utilitarian Motives and Other Correlates of Canadian Attitudes Toward the Death Penalty," (1974) 15 *The Canadian Psychologist* 337. For a discussion of public opinion polls and capital punishment in the United States see Vidmar and Ellsworth, "Public Opinion and the Death Penalty," (1974) 26 Stanford L. Rev. 1245.

opinion,[38] but also to show that they have very wide support and therefore represent a large body of opinion.[39] Legislators often probe representatives of pressure groups to discover whether this is, in fact, true. For example, the Canadian Civil Liberties Association and the Canadian Federation of Civil Liberties and Human Rights Associations were closely questioned about the extent of their membership when they appeared before the Justice and Legal Affairs Committee studying the proposed Human Rights Bill.[40]

Legislators also wish to make sure that those speaking for the group do, in fact, represent the group. Presthus writes[41]:

> In some cases governmental elites require that directors appear armed with a resolution from their members. Such action not only commits members to the collective group position and tactics, it also assures governmental elites that the director really has the green light from his group. . . . It is a common belief among M.P.'s that group leaders do not always represent the wishes of their members.

So, for example, the Canadian Labour Congress, representing at the time one-and-a-half million members, was carefully questioned[42] by members of the Parliamentary Committee considering the legislation that led to the abortion reforms in 1969 as to whether their position reflected the views of the members.

There is a constant interplay between public opinion, pressure groups and influential individuals. This can be seen in the liberalization of the English laws against homosexual conduct. The Wolfenden Committee studying homosexual conduct reported in 1957 that they had "not succeeded in discovering an unequivocal 'public opinion', and . . . felt bound to try to reach conclusions for ourselves rather than to base them on what is often transient and seldom precisly ascertainable."[43] The Committee's view was, in fact, consistent with opinion polls conducted

---

38 Presthus, R., "Interest Groups and the Canadian Parliament: Activities, Interaction, Legitimacy, and Influence," (1971) 4 C.J.P.S. 444 at p. 450: 56% of the M.P.s he surveyed ranked "mobilizing public opinion" as the most effective activity by a pressure group.

39 See *e.g.* the presentation by The Advocates' Society of Ontario to the Justice and Legal Affairs Committee on amendments to the wiretapping provisions of the Criminal Code: 9 June, 1977, (No. 20), oral testimony at pp. 24 *et seq.*, in particular at p. 24 and p. 37, and the brief in Appendix "JLA-10" at p. 1.

40 28 April, 1977 (No. 10) at pp. 19-20 and 32-33.

41 Presthus, R., *Elite Accommodation in Canadian Politics* (Toronto 1973) at p. 198.

42 See the proceedings of the Standing Committee on Health and Welfare (27th Parliament — Second Session) (20 Feb., 1968) at pp. 777 *et seq.* In 1977 the C.L.C. claimed 2.3 million members in an appearance before the Justice and Legal Affairs Committee, 29 March 1977 (no. 7) p. 6.

43 Report of the Committee on Homosexual Offences and Prostitution, Cmnd. 247 (1957) at p. 10.

shortly after the release of the report.[44] Lord Devlin, however, in his provocative Maccabaean Lecture in 1959 stated that there was "a general abhorrence of homosexuality."[45] But in 1965 he signed a crucial letter to *The Times* which referred to some of the influential bodies that had endorsed the Wolfenden Report, and expressed the "hope that . . . Her Majesty's Government will now recognize the necessity for this reform and will introduce legislation."[46]

This letter, as Jerome Skolnick has said, "suggests that although the public opinion polls may not have had a direct effect, their findings may have influenced leading groups in the community, which, in turn, influenced some of those initially opposed to the report, such as Lord Devlin."[47]

3. THE RANGE OF PRESSURE GROUPS

This and the next section on pressure group tactics focuses on the Canadian controversy concerning gun control, which, because of the extent of the pressure group activity on both sides can serve as a model to illustrate some of the organizations and tactics found in other areas as well.

At the same time that the Government introduced Bill C-84 to abolish capital punishment (24 February, 1976) it introduced another bill, Bill C-83, relating to gun control, wiretapping, dangerous offenders, parole and a number of other issues. This omnibus bill which together with Bill C-84 was known as the Peace and Security Program, was intended to give the public some assurance that crime would be effectively dealt with even though capital punishment was to be abolished. In particular, the police, who were strongly against the abolition of capital punishment, were to be protected by the further control of firearms since guns provide the one real threat to a policeman's life.[48] The police had been advocating strong gun control measures for a number of years[49] and general public opinion had, as we have seen, been aroused by a series of tragic gun incidents. A similar sequence of events occurred in England in 1965 when capital punishment was abolished: the Government introduced gun con-

---

44 The Gallup Poll reported that 47% believed homosexuality should be a crime, 38% believed it should not be a crime and 15% were undecided: Skolnick, "Coercion to Virtue: The Enforcement of Morals," (1968) 41 S. Cal. L. Rev. 588 at p. 613.

45 Devlin, P., *The Enforcement of Morals* (London 1965) at p. 17. The polls measured whether homosexuality should be a crime, not the citizens' attitude towards the conduct and so Lord Devlin's statement was not necessarily inconsistent with the polls.

46 *The Times*, 11 May, 1965.

47 (1968) 41 S. Cal. L. Rev. 588 at p. 616.

48 Friedland, M. L., (1975) 18 Crim. L.Q. 29 at p. 30, note 6.

49 *Ibid.* at p. 30, note 5.

trol legislation prior to the vote on capital punishment.[50] In Canada, however, capital punishment was in fact abolished[51] prior to passage of the gun control measures.

Bill C-83 was designed to tighten further the control of handguns, to prevent the acquisition of machine guns and other automatic weapons, and to introduce a scheme whereby those who possessed long-guns, that is, rifles or shotguns, had to obtain a licence. It did not include the more drastic step of registration of long-guns. The Parliamentary session ended in October, 1976 before Parliament could pass the legislation — the Government was obviously not anxious to force it through — and in April, 1977 a new, and in the case of gun control, weaker, bill, Bill C-51, was introduced. (The bill was weaker in that, amongst other changes, existing long-gun owners would not require a licence.) This bill was given a third reading by the Commons on 18 July, 1977 and quick passage by the Senate in August.[52] The government had attempted to blunt the impact of the pressure groups by using an omnibus bill, a device which had been used in the past for other controversial matters such as abortion and homosexual conduct.[53] Opposition M.P.s with strong support from the gun lobby attempted to split the bill, but were unsuccessful.[54]

Submissions on Bill C-83 from 38 organizations were published by the Justice and Legal Affairs Committee to whom the bill was referred after second reading. A much larger number of submissions and letters were, of course, received but not published. The Committee considering the later Bill, C-51, only heard presentations from six groups. The government, it seems, wanted the legislation back before the House for approval in July, 1977 before the summer recess and limited those who were invited to give evidence. Amongst the groups that had requested a hearing on Bill C-51, but were denied such a hearing were the National Indian Brotherhood, the Canadian Civil Liberties Association and the Canadian Association of Chiefs of Police.[55] The organizations that were heard ranged from ad hoc "issue-oriented"[56] groups such as the National

---

50 Greenwood, C., *Firearms Control* (London 1972), at pp. 76 *et seq.*

51 The House of Commons passed Bill C-84 on 14 July, 1976.

52 Senate Debates, 4 Aug., 1977. Royal Assent was given the next day. The licensing provisions did not come into effect, however, until Jan., 1979.

53 The omnibus bill was, of course, also designed to save parliamentary time: see Justice and Legal Affairs, 9 June, 1977 (No. 20), at p. 96.

54 H.C. Debs. (9 March, 1976) at pp. 11623 *et seq.*, and (9 May, 1977) at pp. 5430 *et seq.*, and (11 May, 1977) at pp. 5522 *et seq.*

55 Minutes of Proceedings and Evidence of the (House of Commons) Standing Committee on Justice and Legal Affairs, 7 June, 1977 (no. 19) at p. 33.

56 See Pross, "Pressure Groups: Adaptive Instruments of Political Communication" in *Pressure Group Behaviour in Canadian Politics* (ed. A. P. Pross) (Toronto 1975) at pp. 10 *et seq.*

Firearms Safety Association specifically formed in June, 1975 to promote effective gun control legislation,[57] to well-established institutional groups such as the Canadian Bar Association[58] and the Canadian Labour Congress.[59]

The National Firearms Safety Association was formed as the result of initiatives by a widow from Vancouver whose son had been killed by a firearm.[60] Like many similar ad hoc groups, it appeared to lack a strong organizational structure and was relatively ineffective on the gun control issue. It claimed to have 3,000 members, mainly from Ontario, a small number considering it was the only such group in existence. No membership fee was required.

Such groups find a substantial membership difficult to achieve. This is a constant problem for, for instance, the Consumers Association of Canada[61] and the Society for the Abolition of Capital Punishment.[62] People usually join groups not for so-called "collective benefits,"[63] but for specific individual benefits, such as a magazine, cheap insurance, or the right to emergency road service. Thus, for example, the Ontario Handgun Association which has approximately 4,000 members offers inexpensive firearms insurance as well as a publication, *Canadian Handgun*. Similarly, the Ontario Federation of Anglers and Hunters, with about 15,000 members[64] offered insurance ($200,000 public liability insurance for $1.25) and a magazine, *The Angler and Hunter in Ontario*.

Ad hoc, issue-oriented groups were formed to lobby against the legislation but these groups differed considerably from the National Firearms Safety Association because they built on existing gun clubs. So, for example, an organization called R.A.G.O. (Responsible Alberta Gun Owners)[65] was formed in August, 1975 and claimed, through group

---

57 *Justice and Legal Affairs* (No. 42) 29 April, 1976, at p. 45.

58 *Ibid.* (No. 47) 11 May, 1976, at pp. 5 *et seq.*

59 See the Canadian Labour Congress submission printed in Appendix "JLA-44" to *Justice and Legal Affairs* (No. 61) 8 June, 1976 at pp. 51 *et seq.* and the supplementary submission printed in Appendix "JLA-45" to *Justice and Legal Affairs* (No. 64) 14 June, 1976, at pp. 47 *et seq.*

   Church groups, which have played important roles in a number of recent criminal law issues, were understandably not involved in the gun control legislation.

60 *Justice and Legal Affairs* (No. 42) 29 April, 1976 at p. 48.

61 Trebilcock (1975) 13 Osgoode Hall L.J. 619 at pp. 624 *et seq.*

62 The Society was not a potent force in the 1976 debate on the abolition of capital punishment.

63 Trebilcock (1975) 13 Osgoode Hall L.J. 619 at pp. 625 *et seq.* See also Olson, M., *The Logic of Collective Action* (Cambridge, Mass. 1971). Of course, those who have very strong religious views on an issue, such as on abortion, may join a group for collective benefits.

64 *Justice and Legal Affairs* (No. 58) 31 May, 1976 at p. 39.

65 *Ibid.* (No. 53) 20 May, 1976 at p. 33.

memberships, a quarter of a million members.[66] Another organization, named C.A.S.A.L. (Canadian Association for Sensible Arms Legislation) was formed in September, 1976 shortly before Bill C-83 died on the order paper at the end of the session.[67] It too was an organization of organizations, being composed of over 25 clubs representing, according to their spokesman, half a million persons.[68] Their brief on Bill C-51 stated: "C.A.S.A.L. is the umbrella organization composed of many organizations of Canadian sportsmen, collectors, hunters, trappers, etc."[69]

Coalitions amongst groups are well-known in the lobbying business. The more persons making the same point the more the legislators will take note. This is particularly so when the groups represent different viewpoints. A particularly effective joint brief in another area of criminal law was that prepared by the Canadian Civil Liberties Association and the Metropolitan Toronto Police Association (described by the President of the Police Association as an "unholy alliance") and presented to the Ontario Solicitor General which called for the independent investigation of complaints against the police. There was nothing comparable to this on the gun control issue.

If the coalition collapses, however, the result may well be worse for the lobbyists than if there had been no coalition in the first place. This appears to have happened with respect to C.A.S.A.L., the coalition of gun groups opposing Bill C-51. When C.A.S.A.L. was formed in 1976 it was designed to include all those interested in guns. In the United States the N.R.A. (National Rifle Association), from its multi-million dollar nine-storey headquarters in Washington, has for years been an effective lobby for the various gun groups.[70] But there has been no organization like the N.R.A. in Canada. In fact there have been three main groups of gun enthusiasts (with a great amount of overlap amongst the three) — hunters, shooters and collectors.

Hunters are interested in long-guns (i.e. rifles and shotguns) whereas shooters are also interested in handguns, as are collectors, who in addition want to collect automatic weapons. The handgun and automatic weapon groups have been concerned for years that they might be abandoned by the hunters' groups, in particular the Canadian Wildlife Federation and its provincial affiliates, the Hunting and Angling Associations.

---

66 An organization called F.A.R.O. (Firearms for Responsible Ownership) claimed about 22,000 paid-up members: *Justice and Legal Affairs* (No. 41) 28 April, 1976 at pp. 27, 32. It is not clear from their presentation whether this included group representation.

67 *The Globe and Mail*, 13 and 14 Sept., 1976.

68 *Justice and Legal Affairs* (No. 19) 7 June 1977, at pp. 9-10.

69 *The Globe and Mail*, 19 Oct., 1976.

70 For a description of the N.R.A., see Sherrill, R., *The Saturday Night Special* at pp. 183 *et seq.*

The handgun group had cause to be concerned. In 1967, the Canadian Wildlife Federation had submitted a "Brief on Firearms Legislation" to the Minister of Justice. The Board of Directors of the Ontario Revolver Association in a special issue of their publication, *Canadian Handgun*,[71] under the heading "Wildlife Brief Proposes Sacrifice of Handgunners" stated that the Wildlife Federation "behaves like a fifth-column within the ranks of Canadian shooters. . . . The restrictions on handguns proposed by the Canadian Wildlife Federation lead this Board to only one conclusion: the Canadian Wildlife Federation is out to destroy our sport." Gun clubs stressed the need for solidarity. A document prepared shortly before Bill C-83 by the Winnipeg Game and Fish Club "in affiliation with the handgun and rifle and antique firearms clubs of Winnipeg" warned gun owners:

> Do not sacrifice any form of shooting sports just because you don't participate in it, or condemn some types of firearms because you don't own them. Remember, to non-shooters and non-hunters, all guns and hunting is unnecessary and stupid. We, as shooters, hunters and collectors, must stand united!

And the *Canadian Handgun* pleaded in a 1975 issue: "Don't Sell Out Your Fellow Shooters."

C.A.S.A.L., the umbrella organization, had Colonel L. H. Nicholson, a former R.C.M.P. Commissioner, as its spokesman. He had been associated with the wildlife groups in the fight over Bill C-83, both as the chairman of the Firearms Legislation Committee of the Canadian Wildlife Federation[72] and as an advisor to one of the Federation's affiliates, the Ontario Federation of Anglers and Hunters.[73] In 1969 he had met with the Minister of Justice and presented a brief on gun control amendments on behalf of the Shooting Federation of Canada, the Dominion of Canada Rifle Association and the Canadian Wildlife Federation.[74]

There had been widespread consultation between government officials and Colonel Nicholson and others.[75] However, when the time came for the presentation of briefs to the Justice and Legal Affairs Committee on Bill C-51 the coalition split apart. Colonel Nicholson appeared on behalf of the Canadian Wildlife Federation and refused to endorse the C.A.S.A.L. position. The wildlife group had no interest in endorsing the C.A.S.A.L. position that there should be the right to collect

---

71 Feb., 1967.

72 *Justice and Legal Affairs* (No. 40) 27 April, 1976.

73 *Ibid.* (No. 58) 31 May, 1976.

74 *Ibid.* (No. 8) 6 March, 1969 at pp. 205, 207, 209.

75 *Ibid.* (No. 20) 9 June, 1977 at p. 72.

automatic weapons,[76] and after the C.A.S.A.L. presentation, it sent a telegram to the Justice and Legal Affairs Committee "dissociat[ing] our organization from any statements or briefs presented in the name of C.A.S.A.L. We reaffirm our position regarding the 14 recommendations presented to your Committee Thursday June second 1977."[77]

One specialized type of collector, the antique collector, did not become organized on a national basis when Bill C-83 was debated.[78] Many pressure groups are organized along provincial rather than federal lines and find it difficult to respond in a united way to a federal initiative. As a result, a number of different groups of arms collectors, such as the Canadian Black Powder Federation and the Lower Canada Arms Collectors Association,[79] had appeared on Bill C-83.

The manufacturers' association, The Canadian Sporting Arms and Ammunition Association, appeared and presented a brief on Bill C-83[80] and like the wildlife groups endorsed "the resolve of the Government to extend the prohibition of clearly dangerous and unjustifiable weapons in Canada which are not of a type now commonly used for legitimate sporting or hunting purposes"[81]: a prohibition which would not affect the activities of the Association's members.[82]

The group, consisting of such well-known names as Browning, Remington and Winchester, was formed in mid-1973.[83] Its approach was typical of that of manufacturers' and similar groups. Like most such organizations, but unlike many of the others involved in the gun control issue, it had a full-time executive secretary in Ottawa. Its brief pointed out the economic consequences (at a time of high unemployment) of harming an industry, which "employs in excess of 1,500 skilled personnel in the primary manufacturing and distribution processes, most of whom are located in Quebec and Ontario, primarily in the smaller communities of Brownsburg in Quebec and Dunville, Lakefield, Cobourg and Cambridge in Ontario where the industry is a principal employer."[84] Moreover,

---

76 Compare the C.A.S.A.L. brief, printed as Appendix "JLA-9" to *Justice and Legal Affairs* (No. 19A) 7 June, 1977 at p. 2, with the Canadian Wildlife Federation's presentation, (No. 18) 2 June, 1977 at p. 8.

77 *Justice and Legal Affairs* (No. 20) 9 June 1977 at p. 90.

78 *Ibid.* (No. 19) 7 June, 1977 at p. 43.

79 *Ibid.* (No. 55) 26 May, 1976.

80 *Ibid.* (No. 42) 29 April, 1976.

81 *Ibid.* at p. 83.

82 The manufacturers in Canada, unlike those in the U.S., did not apparently lobby against restrictions against handguns in the 1930s, no doubt because, as the Minister of Justice stated in the House at the time, "there is no manufacture in Canada of pistols or revolvers": Friedland (1975) 18 Crim. L.Q. 29 at p. 45.

83 *Justice and Legal Affairs* (No. 42) 29 April, 1976 at p. 92.

84 *Ibid* at p. 91.

unlike many of the other groups, it did not complain about lack of consultation. Its officials had met with the Minister of Justice, government officials, and the Chairman of the Justice and Legal Affairs Committee.[85] Having a full-time director in Ottawa makes it much easier to develop a close relationship with government.[86] They avoided major conflicts. The executive secretary told the Justice and Legal Affairs Committee[87]: "Our worries are not related to the principle of the matter but rather to details and definitions."

Unlike most other groups that appeared, the Association did not object to the government filling in some of the details of the legislation through regulations[88] — perhaps because this type of association operates most effectively with the quiet diplomacy practised between its own officials and the government's. In contrast, the gun club officials are not used to this form of "elite accommodation" and prefer the legislative process where voting power becomes important. They and other opponents of the legislation constantly criticized the power to make law through regulations, thus by-passing Parliament. As R.A.G.O. (Responsible Alberta Gun Owners) put it in their brief,[89] "Regulatory powers are more damaging than amendments to the code because effects can be achieved without political problems."[90]

Police groups have become active lobbyists in the last 10 years. In 1971, for example, the Canadian Police Association appeared before the Justice and Legal Affairs Committee on the bail issue.[91] After the passage of the Bail Reform Act groups of police[92] and wives of policemen (1200 wives attended a meeting in Toronto and formed an organization[93]) pressed for a "tightening up" of the legislation. There was not a unanimous front, however, on gun control. The policeman wearing his

---

85 *Ibid.* at p. 22.

86 Dawson, "National Pressure Groups and the Federal Government" in *Pressure Group Behaviour in Canadian Politics* (ed. A. P. Pross) (Toronto 1975) at p. 46: "One thing is clear: groups which do not have full-time staff in Ottawa cannot develop this type of relationship."

87 *Justice and Legal Affairs* (No. 42) 29 April, 1976 at p. 19.

88 *Ibid.* at p. 14.

89 *Ibid.* (No. 53) 20 May, 1976, Appendix "JLA-30," at p. 89.

90 F.A.R.O. (Firearms for Responsible Ownership) placed ads in newspapers complaining about the potential use of regulations: see *The Globe and Mail*, 23 June, 1977. Another argument advanced was that if there had to be regulations, they should come before Parliament for approval. An amendment to this effect was defeated in the Commons: Votes and Proceedings, 13 July, 1977, (no. 163) at p. 1352.

91 *Justice and Legal Affairs* (No. 9) 25 Feb., 1971. The Minister of Justice had earlier addressed the Canadian Chiefs of Police to explain the legislation: *The Globe and Mail*, 4 Sept., 1970.

92 *Eg.* the Ontario Police Association. See *The Toronto Daily Star*, 15 Aug., 1973.

93 *The Globe and Mail*, 12 Feb., 1973.

police hat wants gun control, whereas the policeman wearing his sportsman's cap does not. So The Canadian Association of Chiefs of Police supported Bill C-83[94] while some of the police associations (the equivalent of unions) took a more ambivalent position.[95]

Lawyers are, of course, involved in associations of lawyers. They also make submissions on behalf of other groups. For example, a lawyer, who was not a gun owner, acted as one of the spokesmen for F.A.R.O. (Firearms for Responsible Ownership).[96] A lawyer also acted for the industry group.[97] The Canadian Bar Association's Code of Professional Conduct[98] requires that the lawyer should in such cases make it clear that he is acting for a client. As Harry Arthurs has stated[99]: "Lawyers seeking changes in the law must disclose whether they are acting in their own interest, that of a client, or in the public interest: lobbyists must not masquerade as academic critics."

In each province the most powerful group of lawyers is the association that controls the profession, and to which all practising lawyers must belong. In Ontario this body is the Law Society of Upper Canada. In contrast to the official governing bodies in England, the Law Society does not act as a pressure group for changes in the law unless the change directly affects the interests of lawyers. Its Public Relations Committee stated in 1972 that "the Society should express a view only of matters which affect the profession as a whole,"[100] such as Legal Aid[101] or the

---

94 *Justice and Legal Affairs* (No. 50) 18 May, 1976 at p. 27.

95 See the evidence of the National Police Committee for the Protection of the Citizens, formed to study Bill C-83, composed of representatives of the Canadian Police Association, the Quebec Provincial Police Association and the New Brunswick Police Association: *Justice and Legal Affairs* (No. 43) 4 May, 1976. Individual police officers or former officers were also connected with pro-gun lobbies: *e.g.* C.A.S.A.L., the Ontario Handgun Association and the Canadian Wildlife Federation.

96 *Justice and Legal Affairs* (No. 41) 28 April, 1976 at p. 7.

97 *Ibid.* (No. 42) 29 April, 1976 at p. 9.

98 Canadian Bar Association, Code of Professional Conduct (1974), R. 6, para. 4. The Code was adopted by the Bar Association in 1974 and has since then been adopted in principle by the Law Society of Upper Canada: Arthurs, "Barristers and Barricades: Prospects for the Lawyer as a Reformer," (1976) 15 U.W.O.L. Rev. 59 at pp. 63 *et seq.*

99 (1976) 15 U.W.O.L. Rev. 59 at p. 69.

100 Ontario Reports, 10 March, 1972 at p. ccxlviii. In 1969 a resolution "That the proposed Law Society Act be broadened so that there shall be included in the objects of the Society the consideration and initiation of Law Reform and the making of submissions to the proper authorities on matters of Law Reform on behalf of the Society, and that there be provided from the funds of the Law Society adequate assistance for the foregoing purposes including research," was defeated at the Society's Annual Meeting.

101 See a letter from the Treasurer to *The Globe and Mail*, 10 Sept., 1969 and Report of the Task Force on Legal Aid, Part 1 (1974) (Osler), Appendix D. See also Arthurs, "Authority, Accountability, and Democracy in the Government of the Ontario Legal Profession," (1971) 49 Can. B. Rev. 3 at pp. 9-10.

profession's involvement in plea bargaining.[102] It is not, therefore, surprising that the Law Society expressed no view on gun control. On the other hand, it did express concern over the wiretapping provisions of the Bill (a number of lawyers had had their conversations tapped), but apparently could not meet as a group in time to prepare a formal submission on Bill C-51.[103] However, three of the 40 benchers of the Law Society did appear and present a brief on behalf of The Advocates' Society of Ontario,[104] a group of 700 lawyers engaged in litigation.

A number of voluntary groups of lawyers, like The Advocates' Society, have sprung up in Ontario: the Law Union represents left-wing and the more radical lawyers; and the Ontario Crown Attorneys' Association and the Criminal Lawyers Association, each with their own journal, represent their respective interests. Similar groups can be found in other provinces. There is nothing comparable in Canada, however, with the English group "Justice" (although there is a Canadian section of the International Commission of Jurists); nor is there anything like the American Law Institute. Law teachers in Canada, again unlike England, have as an organized group played only a small role in law reform, though individual law teachers have been very active.

The most active professional organization involved in law reform is the Canadian Bar Association, a voluntary organization established in 1915, on the model of the American Bar Association, and organized through provincial branches.[105] A committee on Uniform Legislation and Law Reform was created in 1918,[106] but by and large the Association's law reform activities have not been particularly notable, although it has taken positions on a large number of issues, principally, perhaps, because it has not usually backed up its positions with adequate study and research. When it has done so, as in the comparatively well-financed study on the Supreme Court of Canada,[107] the results have been impressive. But the Association does not usually proceed, as it surely should, by well-researched reasoned arguments; it usually proceeds by "resolutions." Four tough gun control resolutions were passed at its Annual Meeting in Montreal in August 1972, and these were brought to the attention[108] of the

---

102 Letter from the Treasurer, *The Globe and Mail*, 22 Dec., 1971.

103 *Justice and Legal Affairs* (No. 20) 9 June, 1977, at pp. 24-25.

104 *Ibid.* at p. 24.

105 An earlier group was established in Nova Scotia in 1896 which had, as one of its objects, "to secure proper legislation"; but this body lapsed after three years: Hutchison (1956) 38 *Canadian Bar Association Proceedings* at pp. 103-105.

106 (1918) 3 *Canadian Bar Association Proceedings* at p. 104.

107 The Report of the Special Committee of the Canadian Bar Association on the Caseload of the Supreme Court of Canada (1973) (The MacKinnon Report).

108 The resolutions are set out in *Justice and Legal Affairs* (No. 47) 11 May, 1976 at p. 8.

Justice and Legal Affairs Committee in 1976. But their fragile nature had been exposed in a letter to a newspaper editor shortly after they were approved,[109] which pointed out that one of them was carried by a vote of 65-64 at the plenary session. The writer went on to say: "You should therefore not give the impression that the vote of the Canadian Bar Association taken 31 August represents the views of the bar as a whole. It in fact represents the views of 65 lawyers who had no notice of the motion, or any serious opportunity to consider it." It had in fact been defeated the week before by the Criminal Justice section by a vote of 13-7. The Bar Association was one of the few groups to appear before the Justice and Legal Affairs Committee without a written brief. Moreover the presentation would not appear to have been approved by anybody within the 18,000 member organization.[110] No doubt some of the defects in the Association's law reform activities will be corrected by the appointment of a permanent law reform director.[111]

There were many more groups that publicly expressed an interest in the "Peace and Security" legislation. The Canadian Civil Liberties Association, which plays a very influential role in criminal law matters (mainly because of the carefully prepared and researched positions it puts forward),[112] did not find any civil liberties issues in the substantive provisions on gun control; it saved its fire for the wiretapping and corrections part of Bill C-83.[113] The National Gay Rights' Coalition, a coalition of 27 Gay Rights' organizations, claiming to speak for 2 million persons, also appeared on Bill C-83, but concentrated its attention on the "dangerous offender" provisions.[114] Other groups that appeared and commented on the gun control provisions included the Native Council of Canada,[115] the Canadian Association of Elizabeth Fry Societies,[116] the Canadian Criminology and Corrections Association[117] and the Société de

---

109 *The Globe and Mail*, 29 Sept., 1972.

110 *Justice and Legal Affairs* (No. 47) 11 May, 1976 at p. 6.

111 (1976) 3 *The National* (Nov.) at p. 1.

112 See the article on the association's general counsel, A. A. Borovoy: Schiff, "A Very Civil Libertarian," *The Globe and Mail Weekend Magazine*, 4 Sept., 1976 at p. 14. The organization has 3,500 to 4,000 members: *Justice and Legal Affairs* (No. 10) 18 April, 1977 at pp. 19-20.

113 Some civil liberties writers in the U.S., who are concerned about harassment of the left by the right, do see civil liberties implications in the gun control issue: see *e.g.* Kates, "Why a Civil Libertarian Opposes Gun Control" (1976) 3 *The Civil Liberties Review* at p. 24.

114 See *Justice and Legal Affairs* (No. 48) 12 May, 1976, at pp. 32 *et seq.* and its brief in Appendix "JLA-20," at pp. 46 *et seq.*

115 *Ibid.* (No. 44) 5 May, 1976, at pp. 6-7, 51-52.

116 *Ibid.* (No. 47) 11 May, 1976 at pp. 32 and 60.

117 *Ibid.* (No. 46) 6 May, 1976 at pp. 6 and 51-52.

Criminologie du Québec.[118] Finally, the Canadian Labour Congress, representing 2 million members, put in a submission and a supplementary submission, but chose not to appear before the Committee.

One notes the absence of pressure groups of victims. Although families of victims may help to found a group, as we saw with the National Firearms Safety Association, and other organizations such as Rape Crisis Centres have helped advance the interests of rape victims, victims themselves rarely form a group. [Since the above was written, groups of victims — for example, families of persons killed by drunk drivers — have become a more powerful force in demanding higher penalties and stronger legislation: see the Globe and Mail, Jan. 8 and 19, 1983.] Similarly, the other principal participant in crime, the criminal, has in the past been silent, relying on other organizations to speak for him. More recently, however, groups of potential criminals such as possessors of marijuana have taken part in the formation of pressure groups[119], and those serving sentences have been playing a role in the development of penal policy.[120]

4. GROUP TACTICS

"Pressure without reason may be irresponsible," the general counsel of the Canadian Civil Liberties Association, A. Alan Borovoy, once stated,[121] "but reason without pressure is ineffectual." The tactics used by the pressure groups in the gun control issue included mass meetings, delegations, advertisements, petitions, and letter writing. The lobbying was very intense. An M.P. from Northern Ontario stated on the second reading debate on Bill C-83[122]: "In my riding of Nickel Belt, which is predominantly rural and working class, there is great concern about certain provisions, which concern has resulted in about 180 pieces of mail daily, plus a 6,000 signature petition." And a Manitoba M.P. stated that he received a petition signed by 500 persons from a village with a population of only 1,000.[123] There were, however, no very large petitions, such as the

118 *Ibid.* at p. 64.

119 *E.g.* N.O.R.M.L., National Organization for the Reform of Marijuana Laws in Canada: *The Globe and Mail*, 18 July, 1977 and 15 August, 1977.

120 See the Third Report of the Justice and Legal Affairs Sub-Committee on The Penitentiary System in Canada, (No. 45) 26 May, 1977. Appendix "C" lists among the witnesses who appeared before the Sub-Committee several groups of inmates. See also *The Globe and Mail*, 11 Aug., 1977 describing the day of protest (including refusing food) at maximum security prisons across Canada. Hunger strikes have been used in England by suffragettes and, recently, Irish prisoners: Zellick, "The Forcible Feeding of Prisoners: an Examination of the Legality of Enforced Therapy," [1976] *Public Law* at p. 153.

121 "Civil Liberties in the Imminent Hereafter," (1973) 51 Can. Bar Rev. 93 at p. 94.

122 H.C. Deb. at p. 12747 (12 April, 1976).

123 *Ibid.* at p. 12328 (31 March, 1976).

million signature petition in England in 1969 to restore the death penalty[124] or the half million signatures opposing changes in the abortion law in 1967.[125]

Letter writing may have established a Canadian record. One M.P. said that he had received over 5,000 letters.[126] These letters did not emerge spontaneously. Firearms organizations urged their members to write, and gun club literature contained much advice on the type of letters to write. A 1973 bulletin of the Ontario Revolver Association stated: "The first task of every handgunner in Ontario is to communicate with his member of parliament. Clubs should send a delegation to discuss the matter with their M.P. Individuals should write short, polite and precise letters to their M.P.s." One Senator involved in hearings on an earlier private members' bill on gun control received over 700 pieces of mail — all in English.[127] No doubt the extent of the letter writing was influenced by the example of the effective letter writing campaigns engaged in by the N.R.A. in the United States.[128]

All these techniques are, of course, meant to show legislators the numbers of concerned citizens. Implicit, but quite often explicit, was the threat that they would not vote for a legislator who supported gun control. The Northern Ontario M.P. who has already been mentioned stated in the House[129]: "I support the principle of gun control. Indeed the bill does not go far enough with respect to tightening gun control. I have said this to rod and gun clubs and those interested in my constituency, and there are large numbers of them." In answer to an intervention: "What did they say?" the M.P. replied: "They said they would turn me out."

Gun clubs stressed their power to influence votes. Colonel Nicholson, the spokesman at the time for C.A.S.A.L., the leading pro-gun organization, stated that the M.P.'s "are going to be left with the clear impression that if they support the bill they are going to suffer."[130] M.P.'s in unsafe seats — and few seats are really safe — could not help but be worried by these tactics. As a 1975 issue of the *Canadian Handgun* stated[131]:

124 *The Globe and Mail*, 16 Dec., 1969.

125 Hindell, K. and Simms, M., *Abortion Law Reformed* (London 1971) at p. 97.

126 See H.C. Deb. at p. 7752 (18 July, 1977).

127 See *The Globe and Mail*, 25 Feb., 1975.

128 See Sherrill, R., *The Saturday Night Special* (New York 1973) at pp. 195-196 who points out that in one case six letters of protest regarding a gun control bill had arrived, but after the N.R.A. requested its members to send letters, 12,000 arrived. According to Sherrill, N.R.A. "officials have boasted that they can get their million members to hit Congress with at least half a million letters on 72-hour notice."

129 H.C. Deb. at p. 12747 (12 April, 1976).

130 *The Globe and Mail*, 14 and 22 Sept., 1976. Another tactic which was effectively used was to threaten to block an M.P.'s nomination at the next election.

131 Issue No. 4.

"It is what happens at the ballot box that determines what legislation we get. Every politician knows that a switch of as little as five per cent of the votes can decide whether he wins or loses the riding." In the past prohibitionists had used this technique[132], and it is now being used by those for and against abortion[133] and capital punishment,[134] by homosexuals,[135] and, of course, by labour groups. The use of voting power as a tactic is certainly increasing. It is no longer true to say, as one Canadian writer did, that "Groups appear to have come to the conclusion that threatening politicians with exercise of the franchise is a useless manoeuvre."[136]

The pro-gun groups concentrated on M.P.'s, partly, no doubt, because of the influence of gun groups in the United States who understandably concentrate on the much more independent congressmen, but also because they felt that this is where they could have the greatest impact. The individual M.P. could influence policy through the parliamentary caucus, the Justice and Legal Affairs Committee and, of course, the appropriate ministers and their advisors. The traditional quiet lobbying directed at civil servants, usually "the focal point for pressure group activity in this country,"[137] would have had little effect on the outcome. Moreover, two federal departments, the Department of the Solicitor-General and the Department of Justice, were involved in the legislation and so an understanding with one group of civil servants might not carry over to the other. In any event, the Justice and Legal Affairs Committee would necessarily hold hearings on the bill and so the gun organizations would eventually have to make public submissions.[138]

Many of the groups met with the Minister of Justice and the Solicitor-General. Even the Prime Minister met with one group, the Canadian Wildlife Federation.[139] No group, however, met with the Cabinet on this

---

132 See Quinney, R., *The Social Reality of Crime* (Boston 1970) at p. 91.

133 See *The Globe and Mail*, 19 Nov., 1976. Lord Gardiner, when he was a parliamentary candidate and an adviser to the Abortion Law Reform Association, felt that he could not participate in a pro-abortion bill stating that, "In fairness to my local party I could not properly risk that course in a seat which was lost at the last election by a few hundred votes": Hindell, K. and Simms, M., *Abortion Law Reformed* (1971) at pp. 80-81.

134 *The Globe and Mail*, 23 June, 1976.

135 *Ibid.* 6 June, 1977.

136 Dawson, "National Pressure Groups and the Federal Government" in *Pressure Group Behaviour in Canadian Politics* (ed. A. P. Pross) (Toronto 1975) at p. 48.

137 Pross, "Pressure Groups: Adaptive Instruments of Political Communication" in *Pressure Group Behaviour in Canadian Politics* (ed. A. P. Pross) (Toronto 1975) at p. 2.

138 Another complicating factor is that some provinces had indicated an interest in passing gun control legislation if the federal government did not, and so open lobbying would have an impact on the provinces as well as the federal government.

139 Lewis, "The Hidden Persuaders" in *MacLean's*, 13 June, 1977 at p. 40b.

issue, a privilege normally granted only to powerful well-established groups such as the Canadian Labour Congress.

Of course, many M.P.s and Senators belonged to pressure groups involved in the gun control controversy. Indeed, Ron Basford, the Minister of Justice, was a member of the Canadian Wildlife Federation.[140] Most, if not all, M.P.s belong to some pressure groups.[141] In the nineteenth century pressure groups played a direct role in gaining a parliamentary spokesman.[142] In 1866, for example, there were some 146 directors of railway companies in the British House of Commons.[143] Today the influence of pressure groups is more indirect.

It is not possible to say what role campaign and other contributions played in the gun control controversy. In earlier days in the United States, Samuel Colt gave expensive pistols to deserving congressmen before key votes.[144] Such tactics would now be considered bribery in Canada.[145] However, contributions to the party or to the legislator's campaign are, of course, allowed.[146] Between 1908 and 1930 the Dominion Elections Act[147] prohibited any company — and in 1920 this was extended to associations[148] — from making any political contributions, but this legislation was repealed in 1930 under pressure from the unions.[149] In 1974 the Federal Government amended the Income Tax Act to allow part of such contributions to be deducted from federal taxes payable.[150]

Finally, there are the marches and demonstrations which were common in the 1960s, are still used by some groups on such issues as

---

140 *Justice and Legal Affairs* (No. 45) 6 May, 1976 at p. 10.

141 The Canadian Parliamentary Guide lists, at the member's option, some of the organizations to which he belongs.

142 See *Pressure from Without in Early Victorian England* (ed. P. Hollis) (London 1974) at p. 14.

143 Roberts, G. K., *Political Parties and Pressure Groups in Britain* (London 1970) at p. 85. Many M.P.s and Senators in Canada today are directors of companies: *The Globe and Mail*, 25 July, 1977.

144 Note, "Public Disclosure of Lobbyists' Activities," (1970) 38 Fordham L. Rev. 524 at p. 525.

145 See s. 108 of the Code: "being a member of the Parliament of Canada . . . corruptly . . . obtains . . . any . . . valuable consideration . . . in respect of anything done or omitted or to be done or omitted by him in his official capacity." Civil servants would be caught by s. 110: see *R. v. Cooper* (1977), 34 C.C.C. (2d) 18 (S.C.C.).

146 See now the disclosure provisions in the Election Expenses Act, S.C. 1973-74, c. 51; and also the Election Finances Reform Act (now R.S.O. 1980. c 134.)

147 An Act to amend the Dominion Elections Act, S.C. 1908, c. 26, s. 36.

148 The Dominion Elections Act, S.C. 1920, c. 46, s. 10.

149 Pappin, "Tax Relief for Political Contributions," (1976) 24 Can. Tax. J. 298. See also Paltiel, *Political Party Financing in Canada* (1970) at pp. 115-116.

150 See now s. 127(3) of the Income Tax Act, S.C. 1970-71-72, c. 63. Ontario followed suit with a somewhat similar scheme in 1975.

abortion, homosexual rights and marijuana,[151] but which were not used by the gun lobby. This writer has not seen any evidence that civil disobedience was ever openly advocated by the gun organizations, but there was often the veiled threat that new legislation might not be obeyed.[152]

The activities of the pressure groups have thus far focussed primarily on the legislature. Now that the legislation has passed, the focal point has shifted to the civil servants drafting the regulations and administering the scheme, an attempt by opposition M.P.s to keep the focus of attention on the House of Commons by requiring the regulations to come back before the House[153] having been defeated.

The Government released a document in June 1977 entitled "Policy Directives for Preparation of the Regulations in the Gun Control Provisions of Bill C-51."[154] Not only was it prepared in consultation with a number of interest groups such as the Retail Council of Canada and the Trucking Associations, but it envisaged continuing widespread consultation. "As soon as possible after the bill is passed," it stated, "further consultation will be held with manufacturers, wholesalers, retailers and transporters before the regulations are finalized." Moreover, "A commitment has also been made to the Canadian Wildlife Federation and other interest groups that they would be consulted on the regulations. Finally, the National Advisory Council on Firearms Use will be established to monitor the effectiveness of firearms control laws and regulations, with a view to eliminating unwarranted action." This Council will be made up of licensing officials and persons "interested in gun sports."[155]

Very little has been said so far about the courts and pressure groups. Litigation was not important on the gun control issue, though it may become so in the future, in interpreting the legislation and regulations. We turn now, using examples other than gun control, to pressure groups in the courts.

---

151 See *The Globe and Mail*, 18 July, 1977 describing the protest rally at the Parliament Buildings by N.O.R.M.L. (National Organization for the Reform of Marijuana Laws in Canada). For a discussion of the tactics of disruption, see Borovoy, "Civil Liberties in the Imminent Hereafter," (1973) 51 Can. Bar Rev. 93.

152 *The Globe and Mail*, 23 April, 1976: "The Native Council of Canada, representing an estimated 750,000 non-status Indians and Metis, has told the Government it will not ask its people to abide by the gun laws unless changes are made." See also the evidence of the spokesman for R.A.G.O. (Responsible Gun Owners of Alberta), *Justice and Legal Affairs* (No. 53) 20 May, 1976 at p. 36.

153 *Votes and Proceedings* (No. 163) 13 July, 1977 at p. 1352.

154 *Justice and Legal Affairs* (No. 22A) 16 June, 1977. Appendix "JLA-11."

155 H.C. Deb., p. 7751 (18 July, 1977). See also H.C. Deb. at p. 7213 (30 June, 1977), and *Justice and Legal Affairs* (No. 20) 9 June, 1977 at p. 74.

5. PRESSURE GROUPS AND THE JUDICIARY

The American pattern of pressure group activity is well known.[156] Pressure groups have involved the courts in some of the major issues in American life: electoral redistribution,[157] police practices,[158] civil rights,[159] prison reform,[160] abortion,[161] and capital punishment.[162] What is perhaps not so well known is that the Canadian judiciary has been involved in some of these very same issues, although to a far lesser extent. Judges not only play a key role, in their extra-judicial capacity, in the electoral redistribution process,[163] and regularly head committees and commissions dealing with police practices,[164] they have also, as we will see in the following sections, played a limited role on issues involving civil rights,[165] prison reform,[166] abortion,[167] and capital punishment,[168] with which pressure groups have been concerned.

---

156   Chayes, "The Role of the Judge in Public Law Litigation," (1976) 89 Harv. L. Rev. 1281; Denvir, "Towards a Political Theory of Public Interest Litigation," (1976) 54 N.C.L.R. 1133; Greenberg, "Litigation for Social Change: Methods, Limits and Role in Democracy," (1974) 29 *The Record* 320.

   In "The Independent Judiciary in an Interest-Group Perspective," (1975) 18 J. of Law and Economics 875, Landes and Posner argue interestingly (at p. 879) that "an independent judiciary facilitates rather than, as conventionally believed, limits the practice of interest-group politics." The courts "enforce the 'deals' made by effective interest groups with earlier legislatures" (at p. 894). The trouble with this theory is, as they acknowledge (at p. 893), that it "does not explain why the 'Warren Court' interpreted the Constitution as conferring extra-ordinary rights on the common criminal." Moreover, in Canada and England it is difficult for the courts to discover what the "deal" was because of the limitations on the introduction of evidence of parliamentary proceedings.

157   *Baker v. Carr* (1962), 369 U.S. 186.

158   *Escobedo v. Illinois* (1964), 378 U.S. 478 and *Miranda v. Arizona* (1966), 384 U.S. 436.

159   *Brown v. Board of Education of Topeka, Kansas* (1955), 349 U.S. 294.

160   Prigmore and Crow, "Is the Court Remaking the American Prison System?" (1976) 40 *Federal Probation* 3.

161   *Roe v. Wade* (1973), 410 U.S. 113.

162   *Furman v. Georgia* (1972), 408 U.S. 238.

163   S. 6 of the Electoral Boundaries Readjustment Act, R.S.C. 1970, c. E-2 [am. S.C. 1974-75, c. 28, s. 6; 1978-79, c. 13, s. 20].

164   *E.g.* Canadian Committee on Corrections (1969) (Ouimet); Commission of Inquiry Relating to Public Complaints, Internal Discipline and Grievance Procedure Within the R.C.M.P. (1976) (Marin); Royal Commission into Metropolitan Toronto Police Practices (1976) (Morand).

165   See the Jehovah's Witness cases, *infra*; and also *Re Wren*, [1945] 4 D.L.R. 674 (Ont. S.C.).

166   *McCann v. R.* (1975), 68 D.L.R. (3d) 661 (Fed. Ct.).

167   *Morgentaler v. R.* (1975), 53 D.L.R. (3d) 161 (S.C.C.).

168   *R. v. Miller and Cockriell* (1976), 70 D.L.R. (3d) 324 (S.C.C.).

It is safe to predict that pressure groups in Canada will have more and more opportunities to come before the courts. Even in the United States the current slowing down of the procedures whereby pressure groups can get before the courts may be only temporary[169]: a reflection of the present composition of the Supreme Court.[170] In contrast, changes in the composition of the Supreme Court of Canada under the late Chief Justice Laskin may encourage groups in Canada to pursue judicial remedies more readily than in the past.

Canadian pressure groups will, no doubt, continue to concentrate their attention on the civil service and the legislature, regarding the courts as a last resort.[171] But the groups may not have a choice. Gun clubs, to take one of any number of examples, would have liked to have had the offence of careless handling[172] more fully defined in the legislation. Because it was not, the focus will therefore inevitably shift to the courts. Antique gun clubs were more successful in having the definition of antique firearms set out in the Code. In England, by contrast, the task of definition has been left to the courts.[173]

Groups may also be forced into the courts because the government has referred an issue to them for an opinion. So, for example, when the Federal government referred its anti-inflation legislation to the Supreme Court of Canada in 1976[174] it drew in groups such as the Canadian Labour Congress and the Ontario Teachers' Federation who do not normally use the judicial process to pursue their objectives. Similarly, we find powerful groups such as the potash manufacturers[175] and the Ontario Medical Association[176] using the courts to protect their interests in the face of government action. It is therefore becoming less accurate to state, as Presthus does,[177] that "among the few groups that do turn to the courts, the main ones tend to have somewhat marginal status in the larger society."

Pressure groups may, of course, seek to influence the outcome of legal proceedings by illegitimate means, such as disruptive tactics in

---

169 (1976) Harv. L. Rev. 1281 at pp. 1304 *et seq.*

170 Lewin, "Avoiding the Supreme Court," in *The New York Times Magazine*, 17 Oct., 1976, at p. 31.

171 See Presthus, R., *Elite Accommodation in Canadian Politics* (Toronto 1973) at p. 153 and *Elites in the Policy Process* (Toronto 1974) at p. 148.

172 S. 84(2).

173 *Richards v. Curwen*, [1977] 1 W.L.R. 747 (D.C.).

174 *Re Anti-Inflation Act*, [1976] 2 S.C.R. 373.

175 *Amax Potash Ltd. et al. v. The Govt. of Sask.*, [1977] 2 S.C.R. 576.

176 *Ont. Medical Assn. v. Miller* (1976), 14 O.R. (2d) 468 (C.A.).

177 Presthus, R., *Elite Accommodation in Canadian Politics* (Toronto 1973), at p. 153.

court,[178] mass picketing, and the publication of comments on a case which is being or about to be heard, which may amount to, and be dealt with as, contempts of court.[179] Such activities are, however, outside the scope of this essay, as is the electoral pressure to which some American elected judges may be subject.[180] Judges are, of course, sensitive to public opinion,[181] but that, too, is another subject.

Pressure group activity in the courts can be either encouraged or slowed down by rulings and legislation on such matters as standing, mootness, class actions and costs. But it cannot be stopped because proceedings will be instituted, even when there is little chance of winning, in order to focus public attention on an issue so that the proceedings become a catalyst for legislative or administrative change.[182] It is, accordingly, worth looking more closely at the different ways in which pressure groups have come before the courts.

(a) Private Prosecutions

For many centuries groups have been involved in bringing criminal prosecutions as private prosecutors,[183] though the form of proceeding has made it appear as if there were an individual complainant. In the 1700s, for example, Societies for the Reformation of Manners often acted as prosecutors to encourage observance of laws relating to the Sabbath,

---

178 See *eg. Morris v. The Crown Office*, [1970] 2 Q.B. 114 (C.A.), the case of the Welsh students who disrupted court proceedings in England to highlight the failure to use the Welsh language in court.

179 See Borrie, G. and Lowe, N., *The Law of Contempt* (London 1973); and Lowe, "Freedom of Speech and the Sub Judice Rule," [1977] New L.J. 676. Even the accused is sometimes prevented from commenting on a case as a condition of release from custody pending trial or appeal! Dickens, "The Morgentaler Case: Criminal Process and Abortion Law," (1976) 14 Osgoode Hall L.J. 229 at pp. 233 and 239.

180 The President of the International Conference of Police Associations is reported to have suggested that police associations in the U.S. could keep records of individual decisions which "would be publicly analysed during times of elections." (*The Toronto Globe and Mail*, 22 July 1970).

181 See *e.g. R. v. Sargeant* (1974) 60 Cr. App. R. 74 at 77; *R. v. Ingram and Grimsdale* (1977) 35 C.C.C. (2d) 376 (Ont. C.A.). See also *Baker v. R.* [1975] 3 All E.R. 55 at 59 (D.C.) *per* Lord Diplock.

182 See Denvir (1976) 54 N.C.L.R. 1133 at p. 1140; Greenberg (1974) 29 *The Record* 320 at p. 321. Or for a change in corporate policy because of the adverse publicity: see, *e.g. The Financial Post*, 9 Oct. 1976 on the action brought by the "Ontario Rusty Ford Owners Association."

183 It should also be noted that groups in the form of "grand juries" have in the past played a role in the prosecution process; in the middle ages the grand jury was designed to be a group which was "representative of the community": Plucknett, T. F. T., *A Concise History of the Common Law* (5th ed.) (London 1956) at p. 127.

gaming, disorderly houses, obscenity, and cruelty to animals.[184] These societies were encouraged by the courts: Lord Kenyon stated[185] that they were "societ[ies] of gentlemen, instituted for the most important of all purposes — for preserving the morals of the people." Moreover, in the eighteenth and the nineteenth centuries voluntary associations for the prosecution of felons existed in almost every part of England and Wales.[186] "As late as 1836," writes Sir Leon Radzinowicz,[187] "one hundred and eighty-nine such associations were still in existence in various parts of the country."

The private prosecutor's power continues to be quite wide both in Canada[188] and in England,[189] and private prosecutions can, of course, still be brought by groups. As Peter Burns has pointed out[190]: "Public interest groups throughout Canada have evolved to act as informal watch-dogs and they or their members have been involved in private prosecutions under the relevant legislation." Private prosecutions are used, for example, by such organizations as environmental groups to enforce environmental laws,[191] and by labour groups to discourage unfair labour practices. In many of these cases, however, the legislation requires a public official's consent before the action can be brought,[192] and the government can put an end to a private prosecution by taking over the prosecution and offering no evidence, or by entering a *nolle prosequi* or a stay of proceedings.[193]

Private prosecutors in Canada cannot recover their costs in prosecuting indictable offences, even if they are successful, but they may,

---

184 Radzinowicz, L., *A History of English Criminal Law* (London 1957) Vol. 3, at pp. 166 *et seq.*

185 *Ibid.* at p. 167.

186 *Ibid.* Vol. 2, at p. 122.

187 *Ibid.* at p. 125.

188 Burns, "Private Prosecutions in Canada: The Law and a Proposal for Change," (1974) 21 McGill L.J. 269; Berner, *Private Prosecution and Environmental Control Legislation: A Study* (Faculty of Law, U.B.C. 1972); Kaufman, "The Role of the Private Prosecutor: A Critical Analysis of the Complainant's Position in Criminal Cases," (1961) 7 McGill L.J. 102.

189 Williams, "The Power to Prosecute," [1955] Crim. L. R. 596: "No country leaves more to the private prosecutor if he chooses to act."

190 (1974) 21 McGill L.J. 269 at p. 289.

191 See *e.g.* "*R. ex rel. Mackinnon v. Internat. Nickel Co. of Can. Ltd.*" (1974) Can. Env. Law News 75; Burns (1974) 21 McGill L.J. 269 at p. 290.

192 *E.g.* the Lord's Day Act, R.S.C. 1970, c. L-13, s. 16 (requires consent of the provincial Attorney General); the Labour Relations Act, R.S.O. 1980, c. 228, s. 101 (requires consent of the Board); the Securities Act, R.S.O. 1980, c. 466, s. 119 (requires consent of the Minister).

193 See ss. 508 and 732.1 of the Code. See generally, Friedland, M. L., *Double Jeopardy* (Oxford 1969) at pp. 30 *et seq.*

in the discretion of the court, collect limited costs in successful summary conviction proceedings.[194] These restrictions inhibit, of course, the use of this technique. A recent Ontario task force studying the legal aid system recommended that public funds should be used to support prosecutions by groups: "Many statutes establish public rights which can be enforced by criminal process. We see no reason why this mode of enforcement should be foreclosed to legally aided applicants. Indeed, such prosecutions are frequently the most expedient and economical mode of advancing public rights."[195]

(b) Defending Accused Persons

Groups often support defendants. Pro-abortion groups, for example, have helped raise money to assist Dr. Morgentaler at his various trials in Canada[196], and in England in the well-known case of *Regina v. Bourne*[197] the defence was undertaken by the London and Counties Medical Protection Society of which the doctor was a member.[198] This pattern of assistance with the defence costs can be found in many cases although it is rarely apparent from reading the law reports. Labour unions often assist workmen charged with offences in connection with strikes and picketing; some religious groups, such as Jehovah's Witnesses, defend members prosecuted for their religious beliefs[199]; automobile associations provide counsel to members charged with certain offences; and civil liberties associations sometimes defend accused persons because of the wider civil liberties issues involved in a case. In the United States, for example, the N.A.A.C.P. (National Association for the Advancement of Colored People) Legal Defense Fund and the American Civil Liberties Union (A.C.L.U.) planned the strategy for the attempt at the judicial elimination

---

194   Burns (1974) 21 McGill L.J. 269 at p. 286.

195   Report of The Task Force on Legal Aid, Part I, (1974) (Osler) p. 99.

196   *The Globe and Mail*, 3 Dec., 1976: $50,000 collected by "The Committee for the Legal Defence of Dr. Henry Morgentaler."

197   [1938] 3 All E.R. 615 (C.C.A.).

198   Durand, "Abortion: Medical Aspects of *R. v. Bourne*" (1938) 2 M.L.R. 236 at p. 238. Although such organizations act as insurers, they also attempt to further the interests of their members in other ways and so can be classified as pressure groups. Dr. Bourne wanted to use the case to test and clarify the law that an abortion in the circumstances of the case was proper, but the girl's father apparently wanted the matter to be kept secret. The police found out about the abortion when the girl was required to give evidence in another case: *ibid.* at p. 237. *Cf.* Hindell, K. and Simms, M., *Abortion Law Reformed* (London 1971) at p. 70. Dr. Bourne was a member of the Abortion Law Reform Association's Medico-Legal Council (*ibid.* at p. 69) but it is not clear what role it played in the defence.

199   See Stroup, H. H., *The Jehovah's Witnesses* (New York 1945) at p. 25; Penton, M. J., *Jehovah's Witnesses in Canada* (Toronto 1976) at p. 123.

of the death penalty,[200] following the N.A.A.C.P. Legal Defense and Educational Fund's decision to try to block all executions of murderers and rapists, whites and blacks.[201] As one of the participants in the movement stated[202]:

> The politics of abolition boiled down to this: For each year the United States went without executions, the more hollow would ring claims that the American people could not do without them; the longer death-row inmates waited and the greater their numbers, the more difficult it would be for the courts to permit the first execution.[203]

Not only have groups put up funds to pay for the defence, but they have also put up money so that the accused might be released on bail. This is acceptable in the United States where the courts have been concerned with money and little else, and has in the past been acceptable in Canada. In England, on the other hand, the fact that the sureties are backed by a group may be used as an argument against the granting of bail, since the English theory is that an accused's sureties are held financially responsible for his appearance in court so that they will carefully supervise his activities pending his trial. The inducement to do so would be less effective if a group were allowed to share the financial burden.[204]

(c) Amici Curiae

The *amicus curiae* (literally, "friend of the court") device has provided an important vehicle for pressure groups to attempt to influence the development of judge-made law in the United States[205] and is of growing importance in Canada. Pressure groups have not yet been recognized as *amici curiae* in England, although individuals have often appeared in that capacity to assist the court.[206] Historically, the *amicus curiae* was an

---

200 See Meltsner, "Litigating Against the Death Penalty: The Strategy Behind *Furman*," (1973) 82 Yale L.J. 1111.

201 *Ibid.* at p. 1112.

202 *Ibid.* at pp. 1112-1113.

203 The execution of Gary Gilmore was, however, not blocked by the Supreme Court: *Gilmore v. Utah* (1976), 97 S.Ct. 436.

204 See *Re Butler and others* (1881) 14 Cox. C.C. 530 (Ir. Q.B.) *per* May C.J. at p. 532: "We cannot shut our eyes to the fact that there is in the country a body called the Land League, having under its control very large funds, and acting in concert in order to obtain certain objects."

205 See generally, Angell, "The *Amicus Curiae*: American Development of English Institutions," (1967) 16 I.C.L.Q. 1017; Krislov, "The *Amicus Curiae* Brief: From Friendship to Advocacy," (1963) 72 Yale L.J. 694; *cf.* Hakman, "Lobbying the Supreme Court — An Appraisal of 'Political Science Folklore,' " (1966) 35 Fordham L. Rev. 15; and also Levy, "The Amicus Curiae," (1971) 5 *Law Society Gazette* 110; Weiler, "Two Models of Judicial Decision-Making," (1968) 46 Can. Bar Rev. 406 at pp. 445 *et seq.*

206 See *e.g.* the Attorney General's appearance in the House of Lords cases of *Chapman v. Chapman*, [1954] A.C. 429; *I.R.C. v. Baddeley* [1955] A.C. 572; and *Belfast Corp. v. O.D.*

individual who volunteered to assist the court. In a case in 1686, for example, the court stated, "as *amicus Curiae*, any one may move to quash" a defective indictment.[207]

Pressure groups started appearing as *amici curiae* in the Supreme Court of the United States just after the turn of the century, a time when pressure groups were being recognized as important institutions in the development of policy.[208] As Krislov states,[209] "the increased use of the *amicus* brief mirrors the change in tactics and structure of interest articulation in American politics as a whole that occurred during the latter quarter of the nineteenth century." The famous Brandeis Brief was first presented by Brandeis as *amicus curiae* in *Muller v. Oregon* in 1908.[210] At the time of the First World War groups such as the N.A.A.C.P. and groups advancing the interests of Chinese persons started appearing before the Supreme Court.[211] In the 1960s the Supreme Court of the United States relied heavily on *amicus curiae* briefs. The important extension of the due process clause of the Bill of Rights (to include the prior amendments formerly thought to be applicable only to the federal government) in *Mapp v. Ohio*[212] in 1961 was advanced only by the *amicus curiae*.[213] And in *Miranda v. Arizona*[214] in 1966 the background material on police interrogation practices was taken from the A.C.L.U. brief.[215]

The Supreme Court of Canada has since 1974 been allowing pressure groups to appear in both civil and criminal cases. In *Attorney General of*

Cars Ltd., [1960] A.C. 490, cited by Blom-Cooper, L.J. and Drewry, G. *Final Appeal* (Oxford 1972) at pp. 249-250. Appearances are occasionally also made in Canada by the Attorney General: *Bastien and Doyle*, [1969] 2 C.C.C. 280 (B.C. Co. Ct.); and can be made in Constitutional and Bill of Rights cases: Supreme Court Rule 17, as amended in 1976. The Official Solicitor in England also may appear to represent the public interest: *Rondel v. Worsley*, [1969] 1 A.C. 191 (H.L.); *Re Gale*, [1966] Ch. 236 (C.A.). Occasionally the court appoints a member of the bar not holding an official position to assist the court (*e.g. Williams v. Butlers Ltd.*, [1975] 1 W.L.R. 946 (D.C.)), a procedure which will become more common if moot appeals increase: see *e.g. Re A.G.'s Reference (No. 1 of 1974)*, [1974] 2 All E.R. 899 (C.A.).

207 *R. v. Vaux* (1686), Comb. 13; Krislov (1963) 72 Yale L.J. 694.

208 Bentley, A. F., *The Process of Government* (Cambridge, Mass. 1908).

209 72 Yale L.J. 694 at p. 704.

210 (1908) 208 U.S. 412. In fact, Brandeis also represented Oregon, one of the parties, but the well-known brief was filed by him on behalf of a pressure group, the National Consumers' League: Krislov (1963) 72 Yale L.J. 694 at 708; Vose, "The National Consumers' League and the Brandeis Brief," (1957) 1 Midwest J. of Pol. Science 267.

211 Angell (1967) 16 I.C.L.Q. 1017 at p. 1018; Krislov (1963) 72 Yale L.J. 694 at p. 707.

212 (1961) 367 U.S. 643.

213 Angell (1967) 16 I.C.L.Q. 1017 at pp. 1035 *et seq.*

214 (1966) 384 U.S. 436.

215 Angell (1967) 16 I.C.L.Q. 1017 at p. 1044.

Canada v. Lavell[216] a civil action involving alleged discrimination against Indian women contrary to the Canadian Bill of Rights, the Supreme Court of Canada permitted appearances as *amici curiae* by Indian groups such as the National Indian Brotherhood and women's groups such as the University Women's Club of Toronto.[217] Then in the *Morgentaler* abortion prosecution[218] the Supreme Court allowed appearances as *amici curiae* by several groups: the Canadian Civil Liberties Association and the Foundation of Women in Crisis argued in favour of the defence, and the Alliance for Life and three Quebec-based groups against it.[219] The appearance of the pro-abortion groups was objected to by the Attorney-General of Quebec but was permitted by Chief Justice Laskin[220]; the anti-abortion groups came in later. Subsequently, *amici curiae* have appeared in the death penalty[221] and the movie censorship cases,[222] in both of which the Canadian Civil Liberties Association has been involved. Chief Justice Laskin has stated extra-judicially[223] that interventions would be allowed "where it appeared to the Court that it would be helpful to have as wide a canvass as possible of the public law issues raised by the immediate parties but limiting the intervenors to those issues and not inviting them otherwise to speak to the merits." Lower courts have not yet shown much inclination to follow the example offered by the Supreme Court of Canada, except as we shall see below in reference cases.[224]

Prior to 1974 there had been only one instance of intervention by an

---

216 (1973) 38 D.L.R. (3d) 481 (S.C.C.).

217 *Amicus curiae* had appeared in at least one earlier reported civil case: in *Re Wren supra* note 165 where counsel for the Canadian Jewish Congress argued against a discriminatory restrictive covenant.

218 *Supra* note 167.

219 See Dickens, "A Canadian Development: Non-Party Intervention," (1977) 40 M.L.R. 666; and (1976) 14 Osgoode Hall L.J. 229.

220 *The Globe and Mail*, 4 Sept. 1974.

221 *Miller and Cockriell, supra* note 168.

222 *N.S. Bd. of Censors v. McNeil* (1975), 55 D.L.R. (3d) 632 (S.C.C.).

223 (1975) 9 *Law Society Gazette* 92 at p. 98.

224 See, however, *Re A.G. Alta. and Gares* (1976), 67 D.L.R. (3d) 635 (Alta. S.C.) in which the Alberta Human Rights Commission was given leave to appear as an *amicus curiae*. In *Re Can. Arctic Gas Pipeline Ltd.* (1975), 65 D.L.R. (3d) 660 the Federal Court of Appeal permitted a number of groups to appear, but they had appeared before the National Energy Board which was the subject of the court proceeding. The Ontario Criminal Lawyers' Association unsuccessfully (see the *Toronto Daily Star*, 2 Sept. 1977) sought leave to intervene before the Federal Court of Appeal in *Solosky v. R.*, [1978] 1 F.C. 609 (C.A.) on the issue of whether penitentiary officials may continue to open mail from lawyers to clients who are prisoners. [The Canadian Jewish Congress was given standing to appear as an *amicus curiae* in the Ontario Court of Appeal in the *Rauca* extradition case (later reported (1983) 41 O.R. (2d) 225): see the Globe and Mail, Jan. 19, 1983.]

amicus in a criminal case; *Robertson and Rosetanni v. the Queen*[225] in 1963 in which the Lord's Day Alliance, which had not brought the prosecution, appeared as an intervenor in a prosecution for operating a bowling alley on a Sunday. The Alliance feared[226] that the provincial Attorney-General was not vigorously seeking to uphold the legislation and the Supreme Court gave leave to intervene. Although the Alliance had been involved in court cases seeking to uphold Sunday Observance legislation for over 75 years, this had been because they were constitutional references[227] in which *amici curiae* have normally been permitted.

The original 1891 federal legislation setting up the reference machinery,[228] which is still in force,[229] states:

> The court shall have power to direct that any person interested, or, where there is a class of persons interested, any one or more persons as representatives of such class, shall be notified of the hearing upon any reference under this section, and such persons shall be entitled to be heard thereon.

It has been estimated that perhaps one-third of all important Canadian constitutional cases have arisen as references[230] and pressure groups have appeared in a large number of these. For example, the Distillers and Brewers' Association appeared in the early liquor references,[231] the Co-Operative Committee on Japanese Canadians in the 1946 Japanese Canadian reference,[232] the Dominion Mortgage and Investments Association in the Saskatchewan Farm Security Act reference,[233] the Canadian Association of Consumers and the Canadian Federation of Agriculture — on opposite sides — in the Margarine reference,[234] the Ontario Branch of the Canadian Bar Association on the Planning Act

---

225 (1963), 41 D.L.R. (2d) 485 (S.C.C.).

226 Conversation with I. G. Scott, Q.C., counsel for the Alliance.

227 See *A.G. Ont. v. Hamilton Street Ry. Co.*, [1903] A.C. 524 (P.C.); *Re Legislation Respecting Abstention from Labour on Sunday* (1905), 35 S.C.R. 581; *Lord's Day Alliance of Can. v. A.G. Man.*, [1925] A.C. 384 (P.C.); *Lord's Day Alliance of Can. v. A.G. B.C.*, [1959] S.C.R. 497. The Alliance did not intervene in *Ouimet v. Bazin* (1912), 46 S.C.R. 502 because they must have felt that the Attorney General of Quebec would argue strongly in favour of the legislation.

228 S.C. 1891, c. 25, s. 4.

229 The Supreme Court Act, R.S.C. 1970, c. S-19, s. 55(4).

230 Grant, "Judicial Review in Canada: Procedural Aspects," (1964) 42 Can. Bar Rev. 195 at p. 214.

231 *Re Prohibitory Liquor Laws* (1895), 24 S.C.R. 170, reversed [1896] A.C. 348 (*sub nom. A.G. Ont. v. A.G. Dom.*)

232 *Reference as to the Validity of Orders in Council in relation to Persons of the Japanese Race*, [1946] S.C.R. 248, affirmed [1947] A.C. 87 (P.C.).

233 *Reference re Section 6 of the Farm Security Act, 1944, of Sask.*, [1947] S.C.R. 394, affirmed [1949] A.C. 110 (P.C.).

234 *Re Section 5(a) of the Dairy Industry Act*, [1949] S.C.R. 1.

reference,[235] while, on the recent Anti-Inflation Legislation reference,[236] *amicus curiae* appearances were made by such groups as the Canadian Labour Congress, the Ontario Teachers' Federation and the United Steel Workers of America.

Amici curiae are not mentioned in the Supreme Court Act or the Supreme Court rules. The procedure is simply to file a notice of motion to be added as an *amicus*. The decision is made by the Chief Justice or the judge assigned by him for the purpose. The only authority for an appearance is under Supreme Court Rule 60 which provides: "Any person interested in an appeal between other parties may, by leave of the Court or a Judge, intervene therein upon such terms and conditions and with such rights and privileges as the Court or Judge may determine." But this Rule has in the past been held to require "an interest in the subject-matter of the litigation."[237] It is not clear whether *amici curiae* are coming in under this rule or under the inherent jurisdiction of the Court.

The Supreme Court of Canada has not as yet found it necessary to develop detailed rules governing *amici*. The United States Supreme Court has been forced to do so because of the numbers of applications: unless the parties consent, leave to file a brief is required. The Court limits the length of the application for leave to five pages, and even if it does grant leave the *amicus curiae* cannot participate in the oral argument unless one of the parties is willing to give up some of its own time.[238]

The new approach by the Supreme Court of Canada in allowing *amici curiae* to appear in non-reference cases no doubt reflects Chief Justice Laskin's view of the proper role of the Supreme Court. As Krislov has stated[239] "the Court's attitude, practices, and rules regarding the granting of permission to file *amicus* briefs may indicate the extent to which it desires to engage in quasi-legislative activities and to depart from a role of narrowly resolving adversary disputes."

(d) Civil Proceedings

The criminal law develops through civil proceedings as well as through criminal prosecutions. The laws of arrest and of search, for example, are more frequently tested through civil than criminal proceedings. As in criminal proceedings, it is often difficult to tell from a law report that a pressure group was, in fact, behind a plaintiff or defendant or an ap-

---

235 *Reference re Certain Titles to Land in Ontario* (1973), 35 D.L.R. (3d) 10 (Ont. C.A.).

236 *Re Anti-Inflation Act*, [1976] 2 S.C.R. 373.

237 *Norcan Ltd. v. Lebrock* (1969), 5 D.L.R. (3d) 1 (S.C.C.).

238 U.S. Supreme Court Rule 42 and 44.

239 (1963) 72 Yale L.J. 694, 717.

plicant for a prerogative writ. The fact that the *Gouriet* case[240] was sponsored by a pressure group appears to have been regarded as irrelevant in the House of Lords. Lord Wilberforce[241] stated that Mr. Gouriet "though supported by an association, appears simply as a citizen." Lord Edmund-Davies[242] mentioned the group by simply stating that Mr. Gouriet "is the secretary of an organization calling itself The National Association for Freedom."

In Canada, to pick a specific although unique example, many of the most important civil rights issues have been developed through court proceedings by one group, the Jehovah's Witnesses,[243] who used court actions because of the hostility shown by government officials, particularly in Quebec during the long tenure of office of Premier Maurice Duplessis.

Jehovah's Witnesses successfully challenged steps taken by Quebec authorities to prevent the dissemination of pamphlets,[244] the holding of meetings,[245] and their sending their children to Protestant schools.[246] Actions had earlier been brought in Alberta and Ontario to challenge school boards requiring that Jehovah's Witnesses salute the flag.[247] (The

---

240 *Gouriet v. Union of Postal Workers*, [1978] A.C. 435 (H.L.), reversing [1977] 1 All E.R. 696 (C.A.).

241 *Ibid.* at p. 76.

242 *Ibid.* at p. 101. Lord Denning in the Court of Appeal had mentioned but also had dismissed the relevance of the Association, stating (at p. 711) "there is an association called the National Association for Freedom of which we know nothing except that it has a secretary, Mr. John Prendergast Gouriet. It is said by its critics to be a right wing pressure group. But that is no concern of ours." For a description of the Association, see the *New Statesman*, 15 July, 1977.

243 See McWhinney, "The Bill of Rights, The Supreme Court, and Civil Liberties in Canada," in *The Canadian Annual Review for 1960* (1961) at pp. 261, 271. See generally, Penton, M. J., *Jehovah's Witnesses in Canada* (Toronto 1976).

244 *Saumur v. City of Quebec*, [1953] 2 S.C.R. 299 (testing the validity of a Quebec City By-Law); later nullified by the Quebec Freedom of Worship Act: see Penton, M. J., *Jehovah's Witnesses in Canada* (Toronto 1976) at p. 213. Saumur was not the original plaintiff; he was accepted by agreement on the appeal to the Supreme Court of Canada because the original plaintiff Daviau "became disheartened and refused to proceed with the case": Penton, at p. 211. See also *Lamb v. Benoit*, [1959] S.C.R. 321, an action for false imprisonment and malicious prosecution.

245 *Chaput v. Romain*, [1955] S.C.R. 834, a civil action for damages for breaking up a meeting. Moreover, in the well-known *Roncarelli v. Duplessis* case, [1959] S.C.R. 122, Roncarelli, a Jehovah's Witness who had had his liquor licence cancelled for putting up bail money for other Witnesses, won substantial damages against Premier Duplessis: see Penton, M. J., *Jehovah's Witnesses in Canada* (Toronto 1976) at pp. 220-221.

246 *Perron v. School Trustees of the Municipality of Rouyn* (1955), 1 D.L.R. (2d) 414 (Que. C.A.); see also *Chabot v. School Commrs. of Lamorandière* (1957), 12 D.L.R. (2d) 796 (Que. C.A.); Penton, M. J., *Jehovah's Witnesses in Canada* (Toronto 1976) at pp. 216 *et seq.*

247 *Ruman v. Lethbridge School Bd. Trustees*, [1943] 3 W.W.R. 340 (Alta. S.C.); *Donald v. Hamilton Bd. of Education*, [1945] O.R. 518 (C.A.).

flag salute controversy had been an important constitutional issue in the United States where the Supreme Court had ruled in 1943[248] in favour of the Jehovah's Witnesses, reversing an earlier 1940 case.[249]) Court actions were also brought, although unsuccessfully, on the blood transfusion issue.[250] Nor did the Jehovah's Witnesses in Canada succeed in their argument that certain members had the status of clergy and as such were exempt from military service during the War.[251] They were more successful in ensuring proper treatment for those interned.[252] Conscientious objectors were held in camps even after the Second World War, but this was ended shortly after their lawyer, Glen How,[253] threatened to institute "an extensive test case to probe the authority of the Crown under the Emergency Powers Act."[254]

One potential stumbling block in the path of a group wishing to support a party to litigation is the law of maintenance and champerty. Whereas the policy of the law has been to encourage persons or groups other than the victim to bring *criminal* proceedings against wrongdoers, the courts on the civil side have in the past discouraged outsiders from "intermeddling" in another person's lawsuit. Agreeing to assist a plaintiff or defendant with his costs had, in earlier periods, been considered improper maintenance.[255] Today, however, with the exception in some jurisdictions of the champertous device of contingent fees, maintenance can no longer be considered a serious obstacle to the bringing or defending of actions by pressure groups. Not only has the offence of

---

248 *West Virginia State Bd. of Education v. Barnette* (1943), 319 U.S. 624.

249 *Minersville School District v. Gobitis* (1940), 310 U.S. 586. See generally, Manwaring, D.R., *Render unto Caesar: The Flag-Salute Controversy* (Chicago 1962).

250 See *Wolfe v. Robinson*, [1962] O.R. 132 (C.A.) (application to quash a coroner's verdict); *Forsyth v. Children's Aid Society of Kingston*, [1963] 1 O.R. 49 (H.C.). Actions were also unsuccessful in the U.S. "So by the late 1960s, Jehovah's Witnesses no longer took the initiative in pressing transfusion cases in North American courts,": Penton, at pp. 243-244.

251 For the Second World War, see Penton, *Jehovah's Witnesses in Canada* (Toronto 1976) at pp. 174 *et seq.*; for the First World War, *ibid.* at pp. 56-57 and Appendix B setting out Duff J.'s unreported judgment in *Re Cooke*, 1918.

252 Penton, M. J., *Jehovah's Witnesses in Canada* (Toronto 1976) at pp. 177 *et seq.*

253 Glen How did not restrict his activities to court proceedings: for example, he lobbied by means of influential articles in legal journals (see *e.g.* "The Case for a Canadian Bill of Rights," (1948) 26 Can. Bar Rev. 759; "Religion, Medicine and Law," (1960) 3 Can. B.J. 365) and by appearances before Legislative Committees. In 1971 he appeared before the Manitoba Legislature, sitting as a Committee of the Whole, on the blood transfusion issue: see Penton, M. J., *Jehovah's Witnesses in Canada* (Toronto 1976) at p. 252.

254 Penton, *supra* note 154 at p. 181.

255 *Hill v. Archbold*, [1968] 1 Q.B. 686 at pp. 693-694, *per* Lord Denning M.R. (C.A.). See generally Fleming, J. G., *Law of Torts* (5th ed.) (Sydney 1977) at pp. 611 *et seq.*; Winfield, P. H., *History of Conspiracy and Abuse of Legal Procedure* (Cambridge 1921).

maintenance been abolished in a number of jurisdictions,[256] but in those cases where it is applicable the courts are reluctant to hold that the conduct amounts to maintenance.[257]

Certain groups have attempted to use the "class action" (whereby one party represents others with a similar claim) to obtain redress from and to influence actions by government and industry. An individual's single, small claim[258] will not pose a serious threat to a powerful defendant. Groups therefore look to the "class action" as an important weapon in achieving their objectives. Class actions, though usually employed in civil matters,[259] have been used in, for example, litigation involving the death penalty[260] and pre-trial practices.[261]

For the most part pressure groups back litigants who are directly involved in a controversy and who clearly have "standing" before the courts. It is easier, though, for pressure groups to use the judicial system if they can proceed in their own name or by using a nominal party who does not necessarily have a special pecuniary or other interest in the outcome. The more liberal the law of "standing," the more groups — or individuals acting alone — will be able to employ the judicial system in attempting to

---

256 See the English Law Commission Report, Proposals for Reform of the Law Relating to Maintenance and Champerty (1966) recommending the abolition of the offence of maintenance as well as liability in tort for maintenance, which was enacted by the Criminal Law Act 1967, c. 58, ss. 13 and 14. However, contracts for maintenance may still be rendered illegal: s. 14(2). In Canada the offence of maintenance was eliminated when common-law offences were abolished in the 1955 Revision of the Criminal Code. But maintenance and champerty are still torts and illegal contracts — in at least some provinces: see C.E.D. (Ontario, 3rd ed.) vol. 2, c. VIII, Maintenance and Champerty. And see the Champerty Act, R.S.O. 1897, c. 327.

257 *Hill v. Archbold, supra* note 255; and *Martell v. Consett Iron Co.*, [1955] 1 Ch. 363 (C.A.).

258 American courts allow plaintiffs to use the class action when damages are being claimed. English and Canadian courts have not when there are separate contracts: see, *e.g. Markt and Co. v. Knight Steamship Co.*, [1910] 2 K.B. 1021 (C.A.); Williams, N. J. and Whybrow, J., *A Proposal for Class Actions under Competition Policy Legislation* (Ottawa 1976) at p. 35. See now, to the same effect, *Naken et al. v. Gen. Motors of Can. Ltd. et al.* (1983), 144 D.L.R. (3d) 385 (S.C.C.).

259 This is not the place for a discussion of the many complex issues involved in the class action: for thorough discussions see, *e.g.* the lengthy note, "Class Actions," (1976) 89 Harv. L. Rev. 1318; Williams and Whybrow, *A Proposal for Class Actions under Competition Policy Legislation* (1976); Prichard and Trebilcock, "Class Actions and Private Enforcement," a paper presented at the Canadian Association of Law Teachers' Annual Meeting, Fredericton, June 1977 (1978) 27 U.N.B.L.J. 5.

260 Meltsner (1973) 82 Yale L.J. 1111 at pp. 1126 *et seq.*

261 *Gerstein v. Pugh* (1975), 95 S.Ct. 854.

achieve their objectives.[262] The doctrine of "standing" has, therefore, been the subject of controversy in most jurisdictions.[263]

There has recently been a narrowing of the doctrine in the United States,[264] and a broadening of it in Canada. The Supreme Court of Canada held in the *Thorson* case (1974)[265] that a taxpayer had sufficient standing to challenge the constitutionality of the Federal government's legislation on bilingualism and in the *McNeil* case (1975)[266] that a member of the public deprived of the opportunity to see a movie (*Last Tango in Paris*) had the standing to challenge the provincial government's cinema licensing authority. It would be a mistake, however, to read too much into these cases. As Chief Justice Laskin stated extra-judicially,[267] the *Thorson* case "does not give *carte blanche* for indiscriminate taxpayer standing, but it does invite resort to judicial discretion whereas formerly there was a closed door."[268] In both *Thorson* and *McNeil* the Supreme Court was concerned that a denial of standing would result in the constitutionality of the legislation being "immunized from judicial review."[269] Subsequent cases in Canada[270] and England[271] have confined *Thorson* to constitutional matters.

[The Supreme Court, however, in the *Borowski*[272] case extended *Thorson* and *McNeil* to a citizen's challenge to the abortion legislation as a violation of the Bill of Rights. Martland J. for 7 members of the Court stated that if there is a serious issue of invalidity, "a person need only to show that he is affected by it directly or that he has a genuine interest as a citizen in the validity of the legislation and that there is no other reason-

---

262 See generally, Chayes (1976) 89 Harv. L. Rev. 1281; Orren, "Standing to Sue: Interest Group Conflict in the Federal Courts," (1976) 70 Am. Pol. Science Rev. 723.

263 See Cappelletti, "Vindicating the Public Interest through the Courts: A Comparativist's Contribution," (1976) 25 Buff. L. Rev. 643.

264 *E.g. Warth v. Seldin* (1975), 95 S.Ct. 2197; *Simon v. Eastern Kentucky Welfare Rights Organization* (1976), 96 S.Ct. 1917.

265 *Thorson v. A.G. Can. et al.* (1974) 43 D.L.R. (3d) 1 (S.C.C.). See generally, Johnson, "*Locus Standi* in Constitutional Cases after *Thorson*," [1975] Public Law 137.

266 *N.S. Bd. of Censors v. McNeil supra* note 222.

267 (1975) 9 *Law Society Gazette* 92 at p. 98.

268 *Smith v. A.G. Ont.*, [1924] 3 D.L.R. 189 (S.C.C.) *per* Duff J. at 193-194: "An individual, for example, has no status to maintain an action restraining a wrongful violation of a public right unless he is exceptionally prejudiced by the wrongful act"; *Saumur v. A.G. Que.* (1964), 45 D.L.R. (2d) 627 (S.C.C.).

269 *Per* Laskin J. in *Thorson v. A.G. Can.* (1974), 43 D.L.R. (3d) 1 at 7.

270 *Rosenberg v. Grand River Conservation Authority* (1975), 12 O.R. (2d) 496 (C.A.): Rosenberg was supported by the Canadian Environmental Law Association.

271 *Gouriet v. Union of Postal Workers, supra* note 240.

272 *Min. of Justice, Can. v. Borowski* (1981), 130 D.L.R. (3d) 588 (S.C.C.), Laskin C.J.C. and Lamer J. dissenting. See also *Re Royal Commn. on Nor. Environment and Grand Council of the Treaty 9 Bands* (1983), 144 D.L.R. (3d) 416 (Ont. Div. Ct.).

able and effective manner in which the issue may be brought before the Court."]

Not only do courts require that those bringing actions have "standing," they also want them to continue, through all stages of the litigation, to have a special interest in the outcome. Courts do not usually want to deal with "moot" issues.[273] However, courts have tended to be sympathetic, in cases where there is a public interest in the issue, to applicants who wish to obtain a ruling on a matter which was originally a real controversy, but later became moot.[274] This is particularly so for issues concerning such matters as abortion,[275] pre-trial detention[276] and solitary confinement,[277] which, because of the nature of the subject-matter, will normally become moot before a final appeal can be heard. The test used by the United States Supreme Court in these cases is that the action can continue even if the action becomes moot if the harm is "capable of repetition, yet evading review."[278]

Amici curiae, the class action, the doctrines of standing and mootness, and the question of costs[279] will continue to generate discussion, debate and litigation because they are all important tools used by pressure groups in achieving their objectives through the judicial system. Canadian courts

---

273 *E.g. Coca-Cola Co. v. Mathews*, [1944] S.C.R. 385; *Sun Life Assur. Co. of Can. v. Jervis*, [1944] A.C. 111 (H.L.); *Preiser v. Newkirk* (1975), 95 S.Ct. 2330.

274 *E.g. Switzman v. Elbling and A.G. Que.* (1957), 7 D.L.R. (2d) 337 (S.C.C.) (court dealt with the validity of the Quebec Communistic Propaganda Act, even though the lease which was the subject of the proceedings had expired); *Vic Restaurant Inc. v. Montreal*, [1959] S.C.R. 58; *Internat. Brotherhood of Elec. Wkrs.; Local Union 2085 v. Winnipeg Builders' Exchange*, [1967] S.C.R. 628; *Minister of Manpower and Immigration v. Hardayal* (1977), 75 D.L.R. (3d) 465 (S.C.C.). See also Zamir, I. *Declaratory Judgment* (London 1962); de Smith, S. A., *Judicial Review of Administrative Action* (2nd ed.) (London 1968) at pp. 524-525; Note, "The Mootness Doctrine in the Supreme Court," (1974), 88 Harv. L. Rev. 373. [See also *Re A.G. Que. and A.G. Can.* (1982), 140 D.L.R. (3d) 385 (S.C.C.).]

275 *Roe v. Wade* (1973), 410 U.S. 113.

276 *Gerstein v. Pugh* (1975) 95 S.Ct. 854.

277 *McCann v. R.* (1975), 68 D.L.R. (3d) 661 (Fed. Ct.); compare *Preiser v. Newkirk* (1975) 95 S.Ct. 2330.

278 *Roe v. Wade supra* note 275 at p. 125.

279 As is well known, American courts do not award costs to the successful plaintiff. Many courts in the U.S. had been changing this rule to allow plaintiffs to recover costs in these cases brought on behalf of the public in order to encourage these actions. However, in 1975 the U.S. Supreme Court held that any change from the usual rule was up to the Legislature: *Alyeska Pipeline Service Co. v. Wilderness Society* (1975), 95 S.Ct. 1612; see also *Runyon v. McCrary* (1976), 96 S.Ct. 2586. Recent recommendations by an Ontario Task Force on Legal Aid suggest that plaintiffs who bring these types of "public actions" not be saddled with costs if they lose. Moreover, the Task Force recommends that the Act and regulations be changed to enable government funds to be given to support plaintiffs who bring such actions: Report of the Task Force on Legal Aid (1974) (Osler Report), c. 11.

will no doubt be cautious in encouraging new litigation and the expansion of existing litigation by those without a personal stake in the lawsuit. Nevertheless, one can expect an increase in pressure group activity before the courts, particularly where the courts have a quasi-legislative role, such as in constitutional and Bill of Rights cases.

6. CONCLUSION

Groups will continue to play an important role in the development of the law. The process of consultation with interested parties is becoming increasingly institutionalized. Governments have an interest in meeting with groups not only because groups often have considerable expertise in pointing out drawbacks and problems with legislative proposals, but also because governments can use the groups to help disseminate information on government policy.[280] Pressure groups, therefore, provide a two-way flow of information. Moreover, if a pressure group feels that it has contributed to the development of a proposal, there is a better chance that its members will try to make it work after it has become law, while if it is developed without adequate consultation, this is often used as a basis for attacking it, as indeed happened with the first version of the Canadian gun control legislation, Bill C-83.[281]

There has been a noticeable trend in recent years to more open consultation with pressure groups. Changing governmental structures both reflect the desire for and encourage this public consultation.[282]

Four such changes in the structure of government in Canada can be identified: an increase in the number and the activities of regulatory agencies; the widespread use of independent ad hoc committees and Royal Commissions to assist in the formulation of policy; the establishment of permanent Law Reform Commissions; and the use of Parliamentary Committees to work on the details of legislation. All of them bring pressure groups out into the open.

---

280 Pross, "Pressure Groups: Adaptive Instruments of Political Communication" in *Pressure Group Behaviour in Canadian Politics* (ed. A. P. Pross) (Toronto 1975) at p. 6. *E.g.* in England, trade associations were encouraged during the First World War because they were useful in administering wartime controls: see Richardson, J. J., *The Policy-making Process* (London 1969) at p. 7. In Canada, the Anti-Inflation Board has worked closely with groups in administering the anti-inflation legislation.

281 *E.g.*, the Canadian Wildlife Federation: see *Justice and Legal Affairs* (No. 40) 27 April, 1976, at p. 9; and the Canadian Police Association: see *Justice and Legal Affairs* (No. 43) 4 May, 1976 at p. 31.

282 One change in the structure of government that negatively affects consultation with pressure groups is the use of federal-provincial executive meetings to settle broad policy matters: see Aucoin, "Pressure Groups and Recent Changes in the Policy-Making Process," in *Pressure Group Behaviour in Canadian Politics* (ed. A. P. Pross) (Toronto 1975) at pp. 174, 187.

Many, although unfortunately not most, regulatory agencies now invite public participation before finalizing a policy. So, for example, at the federal level the Canadian Radio-Television Commission (C.R.T.C.) considers public hearings "a vital part of its function as a broadcast regulating agency"[283] and at the provincial level the Ontario Securities Commission invites public participation on such issues as commission rates for members of the Toronto Stock Exchange.[284]

Virtually all Royal Commissions and most committees with membership outside the civil service now consult with the public. At a minimum, written submissions are requested. Many go further and hold public hearings. Interim reports are sometimes issued. This was done by the Federal Commission of Inquiry into the Non-Medical Use of Drugs (LeDain)[285] and the Ontario Royal Commission on violence in the communications industry (LaMarsh),[286] thus giving groups a further opportunity to comment on proposals before they are finalized.[287]

There have been a very large number of committees and commissions set up by all levels of government in Canada over the past 10 or 15 years. There have, for example, recently been three inquiries into police disciplinary procedures: the Maloney Report, commissioned by the Municipality of Metropolitan Toronto[288], the Morand Report, set up by the Province of Ontario[289]; and the Marin Report, established by the Federal Solicitor-General's Department.[290] All asked for public participation; the latter two held extensive hearings.

Law reform commissions have made widespread use of the process of consultation. After consultation with interested groups, the English Law Commission prepares and circulates for comment a working paper with tentative conclusions before preparing its final report.[291] This gives

---

283 Canadian Radio-Television Commission, *Annual Report, 1975-76*, at p. 25.

284 Bulletin of Ontario Securities Commission, May 1976, at p. 120.

285 Interim Report of the Commission of Inquiry into the Non-Medical Use of Drugs (1970) (Le Dain).

286 The Royal Commission on Violence in the Communications Industry, Interim Report (1976) (LaMarsh).

287 The Mackenzie Valley Pipeline Inquiry took the unusual step of releasing a staff report for comment just prior to the formulation of the final report.

288 The Metropolitan Toronto Review of Citizen-Police Complaint Procedure: Report to the Metropolitan Toronto Board of Commissioners of Police (1975) (Maloney).

289 Royal Commission into Metropolitan Toronto Police Practices (1976) (Morand).

290 The Report of the Commission of Inquiry Relating to Public Complaints, Internal Discipline and Grievance Procedure within the Royal Canadian Mounted Police (1976) (Marin).

291 See Scarman, L., *Law Reform: The New Pattern* (London 1968); Gower, "Reflections on Law Reform," (1973) 23 U.T.L.J. 257; Farrar, J. H., *Law Reform and the Law Commission* (London 1974).

interested parties at least two opportunities to influence the Commission's report. The Canadian Law Reform Commission also usually prepares working papers, as well as seeking comments on its Programme of Work.[292] Ontario, on the other hand, rarely uses the working paper technique, although it often publishes study papers. The process of consultation varies therefore from commission to commission and, in many cases, from report to report; but the basic fact of widespread consultation has been clearly established for all commissions.

One can contrast this technique with that employed by the English Criminal Law Revision Committee in its Eleventh Report on Evidence. Although there was some consultation at the beginning there was very little during the inquiry. Subsequent attacks on the Report have effectively scuttled it. Had the Committee followed the practice of consultation used by the English Law Commission it might have had more success in having its conclusions turned into legislation. Members of various pressure groups were, in fact, members of the Committee, but this is rarely a substitute for consultation. Indeed, it may make a report less credible because of the compromises that are made in committee.

Parliament itself has been developing techniques to force pressure groups into the open. In Canada most legislation is referred to a Parliamentary Committee after second reading for clause-by-clause study and the hearing of witnesses. We have already looked at the extensive hearings held on the gun control issue by the Justice and Legal Affairs Committee. Sometimes even reports and Government White Papers are sent to Committee for hearing prior to the introduction of legislation.[293] The increasing willingness of the Government to permit committees to amend legislation[294] means that the committee system will not be ignored by pressure groups.

Government has, in fact, done more than give pressure groups an opportunity to be heard. It has in many cases encouraged their growth and development by formally incorporating them into policy-making and by financial and tax support.

Increasingly, federal legislation specifically mentions the involvement of pressure groups in a consultative or advisory capacity, a form of

---

292 Barnes, "The Law Reform Commission of Canada," (1975) 2 Dal. L.J. 62; Friedland, "The Work of the Law Reform Commission of Canada," (1972) 6 *Law Society Gazette* 58.

293 *E.g.,* the Senate Banking and Commerce Committee and the Commons Finance, Trade and Economic Affairs Committee each held separate hearings on the White Paper on Tax Reform (1969-70).

294 See Dawson in *Pressure Group Behaviour in Canadian Politics* (ed. A. P. Pross) (Toronto 1975) at p. 39; Aucoin, in *ibid.* at pp. 187, 188.

recognition which the groups, of course, prize.[295] A cursory examination of the 1970 Revised Statutes of Canada turned up over 30 such cases.[296] This is a relatively new phenomenon. A comparison with earlier sets of Revised Statutes shows that only about one-third of these found in the 1970 Revision were in the 1952 Revision, and less than one-tenth were in the 1927 Revision. No doubt a similar trend could be seen in provincial legislation.

In some cases the group has the right to nominate a person to a government board or advisory body[297], in others it is involved in a consultative role in selecting members of a board or advisory body[298]; more frequently the legislation simply provides that the government board or advisory body should be composed of representatives of various groups.[299] There are also examples where the legislation provides that the Minister or government body may consult with pressure groups.[300]

The Federal Government also planned, as we have seen, to establish an

---

295 Kwavnick, "Pressure Group Demands and the Struggle for Organisational Status: The Case of Organized Labour in Canada," (1970) 3 C.J.P.S. 56.

296 In addition, in the labour field there are conciliation and arbitration tribunals which have representatives of labour and management: see e.g. the Canada Labour Code, R.S.C. 1970, c. L-1, s. 134; the Public Service Staff Relations Act, R.S.C. 1970, c. P-35, s. 60. And, of course, there are many provincial Acts regulating and thereby formally recognizing an activity or a professional body: see, e.g. the Architects Act, R.S.O. 1980, c. 26; the Chiropody Act, R.S.O. 1980, c. 72; the Real Estate and Business Brokers Act, R.S.O. 1980, c. 431.

297 E.g., the Royal Canadian Legion: see s. 4(1) of the Army Benevolent Fund Act, R.S.C. 1970, c. A-16; see also Veterans' Land Act, R.S.C. 1970, c. V-4, s. 21(1).

298 Eg. the Canada Manpower and Immigration Council Act, R.S.C. 1970, c. C-4, ss. 4(2) and 13(2); the Economic Council of Canada Act, R.S.C. 1970, c. E-1, s. 4(2): "shall be appointed after consultation with appropriate representative organizations"; see also the Unemployment Insurance Act, 1971, S.C. 1970-71, c. 48, s. 5(2).

299 See, e.g. the Agricultural Stabilization Act, R.S.C. 1970, c. A-9, s. 5(1), providing for an Advisory Committee consisting, in part, of "representatives of farm organisations"; the Canada Film Development Corporation Act, R.S.C. 1970, c. C-8, s. 14: "an Advisory Group broadly representative of the professional associations, exhibitors, distributors and unions in the Canadian film industry"; the Canadian Wheat Board Act, R.S.C. 1970, c. C-12, s. 10(1): "an Advisory Committee . . . of whom six shall represent wheat producers." See also the Farm Credit Act, R.S.C. 1970, c. F-2, s. 9(1); the Fish Marketing, Freshwater Act, R.S.C. 1970, c. F-13, s. 18(1); the Canada Labour Code, R.S.C. 1970, c. L-1, ss. 85 and 160(1) [re-en. 1972, c. 18, s. 1]; the Public Service Staff Relations Act, R.S.C. 1970, c. P-35, s. 11(1) [re-en. 1974-75, c. 67, s. 2]; the Saltfish Act, R.S.C. 1970, c. 37 (1st Supp.), s. 18(1).

300 See e.g. the Forestry Development and Research Act, R.S.C. 1970, c. F-30, s. 3(4); the Department of Industry, Trade and Commerce Act, R.S.C. 1970, c. 1-11, s. 6(c); the Law Reform Commission Act, R.S.C. 1970; c. 23 (1st Supp.), s. 15; the National Transportation Act, R.S.C. 1970, c. N-17, s. 22(4); the Resources and Technical Surveys Act, R.S.C. 1970, c. R-7, s. 7(3).

Advisory Council to help monitor the new gun control legislation,[301] though this Council, unlike the others that have been mentioned, was not provided for in Bill C-51.

The Canadian Criminal Code incorporates references to non-governmental bodies which are involved in regulating some of the activities covered by the Criminal Code. The Code exempts conduct controlled by these bodies from the prohibition otherwise applicable. One sees this with racing associations in connection with horse racing,[302] charitable or religious organizations with lotteries,[303] agricultural fairs and exhibitions with games of chance,[304] accredited or approved hospitals with abortions,[305] and shooting clubs with gun control.[306] But these bodies are not built into the policy-making structure.

Pressure groups are also recipients of government money. Many groups have received federal government funding through special programmes such as Opportunities for Youth (O.F.Y.) and Local Initiatives Programmes (L.I.P.). The public accounts of Canada for 1974-75[307] show a large number of groups receiving grants from the federal government. Although it is doubtful whether many of the grants are specifically designed to assist the groups in their lobbying activities, it necessarily has this effect by assisting them in maintaining organizational frameworks. The 1975 Public Accounts include the following grants to organizations that engaged in lobbying activities on the gun control issue: Environment Canada appropriated $10,000 to the Canadian Wildlife Federation; the Department of Justice appropriated $10,000 for the Law Amendments Committee of the Canadian Association of Chiefs of Police, and the Department of the Solicitor-General appropriated $50,000 for the same Association; the Department of Indian Affairs and Northern Development appropriated over 14 million dollars to land councils and Indian associations; and the Department of National Defence appropriated $90,000 for rifle associations. And no doubt there are others.

A comparison of grants (in terms of numbers and amounts) in the two earlier periods of 1927 and 1952 (the dates of the Revised Statutes of Canada) shows, not surprisingly, that direct grants to pressure groups have increased substantially in the last 50 years. There were only a few dozen grants in each year in the mid-1920s and the majority of these were

---

301 See *Justice and Legal Affairs* (No. 20) June, 1977, at p. 74; H.C. Debs., p. 7213 (30 June, 1977).

302 S. 188. See also s. 81.

303 S. 190(1)(c).

304 S. 189(3).

305 S. 251(2).

306 S. 106.2(2)(c).

307 Receiver General for Canada, Public Accounts of Canada, 1974-75, vol. II, Details of Expenditure and Revenues.

to such established service agencies as the St. John Ambulance Association, the C.N.I.B., and the Victorian Order of Nurses.

Government funds are now used to assist groups involved in preparing submissions on matters such as the Berger Inquiry into the Mackenzie Valley Pipeline[308] and the Hartt Inquiry into Development in Northern Ontario.[309] The Consumers' Association of Canada receives increasingly large sums of money, some of it specifically for advocacy before courts and tribunals.[310] The Association's annual government grant has grown from $150,000 in 1972-73 to $440,000 in 1976-77.[311] The Canadian Labour Congress recently agreed to accept $10 million over five years from the federal government for union leadership training.[312] One organization, however, that consistently refuses any government grants is the Canadian Civil Liberties Association.[313]

Yet, even the Civil Liberties Association in effect receives government assistance through the charitable deduction provisions in the Income Tax Act.[314] Although the Association itself is not a registered charity, its "education trust" is. The result is that donations to the "trust" can be deducted for the purpose of computing the donor's taxable income.[315] Donations to many of the organizations involved in the gun control controversy, such as the various wildlife federations, could be claimed as charitable deductions.[316]

Trusts set up for the purpose of lobbying for a change in the law are not considered charitable, although it should be noted that prior to the First World War it was otherwise and courts upheld trusts to groups promoting such activities as anti-vivisection[317] and temperance legislation.[318] Subsequently, however, both these purposes were held to be non-

---

308 Berger, "The Mackenzie Valley Pipeline Inquiry," (1976) 3 Queen's L.J. 3, 10. See also the Public Accounts, 1974-75, at pp. 9.7-9.8.

309 *The Globe and Mail*, 7 March, 1977.

310 Trebilcock (1975) 13 Osgoode Hall L.J. 619, at p. 631.

311 H.C. Deb., at p. 4699 (6 April, 1977).

312 *The Globe and Mail*, 20 May, 1977.

313 *Justice and Legal Affairs* (No 10) 28 April, 1977, at p. 19. Note that the Canadian Federation of Civil Liberties and Human Rights Associations will accept government funds: *ibid.* at p. 35.

314 S.C. 1970-71-72, c. 63.

315 S. 110(1)(a). In addition, the trust is not taxable (s. 149(1)(f)), but this benefit is available to a number of non-profit bodies, whether or not they are true "charities" (s. 149(1)(l)).

316 Lewis, "The Hidden Persuaders," in *MacLean's,* 13 June, 1977 at pp. 40 *et seq. Cf. Hobson v. M.N.R.* (1959), 59 D.T.C. 211.

317 *Re Fouveaux; Cross v. Anti-Vivisection Soc.* [1895] 2 Ch. 501; *Re Gwynne* (1912), 5 D.L.R. 713 (Ont. H.C.).

318 *Farewell v. Farewell* (1892), 22 O.R. 573 (Ch.D.).

charitable.[319] The reason for the change of approach was undoubtedly the introduction in Canada, and the immense expansion in England, of the income tax system during the First World War and the effect that a charitable designation would have on their, and their supporters, liability for tax.[320] As Lord Wright said in 1948 in the *Anti-Vivisection* case,[321] denying these groups the status of charities prevents them "from claiming the benefit of being immune from income tax, which would amount to receiving a subsidy from the state to that extent."

The law of "charities" for the purpose of tax law is virtually the same as the law of charities in the law of trusts.[322] But Lord Cross[323] was surely correct to say that it is "unfortunate that the recognition of any trust as a valid charitable trust should automatically attract fiscal privileges, for the question whether a trust to further some purpose is so little likely to benefit the public that it ought to be declared invalid and the question whether it is likely to confer such great benefits on the public that it should enjoy fiscal immunity are really two quite different questions." The question whether a particular — or every[324] — lobbying activity should receive tax consideration should be faced directly.

Pressure groups are clearly a potent force in the formulation of the law. When they put forward well thought-out special points of view they make an important contribution to the development of government policy. Even if it were possible to do so, it would be unwise to attempt to

---

319 For temperance cases see *Commissioners of Inland Revenue v. Temperance Council of the Christian Churches of England and Wales* (1926), 136 L.T. 27, and *Knowles v. Commissioner of Stamp Duties*, [1945] N.Z.L.R. 522; and for anti-vivisection: *National Anti-Vivisection Society v. Inland Revenue Commissioners*, [1948] A.C. 31 (H.L.).

320 *Cf.* Sheridan, "Charity versus Politics," (1973), 2 Anglo-Amer. L. Rev. 47 who does not stress the tax considerations, but argues (at p. 59) that "it is not for the public benefit, as that expression is understood in charity law, to have pressure groups, propaganda campaigns, lobbying, picketing, and so on, for the purpose of inducing a change of national policy"; see also Keeton, G. W. and Sheridan, L. A., *The Modern Law of Charities* (2nd ed.) (Belfast 1971) at pp. 36-37; Waters, D. W. M., *Law of Trusts in Canada* (Toronto 1974) at pp. 494 *et seq.*

321 *Supra* note 221 at p. 52.

322 See generally ss. 149(1)(*f*) and 149.1(1)(*a*)-(*d*) of the Income Tax Act and note that para. 4 of Information Circular 73-11R (27 Oct., 1975) follows closely the definition given in *Income Tax Special Purposes Commr. v. Pemsel*, [1891] A.C. 531 (H.L.) Para. 7(c) of the Information Circular specifically excludes the "advocacy of political action" from charitable purposes.

323 *Dingle v. Turner*, [1972] A.C. 601 at 624-625 (H.L.). U.S. cases have drawn a distinction between the tax aspects and the validity of the trust: see *e.g. Slee v. Commr. of Internal Revenue* (1930), 42 F. 2d 184 (2nd cir.); Scott, A. W., *Trusts* (3rd ed.) (Boston 1967) vol. 4, at pp. 2912-2913.

324 Freeman, "The Poor and the Political Process: Equal Access to Lobbying," (1969) 6 Harvard J. on Legislation 369; Caplin and Timbie, "Legislative Activities of Public Charities," (1975) 39 *Law and Contemporary Problems* 183.

curtail their activities. At times, however, the powerful voice of a pressure group may have an undue influence on policy makers. As Chief Justice Warren once said[325]: "the voice of the people may all too easily be drowned out by the voice of special interest groups seeking favoured treatment while masquerading as proponents of the public weal." It is important, therefore, to understand how pressure groups operate so that policy makers will be aware of this danger.

It is sometimes suggested that it would be desirable to have lobbyists register with the government, as in the United States,[326] but it is doubtful whether this would affect their activities to any considerable extent. It would be more fruitful to direct any regulations at those being lobbied rather than those doing the lobbying. The enactment of conflict of interest rules for members of Parliament and others would help ensure that those lobbied derived no financial advantage from their actions.[327] The recently enacted rules relating to the disclosure of campaign contributions are also important.[328]

Perhaps the most significant step governments can take to decrease the possibility of inordinate influence by powerful pressure groups is to allow greater public access to government documents.[329] Because information is one of the most effective weapons that a pressure group has (whether generated by itself or because of its ability to obtain it from the government), any steps to make information more widely available to the public and other less powerful groups would help both to equalize the influence of competing pressure groups, and to help decrease the reliance of opposition parties on them for information.[330]

325 *U.S. v. Harriss* (1954) 347 U.S. 612 at 625.

326 Note, "Public Disclosure of Lobbyists' Activities," (1970) 38 Fordham L. Rev. 524.

327 See generally the, as yet unimplemented, Canadian Privy Council Green Paper of July, 1973, Members of Parliament and Conflict of Interest. The government has rules for government employees and has recently implemented rules for ex-employees: see H.C. Deb., p. 2104 (17 Dec., 1976). See also the *Report of the Royal Commission on Standards of Conduct in Public Life 1974-1976,* Cmnd. 6524 (1976).

328 Paltiel, "Improving Laws on Financing Elections" in *Political Corruption in Canada: Cases, Causes and Cures* (eds. K. M. Gibbons and D. C. Rowat) (Toronto 1976) at p. 298. The 1973 Green Paper also recognized (at p. 17) that "conflict of interest provisions will remain incomplete unless there are also provisions in the area of campaign contributions." See now the Election Expenses Act, S.C. 1973-74, c. 51; and the Election Finances Reform Act, S.O. 1975, c. 12.

329 See generally, the green paper issued by the Secretary of State of Canada in June, 1977, *Legislation on Public Access to Government Documents,* referred to the House and Senate Standing Joint Committee on Regulations and Other Statutory Instruments on 16 Dec., 1977. For a critique of the Report see the research study prepared for the Canadian Bar Association, Rankin, T. M., *Freedom of Information in Canada: Will the Doors Stay Shut?* (Ottawa 1977). "Freedom of Information" legislation came into force in Canada on July 1, 1983: see The Access to Information and Privacy Acts, S.C. 1980-81-82-83, c. 111.

330 Finer, S. E., *Anonymous Empire* (2nd ed.) (London 1966) at p. 20.

4

GUN CONTROL IN CANADA: POLITICS AND IMPACT*

1. INTRODUCTION: CRIME AND GUN OWNERSHIP IN CANADA

In 1979 there were fewer than 60 homicides committed with handguns in all of Canada.[1] Metropolitan Toronto, with more than 2,000,000 persons, had only four handgun homicides that year.[2] In contrast, in 1979, handguns were used in almost 900 killings in New York City,[3] about 300 in Metropolitan Detroit, and 75 in Metropolitan Boston,[4] the latter being an area having "historically . . . low levels of firearm ownership, as well as low rates of firearm use in crime"[5] and, moreover,

---

* This essay will also appear in A. Doob and E. Greenspan, eds., *The Future of Criminal Law* (tentative title), forthcoming. An earlier version of this paper was presented on March 3, 1981, at a Seminar on Canadian-U.S. Relations, sponsored by the University Consortium for Research on North America, Harvard Center for International Affairs. The research for this paper was supported, in part, by the Ministry of the Solicitor General, Ottawa. I am grateful for the help given to me on various aspects of the paper by Mary Alex, Nick Austin, Calvin Becker, Tanner Elton, Arthur Graham, Virginia Kuash and Gerry Leger, of the Solicitor General's Department, by S/Sgt. Ron Knowles and Supt. Bill Schindeler of the R.C.M.P., by Philip Stenning, Centre of Criminology, University of Toronto, and by J.R.S. Prichard and R.J. Sharpe, Faculty of Law, University of Toronto. The opinions expressed in the paper are, of course, my own, and do not necessarily reflect the view of the Government.

1 Statistics Canada, Homicide Statistics, 1981. The handgun figure shown is 54, but there were also 14 cases where the type of weapon was not known, and I have assumed that these are divided in the same ratio as the known firearms figure.

2 Metropolitan Toronto Police Department statistics, set out at p. 27 in the Report by Decision Dynamics Corporation to the Solicitor General of Canada, "Evaluation of the Canadian Gun Control Legislation: First Progress Report", tabled in the House of Commons, May 20, 1981, hereafter cited as the First Evaluation Report, 1980. A very brief Second Progress Report is published in Focus on Firearms, vol. 2, March, 1983, a newsletter of the Firearms Policy Centre of the Solicitor General of Canada. The Final Report, Evaluation of the Canadian Gun Control Legislation: Final Report (Ottawa 1983) (written by Elisabeth Scarff), published in Aug. 1983 is hereafter cited as the Final Evaluation Report, 1983.

3 The New York Times, Aug. 17, 1980.

4 There is no actual breakdown between handguns and long-guns in the F.B.I.'s Uniform Crime Reports, Crime in the United States, 1979, apart from the statement at p. 7 that handguns are used in 50% of all homicides.

5 Beha, " 'And *Nobody* Can Get You Out': The Impact of a Mandatory Prison Sentence for the Illegal Carrying of a Firearm on the Use of Firearms and on the Administration of

having tough laws against illegal possession introduced in 1974 by the "Bartley-Fox" amendment.[6] The six New England States had over 200 handgun homicides in 1979;[7] the four Canadian Maritime Provinces did not have a single handgun homicide in 1979.[8] There were over 10,000 handgun homicides in the U.S. in 1979, almost 20 times the Canadian *per capita* rate. Statistics for recent years are, in general, not dissimilar to the 1979 figures.[9]

The handgun homicide rate in Canada hovers around 10% of all homicides; in the early 1970's it was a bit above 10%; in the late 1970's a bit under 10%.[10] In the United States, it is about 50% of all homicides.[11]

A similar relatively low use of handguns can be seen in other offences. In Metropolitan Toronto the handgun is used in only 2 or 3% of all woundings. Further, in Metropolitan Toronto there were only 15 reported rapes in which handguns were used during the total eight-year period from 1974 to 1981. The handgun is used in Metropolitan Toronto in under 15% of all robberies.[12] In the United States firearms are used in about 40% of robberies[13] and the handgun is used in over 90% of these cases.[14]

Criminal Justice in Boston — Part 1" (1977) 57 Boston University Law Rev. 96 at p. 100.

6   The amendment took effect April 1, 1975. *Ibid.* See also G. L. Pierce and W. J. Bowers, "The Impact of the Bartley-Fox Gun Law on Crime in Massachusetts", Center for Applied Social Research, Northeastern University, 1979, a revised version of which can be found in The Annals, May, 1981, at p. 120; and Rossman, Froyd, Pierce, McDevitt, and Bowers, "Massachusetts' Mandatory Minimum Sentence Gun Law: Enforcement, Prosecution, and Defense Impact" (1980) 16 Crim. L. Bulletin 150.

7   F.B.I. Statistics, 1979.

8   Statistics Canada, Homicide Statistics, 1979. There were 2 handgun homicides in each of 1980 and 1981.

9   See Statistics Canada, Homicide Statistics, 1981: there were 62 known handgun homicides in 1980 and 59 in 1981. The preliminary 1982 figures made available to the writer by Statistics Canada show a disturbing increase in handgun homicides of 88, a figure similar to the handgun homicides in 1975: see the chart set out later in this paper. In 1981 murder offences accounted for over 90% (599 out of 647) of criminal homicides: Homicide Statistics, 1981.

10   See the chart, *infra.* The 1982 figure was 13%.

11   In the U.S., firearms are used in about two thirds of all homicides, and handguns in over three quarters of all firearm homicides: see generally, G. D. Newton and F. E. Zimring, Firearms and Violence in American Life (1969) (A Staff Report submitted to the National Commission on the Causes and Prevention of Violence). The *per capita* homicide rate in the United States is four times greater than in Canada.

12   Final Evaluation Report, 1983, Table A1.4.

13   F.B.I. Statistics, 1979.

14   See P. J. Cook and J. Blose, "State Programs for Screening Handgun Buyers", The Annals, May, 1981 at p. 80. The May, 1981 issue of The Annals, edited by Philip Cook, contains a very valuable analysis of Gun Control in the United States.

For almost 100 years Canada has controlled the possession of handguns. Further and tighter controls were introduced into the Canadian Criminal Code in 1977.[15] The total number of registered handguns in Canada at the end of 1980 was approximately three quarters of a million weapons.[16] This includes handguns owned by security agencies, by collectors and some owned by the police.[17] So the number of private individuals owning handguns would be far below three quarters of a million. The stock of registered handguns had been increasing at the rate of 20 or 25 thousand a year (including some new police guns).[18] In contrast, there were two million *new* handguns sold in the United States in 1980.[19] In Detroit in 1968 there were 17,760 new *official* handgun possession permits issued (and it is well known that there were a large number of unofficial handguns brought in from other States),[20] whereas in all of Canada in the same year there were only 14,000 new registrations for handguns.[21] There are almost as many new persons licensed each year as *dealers* in the United States[22] as there are new *handguns* registered in Canada. One quarter of all households in the United States have at least one handgun.[23]

There are two main comparisons that should be stressed. The *per capita* acquisition rate for handguns is about ten times as high in the United States as it is in Canada. The *per capita* homicide rate with handguns is almost 20 times as high in the United States as it is in Canada.

Is there a cause and effect relationship between uncontrolled ownership of handguns and the crime rate? Such a relationship does appear to exist, although it is difficult to prove. The more guns there are in irresponsible hands, the more likely that the guns will be irresponsibly

---

15 S.C. 1976-77, c. 53, s. 3. For a discussion of gun control in Canada before the legislation see the author's study prepared for the Ministry of the Solicitor General of Canada, "Gun Control: The Options" (1975-76) 18 Crim. L.Q. 29.

16 Annual Firearms Report to the Solicitor General of Canada by the Commissioner of the R.C.M.P., 1980. By the end of 1982 there were 776,323 restricted weapons: 1982 R.C.M.P. report.

17 Some police forces do not register their handguns because s. 90 of the Canadian Criminal Code exempts peace officers from the registration requirements of the Act.

18 Annual Firearms Reports. In 1982, for example, a net increase of just under 20,000 new handguns is shown by the registry. The figures for 1980 and 1981 are out of line. In 1980 there was a dramatic — and surprising — decrease in new registrations: there were only about 8,000 new restricted weapons registered in Canada that year and over 10,000 were withdrawn from the registry, a net decrease of 2,000 guns! In 1981 the net addition was under 7,000 restricted weapons.

19 See Cook and Blose, "State Programs", *supra* note 14.

20 See R. Sherrill, *The Saturday Night Special* (1973) at p. 98.

21 Friedland, "Gun Control: the Options", *supra* note 15 at p. 34.

22 Cook and Blose, "State Programs", *supra* note 14.

23 *Ibid.*

used. As we will see, Canada has been careful not to permit potentially irresponsible persons from possessing handguns; in the United States many States have had, and still have, very lax laws.

But even if guns are in otherwise responsible hands the number of homicide incidents will rise with the number of guns in existence. If a gun is readily available, for example, it may be used on the spur of the moment to settle an argument. The F.B.I. statistics for 1979 show that the majority of victims of homicide (52%) were acquainted with their assailants, and that the greatest percentage of homicides (43%) resulted from arguments.[24] Of course, knives and other objects can be substituted for guns, but studies have demonstrated that death is less likely if a weapon other than a gun is used — two and a half times less likely in the case of a determined knife attack, and five times less likely for knife wounds in serious areas compared to gun wounds in serious areas.[25] Moreover, if a gun is not available it cannot be stolen, accidentally discharged, or mistakenly used.

The low level of handgun ownership in Canada has meant that citizens have not felt the necessity to acquire handguns for protection, and the government and licensing authorities have not been under pressure to issue certificates for the protection of person or property. The Canadian experience seems to support Franklin Zimring's conclusion that "when ownership levels are low enough to have an impact on handgun availability . . . low aggregate ownership will depress handgun involvement in rates of subcultural violence."[26]

Canadians do, however, possess a large number of long-guns; some of the estimates vary from five to ten million guns.[27] So, it cannot be said that Canada is not a "gun-toting" society. The difference is that we do not "tote" handguns. Until recently there had been relatively no control over the purchase or possession of long-guns. Have these been used as substitutes for handguns in Canada? There are, it is believed, no studies of the issue. No doubt there would be some substitution, but because of the nature of the weapon, it would not be substantial. A long-gun cannot be easily concealed and cannot be used with one hand. (The definition sections of the Canadian Criminal Code have been careful to bring into the restricted weapon category long-guns which can be easily concealed or

---

24 F.B.l. Statistics, 1979.

25 See Zimring, "Is Gun Control Likely to Reduce Violent Killings?" (1968) 35 U. Ch. L. Rev. 721 at pp. 734-5.

26 Zimring, "Firearms and Federal Law: The Gun Control Act of 1968" (1975) 4 J. of Legal Studies 133 at p. 196.

27 See P. C. Stenning and S. Moyer, *Firearms Ownership and Use in Canada: A Report of Survey Findings,* 1976, Centre of Criminology, Toronto, 1981, at pp. 29 and 33. See also Friedland, "Gun Control: the Options", *supra* note 15 at p. 31.

fired with one hand).[28] So it is not surprising that in the United States over 90% of firearm robberies are committed with handguns. In personal encounters the use of long-guns will give greater warning to the victim and a greater opportunity to take defensive action. The long-gun is not well suited for some crimes, such as rape. Long-guns, therefore, are not easily substitutable for handguns in ease of use or effectiveness.

Of course long-guns can be cut down, but this does not seem to occur very frequently. Sawed-off weapons, now prohibited under the Criminal Code,[29] were used in only two out of 648 homicides in Canada in 1981 and in only four the year before.[30] Sawing down a weapon requires the type of planning and determination that is usually absent in homicide cases. Only about 20% of homicides in Canada take place during the commission of other criminal acts.[31] As in the United States, most arise from spur-of-the moment fights and arguments. In Canada about two thirds of the assailants knew the victim of the homicide.[32] Moreover, it makes the firearm — a not inconsiderable investment — unusable for legitimate purposes. Further, being found in illegal possession of a sawed-off weapon is a clear statement that the accused is up to no good and this would be reflected in the sentence of the court. So it is not surprising that sawed-off weapons are not widely used.

Let us now look at the Canadian legislation. I will then examine briefly the historical development of our gun laws and comment on the possible impact of the recent changes in our legislation. Finally, I will speculate on some of the reasons why Canada has been able to pass relatively tough measures.

2. THE CANADIAN LEGISLATION

There are three categories of firearms in Canada: prohibited weapons; restricted weapons — for the most part handguns; and long-guns.

Prohibited weapons include machine guns, sawed-off shot-guns and rifles. Prior to January 1, 1978, these weapons were not in fact prohibited in Canada, although devices such as silencers were. Machine guns and sawed-off weapons were, however, in the restricted category[33] and thus

---

28 Criminal Code, s. 82.

29 *Ibid.,* s. 82(1).

30 Homicide Statistics, 1981. Statistics Canada does not provide a similar breakdown for robberies, but the use of sawed-off weapons would certainly be much higher than for homicides.

31 *Ibid.*

32 *Ibid.*

33 Prior to 1969 sawed-off weapons were prohibited: see Friedland, "Gun Control: the Options", *supra* note 15 at p. 46.

carefully controlled. The 1977 legislation did not, in fact, eliminate existing collections of automatic weapons. One could retain a collection, but could not add to it — a grandfather or, if you prefer, a "godfather" clause.

As a result of the 1977 legislation, a person now requires what is called a Firearms Acquisition Certificate to buy long-guns, that is, rifles or shot-guns. Registration of the guns is not required. The certificate, valid for 5 years, covers an unlimited number of long-guns. Existing long-gun owners do not require a certificate for the guns they possessed on the date the legislation came into force. No reason need be given by the applicant to possess a long-gun. A certificate will be refused, however, if the issuer has "notice of any matter that may render it desirable in the interests of the safety of the applicant or any other person that the applicant should not acquire a firearm."[34] I will return to this question later.

Restricted weapons include all handguns; each gun must be separately registered. The registration certificate only permits the gun to be kept in the person's home or place of business.[35] A special permit is needed to be able to carry the weapon.[36] Control is exercised over the issuing of certificates in two ways: by requiring a valid reason for possessing the handgun, and by requiring that the applicant be a fit person to possess the weapon.

What are the reasons a person can give for desiring a handgun? He can acquire one "in connection with his lawful profession or occupation",[37] that is, as a police officer or security guard. He can also require one for use in "target practice under the auspices of a shooting club approved ... by the Attorney General of the province".[38] So far the reasons are not controversial. The next one is more difficult.

An applicant can acquire a handgun if it "will form part of a gun collection of the applicant who is a *bona fide* gun collector."[39] The collector category is dangerously broad if it permits anyone to *start* a collection. How can one distinguish between the *bona fide* collector and the person who wishes a handgun for other reasons? An English Green Paper in 1973 recommended that the collector category be closed off for the future for all firearms on the basis that "if a desire to collect firearms is accepted as a good reason to justify the grant of a certificate, then virtually any person

---

34 Criminal Code, s. 104(1).

35 Criminal Code, s. 106.1(8).

36. S. 106.2.

37. S. 106.1(3)(*c*)(ii).

38 S. 106.1(3)(*c*)(iii); or under (iv), other target practice under certain conditions.

39 S. 106.1(3)(*d*).

who wanted to keep a few weapons could make out a case for having a certificate."[40]

The Canadian legislative language — "will form part of a gun collection of the applicant who is a *bona fide* gun collector" — first introduced in 1977 could, as a matter of construction, be given a very restricted meaning, requiring the applicant to prove that he already *is* a *bona fide* collector. Unfortunately, it has not been so construed. A recent interim evaluation study of the legislation prepared for the Government by a group of outside consultants observed[41] that "if the applicant stated that he required a restricted weapon to start a collection, and there were no concrete grounds to prove otherwise, the certificate was generally issued."

The most controversial ground for permitting the possession of a handgun — and the one that would account for most handguns in the United States — is for protection. The 1977 Canadian legislation restricted this category to the protection of "life".[42] Formerly it had read "to protect life or property".[43] Relatively few handgun certificates are now issued in Canada to protect life. In 1979 there were fewer than 5,000 issued — and this included some police firearms.[44]

Granting a certificate only allows the gun to be kept in one's home or place of business. As previously mentioned, to carry the gun requires a "permit to carry". It is difficult to obtain a permit to carry for the protection of life — out of 10,000 carrying permits issued in Ontario in 1979 (the vast majority of which are issued to members of gun clubs) fewer than 20 were given to protect life.[45]

The legislation is designed not only to ensure that the applicant has a valid reason for having a handgun, but also that he is a fit person to have one. Applicants for all firearms now require a "Firearms Acquisition Certificate". A certificate will not be granted if the issuer "has notice of any matter that may render it desirable in the interests of the safety of the applicant or of any other person that the applicant should not acquire a

---

40 The Control of Firearms in Great Britain: A Consultative Document, May, 1973, Cmnd. 5297 at p. 16. This Report, which recommended further tightening of English gun controls, has not yet been implemented.

41 First Evaluation Report, 1980, at p. 93.

42 S. 106.1(3)(c)(i).

43 Canadian Criminal Code, R.S.C. 1970, c. C-34, s. 97(2). The provision applied to permits to carry, not to certificates of possession, so the 1977 legislation was even more restrictive than it had previously been.

44 First Evaluation Report, 1980, p. 95.

45 First Evaluation Report, 1980, p. 100.

firearm.''[46] The legislation specifically spells out[47] that the applicant should not acquire a firearm if he has been convicted within the previous five years of "an offence in the commission of which violence against another person was used, threatened or attempted" or an offence relating to firearms.

Moreover, a certificate will not be granted if the applicant within the previous five years has been "treated for a mental disorder, whether in a hospital, mental institute or psychiatric clinic or otherwise and whether or not he was, during that period, confined to such a hospital, institute or clinic, where the disorder for which he was so treated was associated with violence or threatened or attempted violence on the part of the applicant against himself or any other person."[48] Further, the certificate will be refused if he has a history of behaviour within the previous five years that included "violence or threatened or attempted violence . . ."[49] Although the issuer *must* refuse a certificate in the above cases the applicant can appeal to a magistrate who has greater latitude to approve the application.[50]

What steps are taken to determine whether the applicant is caught by the above provisions? In the first place the applicant is required to indicate on the application whether he fits within any of the categories, and there is a criminal penalty provided for a false application.[51] Secondly, all applications are run through the centralized criminal record centre (Canadian Police Information Centre, or CPIC), a system which, unlike the F.B.I. central system, does not have to rely on fingerprint identification. In addition, all applications are sent to the local police division in the area where the applicant lives. The local officers are the ones most likely to know if he has had problems, mental or otherwise, in the past. There is no official check of psychiatric records, and in view of the recent controversy surrounding abuses with respect to hospital records,[52] probably now no unofficial check. Access to such records is at present illegal. Whether it should be is another matter. New York and Illinois, for example, give the

---

46 S. 104(4). In addition, the legislation provides that the applicant for a Firearms Acquisition Certificate must show that he has completed a course or a test relating to the "safe handling and use of firearms" (s. 104(2)(c)), but this has not yet come into force in any province.

47 S. 104(3)(a).

48 S. 104(3)(b).

49 S. 104(3)(c).

50 S. 104(4).

51 S. 106.5.

52 See the Report of the Commission of Inquiry into the Confidentiality of Health Information, 1980 (the Krever Report).

police access to records of mental commitments in the course of handgun licence investigations.[53]

Even though an applicant has a Firearms Acquisition Certificate, a further and more thorough check is made before a handgun certificate is granted. It is not uncommon (in Toronto it is common) for the local police to visit the applicant at home, inspect how he plans to store the gun, and in some cases talk with neighbours and others.[54]

The U.S. 1968 Gun Control Act, the most recent federal legislation, contains similar categories of ineligible handgun purchasers, but, unlike Canada, fewer than half the States require that the police be notified of the purchase, and thus given a chance to check up on a handgun purchaser before the transfer is made.[55] Only three States have such a system for long-guns.[56] The F.B.I. criminal record files are not used because, unlike the practice in Canada, they require fingerprints and a number of weeks waiting time.[57] It is doubtful if any American jurisdiction in practice approaches the Canadian standards for the acquisition of firearms.[58]

Moreover, there are provisions in the Canadian legislation permitting the revocation of handgun certificates and carrying permits.[59] In addition there is a provision for the search for firearms, with or without a warrant, when there are "reasonable grounds for believing that it is not desirable in the interests of the safety of that person, or of any other person, that that person should have in his possession custody or control any firearm or other offensive weapon . . .".[60] The firearms can be disposed of by the court and the person prohibited from possessing firearms for five years.[61]

Another provision in the recent Canadian gun control legislation designed to keep firearms out of dangerous hands is a section making mandatory a prohibition order for at least five years whenever a person is convicted of an offence carrying a possible ten-year penalty "in the

---

53 Cook and Blose, "State Programs", *supra*. The Krever Report, Vol. II, p. 87, suggests that the application for a permit should contain an authorization to release health information.

54 First Evaluation Report, 1980, p. 92.

55 Cook and Blose, "State Programs", *supra*.

56 *Ibid.*

57 *Ibid.*

58 There are also sections dealing with finding or losing a restricted weapon, and a penalty section for careless storage of any firearm or ammunition which should, it is suggested, also result in the imposition of civil liability if the firearm causes damage as a result of not meeting the statutory standards. There is, unfortunately, no requirement that the owner carry insurance.

59 Criminal Code s. 106.4.

60 S. 101(1) and (2).

61 S. 101(6).

commission of which violence against a person is used, threatened or attempted."[62] The section was not, in fact, widely used during the first three years of its existence. R.C.M.P. records showed only a few hundred mandatory prohibitions in 1979 and about 500 in 1980,[63] a very small fraction of those who could have been so prohibited. Was it that prosecutors and judges were unaware of the provision? This might account for part of the answer, as would the problem of poor reporting, but it is likely that the real reason is that prosecutors just did not bother asking for an order. The situation has now improved; there were almost 2,000 mandatory prohibitions in 1982. The section would obviously be more effective if it operated without a special judicial order for, say, a five-year period, but provided the court with the power to make an order for a shorter or longer period.

The final aspect of the Canadian legislation to which reference should be made is section 83 of the Code, which came into force on January 1st, 1978 and provides for a minimum consecutive one-year penalty in the case of a first offence, and a minimum three year penalty in the case of a subsequent offence, for anyone "who uses a firearm . . . while committing or attempting to commit an indictable offence."

This is similar to section 924(c) of the U.S. Federal Criminal Law[64] introduced by the 1968 Gun Control Act. There are two differences, however. The U.S. provision applies to a person who "uses" or "carries" a firearm during the commission of a felony; the Canadian section is restricted to "use", and however widely "use" is interpreted it surely will not encompass mere possession.[65]

Although the U.S. provision is wider in its application, it properly gives the judge discretion to suspend the sentence for a first offence under the section, thereby tending to ensure that persons who should not be sent to jail are not. There is no such discretion in the Canadian section. It is likely, however, that in practice the Canadian section is used in the same manner as the American section. But instead of the judge exercising his discretion it is the prosecutor who does so, by not bringing a charge or by

---

62   S. 98(1). S. 98(2) provides for a discretionary prohibition in certain other cases.

63   Annual Firearms Report to the Solicitor General of Canada by the Commissioner of the R.C.M.P., 1979 at p. 11; 1980 at p. 12. There were 791 in 1981, Report at p. 12. See also Final Evaluation Report at pp. 57-60.

64   18 U.S.C. For an analysis of the comparable Michigan statute see Loftin, Heumann and McDowall, "Mandatory Sentencing and Firearms Violence: Evaluating an Alternative to Gun Control" (1983) 17 Law and Society R. 287; Loftin, Heumann and McDowall, "Federal Firearms Policy and Mandatory Sentencing" (1982), 73 J. Crim. L. and Criminology 1051.

65   See *R. v. Langevin* (1979), 47 C.C.C. (2d) 138 (Ont. C.A.) drawing a distinction between "use" and "being armed", found in an earlier section. The section has been applied to accomplices (*McGuigan v. R.* (1982), 66 C.C.C. (2d) 97 (S.C.C.)) and to unloaded firearms (*R. v. Cheetham* (1980), 53 C.C.C. (2d) 109 (Ont. C.A.)).

asking for its withdrawal or dismissal if a charge is brought. Of course, this gives the prosecutor great power in plea bargaining — perhaps too much power. Relatively few charges are brought under section 83 and in some provinces a large number of those that are brought are dismissed or withdrawn, indicating that section 83 charges are being used as a plea-bargaining tool by prosecutors.[66] In Ontario, for example, only a little over 300 such charges were brought in 1982 and over half of these were withdrawn or dismissed.[67]

As in the United States, "double jeopardy" issues have arisen because of the section. The provincial appellate courts have had no difficulty in upholding[68] convictions under both section 83 and other offences which involve firearms, such as robbery[69] or attempted robbery.[70] Mr. Justice Martin for the Ontario Court of Appeal stated in an armed robbery case:[71]

> It is clear to me that Parliament intended by section 83 to repress the use of firearms in the commission of crimes by making such use an offence in its own right, and one which attracts a minimum sentence of one year consecutive to that imposed for the offence which such use accompanies. The use of firearms in the commission of crimes is fraught with danger and gravely disturbing to the community, and Parliament has sought to protect the public from the danger and alarm caused by that use by enacting the present legislation.

The Supreme Court of Canada agreed with this view in *McGuigan v. The Queen* in 1982, Dickson J. stating for the court[72] that the section "formed part of a comprehensive 'gun control' legislative scheme intended to discourage the use of firearms by the criminal element of our society." Chief Justice Laskin, with whom Ritchie J. concurred, dissented, stating[73] that he was not "as certain as was Martin J.A. . . . that Parliament

---

66 First Evaluation Report, 1980 at p. 164.

67 Annual Firearms Report, 1982 at p. 15. See also Final Evaluation Report, 1983 at pp. 48-9.

68 Distinguishing the Supreme Court of Canada case of *R. v. Quon* (1948), 92 C.C.C. 1, decided under similar legislation enacted in the 1930's, but repealed in 1951.

69 See *e.g., R. v. Langevin supra* note 65; *R. v. Matheson* (1979), 50 C.C.C. (2d) 92 (Man. C.A.), appeal allowed on a different ground (1981), 59 C.C.C. (2d) 289 (S.C.C.); *R. v. Nicholson* (1980), 52 C.C.C. (2d) 157 (Man. C.A.), aff'd (1981), 64 C.C.C. (2d) 116 (S.C.C.).

70 *R. v. McGuigan, Lawson and Tatum* (1979), 50 C.C.C. (2d) 306 (Ont. C.A.), aff'd (1982), 66 C.C.C. (2d) 97 (S.C.C.); *R. v. Eby* (1979), 49 C.C.C. (2d) 27 (N.S.C.A.).

71 *R. v. Langevin supra* note 65 at 146.

72 *McGuigan v. R. supra* note 65 at 123. Will s. 11(*h*) of the Canadian Charter of Rights and Freedoms make a difference on this question? The Supreme Court gave leave to appeal in 7 C.C.C. (3d) 337n from the decision of the Ontario Court of Appeal in *R. v. Krug* (1983), 7 C.C.C. (3d) at 337 in which the court adopted the trial judge's view that multiple convictions are permissible for theft and for an offence under s. 83 and do not violate the Charter.

73 *Ibid.* at 110.

had shown its clear intention to make use of firearms in the commission of an offence culpable in its own right and expressed it in language which reflected that intention." In spite of the Supreme Court decision convictions will probably not be upheld in all cases covered by the language of the section. For example, it would not be reasonable to convict for a section 83 offence and also an offence necessarily involving a firearm such as section 84, pointing a firearm.[74] Parliament surely did not intend to turn such an offence (which can be proceeded with summarily) into one with a minimum one-year penalty.

American courts have also wrestled with double jeopardy problems under section 924. One U.S. Supreme Court decision, *Simpson v. United States* (1978),[75] held that there could not be multiple convictions under section 924 and a section (in that case bank robbery) that already provided an enhanced penalty for the use of a firearm. In *Busic v. United States* (1980)[76] the court held that in such a case the prosecution did not have the choice of weapon: section 924 could not be used even though it provided a more severe penalty. That particular issue cannot, however, arise in Canada because no other section, it appears, provides an enhanced penalty when a firearm is used. It should be noted that the Supreme Court of the United States recently held in *Missouri v. Hunter* (1983)[77] that, if legislative intent is clear, multiple sentences do not violate the double jeopardy provision.

There is nothing in Canada comparable to Massachusetts' 1974 "Bartley-Fox" amendment requiring a minimum one-year prison sentence for a person who is found in possession of a firearm (a handgun *or* long-gun) outside his home or place of business without the appropriate permit. Unlike the federal provision we have just seen, this is not related to the commission of another offence and, moreover, the sentence cannot be suspended. If firearms had been around in Draco's time it would have been called Draconian. But it would seem, according to two thorough studies,[78] that it has had some effect in reducing the illegal possession of

---

74 *R. v. Langevin supra* note 65 at 145; *R. v. Allison and Dinel* (1983), 5 C.C.C. (3d) 30 (Ont. C.A.). *Cf. R. v. Pineault* (1979), 55 C.C.C. (2d) 328 (Que. C.A.) permitting convictions under s. 83 and discharging a firearm with intent to wound under s. 228; *R. v. Yurkiv* (1980), 18 C.R. (3d) 287 (Ont. C.A.) (s. 83, and possessing weapon dangerous to the public peace under s. 85).

75 (1978), 435 U.S. 6.

76 (1980), 100 S. Ct. 1747.

77 (1983), 103 S. Ct. 673.

78 See Beha, "And *Nobody* Can Get You Out", *supra* note 5 and Pierce and Bowers, "The Impact of the Bartley-Fox Gun Law", *supra* note 6. The earlier study was not able to see any effect of the legislation on premeditated, predatory crime stating (at p. 325): "We detected no effect on the use of guns in robbery but did find a reduction in the proportionate use of guns in assaults and a resulting impact on the level of firearm homicides." The second study, which was able to include more recent data, showed a

firearms, and more importantly, of course, the commission of offences with firearms. New York has now introduced a similar law.[79] Society, however, pays a high price for such a deterrent: persons who otherwise would not be sent to jail spend at least a year in custody. If the law is not, in fact, administered in this way, it will eventually lose its effectiveness. The only minimum sentences for first offenders in serious cases in Canadian law are for murder and for importing narcotics. The gun problem in Canada certainly does not warrant such severe legislation as the "Bartley-Fox" amendment.

3. HISTORY OF CANADIAN LEGISLATION

How did we end up where we are? The following is a brief sketch of the developments in Canada over the past one hundred years.[80]

The first nation-wide permit system relating to handguns was introduced in 1892.[81] A minor penalty (between $5 and $25) was provided for anyone who had a pistol outside his home or place of business without a certificate of exemption granted by a Justice of the Peace unless the person had "at the time reasonable cause to fear an assault or other injury to his person, family or property". The Justice of the Peace's certificate, valid for 12 months, was issued if the Justice was satisfied by evidence under oath of the "discretion and good character" of the applicant. Permits were required at an even earlier date in the Northwest Territories, where it was an offence (with up to six months' imprisonment) for anyone to possess a firearm except a shotgun without the permission of the Lieutenant Governor or a commissioner appointed by him.[82] Formerly, the Canadian legislation had taken the more traditional criminal law ap-

---

delayed-reaction reduction in gun robberies (at p. 92): "The relatively immediate changes in gun and non-gun assault rates suggest that it was the law's punishment potential that altered assaultive behaviour. The more delayed reduction in gun robberies suggests that the actual implementation of the law in the courts may have been more important in altering robbery behaviour." This latter study was part of a comprehensive study of Massachusetts' minimum sentence gun law, a summary of which can be found in Rossman, Froyd, Pierce, McDevitt, and Bowers, "Massachusetts' Mandatory Minimum Sentence Gun Law: Enforcement, Prosecution, and Defense Impact" (1980) 16 Crim. L. Bulletin 150. See also P. J. Cook, "The Role of Firearms in Violent Crime: An Interpretive Review of the Literature, with Some New Findings and Suggestions for Future Research, 1981, Institute of Policy Sciences and Public Affairs, Duke University. Caution is necessary because, as Cook points out at p. 69, "the implementation of this amendment coincided with a reversal in the national violent crime trends of the preceding decade."

79 See The New York Times, Aug. 17, 1980.

80 The discussion in this section draws on my earlier paper, "Gun Control: the Options", *supra* note 15.

81 Canadian Criminal Code, S.C. 1892, c. 29, s. 105.

82 S.C. 1885, c. 51, s. 14.

proach of dealing with conduct after the event; for example, it was an offence for a person to have "in his custody or possession . . . any offensive weapons for any purpose dangerous to the public peace."[83]

The 1892 legislation was tightened in 1913,[84] perhaps influenced by the recent New York Sullivan legislation,[85] so that a permit was required for carrying any small arm — whether or not there was "reasonable cause to fear an assault". The legislation, which raised the penalty from the relatively insignificant maximum of $25 found in the 1892 Code to a potential three months' imprisonment, also required a permit for purchasing handguns, but did not affect existing handguns kept in the home or place of business.

In 1933 the legislation was further strengthened by increasing the possible penalty for carrying a handgun from three months to five years.[86] In fact, the Government wanted to make the provision even stronger by providing a minimum one-year penalty. Massachusetts was not the first jurisdiction to consider such a scheme. Indeed, as originally introduced, the Canadian legislation provided a minimum five-year penalty.[87] The Canadian Senate did not agree to any minimum penalty in these circumstances and the Commons accepted the Senate's position.[88] The 1933 legislation did, however, provide a minimum two-year sentence in addition to any other sentence if the offender carried a handgun while committing a criminal offence.[89] This was not objected to by the Senate. A further change introduced by the 1933 Act was to bring sellers of handguns within the permit system and to limit the issuing of permits to carry handguns to certain specified categories.

The following year, 1934, the Government, no doubt influenced by Roosevelt's gun control proposals, brought in a new Bill providing for the registration of all handguns, wherever kept.[90]

By 1934, therefore, the control of handguns was virtually complete,

---

83 S.C. 1892, c. 29, s. 102. See also S.C. 1867, c. 15.

84 S.C. 1913, c. 13, s. 4.

85 See L. Kennett and J. L. Anderson, *The Gun in America: The Origins of a National Dilemma* (1975), chapter 7, "The Beginnings of Controversy: The Sullivan Law". The 1911 Sullivan Act, in fact, went further than the Canadian legislation because it applied to *existing* handguns: see Kennett and Anderson at pp. 181-2. Massachusetts' law did not require a licence for existing guns until 1968; in 1906 it had prohibited carrying a *loaded* handgun without a licence, and in 1911 an unloaded handgun; in 1926 it prohibited purchases of handguns without a licence: see Beha, "And *Nobody* Can Get You Out", *supra* note 5 at pp. 101-2.

86 S. 118 of the Code, as enacted by S.C. 1933, c. 25, s. 1.

87 Hansard, House of Commons, March 29, 1933 at p. 3512.

88 Hansard, House of Commons, April 28, 1933 at p. 4397.

89 The provision was extended to long-guns in 1938: S.C. 1938, c. 44, s. 7.

90 S. 121A of the Code, as enacted by S.C., 1934, c. 47, s. 3.

although a number of important changes were subsequently made further tightening their control. In 1951, for example, a single central registry system was set up under the Commissioner of the R.C.M.P.;[91] the 1934 legislation had attempted to achieve this administratively through cooperative efforts by the provinces. Further changes were made in 1969,[92] again influenced by American initiatives brought about by events in the United States, in particular the shooting of Robert Kennedy and Martin Luther King. The 1977 Canadian legislation further tightened handgun control by limiting the categories of handgun owners and, as we have seen, providing a minimum one-year penalty for using a firearm during the commission of an offence. A similar minimum penalty provision had been, as previously mentioned, in the 1933 legislation, but it had been repealed in 1951[93] following a Supreme Court of Canada case[94] refusing to apply it to armed robbery. Another reason for its repeal may have been because in 1947[95] a potentially more powerful deterrent was added to the Code: it was to be murder (at that time capital) if a gun discharged, even accidentally, and killed somebody during the course of a robbery or a number of other specified offences.[96]

It can be seen that in general legislation in Canada closely parallels movements for reform in the United States. The difference, of course, is that Canada has been able to pass strong legislation, whereas the United States has not. I will return to the possible reasons for this later.

Long-guns were not brought into a system of control until the 1977 legislation.[97] There had been special legislation following the First World War which had required a permit for rifles and shotguns, with the exception of shotguns already owned by British subjects. This legislation, the result of the "red scare" of the time, and no doubt influenced by the far-reaching U.K. legislation enacted in 1920, was short-lived and was repealed in 1921.[98]

The 1977 legislation relating to long-guns, which became operative January 1st, 1979, requires, as we saw earlier, all purchasers to first obtain a Firearms Acquisition Certificate. As originally proposed, the legislation would have required a licence for those who already possessed long-

---

91 S. 124, as enacted by S.C. 1951, c. 47, s. 7.

92 S.C. 1968-69, c. 38, s. 6.

93 S.C. 1951, c. 47, s. 7.

94 *R. v. Quon, supra* note 68.

95 S.C. 1947, c. 55, s. 7.

96 See *e.g., Rowe v. R.* (1951), 100 C.C.C. 97 (S.C.C.). There are no Canadian decisions on the question raised in a number of American cases as to whether the section extends constructive murder to a death caused by a person in retaliation.

97 S.C. 1976-7, c. 53, s. 3.

98 See Friedland, "Gun Control: the Options", *supra* note 15 at pp. 42-3.

guns.[99] This would have been a mistake, as it may have resulted in substantial non-compliance with the law and therefore potential intrusive police activity in order to force compliance. The dangers, recently outlined by John Kaplan,[100] of turning the gun control issue into another liquor "prohibition" situation, are real. Even controlling purchasers of ammunition runs the serious risk of creating underground production — the equivalent of illegal stills. Even so, requiring a permit for "use" might have been a workable system.

Canada has been fortunate in having had a gradual development of control over firearms for the past 100 years. We have never had to face a situation as in the United States today, which appears to many observers to be almost out of control.

4. IMPACT OF RECENT LEGISLATION

It is too early to say whether the recent Canadian legislation will have a long-term effect on the use of guns in criminal activities. There is no question that the cumulative effect of all the legislation over the years has been significant. Here only the recent changes are examined. The Solicitor General of Canada retained a firm of private consultants[101] to evaluate the effectiveness of the legislation over a three-year period. Its first report, officially released in May, 1981, after one full year of data collection, was cautious in its overall conclusions:

> Unfortunately, we do not have sufficient data to draw firm conclusions on whether Bill C-51 has promoted a reduction in firearm incidents. Nevertheless, we have been able to identify some historic trends in gun usage which indicate that the 'gun problem' *per se*, was less serious in the late 1970's than in the early and middle years of the decade. Generally, these favourable trends have continued through the first full year of firearm control in Canada.

The final report, released in 1983, concluded that the new legislation was effective:[102]

> In a considerable number of cases, a decline in the proportion of occurrences with firearms subsequent to the legislation has been found. Most of these declines were modest, but in view of the consistency among the various statistics, it is concluded that the legislation did have a moderate impact on the use of firearms in Canada.

Let us look at the homicide statistics published by Statistics Canada. Preliminary figures for 1982 were obtained in early January, 1984 from Statistics Canada, whose published homicide statistics for 1982 will not be

---

99   Bill C-83, Feb. 24, 1976.

100   "Controlling Firearms" (1979) 28 Cleveland State Law Rev. 1; "The Wisdom of Gun Prohibition" The Annals, May 1981 at p. 11. See also J. D. Wright, P. H. Rossi and K. Daly, Under the Gun: Weapons, Crime, and Violence in America (1983).

101   Decision Dynamics Corporation, *supra* note 2.

102   Final Evaluation Report, 1983, at p. xiii.

available for some time. The Canadian homicide figures for the past nine years are as follows:[103]

FIREARMS

Year	Handguns	Long-guns	Sawed-off weapons	Unknown	Total Shooting	Total homicide victims
1982	88	147	8	5	248	670
1981	59	123	2	15	199	648
1980	62	120	4	9	195	593
1979	54	135	4	14	207	631
1978	63	177	2	8	250	661
1977	61	161	14	24	260	712
1976	67	165	5	21	258	668
1975	88	183	10	11	292	701
1974	76	180	12	15	283	600

It will be recalled that the legislation came into effect on January 1, 1978, but that the licensing requirements for long-guns were not operative until January 1, 1979.

The use of both handguns and long-guns in homicide cases has in general been decreasing since 1975, although there was a disturbing jump in the figures for 1982. There was no significant change in the rate of homicides by shooting between 1977 and 1978, the year in which the minimum penalty was first operative. This is not surprising. The parts of the legislation that came into force at the beginning of 1978 did not materially affect gun ownership; rather, they provided for more severe penalties.

It is likely that the impact of judicial concern over firearms which had started in 1975 with the movement for tighter controls had already had its major effect. An incident in Montreal in January, 1975 in which 13 persons died of gunfire and arson focussed public attention on the issue of firearms.[104] In early 1975, the Chairman of the Metropolitan Toronto Police Commission, to take one example, advocated a mandatory five-year sentence without parole for anyone convicted of a crime with a firearm.[105]

This concern expressed by the public, the media and in Parliament

103 See Homicide Statistics, 1981. See also the Final Evaluation Report, 1983 at pp. 3-6. Preliminary statistics released May, 1984, without firearm breakdowns, show 679 homocides for 1983.

104 See Friedland, "Gun Control: the Options", *supra* note 15 at p. 30.

105 *Ibid.*

was, no doubt, reflected in the sentencing pattern of the courts long before section 83 was introduced. In the 1975 case of *Regina v. Auerswald,*[106] for example, the trial judge sentenced the accused (a member of a Nazi-oriented group) to 18 months imprisonment for the possession in his home of two unregistered but loaded pistols. Two loaded but registered pistols were also seized at the same time. The Ontario Court of Appeal reduced the sentence but agreed that a custodial sentence was warranted, stating:[107]

> Despite the fact that the appellant has no criminal record, and has been an industrious worker and has supported his family, we are, nevertheless, of the view that the trial Judge in all the circumstances did not err in imposing a custodial sentence. . . . The sentence imposed ought to reflect general deterrence as a major consideration.

This comes close to the Massachusetts "Bartley-Fox" legislation. Indeed, it is in one sense more stringent because the guns were found in the accused's home.

The chart indicates, however, a fairly large drop in homicides with firearms from 1978 to 1979. This is consistent, and probably the result of requiring a certificate for the acquisition of long-guns on January 1, 1979. Although the legislation did not affect existing long-guns it made it difficult for a person to obtain a new gun. Homicides with long-guns dropped from 177 in 1978 to 135 in 1979, with a further drop to 123 in 1981. The figure rose substantially in 1982 to 147. Does this latest figure indicate a trend towards greater use of long-guns for homicide, or will the data in future years show a continuation of the lower figures of 1979 to 1981? If it is the latter, then the Canadian experience will support Philip Cook's conclusion[108] with respect to the United States that "despite the apparent ease with which screening systems can be circumvented, such systems may be capable of effecting a modest reduction in gun violence rates."

The Final Evaluation Report also concluded that the new legislation had a positive effect on the use of firearms in robberies:[109]

> National statistics on firearms robberies are available for 1977 to 1981. . . . Over these five years, total robberies have increased about 35 percent . . . whereas robberies with firearms increased only 20.4 percent. . . . In summary, while total robberies have increased, the relative use of firearms in robberies has decreased nationally and in three of the four local jurisdictions (Calgary, Toronto and Vancouver; but not Ottawa) since the start of the legislation. On the other hand, there does not appear to have been any major change in the relative use of handguns in this crime (handgun data are only available from city jurisdictions).

---

106 (1976), 28 C.C.C. (2d) 177 (Ont. C.A.).

107 Ibid at 179.

108 Cook and Blose, "State Programs", *supra* note 14.

109 At p. 8.

Another indication tending to show that the new long-gun licensing provisions are effective can be found in the suicide statistics. The Canadian figures for suicides for 1979 showed a decrease of firearm suicides from 37% in 1978 (and this figure had been relatively constant for a number of years)[110] to 33% in 1979, i.e. from 1287 out of 3475 suicides in 1978 to 1100 out of 3357 in 1979.[111] Similar results occurred in 1980 and 1981.[112]

These homicide, robbery and suicide statistics should engender cautious optimism that the additional controls introduced in 1977 were justified.

5. ACCEPTANCE OF TOUGH LEGISLATION

Why has Canada been able to pass effective gun control legislation whereas the United States has not? In this section some of the more important factors permitting tough legislation in Canada are discussed.

Near the top of the list is the fact that criminal law power was given in the 1867 British North America Act[113] to the federal government. The American model was deliberately rejected. Sir John A. Macdonald stated in the Confederation Debates:[114]

> It is one of the defects in the United States system, that each separate state has or may have a criminal code of its own . . . [U]nder our Constitution we shall have one body of criminal law, based on the criminal law of England, and operating equally throughout British America. . . . I think this is one of the most marked instances in which we take advantage of the experience derived from our observations of the defects in the Constitution of the neighbouring Republic.

This means, of course, that legislation need be passed by only one government, not fifty, as in the United States. Canada does not have to face the difficult problem of widely varying standards from one jurisdiction to another. The main reason, according to Zimring,[115] for the limited impact of the 1968 U.S. Gun Control Act is that the "Act has not produced any measurable change in the migration of handguns from loose-control to tight-control jurisdictions." Nor is it necessary for the federal government

---

110 See the First Evaluation Report, 1980 at p. 8.

111 Statistics Canada, *Causes of Death,* 1979. The drop in the west, where suicides with firearms are higher than in the east, was less pronounced.

112 *Causes of Death,* 1980 (1121 out of 3358 suicides) and 1981 (1172 out of 3403 suicides). See also Final Evaluation Report 1983, at pp. 29-32.

113 S. 91(27).

114 See M. A. Lapin and J. S. Patrick, *Index to Parliamentary Debates on Confederation,* 1865 (1951) at p. 41.

115 Zimring, "Firearms and Federal Law: The Gun Control Act of 1968" (1975) 4 J. of Legal Studies 133 at p. 191.

in Canada to steer a particularly careful course around constitutional obstacles. A recent lower court judgment in British Columbia[116] upheld the constitutional validity of the new licensing aspects of the gun control legislation as "part of the criminal law" and the Alberta Court of Appeal has upheld the search and seizure provisions.[117] Other courts have upheld the prohibition provisions.[118] The Supreme Court of Canada will no doubt arrive at similar conclusions.[119]

Not only can the federal government in Canada set a uniform standard, but through the Royal Canadian Mounted Police it plays a greater role in administering the legislation than is usual in the criminal law, as control over the "administration of justice" was specifically given by the B.N.A. Act to the provinces.[120] It is the Commissioner of the R.C.M.P., for example, who is ultimately responsible for registering the handgun. It is the Commissioner who has the power to appoint the local registrars of firearms.[121] And it is the Commissioner who keeps the central handgun registry and reports to Parliament.

The Mounties have been important for another reason. They were the vehicle used by the federal government to help ensure the peaceful development of the Canadian west. Canada did not have a "wild west" because, as every Canadian school child knows, the law preceded development. The establishment in 1873 of the North-West Mounted Police[122] (now the Royal Canadian Mounted Police) helped ensure peaceful settlement and good relations with the Indians.[123] The role of the Mounties in the west is one of those myths that turns out to be true. The

---

116 *R. v. Northcott,* [1980] 5 W.W.R. 38 (B.C. Prov. Ct.).

117 *A. G. Can. v. Pattison* (1981), 59 C.C.C. (2d) 138 (Alta. C.A.).

118 *R. v. Anderson* (1981) 59 C.C.C. (2d) 439 (Ont. Co. Ct.); *Re Motiuk and R.* (1981), 60 C.C.C. (2d) 161 (B.C.S.C.).

119 The Supreme Court will probably either ignore, not follow, or distinguish as a case upholding concurrent power, Lord Watson's statement in 1896 in *A. G. Ont. v. A. G. Can. (Local Prohibition Case),* [1896] A.C. 348 (P.C.) at 361-2 that "An Act restricting the right to carry weapons of offence, or their sale to young persons, within the province would be within the authority of the provincial legislature."

120 S. 92(14).

121 The power is not, in fact, exercised; the Provincial Attorneys-General appoint the registrars.

122 See R. C. Macleod, "Canadianizing the West: The North-West Mounted Police as Agents of the National Policy, 1873-1905" in L. H. Thomas (ed.), *Essays on Western History* (1976); "The Mounted Police and Politics" in H. A. Dempsey (ed.), *Men in Scarlet* (1974); *The NWMP and Law Enforcement 1873-1905* (1976).

123 See J. Jennings, "The Plains Indians and the Law" in H. A. Dempsey (ed.), *Men in Scarlet* (1974).

development of the American frontier described by Turner[124] found no counter-part in Canada. A Canadian historian recently wrote:[125]

> The presence of the police, coupled with their firm insistence that they alone were the sole agents of Her Majesty's law, ensured that "frontier justice" did not gain currency, and that the extra-legal voluntary associations described by Turner were not only vigorously discouraged but were also unnecessary. Violence in the Canadian cattle country was most uncommon. Between 1878 and 1883 only five murder cases were brought before the courts. An incident in December 1895 in which the Texas foreman of [a] Ranch beat an adversary to the draw and shot him in the stomach caused the editor of the Fort Macleod Gazette to call attention to the rarity of such incidents with the observation that this was only the second time since the paper was established in 1882 that it had been able to report a gun fight. The police vigorously discouraged the carrying of side arms and the mere pointing of a revolver was sufficient to bring imprisonment.

Not only did the Mounties enforce the law — and it should be noted that for most offences they had the now unthinkable power of being judges in their own causes[126] — but many of them settled in the west when their tour of duty was completed. By 1880, former Mounties comprised the principal element within the ranch community,[127] giving stability to a potentially volatile group. The pattern of settlement of the west was different from the egalitarian American west. To a considerable extent the Canadian west mirrored eastern society and its social structure. "The hope was that a loyal and intelligent élite would further stabilize and civilize the frontier."[128]

Is this point about the development of the west overstressed? I do not think so. The "six-gun mystique"[129] in the American west permeated U.S. society[130] and has left a long, unfortunate legacy, a legacy not found in Canada. It is interesting to note that the hand-gun was sufficiently foreign to Canadian society that the Mounties were unsure where to wear their own pistols. Those of us brought up on Westerns *know* how a six-shooter is

---

124 F. J. Turner, "The Significance of the Frontier in American History" in *The Frontier in American History* (1920).

125 D. H. Breen, "The Turner Thesis and the Canadian West: A Closer Look at the Ranching Frontier" in L. H. Thomas (ed.), *Essays on Western History* (1976) at p. 150; see also P. F. Sharp. *Whoop-up Country: The Canadian-American West 1865-1885* (1955).

126 See P. F. Sharp, *Whoop-up Country, supra* at p. 110.

127 See D. H. Breen, "The Mounted Police and the Ranching Frontier" in H. A. Dempsey (ed.), *Men in Scarlet* (1974) at p. 118: D. H. Breen, *The Canadian Prairie West and the Canadian Ranching Frontier* (1982).

128 D. Owram, *Promise of Eden: The Canadian Expansionist Movement and the Idea of the West 1856-1900* (1980) at pp. 142-3.

129 See J. Cawelti, *The Six-Gun Mystique* (1975).

130 See Kennett and Anderson, *The Gun in America, supra* note 85, chapter 5, "Firearms and the Frontier Experience".

worn. The following excerpt from a Report in 1887 by an R.C.M.P. officer, S. B. Steele, speaks for itself:[131]

> At present when the man attempts to draw while holding the reins he experiences great difficulty in reaching the pistol, unless it is hung further forward where it would be perhaps dangerous, as the muzzle would hang over the thigh just below the groin, in which position a premature discharge would, most likely, result in making the man a cripple for life. . . . The men of the western plains of the United States, who are acknowledged to be the most expert pistol shots in the world, invariably wear it on the right side, with the butt at the rear. . . .

Let me offer one more observation on the west before I move back east. The different attitudes towards law and order on each side of the border are reflected in the literature of each area. This has been admirably demonstrated by Dick Harrison, a Professor of English from western Canada.[132] The hero of American fiction is often the stranger who takes the law into his own hands. Contrast that with the following excerpt from a popular Canadian western novel by Ralph Connor published in 1912.[133] The hero is the Mountie who walks into a gambling den where a "bad-man" is flourishing his gun:

> "Put it down there, my man. Do you hear?" The voice was still smooth, but through the silky tones there ran a fibre of steel. Still the desperado stood gazing at him. "Quick, do you hear?" There was a sudden sharp ring of imperious, of overwhelming authority, and, to the amazement of the crowd of men who stood breathless and silent about, there followed one of those phenomena which experts in psychology delight to explain, but which no man can understand. Without a word the gambler slowly laid upon the table his gun, upon whose handle were many notches, the tally of human lives it had accounted for in the hands of this same desperado. . . . The man, still silent, slunk out from the room. Irresistible authority seemed to go with the word that sent him forth, and rightly so, for behind that word lay the full weight of Great Britain's mighty empire.

The development of the west reflected attitudes in the east. I will leave it to historians and others to discuss in detail the grand historical themes that are important in understanding the development of gun control legislation in Canada. Only some of the ideas will be touched on here.

Both countries came into existence as a result of the American Revolution.[134] But whereas the United States was founded as a result of defiance of authority, Canada was the result of obedience to the Crown.

---

131 Report of the Commissioner of the North-West Mounted Police Force, 1887, (Ottawa, 1888) at p. 70.

132 Dick Harrison, *Unnamed Country: The Struggle for a Canadian Prairie Fiction* (1977). I am grateful to Professor Carl Berger for directing me to this book as well as to a number of other historical references.

133 Ralph Connor, *Corporal Cameron of the North West Mounted Police:* see Harrison, *supra,* at p. 77.

134 See S. M. Lipset, "Revolution and Counterrevolution" in R. A. Preston (ed.), *Perspectives on Revolution and Evolution* (1979).

Moreover, the Revolution resulted in a large number of United Empire Loyalists coming to Canada. Their views dominated Canadian attitudes over the next century. In 1838, Chief Justice Robinson, a Loyalist, addressed the two accused found guilty of treason (and later hanged) in the abortive Mackenzie uprising:[135] "You lived in a country where every man who obeys the law is secure in the protection of life, liberty, and property; under a form of government, which has been the admiration of the world for ages." Then turning to Lount, who had been a member of the Legislative Assembly, Chief Justice Robinson said:

> In a country in which you have been admitted to the honourable privilege of making laws to bind your fellow subjects, it was due from *you* to set an example of faithful obedience to public authority . . . as a man, as a subject, and as a Christian.

There has been resort to violence on many occasions in Canada's history, but there has also always been a quick response by the authorities to that violence.[136] Throughout the 19th century the Loyalists drew attention to lawlessness in the United States. In 1896 the president of the United Empire Loyalists Association stated[137] in his Inaugural Address that there should be no surprise over violence in the United States for "did not the Revolution teach Americans that if your neighbour does not agree with you, you may shoot him, confiscate his property, and injure him to the utmost of your ability?"

There is no right to revolution in Canada, no declaration of independence, no "right to bear arms",[138] no tradition of civil disobedience, and no violent civil war. What we have, instead, is the simple phrase in the British North America Act, "Peace, Order and Good Government." As Kenneth McNaught has written,[139] "We have certainly shown deference to the concept of *established* authority and procedures and even to the legal idea that valid authority flows downward from the crown."

One can see these attitudes reflected in other parts of our legal system, apart from gun control legislation. The law of self-defence is a

---

135 See K. McNaught, "Political Trials and the Canadian Political Tradition" in M. L. Friedland (ed.), *Courts and Trials: A Multi-disciplinary Approach* (1975), at p. 142.

136 *Ibid., passim.* See also K. McNaught, "Violence in Canadian History" in J. S. Moir (ed.), *Character and Circumstance* (1970).

137 See C. Berger, *The Sense of Power* (1970) at p. 161.

138 The Second Amendment to the U.S. Constitution states: "A well-regulated militia being necessary to the security of a free state, the right of the people to keep and bear arms shall not be infringed." Fear of a standing army has not been a matter of great concern in Canada. The militia has therefore been less prominent than in the United States. In the war of 1812, for example, the regular British forces were more important than the Canadian Militia and outnumbered the U.S. full-time soldiers: C. P. Stacey, *Canada and the British Army 1846-1871* (revised ed., 1963) at pp. 11-12.

139 "Political Trials" *supra* note 135 at p. 138.

particularly good example. The Canadian Criminal Code has always expected one acting in self-defence to withdraw if it is safe to do so. Section 34 of the Code provides that "Every one who is unlawfully assaulted and who causes death or grievous bodily harm in repelling the assault is justified if . . . he believes, on reasonable and probable grounds, that he cannot otherwise preserve himself from death or grievous bodily harm." In contrast, American law in the past, and even in the majority of American jurisdictions today,[140] does not expect the innocent person to withdraw even if he can safely do so. In 1895 the Supreme Court of the United States[141] quoted with approval the following words of the Supreme Court of Ohio:

> a true man who is without fault is not obliged to fly from an assailant, who by violence or surprise maliciously seeks to take his life or do him enormous bodily harm.

Another consideration is the structure of government. The Canadian political system makes it easier to pass controversial legislation than the American congressional system. If the executive government in Canada, the Cabinet, wishes to have a particular piece of legislation enacted it usually can do so because it can control the House of Commons by imposing party discipline on its members in the House. Members of Parliament in Canada do not usually disregard the party whips. Of course, it may be a minority government which does not have control of the House, or the parliamentary caucus may privately discourage the government from going ahead with its plans, or in the past the Senate might have blocked the legislation. But, in general, particularly with the closure rules introduced in 1969, the Cabinet gets its way.

This gives the Prime Minister and the Cabinet Ministers responsible for the subject matter great influence on whether a measure will be proposed. With respect to the recent legislation, the impetus in the Cabinet came from two sources, the Prime Minister and the Solicitor-General. The then Solicitor-General, Warren Allmand, from a riding in Montreal, was strongly committed to stronger gun control legislation and had introduced a private member's Bill in 1972, before he was Solicitor-General. The Prime Minister as well as the Cabinet were interested in abolishing capital punishment, and in order to do so it was necessary to give the public, which, it should be added, was opposed to abolition, some assurance that crime would be effectively dealt with even though capital punishment was to be abolished.[142] In particular, the police, who were strongly against abolition, were to be protected by the further control of

---

140 W. R. LaFave and A. W. Scott, *Criminal Law* (1972) at p. 395.

141 *Beard v. U.S.* (1895), 158 U.S. 550 at p. 561. *Cf. Allen v. U.S.* (1896), 164 U.S. 492 at p. 498.

142 See chapter 3 of this text.

firearms since guns provide the one real threat to a policeman's life.[143] So, at the same time that the Government introduced a Bill to abolish capital punishment (February, 1976) it introduced an Omnibus Bill relating to gun control, and a number of other subjects such as wiretapping, dangerous offenders, and parole. A similar sequence of events occurred in England in 1965 when capital punishment was abolished: the Government introduced gun control legislation prior to the vote on capital punishment. In Canada, however, capital punishment was in fact abolished prior to the passage of the gun control measures. (As an aside, it can be seen from the homicide figures set out earlier that the abolition of capital punishment in mid-1976 did not have much effect on the homicide rate. It went up slightly in 1977 and then down in the following years to below the 1976 level.)

If the public was against the abolition of capital punishment, it was in favour of stronger gun controls, more so than in the United States. This, of course, assisted in helping to offset the impact of the pressure groups. A Gallup Poll taken in Canada in July, 1975, revealed that 83% in Canada compared to 67% in the United States favoured the registration of all firearms; and 81% in Canada compared to 41% in the United States favoured prohibiting possession of handguns.[144] Of course, public opinion polls vary according to specific events covered by the media. The shooting of President Reagan, the Pope, and John Lennon no doubt raised — at least in the short run — the percentage in the United States who wished stronger controls.

Opinion polls, however, do not usually indicate the strength of the views held. Let us now look at the role of pressure groups who manifest an intensity of feeling absent from public opinion polls. The discussion of pressure groups has been left to the end. It is certainly appropriate to say "last, but not least".

Pressure groups in Canada, as in the United States, are a potent force in the development of the law.[145] On the gun control issue, however, they have been less successful in blocking legislation than in the United States. Why is this so?

There are a number of reasons. In the first place the Canadian political structure makes the Member of Parliament less vulnerable to pressure than the Congressman. Because of party discipline, the M.P. will not be seen by his constituents as having the same degree of responsibility

---

143 See Friedland, "Gun Control: the Options" *supra* note 15 at p. 30: 35 out of 37 policemen killed in Canada between 1961-70 were killed by firearms. In 1979, 100 of the 106 police officers killed in the United States were slain with firearms (76 with handguns): see F.B.I. Statistics, 1979 at p. 311.

144 See Friedland, "Gun Control: the Options", *supra* note 15 at p. 32.

145 See chapter 3, for a fuller discussion of the topic and for detailed footnote references.

in supporting a measure as the Congressman in the United States. Moreover, recent criminal legislation has been presented in an omnibus package — this was the case with the recent gun control legislation — and this makes the M.P.'s responsibility for each part of the package less direct. Opposition M.P.'s with strong support from the gun lobby attempted to split the Omnibus Bill, without success. The use of voting power as a tactic is increasing in Canada, and no doubt played a role in the poor showing by the Liberal party in the west in the two federal elections since the gun control legislation was enacted, but it is still far less important than in the United States.

The Canadian pressure groups relating to gun control are less powerful than the American groups. There is nothing at all comparable to the National Rifle Association with its nine-storey headquarters in Washington. No doubt one important reason why the gun lobby has been weaker in Canada over the years than in the United States is because there are no manufacturers of handguns in Canada. When the anti-handgun legislation was going through Parliament in the 1930's the Minister of Justice specifically noted in the House that "there is no manufacture in Canada of pistols or revolvers."

A further reason for their weakness was that many of the pressure groups were organized along provincial lines and thus could not respond as quickly or effectively to federal action as could the N.R.A. Coalitions of groups were formed to lobby against the legislation, but in the end the principal coalition collapsed. The spokesman for the coalition, a well-respected former R.C.M.P. Commissioner, who represented wildlife groups, could not support the more extreme views of the shooters and collectors. The Canadian Wildlife Federation, for example, had no interest in endorsing the right to collect automatic weapons. The Federation sent a telegram to the Justice and Legal Affairs Committee, then holding hearings on the legislation, "dissociat[ing] our organization from any statements or briefs presented in the name of C.A.S.A.L. [the umbrella organization for the pro-gun groups]". The coalition collapsed and the legislation was passed the next month. No doubt the same debates among the spectrum of interests represented are voiced within the N.R.A. but dissent is more easily submerged in such a powerful organization, which can then appear to speak with one voice.

Nevertheless, the pressure groups, with the support of the Conservative opposition, were able to obtain a number of important modifications in the legislation. Existing long-gun owners were not made subject to the new law. Moreover, the ten dollar fee required for a five-year "Firearms Acquisition Certificate", was placed directly in the legislation rather than in the regulations, thereby making it impossible to have an increase without a legislative debate.

Pressure groups may also be less powerful in Canada because the political system has brought them more openly into the decision-making process, by giving them the opportunity to present briefs before Parliamentary and other Committees, by involving them directly in a consultative or advisory capacity and even by providing them with grants. In addition, organizations defined as "charitable" in effect receive a government subsidy through tax exemptions to the organization and its supporters. However, the Department of National Revenue specifically excludes from charitable purposes (and tax exemption) the "advocacy of political action."[146] The result is that Canada has fostered and encouraged pressure groups, but has discouraged them from going too far as active lobbyists. Canada's willing accommodation of pressure groups is seen by some as one more result of Canada's counter-revolutionary past.[147]

6. CONCLUSION

Canada has learned much from the United States on the issue of gun control. We have learned, for example, that the absence of strong controls over handguns will permit their widespread use for criminal activities. If Canada had not carefully controlled the possession of handguns for the past century it is likely that the Canadian crime rate for serious offences would be substantially higher than it is today, although for the historical and cultural reasons advanced in the previous section it would, no doubt, still be far below the American rate. The Canadian system combines limitations on the reasons for possession of handguns, careful screening of applicants, vigorous judicial sentencing, and strong federal action. It may be that the United States has something to learn from Canada on this issue.

---

146 The Secretary of State, Francis Fox, stated in 1981 (Notes for an Address, Jan. 31, 1981, Ottawa) that this limitation may be reconsidered.

147 See R. Presthus, "Evolution and Canadian Political Culture: The Politics of Accommodation" in R. A. Preston (ed.), *Perspectives on Revolution and Evolution* (1979) at p. 109.

5

NATIONAL SECURITY: SOME CANADIAN LEGAL PERSPECTIVES*

1. INTRODUCTION

Canada is never very far behind the United States on most matters. Investigations into national security issues in the United States — in particular by the Senate's Church Committee[1] — took place in the mid-1970s. Canada recently completed its own investigation into similar issues by a Royal Commission, officially designated the "Commission of Inquiry concerning certain activities of the Royal Canadian Mounted Police",[2] but popularly known after its Chairman as the McDonald Commission.[3]

A number of revelations concerning the activities of the Royal Canadian Mounted Police (R.C.M.P.) showed that the Mounties had not been spending all their time singing love songs in the Rockies — or perfecting their much-heralded musical ride. It was revealed, for example, that in the early 1970s in Quebec the Mounties had, without a

---

* This essay is based on the text of a University of London Special University Lecture delivered at Queen Mary College on Feb. 26, 1980, later published in (1980) 10 Israel Yearbook on Human Rights 257. An earlier version of that paper had been given at a Faculty Seminar in the Faculty of Law at Tel Aviv University on Nov. 6, 1979. The paper has been updated to take into account the Report of the McDonald Commission as well as the Government's response to the McDonald Report, Bill C-157, introduced May 18, 1983, and the Special Senate Committee established on June 29, 1983 under the chairmanship of Senator Michael Pitfield to examine the subject matter of the Bill. The Senate Committee issued its report, Delicate Balance: A Security Intelligence Service in a Democratic Society, in Nov., 1983. A new revised Bill was introduced on Jan. 18, 1984, and at the time of writing is before the Justice and Legal Affairs Committee.

1 See the Final Report of the U.S. Senate Select Committee to Study Governmental Operations with respect to Intelligence Activities. The Church Committee was established in Jan., 1975 to "conduct an investigation and study of governmental operations with respect to intelligence activities and the extent, if any, to which illegal, improper, or unethical activities were engaged in by any agency of the Federal Government". The Committee's final report is divided into two main volumes. Book II covers domestic activities of intelligence agencies and their activities overseas to the extent that they affect the constitutional rights of Americans. Book I covers all other activities of United States foreign and military intelligence agencies. See the preface in Book II. Book III and later volumes contain detailed staff studies.

2 Established July 6, 1977. The Commission's terms of reference are contained in P.C. 1977-1911.

3 Mr. Justice David McDonald, Supreme Court of Alberta. The two other lawyer Commissioners were Guy Gilbert of Montreal and Donald Rickerd of Toronto.

warrant, entered and removed documents from the premises of a press agency; had similarly removed from private premises computer tapes containing membership lists of the Parti Québecois; had issued a fake communiqué urging F.L.Q. extremists to continue on a course of revolutionary action; had burned down a barn to prevent a meeting taking place; and had engaged in many more questionable activities.[4]

As a result of these disclosures, the Trudeau Government appointed a Royal Commission in July 1977 to inquire into R.C.M.P. activities "not authorized or provided for by law" as well as to advise on policies for the future. This latter aspect of its mandate — and the one under consideration here — reads as follows:

> to advise and make such report as the Commissioners deem necessary and desirable in the interest of Canada, regarding the policies and procedures governing the activities of the R.C.M.P. in the discharge of its responsibility to protect the security of Canada, the means to implement such policies and procedures, as well as the adequacy of the laws of Canada as they apply to such policies and procedures, having regard to the needs of the security of Canada.

I was asked by the Commission to prepare a background study on the Legal Dimensions of National Security, which was completed in June 1979 and published, along with several other studies.[5] The comments in this paper have, for the most part, been drawn from that study. The study and these comments express my own views and do not necessarily reflect the views of the Commission.

The McDonald Commission reported its findings in a three-volume Report in August, 1981.[6] An earlier Report, entitled *Security and Information*, was published in October, 1979. On May 18, 1983 the Government introduced Bill C-157, the Canadian Security Intelligence Service Act, which adopted the major McDonald Commission recommendation that the Security Service be separated from the R.C.M.P. A Special Committee of the Senate was appointed on June 29, 1983 under the Chairmanship of Michael Pitfield (who had earlier been the Clerk of the Cabinet) to examine the subject matter of the Bill.[7] Its Report was issued in November, 1983, and a further revised Bill was introduced by the government in January, 1984.

---

4 See the document dated October, 1978, "Freedom and Security: An Analysis of the Policy Issues Before the Commission of Inquiry", prepared by the Commission's Director of Research, Peter Russell.

5 Friedland, *National Security: The Legal Dimensions* (1980); Edwards, *Ministerial Responsibility* (1980); and Franks, *Parliament and Security Matters* (1980).

6 Second Report, Volumes 1 and 2, *Freedom and Security under the Law;* Third Report, *Certain R.C.M.P. Activities and the Question of Governmental Knowledge.*

7 See Issue No. 1 of the Proceedings of the Senate Committee, June 30, July 7, July 8, 1983. The writer gave evidence to the Committee on Sept. 12, 1983, reported in Issue No. 6 of the Proceedings.

A previous Canadian Royal Commission dealing with security, the Mackenzie Royal Commission, had also recommended in its Report[8] in 1969 that the Security Service be separated from the R.C.M.P. and, as with MI5 in England, be under civilian control. This key recommendation was, however, never implemented. Instead, a civilian director was brought in to head the Service. So, the Security Service remained an integral part of the Canadian national police force. A small civilian policy unit within the Solicitor General's Department, the Government Ministry to which the R.C.M.P. reports, was set up in 1971 to provide a further source of input on security matters. There is no intelligence agency, like the CIA in the United States or MI6 in England, for external espionage.[9]

The title of this paper, "National Security", has caused me considerable concern because, quite frankly, I do not know what national security means. It is one of those terms after which one should add the phrase "whatever that means", as Mr. Justice Black once did in the United States Supreme Court.[10] Some view the concept as one that they cannot define, but, like obscenity,[11] they know it when they see it. This was the view of the U.K. Committee of Privy Counsellors on Ministerial Memoirs, which in 1976 stated:

> National security is a vague enough idea in the conditions of the modern world and its subjects range much further afield than the simpler categories of earlier days, such as the plans of fortresses or the designs of warships or aeroplanes. Nevertheless, experience has shown that, when it comes to a practical issue turning on a particular set of facts, it is not usually difficult to agree whether they fall within or without the security net.[12]

However, the term "national security" is used here as a convenient way of describing a range of problems that come under that label.

Three topics have been chosen for the purpose of this paper: the Official Secrets Act, wiretapping, and emergency legislation. These three topics — if my reading of the *New Statesman* is accurate — are also relevant in Britain today.

2. THE OFFICIAL SECRETS ACT

The Canadian Official Secrets Act[13] passed in 1939 is very similar to

---

8 Report of the Royal Commission on Security (abridged), June, 1969.

9 See Wm. and Nora Kelly, *Policing in Canada* at p. 510 (1976).

10 *Berger v. N.Y.* (1967), 388 U.S. 41 at 88.

11 See the comment of Mr. Justice Potter Stewart in *Jacobellis v. Ohio*, (1964), 378 U.S. 184 at 197.

12 Cmnd. No. 6386, at p. 18 (1976).

13 R.S.C. 1970, c. O-3, as amended.

the present British Official Secrets Acts. The Canadian 1939 Act combined into one Act the 1911[14] and 1920[15] British Acts.

The Act is complicated because it deals with two separate, although sometimes related, concepts: espionage (section 3) and leakage (*i.e.* the improper disclosure of government information) (section 4). To add to the complication, the comparable sections in the British legislation are numbered differently: the British espionage section is section 1 and the leakage section is section 2.

Most of the concern over the Act in recent years has related to the leakage provisions. Recent prosecutions in Canada against an engineer, Peter Treu,[16] and a newspaper, the Toronto *Sun*,[17] involved the leakage sections. In Britain, concern over the Act also relates to the leakage provisions. This led to a report in 1972 by a Departmental Committee under the Chairmanship of Lord Franks,[18] which recommended a number of changes in the Act. In July 1978 the British Government issued a White Paper on the subject.[19]

A brief history of the legislation will assist in understanding why it was passed. The first Official Secrets Act was promulgated in Britain in 1889.[20] In the decade before that Act there were a number of incidents that caused the British Government considerable concern about the improper use of secret government information.[21] For example, in 1878 a disgruntled clerk by the name of Marvin divulged to a newspaper for compensation a secret Anglo-Russian treaty concerning the Congress of Berlin. He was charged with stealing the paper upon which the treaty was written, but because he had only memorized the treaty the prosecution was unsuccessful. Another government employee, Terry, in 1887, had escaped a conviction for selling, possibly to a foreign power, tracings of warships. This latter incident led the First Lord of the Admiralty to make the obvious point in the House of Commons that "The law at present is

---

14   Official Secrets Act, 1911, 1 & 2 Geo. 5, c. 28.

15   Official Secrets Act, 1920, 10 & 11 Geo. 5, c. 75.

16   The judgment of Trudel J. is appended to the House of Commons Debate of June 9, 1978. Treu's convictions were reversed on appeal to the Quebec Court of Appeal and acquittals entered; *R. v. Treu* (1979), 49 C.C.C. (2d) 222.

17   *R. v. Toronto Sun Publishing Ltd.* (1979), 47 C.C.C. (2d) 535 (Ont. Prov. Ct.).

18   Report of the Departmental Committee on Section 2 of the Official Secrets Act 1911, Cmnd. No. 5104 (London 1972) (hereinafter cited as "The Franks Report").

19   Reform of Section 2 of the Official Secrets Act 1911, Cmnd. No. 7285 (July, 1978). A Summary of the White Paper appears in *The Times,* July 20, 1978 at p. 4.

20   Official Secrets Act, 1889, 52 & 53 Vict., c. 52.

21   For the background to the Acts, see generally Williams, *Not in the Public Interest: The Problem of Security in Democracy* at pp. 15-20 (1965); Aitken, *Officially Secret* 7-14 (1971); Bunyan, *The History and Practice of the Political Police in Britain* 5-6 (1977); The Franks Report, Appendix III.

not, in my judgment, in a satisfactory state so far as it bears upon offences of this kind."[22]

As the First World War approached, there was concern that the espionage parts of the Act did not go far enough. The Act did not prevent German agents from holidaying in England and photographing harbours and other strategic, although not technically "prohibited", areas. Moreover, it was thought to be too difficult to prove under the 1889 Act that the accused possessed the information with the intention of communicating it to a foreign State or to any agent of a foreign State. A new Act was therefore introduced and passed with very little debate in 1911 at the time of the Agadir incident (a German gunboat had entered Agadir harbour in Morocco, thereby threatening French, and consequently British, interests).[23] The Act created a number of presumptions in the Crown's favour relating to assisting a foreign State, and also made it an offence, with a three year *minimum* penalty, to obtain or communicate "any . . . information which . . . might be . . . useful to an enemy". The latter provision prevented Germans from openly obtaining strategic information. Although the Act used the word "enemy", it was later interpreted as including a "potential enemy".[24] The Government, while stressing the espionage sections, used the occasion to broaden the anti-leakage section to make those who *received* official information (often the press) also guilty of an offence. It is, in fact, this extension in 1911 to the receiver that has turned out to be the most controversial section of the Act.

This 1911 Act was made applicable to the Dominions overseas and thus became part of the law of Canada. Further British legislation enacted in 1920 made permanent certain wartime Defence of the Realm regulations which the Government wished to preserve in peacetime. Not only was there the threat of communism made vivid by the Russian Revolution,[25] but there was great concern over the activities of the I.R.A. and the possibility of civil war in Ireland. The 1920 legislation was not applied to Canada because, in the words of the Attorney General, Gordon Hewart, "the Dominions and India have under contemplation legislation

---

22 3 Parl. Deb., H.C. (Brit.) col. 20 (1887). Note that the Ontario Court of Appeal would probably arrive at a different result if the question arose today: see *R. v. Stewart* (1983), 10 W.C.B. 150 holding that information consisting of a copy of a list of employees can be the subject of a charge of theft.

23 Aitken, *supra* note 21 at p. 19.

24 *R. v. Parrott* (1913), 8 Cr. App. R. 186. See also Williams, *supra* note 21 at pp. 31-32.

25 See Bunyan, *supra* note 21 at p. 10. "Many observers", writes Iain McLean, "both at the time and later, thought that 1919 marked the high point for the prospects of the British revolution." ("Red Clydeside, 1915-1919", in *Popular Protest and Public Order* (Quinault and Stevenson eds. 1974).)

which goes somewhat further".[26] However, no such legislation was ever enacted.

As mentioned above, the 1939 Canadian legislation combined into one Act the 1911 and 1920 British Acts. The Minister of Justice, Ernest Lapointe, stated in the House of Commons in introducing the legislation on April 12, 1939 that "the purpose of the Bill is to consolidate the two Acts and, by an Act of the Parliament of Canada, make them the law of this country".[27]

The 1969 Report of the Royal Commission on Security (the Mackenzie Report) accurately described the Act as "an unwieldy statute, couched in very broad and ambiguous language",[28] and concluded that "Consideration should be given to a complete revision of the Canadian Official Secrets Act".[29] There seems to be general agreement with that conclusion. The question is: what revisions should be made?

One of the most difficult questions that has to be faced under the espionage section — and the only one to be discussed here — is the type of information that is, or should be, subject to a criminal penalty.[30]

Canadian courts on a number of occasions have stated that only "secret official" information is subject to the Act.[31] The Canadian espionage section, like the British section, provides that "Every person is guilty of an offence . . . who, for any purpose prejudicial to the safety or interests of the State, . . . communicates to any other person any *secret official* code word, or pass word, or any sketch, plan, model, article, or note, or other document or information that . . . might be . . . directly or indirectly useful to a foreign power."[32] The question is, do the words "secret official", italicized here, refer only to code words and possibly passwords or do they qualify all of the list including the word "information"? As mentioned above, the courts in Canada have opted for the latter interpretation. But this interpretation cannot be correct. The words "secret official" did not appear in Britain in the 1889 or 1911 Acts. They were, in fact, added by a Schedule at the end of the 1920 Act and were referred to in the Act itself as "minor

---

26 12 Parl. Deb., H.C. (Brit.) col. 969 (1920).

27 4 Parl. Deb., H.C. (Can.) at p. 2705 (1939).

28 Report of the Royal Commission on Security (abridged), 1969, at p. 75.

29 *Ibid.,* at p. 78.

30 For the U.S. experience see Edgar and Schmidt, "The Espionage Statutes and Publication of Defense Information", (1973), 73 Colum. L. Rev. 929 who devote 150 printed pages to this issue.

31 See *Regina v. Biernacki,* 1961, Judgment No. 5626, Court of Preliminary Inquiry, District of Montreal, reported on another point in 37 C.R. 226 (Que.); *Boyer v. R.* (1948), 7 C.R. 165 (Que. C.A.); *R. v. Toronto Sun Publishing Ltd.,* (1979), 47 C.C.C. (2d) 535 (Ont. Prov. Ct.); see also the Report of the Commission of Inquiry into Complaints Made by George Victor Spencer (Ottawa 1966), at p. 57.

32 S. 3(1). Italics added.

details".[33] No one suggested that by adding these words they were changing the meaning of the 1911 Act. It is known that the 1911 Act was introduced in part to control the activities of German agents who were openly collecting information that was clearly not secret or official information (*e.g.*, sketching harbours). So it is not at all surprising that in Britain, to quote the Franks Committee, "it is clear that the words 'secret official' qualify only the words 'code word, or pass word' ".[34] Not only is this the interpretation given to the espionage section, but in the leakage section, where the words "secret official" are also used, it has been held in Britain that the information under the section need be only "of an official character" and not necessarily secret.[35] When Canada enacted the Official Secrets Act in 1939 there was no indication that a substantial departure from the 1911 and 1920 British legislation was intended. Nevertheless, the espionage section has been judicially restricted to "secret official" information.

If the information need not be "secret official", are there any limitations? Should all information be subject to the espionage legislation? Should it be an offence, for example, for a person, as in one Canadian case,[36] to supply the Russians with outwardly innocuous information on such matters as names, with dates of birth and death, gathered from tombstones in local cemeteries? This can be important information. The Russians would then be able to send in an agent with a birth certificate and other fake documentation who would take on the identity of one of the deceased. Since the real person is dead, the chances of detection are lessened. Should it be an offence to provide the Russians with clippings from newspapers and magazines?

Perhaps the solution to these problems is to include in the section all information which is given for a prejudicial purpose but to provide a defence similar to that found in the wartime Defence of Canada Regulations, which provided that no one would be guilty if he communicated information that "has, before being so ... communicated, appeared, or is fairly deducible from information which has appeared, in any printed publication or publications distributed to the

---

33 Official Secrets Act, 1920, 10 & 11 Geo. 5, c. 75, s. 10.

34 The Franks Report, at p. 125.

35 See *R. v. Crisp and Homewood* (1919), 83 J.P. 121, where a government employee who supplied and a tailor who received information relating to contracts for military uniforms were found guilty of violating the leakage section. It should be noted, however, that the trial judge, Avory J., said that "there is evidence that these documents were official secrets". See also the same interpretation as in *Crisp and Homewood* by Mars-Jones J. in the *Aubrey, Berry and Campbell Case,* discussed in Nicol, "Official Secrets and Jury Vetting", [1979] Crim. L. Rev. 284, at pp. 288-89.

36 See the Report of the Commission of Inquiry into Complaints Made by George Victor Spencer (Ottawa 1966).

public in Canada through government or normal commercial channels".[37]
This would allow foreign agents, including, of course, those with diplomatic immunity, to collect information from newspapers, books, and
official published reports, which foreign Governments undoubtedly do
now, but would prevent them from going out to collect this information
themselves if it was to be used *for a prejudicial purpose*. The Security Service
could still, therefore, consider it a breach of the Official Secrets Act for a
foreign agent to take photographs of pipelines, dams, and harbours which
could be used by the foreign country for sabotage purposes or for
bombing in the event of a war. (This may be an unrealistic example today
because of satellite reconnaissance; other examples might include
collecting unpublished scientific matters.) In the event of an actual war,
regulations could be brought in making the disclosure of *any* information
for a prejudicial purpose an offence.

Another approach which attempts to achieve much the same result is
that found in the as yet unimplemented U.S. Report on Reform of the
Federal Criminal Laws of 1971, the Brown Commission Report.[38] The
Report provides that a person should be guilty of the offence of espionage
if he "reveals national security information to a foreign power or agent
thereof with intent that such information be used in a manner prejudicial
to the safety or interest of the United States".[39]

The word "reveals" is used, according to the Commission's comment on the section, "to deal with problems raised in connection with the
transmittal of information in the public domain. It permits a court to
distinguish between the assembly and analysis of such information so as to
constitute a revelation, and the simple transmittal of, for example, a
daily newspaper."[40]

As in Canada, the judicial construction of the type of information
covered in the U.S. Espionage Act of 1917, *i.e.* "information relating to the
national defence",[41] has caused problems in the past. The U.S. Supreme
Court suggested in *Gorin v. U.S.* in 1941[42] that communicating to a foreign
power information already made public would not be an offence. This was
extended by Judge Learned Hand in *U.S. v. Heine*[43] to the compilation

---

37 S. 16(3)(a). See *Boyer v. R.,* *supra* note 31.

38 Final Report of the National Commission on Reform of Federal Criminal Laws
    (Proposed New Federal Criminal Code), 1971.

39 *Ibid.,* s. 1112(1)(a). The latest version, s. 1437, which was passed by the Senate in Jan.,
    1978 (but has been stalled in the House) does not attempt reform along these lines, but
    maintains the *status quo*; see ss. 1121 ff.

40 *Ibid.* at p. 87.

41 The U.S. Espionage Statutes are codified in 18 U.S.C. ss. 793-98.

42 (1941), 312 U.S. 19, at 28.

43 (1945), 151 F. 2d 813 (2d Cir.), *cert.* to the Supreme Court denied.

before war broke out in 1940 of extensive reports on the U.S. aviation industry for use by Germany. The information came from such sources as newspapers, catalogues, correspondence and interviews. The Brown Commission, like a number of critics of the decision, would, however, prohibit Heine's conduct in the future because of the interpretation that the courts would likely give to the word "reveals". Of course, if information is communicated to the enemy in wartime, then any simple disclosure of information, whether accompanied by any analysis or not, would be prohibited under another section. The well thought-out Brown Commission provisions are worth very careful consideration in any future redrafting of the Canadian — or British — espionage sections.

The more controversial aspect of the Official Secrets Act in Canada — and in Britain — is the leakage provision of the Act.

Under section 4(1)(a) of the Canadian Act, if a government employee or former employee "communicates . . . information to any person, other than a person to whom he is authorized to communicate with, or a person to whom it is in the interest of the State his duty to communicate it", he is guilty of an offence and liable to a fourteen-year penalty,[44] a ridiculously high penalty for such an offence.

Although the words "secret official" are used in the section, as was already seen, historically (and, one should add, grammatically) these can qualify only the words "code word" and possibly "pass word". Thus all government information, whether "classified" or not, is subject to the section. This is clearly the interpretation in England of section 2, the comparable section.[45] Although the espionage section requires a "purpose prejudicial to the safety or interests of the State", no such purpose is required for the leakage section. Thus the latter section is very broad.

The Franks Committee stressed the "catch-all" nature of the leakage section:

> The leading characteristic of this offence is its catch-all quality. It catches all official documents and information. It makes no distinctions of kind, and no distinctions of degree. All information which a Crown servant learns in the course of his duty is "official" for the purposes of section 2, whatever its nature, whatever its importance, whatever its original source. A blanket is thrown over everything; nothing escapes.[46]

A former Attorney General of England described the breadth of the British section by stating that section 2 "makes it a crime, without any possibility of a defence, to report the number of cups of tea consumed per week in a government department, or the details of a new carpet in the

---

44 Official Secrets Act, R.S.C. 1970, c. O-3, s. 15(1).

45 See The Franks Report, at 125 and *R. v. Crisp and Homewood* (1919), 83 J.P. 121.

46 The Franks Report at p. 14.

minister's room . . . The Act contains no limitation as to materiality, substance, or public interest."[47] If one substitutes "coffee" for "tea", the comment would be equally applicable in Canada.

The most controversial section of the Official Secrets Act is the one that affects the Press, section 4(3). This subsection provides that

> Every person who receives any . . . information, knowing, or having reasonable ground to believe, at the time when he receives it, that the . . . information is communicated to him in contravention of this Act, is guilty of an offence under this Act, unless he proves that the communication to him of the . . . information was contrary to his desire.

A recent prosecution against the Toronto *Sun*[48] was the first such prosecution against a newspaper in Canada. There have been a number in Britain.[49] The *Sun* had published a document designated as "top secret" which outlined suspected Russian espionage activity in Canada. The Judge dismissed the prosecution at the preliminary hearing on the ground that the information was already in the public domain (to use his phrase, the document was now "shopworn"). But the information had not been officially released and one wonders whether it is a correct interpretation of the section to give *carte blanche* to publish information merely because some of it has already been improperly leaked.

The recent British White Paper sensibly proposes that the "mere receipt of protected information" should not be a criminal offence, but that communication by the recipient should be.[50] This, of course, may not satisfy the desire of some sections of the Press to be able to print improperly leaked information without fear of prosecution.

There is no question that the leakage section is too wide and imposes criminal liability in many unnecessary cases. Most of these cases could be handled as they now are by disciplinary action. The proposal in the British White Paper limiting criminal liability to a narrow range of cases in a new Official Information Act makes good sense. The Franks Committee in 1972 had made recommendations with respect to criminal liability. The British Government White Paper in general adopted the Franks Committee Report. The White Paper would not, however, use the criminal law in a number of areas proposed by the Franks Committee, such as improper disclosure of the value of sterling and most Cabinet documents,[51] but

---

47 Sir Lionel Heald, Q.C. in *The Times,* March 20, 1970 at p. 13, cited by Williams, "Official Secrecy and the Courts", in *Reshaping the Criminal Law* 160-61 (Glazebrook ed. 1978).

48 *R. v. Toronto Sun Publishing Ltd. supra* note 17.

49 See Aitken, *supra* note 21, for a discussion of the *Sunday Telegraph* prosecution. See also Crane, "Freedom of the Press and National Security" (1975), 21 McGill L.J. 148 at p. 152, and Bunyan, *supra* note 21, at p. 10.

50 Reform of Section 2 of the Official Secrets Act 1911, Cmnd. No. 7285, at p. 17 (1978).

51 *Ibid.,* at pp. 9-10.

would extend criminal liability in other areas such as confidences held by, and not as the Franks Committee had recommended just to confidences given *to*, the Government. The White Paper recommended that the criminal law be used to protect government information relating to defence and internal security, international relations, law and order, and confidences of the citizen, which had all been recommended by the Franks Committee, and added a further category, intelligence and security.

Criminal liability for disclosure of information, according to the British White Paper, would not be uniform and would vary from category to category. In the case of defence, internal security and international relations, criminal liability would be restricted to the disclosure of information which would "seriously damage" the interests of the State (i.e., the "secret" classification), whereas all confidences held by the Government would be protected, whatever harm their disclosure might cause. In the case of security and intelligence information, the White Paper concludes that "information relating to security and intelligence matters is deserving of the highest protection whether or not it is classified". "This is pre-eminently an area", states the White Paper, "where the gradual accumulation of small items of information, apparently trivial in themselves, could eventually create a risk for the safety of an individual or constitute a serious threat to the interests of the nation as a whole".

One key question is whether a court should be able to review the classification given to a document. In the past this has not been an issue in Britain or, I suggest, in Canada because all Government information, whether classified or not, is covered by the Act. The Mackenzie Commission had recommended that in any new legislation the Minister's designation be conclusive.[52] The Franks Committee also took the position that decisions about classification should be reserved to the Government,[53] but recommended a safeguard[54] which required the appropriate Minister to certify that "at the time of the alleged disclosure" (as distinct from the time of classification) the information was properly classified. In my opinion, before criminal liability is imposed, the court, and not just the Minister, should be satisfied that the information fits the definition in the Act.

Legislation was introduced by the Conservative Government in Britain in October 1979,[55] but was withdrawn by the Government shortly

---

52 Report of the Royal Commission on Security, at p. 77.

53 The Franks Report, at p. 55 ff.

54 *Ibid.,* at p. 61.

55 Protection of Official Information Bill; see (1979), 129 New L.J. at p. 1063.

after the Anthony Blunt affair brought the proper scope of the proposed legislation into question.

In Canada, the McDonald Commission[56] recommended that "the espionage offences be placed in the Criminal Code or in a separate statute" and that the Official Secrets Act be repealed. The Commission recommended a wide definition of "information", stating:[57] "We are convinced that any provision relating to espionage should cover the disclosure of, or an overt act with the intention to disclose, information whether accessible to the public or not, either from government sources or private sources, if disclosure is, or is capable of being, prejudicial to the security of the state." No legislation along these lines has yet been introduced. The responsibility for producing draft legislation seems to have fallen to the Law Reform Commission of Canada as part of its overall review of the Criminal Code.

Canada has, however, unlike England, recently passed Freedom of Information legislation.[58] There is an interrelationship between Freedom of Information legislation and the Official Secrets Act. They deal with the opposite sides of the same coin. A Freedom of Information Act says what Government information *must* be released on request. The Official Secrets Act says what *must not* be improperly released. Thus the two Acts deal with different concepts. Yet they are interrelated in that the Official Secrets Act creates, as the Franks Committee points out, "a general atmosphere of unnecessary secrecy . . . a general aura of secrecy".[59] Similarly, a Canadian Government Green Paper of 1977, *Legislation on Public Access to Government Documents*,[60] points out that the "broad scope of the Official Secrets Act", *inter alia*, "constitutes a substantial disincentive to any public servant releasing government documents to a citizen".

3. WIRETAPPING

The second major area to be discussed here is wiretapping. Canadian legislation giving the police the right to wiretap came into force in June, 1974. This law, named, or, arguably,[61] misnamed, the Protection of Privacy Act, has two main components. It amends the Criminal Code to enable the police — and only the police — to wiretap with a judicial

---

56 Second Report at p. 939.

57 First Report at p. 14.

58 Access to Information and Privacy Acts S.C. 1980-81-82-83, c. 111.

59 Report of the Departmental Committee on Section 2 of the Official Secrets Act 1911, at p. 31.

60 June, 1977, at pp. 14-15.

61 An opposition amendment in Committee to entitle the Act the Interception of Private Communications Act was defeated only by the Chairman's deciding vote; *Justice and Legal Affairs* (No. 29) at 5 (Nov. 13, 1973).

warrant in ordinary criminal cases, and it also amends the Official Secrets Act to allow for the interception and seizure of communications with a Solicitor General's warrant in certain cases involving national security.

The wiretapping law was designed to control improper electronic surveillance and at the same time to make it clear that in certain circumstances wiretapping and other forms of electronic surveillance were permitted. Before then the legality of wiretapping was said not to be clear.[62] It was clear, however, that wiretapping was taking place.[63] The United States had introduced wiretapping legislation in 1968,[64] and the Canadian Ouimet Committee in 1969,[65] as well as the Federal Justice and Legal Affairs Committee in 1970,[66] recommended that comparable legislation be enacted in Canada. Once again Canada followed closely behind the U.S. Legislation was passed in 1973[67] and came into force in June, 1974. (Amendments were proposed in 1976, the so-called "Peace and Security" legislation, and were eventually passed in August, 1977.[68])

The procedure for wiretapping in cases involving national security differs from that for ordinary police matters. The Ouimet Committee considered "that wiretapping and electronic eavesdropping in matters affecting national security is within the sphere of the executive branch of government".[69] The Mackenzie Commission on security, which reported at about the same time as the Ouimet Committee, stated: "We think it important that any such legislation should contain a clause or clauses exempting interception operations for security purposes from the provisions of the statute" and further that "control should be ministerial rather than judicial".[70] Electronic surveillance in national security matters, in line with these studies, was therefore handled separately, with separate procedures set out in section 16 of the Official Secrets Act.[71] Section 16 reads in part as follows:

> 16. (2) The Solicitor General of Canada may issue a warrant authorizing the interception or seizure of any communication if he is satisfied by evidence on oath that

---

62 See the Report of the Canadian Committee on Corrections (1969), at 82; Beck, "Electronic Surveillance and the Administration of Criminal Justice", 46 *Can. B. Rev.* 643 (1968).

63 Report of the Canadian Committee on Corrections (1969), at p. 82.

64 Title III of the Omnibus Crime Control and Safe Streets Act, 18 U.S.C. Secs. 2510-20.

65 Report of the Canadian Committee on Corrections (1969), at pp. 80-88.

66 116 H.C. Jour. (No. 84) at p. 553 ff. (March 11, 1970).

67 Protection of Privacy Act, S.C. 1973-74, c. 50.

68 Criminal Law Amendment Act, 1977, S.C. 1976-77, c. 53.

69 *Supra* note 63 at p. 83.

70 Report of the Mackenzie Commission at p. 102.

71 As enacted 1973, c. 50, s. 6.

such interception or seizure is necessary for the prevention or detection of subversive activity directed against Canada or detrimental to the security of Canada or is necessary for the purpose of gathering foreign intelligence information essential to the security of Canada.

(3) For the purposes of subsection (2), "subversive activity" means

(a) espionage or sabotage;

(b) foreign intelligence activities directed toward gathering intelligence information relating to Canada;

(c) activities directed toward accomplishing governmental change within Canada or elsewhere by force or violence or any criminal means;

(d) activities by a foreign power directed toward actual or potential attack or other hostile acts against Canada; or

(e) activities of a foreign terrorist group directed toward the commission of terrorist acts in or against Canada.

One obvious difference in procedure is with respect to notice of the wiretap. Under the Criminal Code, notice must be given to the person whose telephone has been tapped or whose place has been electronically monitored ninety days after the surveillance has ended (with the possibility of extension).[72] This is a desirable technique for limiting the extent of police wiretapping. But the Security Service cannot, without serious international repercussions, notify a foreign government that the Government has been electronically monitoring its embassy. So section 178.23(2) of the Code exempts these cases from the disclosure requirement. It is left for others to analyze the question whether it is proper or legal to monitor embassies electronically. The Canadian Diplomatic and Consular Privileges and Immunities Act of 1977 provides that certain international conventions "have the force of law in Canada in respect of all countries".[73] One of these conventions provides that "The premises of the mission shall be inviolable."[74] But one should take note of section 2 of the Act, as follows:[75]

> If it appears to the Secretary of State for External Affairs that the privileges and immunities accorded to the Canadian diplomatic mission or to a consular post in any country, or to persons connected therewith, are less than those conferred by this Act on that country's diplomatic mission or consular post, as the case may be, or on persons connected therewith, he may by order withdraw from that country's mission or from any or all of that country's posts or from any or all persons connected therewith such of the privileges and immunities so conferred as he deems proper.

In any event, the Official Secrets Act covers a much wider area than the electronic monitoring of members of foreign embassies and consulates. It involves, for example, "sabotage" and solely internal

---

72 Code s. 178.23.

73 S.C. 1976-77, c. 31, which incorporates parts of the Vienna Convention on Diplomatic Relations and the Vienna Convention on Consular Relations.

74 Art. 22, Convention on Diplomatic Relations.

75 S. 2(4), as re-enacted 1980-81-82-83, c. 74, s. 1.

subversive "activities directed toward accomplishing governmental change within Canada or elsewhere by force or violence or any criminal means". There is no reason why notice of wiretapping should not be given in such cases. There can be no "official" embarrassment in giving notice and it would help ensure that abuses did not take place. Of course, the Security Service would likely object to giving notice; but even with respect to wiretapping in ordinary criminal cases the police are far from happy with the notice provisions.

A further difference between taps and electronic monitoring under the Code and those under the Official Secrets Act is that the former are to investigate a specific offence whereas under the Official Secrets Act the surveillance can be for broader purposes, such as "gathering foreign intelligence information essential to the security of Canada".[76] Even in relation to "subversive activity" the electronic surveillance may be for "prevention" as well as "detection". Thus the 60-day limit on taps[77] under the Criminal Code may well be too short for the type of operations conducted under the Official Secrets Act. The Annual Report for 1978 by the Solicitor General of Canada under the Official Secrets Act shows that there were just under 400 warrants issued in 1978 with an average length of almost 250 days.[78] In contrast, the approximately 700 warrants issued under the Criminal Code in 1978 had an average length of almost 75 days.[79] If an electronic monitor is placed in an embassy, one would expect it to stay in place for a lengthy period of time. But once again, this same lengthy time-frame might be unreasonable for internal subversive operations for which a time limit closer to that found in the Criminal Code might be more reasonable.

The Solicitor General's Annual Report under the Official Secrets Act[80] is far less detailed than the Annual Reports under the Code.[81] When the legislation was first introduced in 1972 no Report to Parliament was envisaged: the reporting section merely stated that "The Commissioner of the Royal Canadian Mounted Police shall from time to time make a report to the Solicitor General of Canada with respect to each warrant issued . . . setting forth particulars of the manner in which the warrant was used and

---

76 S. 16(2), as enacted 1973, c. 50, s. 6.

77 Code s. 178.13(2)(e); but with further 60-day renewals.

78 Solicitor General's Annual Report, 1978, to the Governor-General as required by s. 16(5) of the Official Secrets Act. In 1977, 471 warrants were issued, with an average length of 244.55 days.

79 Solicitor General's Annual Report, 1978, to Parliament as required by the Criminal Code of Canada, s. 178.22. These figures do not include 10 warrants granted under the emergency provision, s. 178.15, which last a maximum of 36 hours. In 1977, 605 warrants were issued, with an average length of 61.3 days.

80 As required by s. 16(5).

81 As required by s. 178.22.

the results, if any, obtained from such use."[82] But the Justice and Legal Affairs Committee inserted the reporting provision contained in the present legislation.[83]

In Britain, figures are not released on a regular basis. The Birkett Report of 1957, a Report by a Committee of Privy Councillors which approved the use of wiretapping with a warrant from the Secretary of State, said:

> We are strongly of the opinion that it would be wrong for figures to be disclosed by the Secretary of State at regular or irregular intervals in the future. It would greatly aid the operation of agencies hostile to the State if they were able to estimate even approximately the extent of the interceptions of communications for security purposes.[84]

A further difference between the Code and the Official Secrets Act is that while the Criminal Code is directed only at the *interception* of communications, the Official Secrets Act refers to the interception *or seizure* of any communication. The word "communication" is not defined; however, there is no reason to limit it to auditory or visual communications. It could encompass written documents as well. It would not seem to be wide enough, however, to include non-documentary "physical intelligence".

The main difference between the Official Secrets Act and the Code provisions is, of course, that the Solicitor General (in Canada a member of the Cabinet), rather than a judge, grants the authorization. This is in line with the Mackenzie and Ouimet recommendations mentioned above. There is likely no constitutional argument in Canada, as there is in the United States,[85] against Parliament adopting this distinction. The question of the wisdom of doing so is another matter.

, In my opinion, judicial warrants should be required in these cases, with the possible exception of the surveillance of foreign embassies and foreign agents. This use of the judiciary will act as a barrier to a Government using electronic surveillance for internal political purposes. The concept of "subversion" is open to political abuse because, as U.S. Supreme Court Justice Robert Jackson said in 1940 when he was Attorney

---

82 Bill C-6, s. 6 (Feb. 21, 1972).

83 *Justice and Legal Affairs* (No. 29) at p. 4 (Nov. 13, 1973).

84 Report of the Committee of Privy Councillors Appointed to Inquire into the Interception of Communications, Sept. 18, 1957, Cmnd. No. 283, at 27. In April, 1980 the British Government released an 8-page White Paper, The Interception of Communications in Great Britain, Cmnd. No. 7873, bringing "up to date the account given" in The Birkett Report. The White Paper stated that "the Government does not propose to disclose figures regularly in the future". As an exceptional measure, however, it gave figures in the Report indicating the extent of interceptions in the past. In 1979, for example, there were 411 telephone warrants issued in England and 56 in Scotland.

85 See *U.S. v. U.S. Dist. Ct.* (1972), 92 S. Ct. 2125, usually referred to as the *Keith* case.

General: "Those who are in office are apt to regard as 'subversive' the activities of any of those who would bring about a change of administration."[86] The U.S. Church Committee stated that its "examination of forty years of investigations into 'subversion' has found the term to be so vague as to constitute a license to investigate almost any activity of practically any group that actively opposes the policies of the administration in power".[87] A former R.C.M.P. Deputy Commissioner recently gave the following definition: "To subvert is to overturn, upset, effect the destruction or overthrow of such things as religion, monarchy, the constitution, principles or morality".[88] Few people could escape being caught by that definition. Section 16 of the Official Secrets Act does define subversion, but any definition will necessarily be vague. The best control is judicial control.

In the United States, domestic security surveillance can be done only *with* a judicial warrant. The U.S. Foreign Intelligence Surveillance Act of 1978,[89] however, permits a very limited amount of electronic surveillance without a warrant. The Act provides that the President, through the Attorney General, can authorize electronic surveillance without a court order to acquire foreign intelligence information for periods of up to one year if the Attorney General certifies in writing under oath that the communication is between or among foreign powers and that there is no substantial likelihood that the surveillance will acquire the contents of any communication to which a United States person is a party.[90] In other cases foreign intelligence information is obtained in the United States by virtue of a court order issued by one of seven district court judges publicly designated by the Chief Justice of the United States from seven of the U.S. judicial circuits. Each application, which requires the approval of the Attorney General, must contain certification by a very senior executive officer that the purpose of the surveillance is to obtain foreign intelligence information which cannot reasonably be obtained by normal investigative techniques. Similar procedures, including the transfer of the hearing to a place that would guarantee full security,[91] could be adopted in Canada — or Britain. Wiretapping in national security matters should, as far as possible, be brought more closely in line with the Criminal Code wiretapping provisions.

86 Cited in Final Report of the Select Committee to Study Government Operations with Respect to Intelligence Activities, U.S. Senate, April 26, 1976, Bk. 2, at p. 4.

87 *Ibid.,* at p. 319.

88 See Kelly, *supra* note 9, at p. 570.

89 Public Law, 95-511.

90 Ss. 102 ff.

91 See *U.S. v. U.S. Dist. Ct.,* *supra* note 85, and *Zweibon v. Mitchell,* (1975), 516 F. 2d 594 (C.A., D.C.).

Wiretapping has recently been the subject of intense discussion in Britain. There have been allegations that the extent of wiretapping is much greater than was contemplated at the time of the Birkett Report in 1957.[92] Moreover, Sir Robert Megarry examined the issue of wiretapping in the *Malone* case in 1979[93] and concluded that the present situation "cries out for legislation".[94] He upheld the right of the police to tap telephones, finding a statutory recognition (not, it should be noted, a very clear authorization) for the practice in section 80 of the Post Office (Reorganization) Act of 1969 which specifically refers to telecommunications. Unlike the position in Canada, the police in Britain do not attempt to use the wiretapping evidence in court, although they will use evidence discovered as a result of the tap.

The Birkett Report of 1957 recommended that the Secretary of State continue to issue warrants authorizing wiretapping as well as the opening of mail.[95] Mail opening has been engaged in for centuries in Britain, and has been recognized in successive Postal Acts.[96] The Home Secretary had argued that the power was based on the Royal Prerogative.[97] It was

---

92 *See e.g., New Statesman,* Feb. 1, 1980; *The Sunday Times,* Feb. 3, 1980; (1980) 13 New L.J. 126. The Government White Paper of April 1, 1980, The Interception of Communications in Great Britain, Cmnd. No. 7873, indicates that the number of warrants has not gone up dramatically, but it is not clear how comprehensive the figures are. Do they cover electronic interceptions outside the post-office? Or wiretapping for purposes of foreign intelligence?

In May, 1980, Lord Diplock, a senior Law Lord, was appointed by the Prime Minister to be the "continuous independent" monitor of that part of communications interception which is authorized by the Home Secretary. His terms of reference are: "To review on a continuing basis the purposes, procedures, conditions and safeguards governing the interception of communications on behalf of the police, H.M. Customs and Excise and the Security Service as set out in [the White Paper of 1 April] and report to the Prime Minister." *See The Times,* May 6, 1980. Lord Diplock's first report found that the procedures and controls were working satisfactorily: see The Interception of Communications in Great Britain (1981, Cmnd. 8191); *The Times,* March 4, 1981. Lord Diplock's second report in 1982, which was not published, again found that procedures continued to operate satisfactorily: see Duffy, "Secret Surveillance" [1982] Public Law 381. An attempt to place wiretapping on a legislative footing was defeated in the Commons in 1981: see "The Telephone Tapping Debate" (1981) 131 New Law J. 409.

93 *Malone v. Metro. Police Commr. (No. 2)* (1979) 69 Cr. App R. 168. See Williams, "Telephone Tapping", (1979) 38 Camb. L.J. 225. The *Malone* case was taken to the European Commission on Human Rights (see (1980) 130 New L.J. 126) which in January 1983 ruled 11-1 against Britain; the European Court of Human Rights was to hear the matter on Feb. 20, 1984: see the Sunday Times, Feb. 19, 1984.

94 *Ibid.* at 199.

95 Report of the Committee of Privy Councillors Appointed to Inquire into the Interception of Communications, 18 September 1957, Cmnd. No. 283.

96 *See, e.g.,* the Post Office Act of 1953, 1 & 2 Eliz. 2, c. 36, s 58.

97 The Government did not advance prerogative claims in the *Malone* case; see Williams, *supra* note 93, at 225.

necessary for him to stress the prerogative because if the basis was simply the language of the Postal Act then it would not apply to telephones. The Birkett Committee was obviously sympathetic to the view that the power to intercept rested on the prerogative, stating: "We have been impressed by the fact that many Secretaries of State in many Administrations for many years past have acted upon the view that the power to intercept communications was in the nature of a prerogative power."[98] But in the end the Committee did not decide the source of the power and simply said, "We favour the view that it rests upon the power plainly recognized by the Post Office statutes as existing before the enactment of the statutes, by whatever name the power is described."[99] This conclusion, however desirable, is inconsistent with *Entick v. Carrington,*[100] the celebrated 1765 decision in which Lord Camden held that search warrants could not be authorized by a Secretary of State, but only by a judicial officer. In order to distinguish the *Entick* case, the Committee did not read it as banning search warrants by the Secretary of State, but rather as banning the practice of issuing *general* warrants.[101] Having read *Entick v. Carrington* in this way, it was easy to accept the Home Secretary's argument that "there is a distinction to be drawn between the general warrants condemned by Lord Camden, and the limited, strictly governed use of the Secretary of State's warrant" in these cases.[102]

If the legislative route were to be followed in Britain, the procedures and safeguards found in the Canadian Criminal Code should be carefully examined. Judicial authorization in advance (at the Supreme or County Court level), notification to the object of the tap that his phone was tapped, limiting the duration of the tap, and reporting the extent of wiretapping have already been mentioned above. Additional controls found in Canadian legislation involve a criminal penalty for illegal tapping; a punitive civil penalty which can be awarded by the judge to the person subject to an illegal tap at the time that the tapper is sentenced; and the exclusion at any trial of evidence of any conversation obtained through an illegal tap, with a discretion in the trial judge also to exclude other evidence found as a result of the illegal tap.

Before leaving the topic of wiretapping, I would like to raise one obvious question that was neither squarely raised in Parliament in Canada nor in Congress in the United States. Can the police who have a warrant to tap surreptitiously enter a place in order to engage in electronic surveillance?

---

98 *Supra* note 95, para. 38.

99 *Ibid.,* para. 50.

100 (1765), 19 St. Tr. 1030.

101 *Supra* note 95 para. 23.

102 *Ibid.,* para. 25.

The question should have been dealt with because the Ouimet Committee had pointed out that "frequently electronic eavesdropping involves a trespassory invasion".[103] And the 1967 U.S. Supreme Court case of *Berger v. New York*,[104] which was brought to the attention of the Justice and Legal Affairs Committee,[105] had involved just such conduct. Nevertheless, the legislative debates in Canada are inconclusive on the point. There are hints both ways.

The U.S. wiretapping legislation also says nothing about the issue and the legislative debates, as in Canada, are inconclusive. Perhaps for political reasons in both countries, the politicians who thought about the issue did not want to face up to this awkward question.

The issue was dealt with by the U.S. Supreme Court in 1979 in *Dalia v. United States*.[106] Prior to this decision, the U.S. cases had gone in a number of different directions. In *Dalia*, seven out of the nine members of the Supreme Court held that it was constitutionally permissible for Congress to authorize covert entries to plant a monitoring device.[107] A majority of the Court also held that Congress had implicitly authorized such entries, stating: "Those considering the surveillance legislation understood that, by authorizing electronic interception of oral communications in addition to wire communications, they were necessarily authorizing surreptitious entries." The dissenting opinion stated that "it is most unrealistic to assume that Congress granted such broad and controversial authority to the Executive without making its intention to do so unmistakably plain". The majority also held that it was unnecessary, though preferable, for the judicial authorization specifically to include such an entry.

In Canada there have been a variety of judicial opinions on this difficult question. For example, a trial judge in Manitoba held that such entries are permissible,[108] but the Manitoba Court of Appeal, in an *obiter* opinion, disagreed.[109] Mr. Justice David McDonald, taking the same view as his McDonald Commission,[110] also held that these entries are not

---

103   Canadian Committee on Corrections (1969), at p. 81.

104   (1967), 388 U.S. 41.

105   Justice and Legal Affairs, June 10, 1969, at p. 1274.

106   (1979), 99 S. Ct. 1682.

107   The majority opinion was delivered by Powell J., concurred in by Burger C.J., and White, Blackmun and Rehnquist JJ. Stevens and Marshall JJ. dissented on all points; they wanted Congress to deal with the matter before the courts ruled on its constitutionality. Stewart and Brennan JJ. agreed with the majority's constitutional argument. Stewart J. did not dissent from the majority opinion that Congress had impliedly authorized entries.

108   *R. v. Dass* (1978), 3 C.R. (3d) 193.

109   47 C.C.C. (2d) 194 (1979). See generally Frankel, "Surreptitious Entry: Its 'Legality' and Effect on Admissibility" (1979), 22 Crim. L.Q. 112.

110   Second Report at p. 173.

permissible[111] and this position was recently upheld (3-2) by the Alberta Court of Appeal.[112] Other courts and federal and provincial Departments of Justice[113] have expressed the opposite view. The matter will likely be determined by the Supreme Court of Canada in a set of appeals from British Columbia[114] or on an appeal from the Alberta Court of Appeal. My prediction is that the Supreme Court of Canada by a bare majority will allow such an entry if the judicial order specifically permits it. It should be noted that in England Sir Robert Megarry did not deal with the legality of the situation "whereby anyone trespasses on to the premises of the subscriber or anyone else to affix tapping devices or the like".[115] It would be reasonably safe to predict, however, that without special legislation the English courts would not allow such activity, even with a warrant by a Secretary of State.

The best solution to this problem for future cases would be to spell out in the legislation whether or not surreptitious entry is permitted.

The McDonald Report recommended such a legislative solution to the surreptitious entry issue. They also recommended that responsibility for authorizing wiretaps be given to Federal Court judges and not to the Solicitor General, as section 16 of the Official Secrets Act now provides. A number of other safeguards were recommended by the Commission.[116] Bill C-157 transferred responsibility for approving national security wiretaps to Federal Court judges, but omitted some important safeguards, such as preventing judge-shopping, adding ministerial responsibility and providing a proper test to determine when warrants should be issued. These inadequacies are more fully spelled out in the writer's submission to the Senate's Pitfield Committee.[117] The Pitfield Committee Report[118] criticized the wiretapping aspects of the Bill, finding that the standard set for obtaining a warrant was "unreasonably low" and setting out criteria for the granting of warrants. The Report also dealt with the issue of potential judge-shopping. These concerns were, for the most part, met in the Bill introduced in January, 1984, which is now before the Justice and Legal Affairs Committee.

---

111 *Re Application for Authorization to Intercept Private Communications* (1982), 31 C.R. (3d) 31 (Alta. Q.B.).

112 *Re Reference to the Alberta Court of Appeal by Order-in-Council 84/83* dated Feb. 2, 1983, reasons for judgment delivered Dec. 7, 1983.

113 See the Report of the Federal/Provincial Committee of Criminal Justice Officials with Respect to the McDonald Commission Report, Ottawa, June 1983 at pp. 59 *et seq.*

114 *R. v. Lyons et al.* (1982), 69 C.C.C. (2d) 318 (B.C.C.A.).

115 *Malone v. Metro. Police Commr. supra* note 93, at 177.

116 Second Report at pp. 551 *et seq.*, 592 *et seq.*, 1019 *et seq.*

117 Sept. 12, 1983.

118 Paras. 56-62.

4. EMERGENCY POWERS

The final area to be dealt with here is Emergency Powers, and, in particular, the Canadian War Measures Act.[119]

The Canadian War Measures Act has been invoked three times, for the First and Second World Wars, and in October, 1970, during the Cross/ Laporte crisis. Pierre Laporte, a Quebec Cabinet Minister, and James Cross, a British diplomat, had been kidnapped by members of the F.L.Q. After Laporte had been found murdered the Trudeau Government invoked the War Measures Act and promulgated regulations at four o'clock in the morning. Hundreds of persons were then arrested under the regulations, which made it an offence to be a member of the F.L.Q. and gave the police special powers of search, arrest, and detention. The use of the War Measures Act in Quebec continues to be the subject of discussion and debate in Canada. The question to be discussed here is whether permanent legislation such as the War Measures Act is needed or whether some less drastic intermediate legislation would be desirable. One should first take a brief look at the history of the legislation.

The origin of the War Measures Act was the need for special powers when the First World War broke out on August 4, 1914. Britain passed its special legislation, the Defence of the Realm Act, known as DORA, on August 8. It took some time for the Canadian Parliament to assemble; the first session to discuss emergency legislation was not held until August 19. The Act was quickly passed without dissent on August 21 with just over half-an-hour of debate[120] and received the Royal Assent on August 22. In the meantime the Government had already acted to cope with the emergency, such as by detaining enemy ships, and the Act validated these actions.

The Canadian War Measures Act, passed a few weeks later, followed much the same pattern as DORA, permitting the Government to invoke the Act during "war, invasion, or insurrection, real or apprehended" and giving the executive broad power to pass regulations. It was, however, more all-embracing than the British legislation, and allowed the executive to make orders and regulations deemed "necessary or advisable for the security, defence, peace, order and welfare of Canada".[121] The regulations were to be in force only during "war, invasion or insurrection, real or apprehended",[122] but "the issue of a proclamation" by the Government was "conclusive evidence that war, invasion, or insurrection, real or ap-

---

119 S.C. 1914 (2nd sess.), c. 2; see now R.S.C. 1970, c. W-2.

120 See generally Haggart and Golden, *Rumours of War* (1971).

121 See now R.S.C. 1970, c. W-2, s. 3.

122 *Ibid.*, s. 6.

prehended, exists".[123] The draftsman of the Act[124] later stated that it was drafted in this form because "no man could foresee what it would need to contain to be effective and . . . the only effective Act would be one of a 'blanket' character, whereunder the Government could act free of question between Parliaments".[125] The Canadian Act was also more stringent than the British Act, permitting penalties of up to five years for breaches of the regulations compared to a three month penalty in England. Moreover, the Canadian Act permitted courts-martial of civilians, whereas in England this was not permitted except under very limited circumstances.[126]

The British legislation expired about a year after the end of the First World War, whereas the Canadian Act was never repealed. It is not clear whether the original intent was to make the Canadian Act a permanent one.[127] By way of contrast, DORA specifically applied only "during the continuance of the present war".[128] The language of the Canadian Act has specific reference to the existing hostilities; yet it refers to "war, invasion, or insurrection, real or apprehended", and if it was only to last during the war there would have been no need to refer to anything but war. So it is likely that the Government intended to keep the statute on the books. If, indeed, there was any thought of repealing the Canadian Act, the Winnipeg General Strike in 1919 would have convinced the Government that it was a desirable Act to have available.

Just before the British legislation expired, special *ad hoc* legislation was passed relating to Ireland,[129] as well as permanent emergency

---

123 *Ibid.*, s. 2.

124 William F. O'Connor. O'Connor was later Parliamentary Counsel to the Senate and in that capacity authored the well-known Report to the Senate in 1939 (O'Connor Report) relating to the British North America Act. Sir Robert Borden described him as "a capable man of strict integrity, but, occasionally somewhat eccentric" (letter dated Nov. 25, 1929, Borden Papers, Post 1921 Series, Folder 191, No. 156431).

125 O'Connor's views on the War Measures Act can be found in the notes he prepared for Sir Robert Borden's memoirs; Borden Papers, Memoir Notes at p. 182. Borden never published his memoirs, but his nephew, Henry Borden, edited *Robert Laird Borden: His Memoirs* (1938); see p. 458 for a brief reference to the introduction of the War Measures Act.

126 DORA as passed and amended in 1914 listed many offences triable by court-martial; see 4 & 5 Geo. 5, c. 29 and c. 63, and 5 & 6 Geo. 5, c. 8. These were drastically curtailed in 1915, trial by court-martial of a civilian British subject being permitted only in the event of invasion or other special military emergency; see 5 & 6 Geo. 5, c. 34.

127 Compare Haggart and Golden, *supra* note 120, at p. 92, who state that the Act was designed for this one emergency, with Tarnopolsky, *The Canadian Bill of Rights* (1975) at p. 324, who states it was "drafted so as to remain on the statute books to be invoked when deemed necessary by the executive".

128 4 & 5 Geo. 5, c. 29, s. 1.

129 Restoration of Order in Ireland Act, 1920, 10 & 11 Geo. 5, c. 31.

legislation relating to essential services. This permanent legislation, the Emergency Powers Act of 1920,[130] permits regulations to be passed if the essential services of the country, for example, the supply and distribution of food, water, fuel or light, are threatened. The British Act has been used in cases of labour unrest. It was first invoked in 1921 and since then in at least ten other cases,[131] including an eight-month period during the 1926 General Strike.

The Canadian War Measures Act was, of course, invoked for the Second World War. This time Canada had its emergency regulations ready. Indeed, the Act was invoked on September 1, 1939, prior to the formal Declaration of War on September 3.

The Canadian Act was amended in 1960 by the Act which introduced the Canadian Bill of Rights.[132] The amendment provides that a proclamation invoking the Act "shall be laid before Parliament forthwith after its issue, or, if Parliament is then not sitting, within the first fifteen days next thereafter that Parliament is sitting". This section further provides for parliamentary debate of a motion, when instituted by ten members, "praying that the proclamation be revoked", and, if both Houses so resolve, the proclamation shall cease to have effect. The 1960 legislation provides, however, that anything done under the authority of the War Measures Act "shall be deemed not to be an abrogation, abridgement or infringement of any right or freedom recognized by the Canadian Bill of Rights". Lester Pearson, then Leader of the Opposition, maintained that an effective Bill of Rights should restrict certain powers of the executive even in an emergency. He submitted that the Governor in Council should be expressly forbidden to act under the War Measures Act to deprive any Canadian citizen of his citizenship or to banish or exile any citizen in any circumstances. He further proposed a "limitation by law on the absolute and arbitrary power of the government to detain persons, even in wartime", but stopped short of recommending that detention without an early trial on properly laid charges should be expressly forbidden.[133] These proposals were not accepted, however. Prime Minister Diefenbaker pointed out that the Government's amendments "assured parliamentary control which has not previously existed under the War Measures Act".[134] Moreover, he suggested that a parliamentary committee should later be established to examine the operation of the War Measures Act. No such committee was ever set up.

---

130   1920, 10 & 11 Geo. 5, c. 55.

131   See Bunyan, *supra* note 21, at p. 54.

132   S.C. 1960, c. 44, s. 6.

133   See Parliamentary Debates, House of Commons (Can.), July 1, 1960, at pp. 5651-52.

134   *Ibid.*, Aug. 3, 1960 at p. 7506.

The third time the War Measures Act was invoked was, as mentioned before, on October 16, 1970, during the Cross/Laporte crisis. It will be left to others to analyze whether the invocation of the Act was, in fact, necessary or was done more for psychological reasons. Similarly it will remain for others to determine whether there was, in fact, an apprehended insurrection at the time.

It was, no doubt, a crisis and the Government wanted special powers to deal with it. In the first place, it wanted to create the offence of membership in the F.L.Q. The Government obtained special powers in the regulations to deal with this target group: power to arrest without warrant on suspicion,[135] to hold without bail[136] and to search on suspicion.[137] Moreover, the regulations made members of the Armed Forces peace officers for the enforcement of the regulations. These regulations were replaced on December 1, 1970 with a special Emergency Act,[138] which was very similar to the regulations, but with certain Bill of Rights safeguards made applicable.

One feature of the Regulations passed in October, 1970 deserves special mention and that is their quasi-retroactive nature. They were brought in at four in the morning and persons were then arrested and charged with being members of the F.L.Q. before they had a chance to renounce their membership. During the Second World War the Government gave notice of the groups that were to be proscribed and this gave persons an opportunity to leave the organizations. The recent and comparable British legislation proscribing the I.R.A. also handled this matter in a sensible way by stating that

> a person belonging to a proscribed organisation shall not be guilty of an offence under this section by reason of belonging to the organisation if he shows that he became a member when it was not a proscribed organisation and that he has not since he became a member taken part in any of its activities at any time while it was a proscribed organisation.[139]

It was the absence of such a provision in Canada which enabled the police to arrest so many persons.

The Government had great difficulty in obtaining convictions, however, for a very technical reason. The Regulations Act requires that a regulation be published in the *Canada Gazette* before a prosecution can be based on it,[140] and because the *Gazette* was not published until later that

---

135 Public Order Regulations, 1970, s. 9(1).

136 S. 7(1).

137 S. 10.

138 The Public Order (Temporary Provisions) Act, S.C. 1970-71-72, c. 2.

139 Prevention of Terrorism (Temp. Prov.) Act, 1976, c. 8, s. 1(6).

140 R.S.C. 1970, c. R-5. See generally Marx, "The 'Apprehended Insurrection' of October 1970 and the Judicial Function", (1972) 7 U. B.C.L. Rev. 55.

day the Government had difficulty in showing that the accused were still then members of the F.L.Q. The Government could have exempted the regulations from the Regulations Act, but perhaps at four in the morning no one thought of this important detail.

The courts have not allowed litigants to challenge the Government's proclamation that war or insurrection, real or apprehended, exists. The wisdom of using the Act is, therefore, left to the political process. The Bill of Rights cannot be used because, as previously stated, the War Measures Act is specifically exempted from its operation. The Canadian Charter of Rights and Freedoms[141] can, however, be used. There is no exemption of the War Measures Act in the Charter. The Government could specifically exempt regulations under the War Measures Act from the Charter by legislation (but not by regulation) under the override provision,[142] but let us assume it has not done so. Section 1 of the Charter is the section that would be used by the Government to justify encroachments. The section provides:

> The Canadian Charter of Rights and Freedoms guarantees the rights and freedoms set out in it subject only to such reasonable limits prescribed by law as can be demonstrably justified in a free and democratic society.

So, it seems, it would be up to the Government to demonstrate that there was an emergency and that the regulations under the War Measures Act were justified.

Both the European Convention on Human Rights, 1950,[143] and the International Covenant on Civil and Political Rights, 1966,[144] permit the overriding of rights in time of "public emergency threatening the life of the nation".[145] In both conventions, however, certain rights cannot be

---

141 Set out in Part I of the Constitution Act, 1982, as enacted by the Canada Act 1982 (U.K.), c. 11.

142 Ibid., s. 33.

143 T.S. No. 71; (1951) 45 Am. J. Int'l L., Supp. 24; entered into force 1953.

144 GAOR, 21st Sess., Supp. No. 16 (A/6316), at p. 49; (1967) 61 Am. J. Int'l L. 870; entered into force 1976.

145 European Convention, Art. 15; the International Covenant, Art. 4 is similar. Both permit derogation only "to the extent strictly required by the exigencies of the situation". The Covenant further requires that the emergency be "officially proclaimed", and that no derogation involve discrimination "solely on the ground of race, colour, sex, language, religion or social origin". Some specific rights can be restricted even though the life of the nation is not threatened. For example, freedom of movement within the territory (Art. 12) can be subjected to restrictions which "are necessary to protect national security, public order (ordre public), public health or morals or the rights and freedoms of others, and are consistent with the other rights recognized in the present Covenant".

overridden in any circumstances.[146] In the case of the International Covenant, to which Canada acceded on May 19, 1976,[147] these are the right to life,[148] the protection against cruel, inhuman, or degrading treatment or punishment,[149] the protection against slavery,[150] against imprisonment for debt,[151] against punishment for acts made crimes retroactively,[152] the right of every individual to be recognized as a person before the law,[153] and the right to freedom of thought, conscience and religion.[154] Since Canada is bound by the International Covenant and could be the subject of an international complaint,[155] regulations under the War Measures Act would have to meet the Standards of the International Covenant.

Should the Government introduce legislation which is less drastic than the War Measures Act? The Government had proposed in 1971 that a Special Joint Committee of the Senate and House "report upon the nature and kind of legislation required to deal with emergencies that may arise".[156] However, the Committee was never set up, probably because the Opposition wanted the Joint Committee to examine the facts surrounding

---

146 See generally Higgins, "Derogations under Human Rights Treaties", (1976-77) 48 Brit. Y.B. Int'l L. 281; O'Donnell, "States of Exception", (1978) 21 I.C.J. Rev. 52; Green, "Derogation of Human Rights in Emergency Situations", (1978) 16 Can. Y.B. Int'l L. 92.

147 Accession in force Aug. 19, 1976; see Order-in-Council P.C. 1976-1155 of May 18, 1976, and Fischer, "The Human Rights Covenants and Canadian Law", (1977) 15 Can. Y.B. Int'l L. 42, who deals with the problem of implementing the Covenant. Little consideration is there given to emergency powers except to note (at p. 50, note 40) that "The War Measures Act . . . does not appear to be entirely consistent with [the Article 4 derogation] requirements".

148 Art. 6.

149 Art. 7.

150 Art. 8(1) and (2).

151 Art. 11.

152 Art. 15. It is arguable, though by no means clear, that the quasi-retroactive regulations concerning F.L.Q. membership made under the War Measures Act in October 1970 would have breached this article had the Covenant been in force in Canada at the time.

153 Art. 16.

154 Art. 18. Subsection 3 adds that freedom to "manifest one's religion or beliefs may be subject only to such limitations as are prescribed by law and are necessary to protect public safety, order, health, or morals or the fundamental rights and freedoms of others".

155 Canada also acceded (Order-in-Council P.C. 1976-1156 of May 18, 1976) to the Optional Protocol to the International Covenant, which in Articles 1 and 2 gives to individuals within Canada who claim to be victims of a violation of the rights set forth in the Covenant the right to submit a written communication to the Human Rights Committee at the UN for consideration by the Committee.

156 Parl. Deb., H.C. (Can.), May 13, 1971, at 5778.

the use of the War Measures Act in October 1970. In 1975 the Government indicated that legislation was going to be introduced on the subject,[157] but no such legislation has yet been brought forward. Justice Minister Jean Chretien indicated in 1982 that he would like to see legislation allowing the police and Armed Forces to have emergency powers to deal with terrorists in Canada, but added that it was not a priority of his at the moment.[158]

Would such an Act be desirable? Presumably it would specify certain emergency powers relating to proscribed organizations and to arrest, bail and search which could be invoked by the Government without prior parliamentary approval when there was a serious threat to the internal security of the country.

There is much force, however, in the position taken by the Canadian Civil Liberties Association in opposing new intermediate legislation: "For the very reason that it is so politically difficult to invoke it is preferable that a Government have to choose between the enforcement of existing criminal legislation and the invocation of the War Measures Act."[159] If special legislation is needed to deal with a particular emergency it can, as in England with respect to I.R.A. terrorism, be passed by Parliament. Indeed, a good argument can be made that all threats to internal security, particularly those that are still in the "apprehended" stage, should be handled by the regular criminal law and by *ad hoc* emergency legislation. The War Measures Act could therefore be restricted to war and invasion, real or apprehended, and possibly also to actual insurrection. In the case of "apprehended" insurrection there would still be time to introduce special legislation. Because of the new closure rules in Canada introduced in 1969,[160] time limits can now more easily be put on the length of legislative debates than was formerly the case. These closure rules had not yet been tested in 1970.

Another change between 1970 and today which makes emergency legislation less necessary is that army personnel can be designated by Order in Council as peace officers under the Code, whether or not a request for assistance has been made by a province.[161] The existing criminal law gives peace officers relatively wide powers of arrest and search. Further, it is no longer necessary for the federal government to give the provinces and municipalities emergency power to prohibit assemblies — a power which was thought not to exist at the time of the invocation of the War Measures Act in 1970 — because the Supreme

---

157 See *ibid.*, Oct. 27, 1975 at p. 8557 and Oct. 29, 1975 at p. 8651.

158 *Globe and Mail,* Sept. 3, 1982.

159 Submissions to the Hon. John Turner Re Emergency Powers From the Canadian Civil Liberties Association, March 29, 1971 at p. 3.

160 See Stewart, *The Canadian House of Commons: Procedure and Reform,* (1977) Ch. 9.

161 S. 2(f) (ii) of the Code.

Court of Canada, in early 1978 in *Attorney General for Canada and Dupond v. Montreal,*[162] by a majority, upheld a Montreal by-law permitting the banning of parades. The decision upheld a section of the by-law which allowed the Executive Committee, when there are "reasonable grounds to believe that the holding of assemblies, parades or gatherings will cause tumult, endanger safety, peace or public order" to prohibit holding them "at all times or at the hours it shall set". Perhaps the one emergency power that might be added to the Criminal Code would permit a High Court judge, or possibly a panel of High Court judges, at the request of the government to issue a search warrant for a short period of time, possibly a few days, to conduct searches in defined areas based on less than reasonable and probable belief if there were a serious threat to public safety caused, for example, by the illegal possession of explosives or other dangerous substances. This would permit the police to search cars and buildings more widely than the existing law would now permit in the case, for example, of terrorist bombings (including the threatened use of nuclear weapons), or the theft of nuclear materials. An emergency provision such as this could also cover the search for victims of a kidnapping, as in the Cross/Laporte cases. Note that this would only widen the right to search under a judicial warrant, not the right to arrest or detain.

It was suggested above that a threat to internal security which is still at the stage of an apprehended insurrection be handled by the regular criminal law and *ad hoc* emergency legislation. If this approach is taken, it would be desirable to have *draft* legislation ready for enactment by Parliament should an internal emergency arise. This draft legislation should have undergone a thorough discussion and analysis by, say, the Justice and Legal Affairs Committee at a time when there was *no* emergency facing the country. This analysis would have no legal effect. The draft would remain a draft — to be enacted by Parliament if an emergency were to arise. The draft Act could include a number of options, both in terms of powers and safeguards, which Parliament could then enact depending on the nature of the emergency. Another possibility is to enact the legislation setting out the range of options, but require Parliament itself, rather than the Executive, to proclaim the parts of the Act which should be brought into operation.

The McDonald Commission Report did not recommend the adoption of legislation less drastic than the War Measures Act, stating[163]

> We are not convinced that a case has been made, from the point of view of national security, for the enactment of additional emergency powers legislation that would give the government special powers in situations falling short of 'war, invasion or

---

162 [1978] 2 S.C.R. 770.

163 Second Report at p. 921.

insurrection, real or apprehended'. When less grave emergencies occur or are apprehended, and the government wishes special powers, it should seek the approval of Parliament to special legislation.

The Commission recommended[164] that emergency powers set out in "draft regulations be debated in public *before* a crisis develops, to ensure that proper attention will be paid to civil liberties." "In our view", stated the Commission, "it would be an appropriate and useful step to have such draft regulations tabled and discussed in Parliament."

5. CONCLUSION

The three areas discussed in this paper raise fundamental issues concerning the conflict between the right of the individual to be free from oppressive government action and the right of the State to protect itself against serious threats to its security. Canada is searching for answers. Whether it will find the right ones remains to be seen.

---

164 *Ibid.* at p. 922.

6

CONTROLLING ENTRAPMENT*

1. INTRODUCTION

The use of undercover police officers and informers is an accepted technique of law enforcement. One danger in their use, however, is that they may go too far in encouraging or actively participating in improper conduct. How far is "too far"? Who determines what should be the dividing line between proper and improper conduct? What are the best techniques for ensuring that the police or their agents do not engage in this form of impropriety? These questions are the subject of this paper.

Undercover agents come in many different shapes and guises, but there are two basic categories: undercover police officers, and informers who co-operate with the police for pay or other consideration. In both

---

* This article was originally published in (1982) 32 U.T.L.J. 1 and is based on a paper prepared under contract for the Federal Commission of Inquiry Concerning Certain Activities of the RCMP (the McDonald Commission) and submitted to the Commission in March, 1980. The opinions expressed are, of course, the author's and do not necessarily represent the views of the Government or the Commission. The important Supreme Court of Canada case of *Amato v. R.* (1982), 69 C.C.C. (2d) 31, which came out after this article was prepared, is dealt with in the Addendum, Part 12 of this chapter, as is the Report of the McDonald Commission.

Some of the more recent law review articles on entrapment are: in Canada, Hutchinson and Withington, "Comment" (1980) 58 Can. Bar Rev. 376; Paterson, "Towards a defence of entrapment" (1979), 17 Osgoode Hall L.J. 261; Gold, "Entrapment" (1977-8), 20 Crim. L.Q. 166; Stober, "Entrapment" (1976), 7 Rev. Générale de Droit 25; Sneideman, "A judicial test for entrapment: The glimmerings of a Canadian policy on police-instigated crime" (1973) 16 Crim. L.Q. 81; in England, Oscapella, "A study of informers in England" [1980] Crim. L.R. 136; Allen, "Entrapment and exclusion of evidence" (1980) 43 Mod. L.R. 450; Heydon, "Entrapment and unfairly obtained evidence in the House of Lords" [1980] Crim. L.R. 129; Barlow, "Entrapment and the common law: Is there a place for the American doctrine of entrapment?" (1978) 41 Mod. L.R. 266; Ashworth, "Entrapment" [1978] Crim. L.R. 137; Smith, "Official instigation and entrapment" [1975] Crim. L.R. 12; Heydon, "The problems of entrapment" [1973] Camb. L.J. 268; in the United States, Gershman, "The 'Perjury Trap'" (1981) 129 U. Pa. L.R. 624; Cohen, "The need for an objective approach to prosecutorial misconduct" (1980) 46 Brooklyn L.R. 249; Cronin, "The law of entrapment in Massachusetts and the First Circuit" (1980) 14 Suffolk U. L.R. 1203; Kleven, "*People v. Barraza*: California's latest attempt to accommodate an objective theory of entrapment" (1980) 68 Cal. L.R. 746; Park, "The entrapment controversy" (1976) 60 Minn. L.R. 163; Dix, "Undercover investigations and police rulemaking" (1975) 53 Texas L.R. 203. See also the articles referred to in footnotes 16 and 195.

cases their conduct ranges from being passive observers to being active participants. But, as one sociologist has warned, "there are pressures inherent in the role that push the informant toward provocation".[1] Indeed, there is a risk that the agent may go even further. "The spy,"stated Chafee, "often passes over an almost imperceptible boundary into the *agent provocateur*, who instigates the utterances he reports, and then into the fabricator, who invents them."[2]

Let us first clear aside one type of informer, the co-operative accomplice who turns "Queen's Evidence" against his confederates. This category of informer raises a number of issues, legal and otherwise: for example, corroboration of the accomplice's testimony; granting immunity from prosecution; plea bargaining for testimony; the extent to which co-operation should be taken into account in sentencing; the timing of the testimony; and the protection by the authorities of those who give evidence. These issues will not be dealt with in this chapter because they do not involve questions of entrapment. An arrested person may, however, for various reasons, agree to co-operate with the police by continuing his association with other criminals. In such a case the danger of improper conduct does arise.

There has been no suggestion by the judiciary in Canada or England that it is improper to use undercover operations. (Indeed, the courts have always been careful to protect the informer's identity from disclosure.)[3] Laskin C.J. wrote in 1977 in *Kirzner v. The Queen*, which involved narcotics: "The use of spies and informers is an inevitable requirement for detection of consensual crimes and of discouraging their commission . . . Such practices do not involve such dirty tricks as to be offensive to the integrity of the judicial process."[4] Similarly, the Lord Chief Justice of England stated in 1974 in *Regina v. Mealey and Sheridan*: "So far as the propriety of using methods of this kind is concerned, we think it right to say that in

---

1 Marx, "Thoughts on a neglected category of social movement participant: The agent provocateur and the informant" (1973) 80 Am. J. Sociol. 402, at pp. 404-5. See also Marx, "Who Really Gets Stung? Some Issues Raised by the New Police Undercover Work" (1982) 28 Crime and Delinquency 165.

2 Chafee, *Free Speech in the United States* (1942), at p. 215, cited in Heydon, "The problems of entrapment" (1973) 32 Camb. L.J. 268 at p. 271.

3 See, *e.g., Marks v. Beyfus* (1890), 25 Q.B.D. 494 (C.A.); *D. v. Nat. Society for Prevention of Cruelty to Children*, [1978] A.C. 171 (H.L.); *cf Re Inquiry into the Confidentiality of Health Records in Ontario* (1979), 47 C.C.C. (2d) 465 (Ont. C.A.), reversed (*sub nom. Solicitor-Gen. Can. v. Royal Comm. of Inquiry into Confidentiality of Health Records in Ont.*) (1981), 23 C.R. (3d) 338 (S.C.C.). See generally, Oscapella, "A study of informers in England" [1980] Crim. L.R. 136, at pp. 137-41.

4 (1977) 38 C.C.C. (2d) 131 at 136 (S.C.C.).

these days of terrorism the police must be entitled to use the effective weapon of infiltration."[5]

U.S. cases have also permitted the use of infiltration. The Search and Seizure provision of the Fourth Amendment has been held not to be violated by such action,[6] although there are some state cases holding that the First Amendment's guarantee of freedom of speech and association might be.[7] While the Canadian Bill of Rights also recognizes "freedom of speech" and "freedom of assembly and association,"[8] it is very unlikely that the Supreme Court of Canada would declare undercover observers illegal on this basis.

2. INSTIGATING CRIMINAL ACTIVITY

Informers and undercover officers and agents are often involved in instigating — to use a relatively neutral term[9] — criminal conduct. Canadian cases, particularly in the drug field, are replete with examples.[10] In many cases, this activity is entirely acceptable. Few would suggest, for example, that it is improper for the police to seek to purchase drugs from a known trafficker to get a conviction against him. As the Ouimet Committee stated, "it is sometimes necessary for law enforcement officers to pose as members of a criminal group or to make purchases of narcotic drugs."[11] To purchase drugs is a form of entrapment, but entrapment is not necessarily improper.[12]

On the other hand, it would not be considered proper for an undercover policeman, in order to charge the person with trafficking,

---

5 (1974) 60 Crim. App. R. 59 at 61. See also R. v. Underhill (1979), 1 Cr. App. R. (S.) 270 at 272: "It is a recognized and legitimate means of detecting crime and bringing the guilty people to justice that infiltration shall take place."

6 See Professor Antonin Scalia's paper prepared for the McDonald Commission, United States intelligence law (1978) at 47. See also Hoffa v. U.S. (1966), 385 U.S. 293; U.S. v. White (1971) 401 U.S. 745. Some argue, however, that it should be so interpreted: see Amsterdam, "Perspectives on the Fourth Amendment" (1974) 58 Minn. L.R. 349 at p. 407.

7 See, e.g., White v. Davis (1975), 533 P. 2d 222 (Cal. S.C.), holding that the use of police undercover agents and informants in classes at U.C.L.A. would in the absence of a "compelling state interest" violate the First Amendment guarantees of both the state and federal constitutions. See Scalia's paper at pp. 52 et seq. for discussion of these cases, including the U.S.S.C. decision of Laird v. Tatum (1972), 408 U.S. 1, which held that the "chilling effect" of the defendant's conduct was not adequate to confer "standing" on the plaintiff.

8 S.C. 1960, c. 44, Appendix 111 to R.S.C. 1970, s. 1(d) and (e).

9 See Wilson, The Investigators (1978), at p. 22.

10 See the Final Report of the Commission of Inquiry into the Non-medical Use of Drugs (the Le Dain Commission) (1973) at p. 952, and the cases cited at p. 966, note 14.

11 Report of the Canadian Committee on Corrections (1969), at p. 75.

12 See Williams, Criminal Law (2nd ed. 1961), at p. 785.

actively to persuade — through, for example, feigned friendship and great need — a user who has, to the knowledge of the police, not been engaged in trafficking before, to sell him a small quantity of narcotic.

The courts in the United States, through the defence of entrapment, which will be discussed in detail later, have attempted to separate proper from improper conduct. English and Canadian courts have barely touched on the question.

Widgery C.J. in *Mealey and Sheridan*, stated that the officer "must endeavour to tread the somewhat difficult line between showing the necessary enthusiasm to keep his cover and actually becoming an agent provocateur, meaning thereby someone who actually causes offences to be committed which otherwise would not be committed at all."[13] Laskin C.J. expressed the same concern in *Kirzner*: "The problem which has caused judicial concern is the one which arises from the police-instigated crime, where the police have gone beyond mere solicitation or mere decoy work and have actively organized a scheme of ensnarement, of entrapment, in order to prosecute the person so caught."[14]

Finding the proper dividing line is not an easy task because it will vary from crime to crime and from fact situation to fact situation. Take the simple question of whether solicitation is proper. The offence of bribery, the subject of recent instigatory tactics by FBI agents against members of Congress,[15] offers some interesting examples. No doubt there will soon be a flurry of Law Review notes in the United States on the subject.[16]

Is it right for a police officer to ask a citizen arrested for, say, careless driving, for a small bribe in exchange for dropping the charge, in order to get evidence to convict the citizen of attempted bribery? No doubt most would say that it is unfair to trap a person in this way. Not only is it "manufacturing" crime by creating too great a temptation for an accused

---

13 *R. v. Mealey and Sheridan* (1974), 60 Crim. App. R. 59 at 62.

14 *Kirzner v. R.* (1977), 38 C.C.C. (2d) 131 at 136.

15 Convictions obtained against defendants in New York and Philadelphia have been upheld by appeal courts, with the Supreme Court of the United States denying certiorari: see *U.S. v. Myers* (1982), 692 F. 2d 823 (2nd Circ. C.A.), certiorari denied (1983), 103 Sup. Ct. 2438; *U.S. v. Jannotti* (1982), 673 F. 2d 578 (3rd Circ. C.A.) certiorari denied (1982), 102 S. Ct. 2906.

16 Some of the articles which have appeared since the above was written are Perelli-Minetti, "Causation and Intention in the Entrapment Defense" (1981) 28 U.C.L.A. L. Rev. 859; Witkes, "Entrapment and Unwitting Intermediaries: Opposition to the Direct Inducement Requirement" (1982) 62 Boston U.L. Rev. 929; Yasuda, "Entrapment as a Due Process Defense: Developments after *Hampton v. United States*" (1982) 57 Indiana L.J. 89; Note, "Entrapment through Unsuspecting Middlemen" (1982) 95 Harvard L. Rev. 1122; Altman and Lee, "Legal Entrapment" (1982) 12 Phil. and Public Affairs 51; Gershman, "Abscam, the Judiciary, and the Ethics of Entrapment" (1982) 91 Yale L.J. 1565; Gershman, "Entrapment, Shocked Consciences, and the Staged Arrest" (1982) 66 Minn. L. Rev. 567; Moloy, "ABSCAM: Time for the United States Supreme Court to Clarify the Due Process Defense" (1983) 16 Indiana L. Rev. 581.

who had no predisposition to engage in such conduct, but to allow it would give a legitimate cover to police corruption by permitting a corrupt officer to say that he was merely testing the accused in asking for money. What if the same accused had, to the officer's knowledge, a reputation for giving bribes, and had even previously been convicted of bribery? Again, the answer should be that the police conduct is improper because a briber can be dealt with when he does, in fact, offer a bribe.[17]

If asking a citizen for a bribe is improper, is it acceptable for the police to trap a fellow officer suspected of accepting bribes into accepting one? Most would say "yes", because of the great difficulty of controlling the conduct in any other way. The corrupt officer and the briber are like the narcotics buyer and trafficker. It is a consensual arrangement where there is no immediate victim. Would the same type of instigation be proper against officers who were not suspected of taking bribes? Most would probably agree with the American writer who stated that "the offence is so grave, the evidence so difficult to obtain, the temptation so constant and recurring that a government is justified in testing its officers by a normal offer."[18] In any event, even if one considers such indiscriminate testing improper for the purpose of charging the officer who succumbs, it should not be so considered for internal disciplinary purposes.

In Canada these questions are rarely the subject of discussion. Nor will they be in the future unless some method of settling the propriety of this conduct is determined.

Before we turn to the questions of techniques of settling and enforcing the boundaries between legal and illegal conduct, we should look at the likely extent of informer and police undercover activity in Canada. The greater the use of undercover activity, the greater the danger that if it is uncontrolled, improper instigation will occur.

3. EXTENT OF INFILTRATION

I know of no published empirical study on the role of the undercover policeman or the informer in Canada. An English study[19] of 150 cases tried at the Old Bailey in the early 1970s turned up only nine instances where it was apparent that an informer had alerted the police. But as the investigator of the study concedes, "there may have been a deliberate concealment by the police of the fact that an informer played any role whatever.[20] Confidentiality — even from the prosecutor — is important in

---

17 See Williams *Criminal Law* (1961), at p. 788.

18 See Note, "Entrapment by government officials" (1928) 28 Col. L.R. 1067 at 1074, cited in *ibid.*, at p. 788.

19 Oscapella, "A study of informers in England", [1980] Crim. L.R. 136.

20 See Oscapella's LL.M. thesis, from which the Crim. L.R. article was drawn, at p. 14. See also Skolnick *Justice Without Trial: Law Enforcement in Democratic Society* (1966) at p. 133.

the world of the informer. Neither the Ouimet Committee[21] nor the Le Dain Commission[22] published empirical data on the use of the undercover agent or informer, although both dealt with the subject. The Le Dain Commission acknowledged their importance in stating: "Because of the difficulty of detecting drug crimes the police rely heavily on undercover agents and informers."[23] The Ouimet Committee, as we have seen, simply stated that "it is sometimes necessary for law enforcement officers to pose as members of a criminal group or to make purchases of narcotic drugs."[24]

Three important American studies, however, one in each of the last three decades, show the pattern in the United States with respect to the role of the informer. There is little reason to believe that the pattern is substantially different in Canada.

William Westley's investigation[25] of the municipal police force in a midwestern city done in 1950 (but not, in fact, published until 1970) set out the importance of informants. One detective graphically summed up their value to Westley: "A dick is as good as his pigeons." Another stated: "Pigeons account for the solution of between 40% and 50% of the tough cases."[26]

A similar conclusion was drawn by Jerome Skolnick in his study of a California city in the early 1960s.[27] Police testimony and his own observation led him to the conclusion that "it almost never happens that an informant is not used somewhere along the line in crimes involving 'vice,' and also in such other secret crimes as subversion, espionage, and counterfeiting."[28]

Finally, James Q. Wilson's study in the mid 1970's of FBI and narcotics agents[29] again shows their importance. About half the FBI matters he examined involved the use of an informant.[30] Informants are even more important for the Drug Enforcement Agency: "Most

---

21 *Report of the Canadian Committee on Corrections* (1969).

22 *Final Report of the Commission of Inquiry into the Non-medical Use of Drugs* (1973). The commission's final report lists a research project on entrapment undertaken for the commission (p. 1145 of the report): B. Anthony, J. Moore, R. Solomon, and M. Green, "Entrapment and violence in the enforcement of drug laws." But this research report, as far as I can tell, was never published.

23 *Ibid.* at p. 951.

24 *Ibid.* at p. 75.

25 *Violence and the Police: A Sociological Study of Law, Custom and Morality* (1970).

26 *Ibid.* at p. 41.

27 *Justice Without Trial* (1966).

28 *Ibid.* at p. 133. Cf Greenwood, Chaiken, and Petersilia *The Criminal Investigation Process* (1977), at p. 126.

29 *The Investigators: Managing F.B.I. and Narcotics Agents* (1978).

30 *Ibid.* at pp. 34-5.

investigations depend on informants; narcotics investigations depend crucially on them."[31]

Thus, it would be surprising if informers — and no doubt undercover policemen — do not play a very significant role in the work of police forces in Canada, particularly the RCMP, perhaps more than is normally realized.

4. TECHNIQUES OF CONTROL

The following sections examine possible techniques of control. These include creating a defence to the criminal charge instigated, excluding evidence, reducing the sentence, creating criminal or civil liability in the person who improperly instigates the offence, and finally setting out rules for disciplinary action. A combination of techniques will be necessary. Disciplinary action, for example, may well have some effect on the police, but not on an informer who is not directly employed by the police.

At the present time, the legality of conduct in this area is not at all clear. The situation is reminiscent of that of ten years ago with respect to wiretapping, where the police engaged in the practice but were unsure whether it was legal to do so.[32] Wiretapping and infiltration are similar in that both intrude on the privacy of the individual. Indeed, the informer can often have access to more personal information than the wiretapper.

A number of techniques to control improper wiretapping were introduced in 1973 in the Protection of Privacy Act.[33] Undoubtedly the most important technique is to require judicial approval in advance. Would such a procedure be desirable to control informants and improper instigation?[34] Probably not. Wiretapping is an extraordinary technique — at least it should be — and so the burden placed on the senior judiciary to hear applications is not a particularly onerous one. Moreover, the authorization generally involves relatively straightforward activity. In contrast, there are so many situations involving undercover agents and various forms of instigation that it would place a very great burden on the

---

31 *Ibid.* at p. 58.

32 See Friedland *National Security: The Legal Dimensions* (1980), at pp. 78 *et seq.*

33 S.C. 1973-4, c. 50.

34 The point is discussed in Dix, "Undercover investigations and police rulemaking" (1975) 53 Texas L.R. 203 at 215, and Zimring and Frase *The Criminal Justice System: Materials on the Administration and Reform of the Criminal Law* (1980), at p. 249. The Quebec Keable Commission (*Rapport de la Commission d'enquête sur des opérations policières en territoire québécois*, 1981, at p. 424) recommends that approval of a request for authorization be required in advance: "Elle devrait faire l'object d'une approbation accordée soit par le Procureur général du Québec (ou son représentant), soit par un magistrat sur demande du Procureur général (ou son représentant)." See also Toronto *Globe and Mail*, 7 March, 1981.

judiciary. Drug purchases alone would require a very large number of applications. If the task were given to the judiciary, it is likely that it would require only the control of a justice of the peace, as with search warrants, and this is not a particularly effective control mechanism.[35] Further, the police would have difficulty in specifying in advance the precise conduct that they or their agents wished to engage in, so there would necessarily be either very vague authorizations or continuing close interaction between the police and the judiciary, which would not be desirable. Moreover, there will be many cases where there will be no time for an authorization, and the legislation would no doubt allow the police to operate in these cases without authorization in advance. As in the case of arrest without a warrant, this would tend to be used far more than the authorization provision.[36] It is far better to find techniques which attempt to control impropriety by examining the conduct and fashioning a remedy after the event.

The wiretapping legislation does, however, contain other techniques which warrant consideration. Some of these, such as creating criminal and civil liability[37] and excluding illegally obtained evidence,[38] will be discussed in later sections. The requirement that the request for an authorization be made by the solicitor general of Canada or the attorney general of a province or by a person specially and personally designated by one of them[39] is another control technique forcing a member of the Cabinet to take political responsibility for the applications. Because of the number of such applications it would be unwise to require approval at such a high level in the case of informers, but it would be sensible to require authorization at a senior level within the police force itself. This is a technique that has been adopted in England, where the latest Home Office Circular requires that "a decision to use a participating informant should be taken at senior level."[40]

Another technique used in wiretapping is to require periodic reports on the extent to which wiretapping is used. Although such reports would be instructive and would inhibit the use of informants in the case of infiltration of suspected subversive organizations, I doubt that figures in other cases would tell us enough to warrant the expense and inconvenience of collecting the data.

Finally, there is the technique of requiring notification ninety days

35 See generally, Friedland *Detention Before Trial* (1965).

36 *Ibid.*, chapter 2.

37 Canadian Criminal Code, ss. 178.11(1), 178.12.

38 *Ibid.*, s. 178.16.

39 *Ibid.*, s. 178.12.

40 *Home Office Consolidated Circular to the Police on Crime and Kindred Matters*, section 1, paragraph 92 (e), set out as appendix 4 to Report No. 83 of the English Law Commission, *Report on Defences of General Application* (1977).

after a person's phone has been tapped that he was the subject of wiretapping.[41] This is very effective in discouraging the widespread use of wiretapping. There is no doubt that a similar procedure would discourage the use of undercover agents, but in the case of informants it would also endanger their safety. Moreover, it might discourage the use of informants and undercover agents to a greater extent than is warranted.

Let us now turn to the device that is used in the United States, an entrapment defence. A brief look at the question of the acceptance of the defence in Canada, England, and the United States will precede a theoretical discussion of the defence.

5. THE DEFENCE OF ENTRAPMENT

(a) In Canada

The Supreme Court of Canada has not yet dealt directly with the question whether entrapment can be a defence to a charge.[42] In 1967 in *Lemieux v. The Queen*, Judson J., speaking for the Supreme Court, stated: "Had Lemieux in fact committed the offence with which he was charged, the circumstances that he had done the forbidden act at the solicitation of an *agent provocateur* would have been irrelevant to the question of his guilt or innocence."[43] The statement was not, however, necessary to the judgment, and might well be considered *obiter* in a future case.[44]

The question of entrapment came up again before the Supreme Court in 1977 in *Kirzner v. The Queen*.[45] The Ontario Court of Appeal had held[46] that no defence of entrapment was available, Brooke J.A. stating for the court: "[We] are convinced . . . that this defence is not available to a criminal charge."[47] Five members of the Supreme Court held, dismissing the accused's appeal, that it was unnecessary for them to discuss the defence, as the evidence was not open to show a "police-concocted plan to ensnare him going beyond mere solicitation."[48] Laskin C.J. with whom three other members of the court concurred,[49] while also holding that the evidence in the case could not amount to entrapment, dealt at length with

---

41 Code s. 178.23.

42 See now *Amato v. R.* (1982), 69 C.C.C. (2d) 31, discussed in the addendum, Part 12 of this chapter.

43 [1968] 1 C.C.C. 187 at 190.

44 See *Peda v. R.*, [1969] 4 C.C.C. 245 (S.C.C.).

45 (1977), 38 C.C.C. (2d) 131.

46 (1977), 32 C.C.C. (2d) 76. See also *R. v. Chernecki* (1971), 4 C.C.C. (2d) 556 (B.C.C.A.).

47 *Ibid.* at 77.

48 *Supra* note 45, per Pigeon J. at 142.

49 Spence, Dickson, and Estey JJ.

the defence and preferred "to leave open the question whether entrapment, if established, should operate as a defence."[50] The *Kirzner* case was not, in fact, a good case in which to analyze the defence of entrapment because the accused's defence was that he was *acting* for the police,[51] not that he was *entrapped* by the police. Protecting an informer or undercover policeman, which will be discussed in a later section, is a different question than providing an entrapment defence.

A number of lower court judgments have dealt with the defence. A provincial court judge in British Columbia in 1976[52] and a county court judge in Nova Scotia provide the only reported cases where entrapment was clearly accepted as a defence, and which resulted in acquittals of the accused. Other provincial court judges have achieved the same result by staying a prosecution as an abuse of the process of the court,[53] a technique which Laskin C.J. specifically leaves open in *Kirzner*.[54]

Some Canadian judgments have dealt with entrapment cases by reducing the accused's sentence.[55] But Canadian courts cannot grant an absolute or conditional discharge in cases where the possible penalty is fourteen years or more,[56] thus cutting out its use in the bribery[57] and trafficking[58] examples used earlier in this paper. In my opinion there is no justification for any restrictions on the granting of discharges.[59] Further, there are still some minimum sentences applicable in Canada, including the seven-year minimum penalty for the offence of importing a narcotic into Canada.[60] So, a sentencing reduction could not handle a case in which a person without any previous conduct with respect to trafficking takes a small amount of a narcotic drug across the border at the urgent insistence of a sick friend, who, in fact, turns out to be a police officer.

The Ouimet Committee concluded that "there should be a clear

---

50 *Supra* note 45 at 141.

51 See Note by Gold, "Entrapment" (1977-8) 20 Crim. L.Q. 166 at p. 167.

52 *R. v. Haukness*, [1976] 5 W.W.R. 420 (B.C. Prov. Ct.); *R. v. Rippey* (1981), 65 C.C.C. (2d) 158 (N.S. Co. Ct.). The defence was put to the jury by the trial judge, Greenberg J., in *R. v. Sabloff* (1979), 13 C.R. (3d) 326 (Que. S.C.), but the jury convicted.

53 See, *e.g. R. v. Shipley*, [1970] 3 C.C.C. 398 (Ont. Co. Ct.).

54 *Supra* at 141.

55 See, *e.g., R. v. Steinberg*, [1967] 3 C.C.C. 48 (Ont. C.A.); *R. v. Price* (1970), 12 C.R.N.S. 131 (Ont. C.A.); *R. v. Chernecki* (1971), 4 C.C.C. (2d) 556 (B.C.C.A.); *R. v. Kirzner* (1976), 32 C.C.C. (2d) 76 (Ont. C.A.).

56 Canadian Criminal Code, s. 662.1.

57 Bribery of a police officer under s. 109 carries a possible 14-year penalty.

58 There is a possible life sentence for trafficking: see the Narcotic Control Act, R.S.C. 1970, c.N-1, s. 4(3).

59 *The Report of the Canadian Committee on Corrections* (1969), at pp. 194-6, did not include such a restriction in its recommendation.

60 Narcotic Control Act, s. 5.

legislative statement with respect to the unacceptability of official *instigation* of crime."[61] In particular, it recommended that legislation be enacted to provide:

1. That a person is not guilty of an offence if his conduct is instigated by a law enforcement officer or agent of a law enforcement officer, for the purpose of obtaining evidence for the prosecution of such person, if such person did not have a pre-existing intention to commit the offence.

2. Conduct amounting to an offence shall be deemed not to have been instigated where the defendant had a pre-existing intention to commit the offence when the opportunity arose, and the conduct which is alleged to have induced the defendant to commit the offence did not go beyond affording him an opportunity to commit it.

3. The defence that the offence has been instigated by a law enforcement officer or his agent should not apply to the commission of those offences which involve the infliction of bodily harm or which endanger life.[62]

A legislative solution to the entrapment defence will be discussed more fully in a later section.

(b) In England

The English Court of Appeal has held in a number of cases that the defence of entrapment does not exist in English law.[63] In *Regina v. Mealey and Sheridan* in 1974 Widgery C.J. stated:

[I]f one looks at the authorities, it is in our judgment quite clearly established that the so-called defence of entrapment, which finds some place in the law of the United States of America, finds no place in our law here. It is abundantly clear on the authorities, which are uncontradicted on this point, that if a crime is brought about by the activities of someone who can be described as an agent provocateur, although that may be an important matter in regard to sentence, it does not affect the question of guilty or not guilty.[64]

The House of Lords in *Regina v. Sang*[65] in 1979 assumed that the defence did not exist. Although the point was not, in fact, argued before the House of Lords, the judgments used sufficiently conclusive language that it would now require legislation to bring the defence into English law. Lord Diplock, for example, stated that "the decisions . . . that there is no

---

61 *Supra* note 21, at p. 76.

62 *Ibid.* at pp. 79-80.

63 See, *e.g., R. v. Sang,* [1979] 2 W.L.R. 439 at 444: "[T]he so-called doctrine of entrapment has no place in English law"; *R. v. Mealey and Sheridan* (1974), 60 Cr. App. R. 59 (C.A.); *R. v. McEvilly* (1973), 60 Cr. App. R. 150 (C.A.).

64 (1974), 60 Cr. App. R. 59 at 62. For a discussion of the background to this case and the role of the police informer, see Robertson *Reluctant Judas: The Life and Death of the Special Branch Informer, Kenneth Lennon* (1976). See also the *Report to the Home Secretary from the Commissioner of Police of the Metropolis on the Actions of Police Officers concerned with the Case of Kenneth Joseph Lennon, Ordered by the House of Commons to be printed 31 July, 1974.*

65 [1979] 3 W.L.R. 263.

defence of 'entrapment' known to English law are clearly right."[66] Viscount Dilhorne stated: "It has been held, rightly in my opinion, that entrapment does not constitute a defence to a charge."[67] And similar statements were made by the other Law Lords.[68] A Court of Appeal decision after the House of Lords' judgment in *Sang* stated: "It has now been established beyond possibility of further argument that the doctrine of entrapment, as it is sometimes called, is not known to the English law."[69]

Legislation is not likely in the near future. The Law Commission, in its 1977 report,[70] did not recommend the introduction of the defence, stating: "[We] have come to the conclusion, after considering the full range of arguments, that a defence would not be the best solution to present difficulties, whether as a matter of principle or in practice."[71] The Law Commission's earlier Working Party on the Criminal Law had been "undecided on the question"[72] and so did not come forward with a positive view on the subject.

The Law Commission favoured instead the introduction of a new criminal penalty to apply to the entrapper.[73] This will be dealt with in a later section.

The English courts will continue to use evidence of entrapment to affect the sentence,[74] and will grant an absolute discharge in appropriate cases.[75] Unlike Canada, England has no restrictions on the use of absolute discharges.[76]

In addition, there is the possibility of stopping a prosecution as an abuse of the process of the courts. Abuse of process was not argued in

---

66 *Ibid.* at 267.

67 *Ibid.* at 276.

68 Per Lord Salmon at 277: "[I]t is now well settled that the defence called entrapment does not exist in English law"; Lord Fraser at 280: Court of Appeal "decisions appear to me to be right in principle"; and Lord Scarman at 285: "[I]t would be wrong in principle to import into our law a defence of entrapment."

69 *R. v. Underhill* (1979), 1 Cr. App. R.(S.) 270.

70 Law Commission Report No. 83, *Report on Defences of General Application* (1977), at p. 32 *et seq.*

71 *Ibid.* at 46.

72 Law Commission Working Paper No. 55 (1974), at p. 48. The Law Commission may, however, "take a fresh look at and consult upon" entrapment in a future report: see their Report No. 102, *Attempt and Impossibility in Relation to Attempt, Conspiracy and Incitement* (1980), at p. 2.

73 *Ibid.* at pp. 51-2.

74 See, *e.g., Browning v. Watson,* [1953] 1 W.L.R. 1172 (Div. Ct.); *R. v. Birtles* (1969), 53 Cr. App. R. 469 (C.A.); *R. v. McCann* (1971), 56 Cr. App. R. 359 (C.A.); *R. v. Sang,* [1979] 3 W.L.R. 263 (H.L.); *R. v. Underhill* (1979), 1 Cr. App. R.(S.) 270.

75 See, *e.g., Browning v. Watson,* [1953] 1 W.L.R. 1172 (Div. Ct.).

76 See Thomas *Principles of Sentencing* (2nd ed. 1979), at pp. 225 *et seq.*

Sang.[77] The Court of Appeal, however, stated, *obiter,* that "a trial judge may have power to stop a prosecution if it amounts to an abuse of the process of the court and is oppressive and vexatious."[78] In the House of Lords only Lord Scarman mentioned the "abuse of process" concept, stating, "Save in the very rare situation, which is not this case, of an abuse of the process of the court (against which every court is in duty bound to protect itself), the judge is concerned only with the conduct of the trial."[79]

(c) In the United States

A series of four United States Supreme Court cases have established the defence of entrapment in American law. In *Sorrells v. United States,* decided in 1932, the defence of entrapment applies, according to the majority opinion, if the result of the governmental activity is to "implant in the mind of an innocent person the disposition to commit the alleged offense and induce its commission in order that they may prosecute."[80] The same view was restated by the majority of the Supreme Court in the subsequent cases of *Sherman v. United States* in 1958,[81] *United States v. Russell* in 1973,[82] and *Hampton v. United States* in 1976.[83] The test focuses on the accused's predisposition and is therefore often labelled the "subjective" test.

The minority view in each of the four cases focuses attention on police conduct and is known as the "objective test." In *Sherman v. United States,* for example, Frankfurter J. stated that an entrapped accused should not be convicted if "the methods employed on behalf of the Government to bring about conviction cannot be countenanced."[84]

No Supreme Court case has established the defence as a constitutional requirement applicable to the federal government or to the states.[85] But this is hardly necessary because of the acceptance of the defence by the Supreme Court and by state courts and legislatures. In 1976, according to one commentator,[86] all states except Tennessee had accepted the defence of entrapment, and Tennessee at the time had legislation pending that would do so.

---

77 [1979] 2 W.L.R. 439 at 443.

78 *Ibid.*

79 [1979] 3 W.L.R. 263 at 288.

80 (1932), 287 U.S. 435 at 442.

81 (1958), 356 U.S. 369.

82 (1973), 411 U.S. 423.

83 (1976), 425 U.S. 484.

84 *Supra* note 81 at 380.

85 See LaFave and Scott, *Criminal Law* (1972), at p. 370.

86 Park, "The entrapment controversy" (1976), 60 Minn. L.R. 163 at pp. 164-5.

The Supreme Court split between those favouring the subjective and those favouring the objective approach is also found, not surprisingly, in the state courts. Most follow the subjective approach, but a small number, including, recently, the Supreme Court of California,[87] use the objective test.[88]

In contrast, almost every commentator on the defence and all the major legislative proposals take the objective approach. The California Supreme Court pointed out in 1979 that only two American law review articles endorsed the subjective view.[89] One of these, however, a lengthy, illuminating analysis published in 1976 in the *Minnesota Law Review*,[90] shows some of the advantages of the subjective approach often overlooked in other articles and argues that the objective "hypothetical-person defense creates a greater risk of unjust treatment of individual defendants than does the federal defense, and that the possibility of beneficial effects upon conduct of police agents is not strong enough to justify taking this risk."[91]

Both the American Law Institute's Model Penal Code of 1962[92] and the proposed U.S. Federal Code prepared by the Brown Commission in 1971[93] adopted the objective approach. The Model Penal Code states that entrapment should be a defence if the police or their agents induce or encourage an offence by "employing methods of persuasion or inducement which create a substantial risk that such an offense will be committed by persons other than those who are ready to commit it."

The Brown Commission proposal is that "entrapment occurs when a law enforcement agent induces the commission of an offense, using persuasion or other means likely to cause normally law-abiding persons to commit the offense." This was the test judicially adopted by the California Supreme Court in the 1979 case mentioned above.[94]

---

87 *People v. Barraza* (1979), 591 P. 2d 947 (Cal. S.C.) See Kleven, *"People v. Barraza:* California's latest attempt to accommodate an objective theory of entrapment" (1980), 68 Cal. L.R. 746.

88 Park, *supra* note 86, at pp. 167-8.

89 See *People v. Barraza supra* note 87.

90 Park, *supra* note 86.

91 *Ibid.* at p. 170.

92 Proposed Official Draft, s. 2.13.

93 *Final Report of the National Commission on Reform of Federal Criminal Laws*, s. 702. The Senate Committee on the Judiciary's S. 1. reverted to the subjective approach: see Schwartz, "Reform of the federal criminal laws: Issues, tactics and prospects" [1977] Duke L.J. 171 at p. 208. The Criminal Code Reform Act of 1977, which passed the Senate but not the House, leaves the defence of unlawful entrapment (along with other defences) to "be determined by the courts of the United States according to the principles of the common law as they may be interpreted in the light of reason and experience."

94 *People v. Barraza, supra* note 87.

The two tests are not as clearly separated in practice as they are in theory.[95] Indeed, Lafave and Scott's view is probably correct that "most cases would come out the same way in the end whichever view is taken."[96] Some cases mix up the tests by construing the objective test as subjective.[97] And some of the supposed theoretical characteristics of each test can be found in practice in the other test as well. So, for example, although the objective test is usually thought to be a question for the judge, the recent California test has left it as a jury question.[98] And although the accused's previous convictions are thought not to be relevant for the objective test, many courts permit their use.[99]

There is a possibility of using the due process clause of the Fifth and Fourteenth Amendments to bar government activity which "shocks the conscience"[100] of the court, whether or not the accused was predisposed to commit the offence. The door for such a defence was left open by Rehnquist J. in *United States v. Russell*, when he stated: "While we may some day be presented with a situation in which the conduct of law enforcement agents is so outrageous that due process principles would absolutely bar the government from invoking judicial process to obtain a conviction . . . the instant case is distinctly not of that breed."[101] But Rehnquist J., speaking for two other members of the court, tried to shut the door firmly again in 1976 in *Hampton v. United States*[102] by not applying the due process clause to an accused who was predisposed to commit the offence. Two other concurring members of the court,[103] however, (who would, of course, be joined by the dissenters on this issue) considered that it was going too far to hold "that the concept of fundamental fairness inherent in the guarantee of due process would never prevent the conviction of a predisposed defendant, regardless of the outrageousness of police behaviour in light of the surrounding circumstances." So the door is still slightly ajar.

The Canadian Bill of Rights[104] also contains a "due process" clause: "There have existed and shall continue to exist . . . the right of the individual to life, liberty, security of the person and enjoyment of

---

95 See generally, Park, *supra* note 86.

96 *Criminal Law* (1972), at p. 372.

97 See Park, *supra* note 86 at p. 168.

98 *People v. Barraza supra* note 87 at 956.

99 Park, *supra* note 86 at pp. 201 *et seq.*

100 Per Frankfurter J. in *Rochin v. California* (1952), 342 U.S. 165 at 172.

101 (1973), 411 U.S. 423 at 431-2.

102 (1976), 425 U.S. 484. See the less onerous "due process" standard in *People v. Isaacson* (1978), 378 N.E. 2d 78 (N.Y.C.A.).

103 Powell and Blackmun JJ. at 492.

104 S.C. 1960, c. 44, s. 1, found in Appendix III to R.S.C. 1970.

property, and the right not to be deprived thereof except by due process of law." This clause has not yet been raised in any reported Canadian entrapment case. If it were, its chance of success would be very slight because of the limited scope the Supreme Court of Canada has so far given to the words "due process."[105] There is a better chance of arguing that entrapment violates section 7 of the Canadian Charter of Rights and Freedoms:[106] "Everyone has the right to life, liberty and security of the person and the right not to be deprived thereof except in accordance with the principles of fundamental justice."

The outcome of applying the various tests will, of course, depend to a great extent on how the tests are interpreted by the courts. Take the Brown Commission proposal "likely to cause normally law-abiding persons to commit the offense." Does "likely" mean possibly or does it mean greater than a 50 per cent chance? If the latter, then the defence is almost a dead letter. Who is the normally law-abiding person? If he is the reasonable man on the Clapham omnibus, will he ever be induced to commit an offence? Presumably, because of the deliberate use of the word "normally," he is less law-abiding than the reasonable man, who I would think would *always*, not just normally, be considered law-abiding.

Does the normally law-abiding person have any of the accused's characteristics? For example, if a paedophile is entrapped into attempting an offence, does one measure the police lure by judging how a normally law-abiding paedophile would react? If not, then it would be very difficult ever to establish the defence in such a case. Similarly, if a person is induced to traffic in narcotics, is the lure measured against the reaction of a normally law-abiding possessor (a contradiction in terms?) or by a non-user? If the latter, then again it is unlikely that the defence will be established in many cases. So, as with the Canadian and English law of provocation, one is forced to build some of the accused's characteristics into the "ordinary" or normally law-abiding person.[107] Once again one sees a merging of the objective and subjective approaches.

Looking at the subjective test, which denies the defence to a person who is "predisposed," what do we mean by "predisposed"? Predisposed to commit that very offence? To commit an offence violating that very law? To commit offences of that type? To commit offences in general? If it is the last, then the defence will be difficult to apply; if the first (committing that very offence) then the defence will apply in a great many cases.

So the test itself does not determine the result. The content of the test is very important, as is the crucial issue of the burden of proof. For ex-

---

105 See *Curr v. R.* (1972), 7 C.C.C. (2d) 181 (S.C.C.).

106 Set out in Part I of the Constitution Act, 1982, as enacted by the Canada Act 1982 (U.K.), c. 11.

107 *D.P.P. v. Camplin*, [1978] A.C. 705.

ample, probably many, if not most, district attorneys in the United States would prefer the objective test with the burden of persuasion on the accused rather than the subjective test with the burden on the prosecution to disprove entrapment beyond a reasonable doubt.

6. THEORETICAL BASIS FOR THE DEFENCE

What is the theoretical basis for the establishment of the defence? Glanville Williams has rightly pointed out that there is "no ready-made doctrine to cover the situation."[108] Except in a few special cases, to quote Lord Diplock in the *Sang* case, "both the physical element (*actus reus*) and the mental element (*mens rea*) of the offence with which he is charged are present."[109]

The special cases in which entrapment affects the *actus reus* are those in which police involvement affects one of the elements of the charge. So, for example, because of police involvement in the case of possession of stolen goods, the goods might no longer be considered stolen goods;[110] in the case of breaking and entering, the house might not have been broken into without the consent of the owner;[111] and in the case of treason, the enemy may not actually have been assisted.[112] However, in Canada (but not in England)[113] it should be possible in these cases to convict the accused of an attempt.[114]

There are other, but not many, isolated instances where traditional concepts might be able to solve entrapment problems. For example, an assurance by a peace officer that the proposed conduct is not illegal might enable the accused to raise a mistake of law defence,[115] particularly if the peace officer acts openly as a peace officer. The Model Penal Code specifically deals with this in the entrapment section, providing a defence if the police make "knowingly false representations designed to induce the belief that such conduct is not prohibited."[116] And there may be cases where the police tactics are so excessive that they can amount to duress.

Estoppel is not applicable as a basis for the defence because, as Glanville Williams has stated: "The strict doctrine of estoppel has not been

---

108 *Criminal Law* (1961), at p. 785.

109 *R. v. Sang*, [1979] 3 W.L.R. 263 at p. 267.

110 See, *e.g., Haughton v. Smith,* [1975] A.C. 476 (H.L.) and *Booth v. State of Oklahoma* (1964), 398 P. 2d 863 (C.C.A., Okla.).

111 See *Lemieux v. R.,* [1968] 1 C.C.C. 187 (S.C.C.).

112 *R. v. Snyder* (1915), 24 C.C.C. 101 (Ont. C.A.).

113 See *Haughton v. Smith*, [1975] A.C. 476.

114 See s. 24 of the Criminal Code: see also *R. v. Scott,*]1964] 2 C.C.C. 257 (Alta. C.A.).

115 See Friedland, *National Security: The Legal Dimensions* (1980) at pp. 101 *et seq.*

116 S. 213(1)(*a*).

applied in criminal law, except in respect of estoppel by judgment; and in any event the situation is not precisely one of estoppel."[117]

The U.S. cases bring in the defence in two ways, depending on whether the subjective or objective approach is taken. Those favouring the subjective approach bring in the defence through the device of statutory interpretation, holding that the legislature could not have intended the statute to cover police-instigated conduct that traps an innocent person. This theory was enunciated by the United States Supreme Court in 1932 in *Sorrells v. United States,*[118] where a prohibition agent induced Sorrells, a law-abiding citizen without previous involvement in such sales, to supply liquor through repeated requests in which, in the language of the majority decision, he took "advantage of the sentiment aroused by reminiscences of their experiences as companions in arms in the World War."[119] Chief Justice Hughes for the majority of the court stated: "We are unable to conclude that it was the intention of the Congress in enacting this statute that its processes of detection and enforcement should be abused by the instigation by government officials of an act on the part of persons otherwise innocent in order to lure them to its commission and to punish them. We are not forced by the letter to do violence to the spirit and purpose of the statute."[120] The minority view, which also led to an acquittal, looked at the conduct of the government, refusing to rely on what they considered the artificiality of using the technique of statutory construction. It "requires no statutory construction, . . . but frankly recognizes the true foundation of the doctrine in the public policy which protects the purity of government and its processes."[121]

The same division is found in the later cases. In *United States v. Russell*[122] Rehnquist J. for the court stated that the defence "is rooted not in any authority of the Judicial Branch to dismiss prosecutions for what it feels to have been 'overzealous law enforcement,' but instead in the notion that Congress could not have intended criminal punishment for a defendant who has committed all the elements of a prescribed offense but was induced to commit them by the government."[123] The minority in *Russell*, dissenting, again looked to the abuse of government power: "[T]he focus of this approach is not on the propensities and predisposition of a specific defendant, but on 'whether the police conduct revealed in the

---

117 *Criminal Law* (1961), at p. 785.

118 (1932), 287 U.S. 435.

119 *Ibid.* at 441.

120 *Ibid.* at 448.

121 Per Roberts J. at 455.

122 (1973), 411 U.S. 423.

123 *Ibid.* at 435.

particular case falls below standards, to which common feelings respond, for the proper use of government power.'"[124]

Would either of these approaches be acceptable to the judiciary in Canada?

Statutory interpretation certainly appears artificial in this situation. We do not usually build the law of defences and excuses in this way, although there are occasions such as the recent *Regina v. Sault Ste. Marie* decision[125] on strict responsibility where it was desirable to do so. A more acceptable approach is to use section 7(3) of the Criminal Code, which provides:

> Every rule and principle of the common law that renders any circumstance a justification or excuse for an act or a defence to a charge continues in force and applies in respect of proceedings for an offence under this Act or any other Act of the Parliament of Canada, except in so far as they are altered by or are inconsistent with this Act or any other Act of the Parliament of Canada.

Although the section, by its very terms, applies only to federal legislation, there is little doubt that if the defence is accepted with respect to federal statutes it would, without too much difficulty or discussion, also be applied by the courts to provincial legislation.

Section 7(3) has been used by the Supreme Court of Canada in the past few years to introduce — or at least to acknowledge the existence of — the defence of necessity in the *Morgentaler* case,[126] to permit the use of the law of duress in the *Paquette* case,[127] and to develop the concept of double jeopardy in the *Kienapple* case.[128]

One hurdle that the court would have to get over is that the section can be interpreted to limit defences to those recognized when the Code was first introduced in 1892 — and entrapment was not then recognized as a defence. But in the above cases the Supreme Court has given a liberal interpretation to the section and, as Laskin C.J. stated in *Kirzner*, "I do not think that s. 7(3) should be regarded as having frozen the power of the Courts to enlarge the content of the common law by way of recognizing new defences, as they may think proper according to circumstances that they consider may call for further control of prosecutorial behaviour or of judicial proceedings."[129] The courts should not be criticized for manufacturing a defence to deal with manufactured crime.

An entrapment defence is akin to the defences of duress and

---

124 Per Stewart J. at 441, quoting in part from the dissenting judgment of Frankfurter J. in *Sherman v. U.S.* (1958), 356 U.S. 369 at 382.

125 (1978), 40 C.C.C. (2d) 353 (S.C.C.).

126 *Morgentaler v. R.* (1975), 20 C.C.C. (2d) 449.

127 *R. v. Paquette* (1976), 30 C.C.C. (2d) 417.

128 *Kienapple v. R.* (1974), 15 C.C.C. (2d) 524.

129 (1977), 38 C.C.C. (2d) 131 at 138.

necessity, but does not fit comfortably with either. In all cases there is an external force which has an effect on the accused, although in this case, unlike the others, the external force is the police. It is, however, not like necessity, where the accused acts to protect a more important value. The defence is closer to duress. As Fletcher has written, "In one case the actor is seduced by the wiles of a duplicitous police officer, in the other he is coerced by the threats of an overbearing will."[130]

The defence also bears some resemblance to the concept of provocation, which provides the accused with a defence to a murder charge if an external event would have made an ordinary person lose his self-control.[131] But provocation only reduces murder to manslaughter and does not result in an outright acquittal. Thus a successful provocation defence affects sentencing, which entrapment can (with some limitations) now do.

No existing defence quite fits. Perhaps all one can say is that if it is to be a defence it is because it is unjust to register a conviction in certain circumstances. We will return to this theme later.

Let us turn to the minority view that the purpose of the defence is to control government power. The potential for this approach in Canada will depend on whether the Supreme Court of Canada accepts that it has a role in controlling prosecutorial power. This issue is still an open question in Canada, although it would seem not to be in England, at least with respect to government harassment through multiple prosecutions by unreasonably splitting a case. In *Connelly v. D.P.P.* [132] the House of Lords developed the concept that it would be an abuse of the process of the court for the Crown unreasonably to split its case. This particular issue has not yet been settled in Canada.[133] If the Supreme Court holds — and as I have written elsewhere[134] it would be unfortunate if it did so hold — that there is no power to bar abusive prosecutorial practices in such cases, then it could not logically stop a prosecuion because of abusive police practices. The case for interference with abusive prosecutorial practice is a far stronger one because it relates directly to the procedure before the court.

But even if the courts do step in to bar prosecutorial harassment they may not take the further and more difficult step of attempting to control police misconduct through a general discretionary power to bar

---

130 Fletcher *Rethinking Criminal Law* (1978), at p. 542.

131 Canadian Criminal Code, s. 215.

132 [1964] A.C. 1254; see also *D.P.P. v. Humphrys*, [1976] 2 All E.R. 497 (H.L.).

133 See *R. v. Osborn* (1970), 1 C.C.C. (2d) 482 (S.C.C.); see also *Rourke v. R.* (1977), 35 C.C.C. (2d) 129 (S.C.C.). Note that in *R. v. Krannenburg (Kranenberg)* (1980), 51 C.C.C. (2d) 205 at 212 (S.C.C.) Dickson J. stated, *obiter,* for the court: "[T]he laying of another information may amount to nothing less than an abuse of process."

134 Friedland *Double Jeopardy* (1969) ch 7.

prosecutions as an abuse of process. Indeed, if the concept, which is often given the convenient label "abuse of process," is given the fuller description of "abuse of the process of the courts" then it is not easy to extend it to the pre-trial stage. In *Rourke v. The Queen*[135] the question was whether it was an abuse of process to delay bringing a charge. Pigeon J., for the majority of the court, stated that he could not "admit of any general discretionary power in Courts of criminal jurisdiction to stay proceedings regularly instituted because the prosecution is considered oppressive."[136] Yet, if the concept of abuse of process can be used to bar a criminal case because it is felt the courts are being used as a collection agency,[137] why should a case not be barred when the Criminal Court is being used to prosecute a state-manufactured crime?[138] Even though there may be no "general discretionary power," it is still quite possible that the Supreme Court might apply it to specific exceptional situations,[139] such as entrapment.

The concept of abuse of process is therefore one possible solution to the entrapment problem. A better solution would be a legislative one in which the various issues can all be faced directly at the same time: the test to be applied; the burden of proof; whether it is to be dealt with by the judge or jury; and whether the accused's record should be admissible when entrapment is in issue.

Before we turn to an examination of such a legislative provision, let us examine a further device which has been used by some courts, that is, barring evidence based on entrapment.

7. EXCLUSION OF EVIDENCE

A number of cases in England[140] and elsewhere[141] had excluded evidence by the entrapper as a method of controlling entrapment. But this technique was unequivocally rejected in England by the Court of

---

135 (1977), 35 C.C.C. (2d) 129 (S.C.C.).

136 *Ibid.* at 145.

137 See the cases cited by Laskin C.J. in *Rourke v. R.*, note 135 *supra* at 137.

138 It will be recalled that only one member of the House of Lords, Lord Scarman, in *R. v. Sang*, [1979] 3 W.L.R. 263 at 288, mentioned abuse of process; see also *R. v. Sang*, [1979] 2 W.L.R. 439 at 443 (C.A.).

139 See the analysis of *Rourke* by Jessup J.A. in *Re Abitibi Paper Co. and R.* (1979), 47 C.C.C. (2d) 487 (Ont. C.A.), and by Krever J. in *R. v. Crneck, Bradley and Shelley* (1980), 30 O.R. (2d) 1 (H.C.); see also *Re Orysiuk and R.* (1977), 37 C.C.C. (2d) 445 (Alta. C.A.); *cf. R. v. Ridge* (1979), 51 C.C.C. (2d) 261 (B.C.C.A.). See now *Amato* in the Addendum.

140 *R. v. Ameer and Lucas*, [1977] Cr. L.R. 104 (C.A.); *Jeffrey v. Black*, [1978] Q.B. 490 (Div. Ct.); *R. v. Foulder, Foulkes and John*, [1973] Cr. L.R. 45 (London Quarter Sess.); *R. v. Burnett and Lee*, [1973] Cr. L.R. 748 (Cent. C.C.).

141 *R. v. Pethig*, [1977] 1 N.Z.L.R. 448 (S.C.); *R. v. Capner*, [1975] 1 N.Z.L.R. 411 (C.A.).

Appeal[142] and the House of Lords[143] in *Sang*. To reject evidence was, in effect, to bring in the defence through the back door. And so the proposal to do so, according to Lord Diplock, "does not bear examination."[144] Lord Salmon stated that such a result would be "inconceivable,"[145] Lord Fraser that it would be "remarkable,"[146] and Viscount Dilhorne that it would be "odd."[147] And so, as Lord Diplock stated, '[w]hatever be the ambit of the judicial discretion to exclude admissible evidence it does not extend to excluding evidence of a crime because the crime was instigated by an agent provocateur.'[148]

The House of Lords went on to deal with this broader question of the extent to which a judge has a discretion to exclude illegally obtained evidence. Their Lordships held, although the result is not as clear as one would like,[149] that there was no discretion to exclude evidence on the ground that it was obtained by improper or unfair means except in the case of confessions and evidence obtained from the accused after commission of the offence. And, of course, they reaffirmed that there is a discretion to exclude evidence if its prejudicial effect outweighs its probative value.

Canadian courts are even less inclined to exclude illegally obtained evidence. In the well-known case of *The Queen v. Wray*[150] in 1970 the Supreme Court of Canada held that there was not even a discretion to exclude real evidence obtained through the accused as the result of oppressive interrogation tactics. And in *Hogan v. The Queen*[151] the Supreme Court held that even a violation of the Bill of Rights did not justify the exclusion of evidence.[152].

Both the Ouimet Committee and the Evidence Code of the Law Reform Commission of Canada recommend that the trial judge have a limited discretion to exclude evidence. The Ouimet Committee recommended that legislation give effect to the principle that "[t]he court may in

---

142   *R. v. Sang*, [1979] 2 W.L.R. 439.

143   *R. v. Sang*, [1979] 3 W.L.R. 263.

144   *Ibid.* at 267.

145   *Ibid.* at 277.

146   *Ibid.* at 280.

147   *Ibid.* at 276.

148   *Ibid.* at 268.

149   See Cross *Evidence* (5th ed., 1979), addendum at p. viii *et seq.*; Ashworth, "The court's discretion to exclude evidence" (1979) 143 J.P. 558; Heydon, "Entrapment and unfairly obtained evidence in the House of Lords" [1980] Crim. L.R. 129.

150   [1970] 4 C.C.C. 1. Three members of the court, Cartwright CJC, Hall and Spence JJ, dissenting, would have allowed the trial judge to exclude the evidence.

151   (1974), 18 C.C.C. (2d) 65.

152   See now s. 24 of the Canadian Charter of Rights and Freedoms.

its discretion reject evidence which has been illegally obtained."[153] And the Law Reform Commission's draft section provides, in part: "Evidence shall be excluded if it was obtained under such circumstances that its use in the proceedings would tend to bring the administration of justice into disrepute."[154] It should also be noted that the Canadian wiretapping legislation includes a provision excluding conversations illegally obtained.[155]

The English Royal Commission on Criminal Procedure considered the exclusion of evidence in its report published in January 1981. "Running as a common thread through all the evidence on police powers," the commission had stated in its earlier consultative paper, "is the question of how the exercise of those powers can be effectively controlled." The report rejects the automatic exclusionary rule as a general means of securing compliance with its proposed statutory rules respecting police questioning. It would, however, use the technique "in order to mark the seriousness of any breach of the rule prohibiting violence, threats of violence, torture or inhuman or degrading treatment and society's abhorrence of such conduct."[156]

Even if the courts were to be given some discretion to exclude evidence, it would not be a sound technique for controlling entrapment. Entrapment does not lead to the creation of evidence in the same way as illegal search and interrogation do. What is to be excluded? Presumably it is the evidence of the undercover agent.[157] So an accused who happens to admit the facts to the police will be convicted, but one who does not will not. Similarly, if another witness happens to be present the accused will be convicted; if the entrapper and the accused are alone, he will not. These distinctions are surely unwarranted. The entrapment should either directly affect the result or it should not. Moreover, it is not possible to say on the basis of the present law what police conduct is legal and what is illegal, and so whether evidence will be excluded will be too dependent on the personal views of the trial judge. It would be far better to develop a limited defence of entrapment to handle the problem.

---

153 *Report of the Canadian Committee on Corrections* (1969), at 74.

154 *Evidence Report* (1977) s. 15(1).

155 Code 178.16(1). Subsection (2) gives the judge a discretion to refuse to admit evidence obtained directly or indirectly as a result of information acquired by an illegal interception "where he is of the opinion that the admission thereof would bring the administration of justice into disrepute."

156 *Report of the Royal Commission on Criminal Procedure*, January 1981, Cmnd. 8092 at pp. 64, 112-18; see also the *Consultative Paper* issued by the Royal Commission on Criminal Procedure (1979), at pp. 15-16.

157 See Heydon, "Entrapment and unfairly obtained evidence in the House of Lords" [1980] Cr. L.R. 129 at 132.

8. A LEGISLATIVE SOLUTION

There is no single simple solution to entrapment problems. A legislative solution which provides a defence to the accused may not also supply a fair test for deciding whether a police officer should be prosecuted for his conduct. Neither test may be the right one for deciding what the borderline should be between proper and improper conduct and whether a police officer should be disciplined for overstepping the line. Again, none of the tests may be the same as that which should be used to decide whether the police officer or agent is an accomplice and thus requires corroboration. In this section we examine possible legislative provisions which would give a defence to the accused.

Neither the objective nor the subjective model is ideal.

The objective model, which is designed to control police behaviour, is inconsistent with the present Canadian judicial philosophy of not using the trial of an accused to control the police, although this may change as a result of section 24 of the Charter which provides for the exclusion of evidence when there has been a violation of the Charter if "the admission of it in the proceedings would bring the administration of justice into disrepute." Even in the area of the law of confessions, where one might have thought that controlling the police was one of the prime considerations, the Supreme Court of Canada has held that evidence obtained as the result of an inadmissible confession — for example, the location of the murder weapon — is admissible, as well as those parts of the confession that are confirmed by the subsequent find.[158] So, introducing the objective test would be a far-reaching step in Canadian law. Moreover, somewhat paradoxically, the test suffers from the disadvantage of making the test in certain cases too difficult for the accused. Not only does the test usually place the onus of proof on the accused, but, because the test has to handle cases of those with and without a pre-existing intent, the judges are likely to err on the side of giving the police greater scope for instigation than is desirable.[159]

The subjective test, such as that suggested by the Ouimet Committee, previously set out,[160] would be preferable.

One of the objections to the subjective test is that it permits the prosecutor to prove previous convictions and other evidence of wrong-doing in order to show a pre-existing intention. But this objection can be overstated because the *actus reus* and *mens rea* will already have been admitted by the very nature of the defence and so the previous conviction cannot prejudice those issues. Moreover, the accused will almost certainly have to go into the witness box to give his version of the transaction, and

---

158 *R. v. Wray*, [1970] 4 C.C.C. 1(S.C.C.).

159 See Park, *supra* note 86.

160 See *supra* at pp. 8-10.

under Canadian law[161] his previous convictions would then be admitted, although for a different purpose.

The Ouimet test may, however, favour the accused to too great an extent in certain cases. Let us suppose that there have been a series of violent sexual assaults at night in a certain park. The police decide to use a female decoy to trap the culprit. Another person, not the suspected culprit, seeing the female sitting in a provocative pose alone on the park bench decides, without any "pre-existing intention," to indecently assault her. Should he have a complete defence? The Ouimet test would give him one. But it does not seem desirable that he should be acquitted. Society expects people like him to exercise restraint. It is, of course, possible to say that the accused had, in fact, a pre-existing intention because he decided to indecently assault her; but if this is the meaning of "pre-existing intention" then the defence will rarely be applicable.

Take another case. If there is widespread corruption in a police force and the police commission decides to test officers with bribes, then the Ouimet test would prevent the conviction of someone who accepted a bribe if he did not have a pre-existing intention to do so. Yet, as previously suggested, most people would feel that a conviction in such a case would be warranted.

Although the Ouimet test, as drafted, is a relatively good one, it may be that a better one would combine elements of both the objective and subjective tests so that the police conduct and the accused's pre-existing intent would both be factors in determining whether a defence should apply. It is the combination of the two factors that makes it unjust to convict in any particular case. Society should allow the police very little scope for entrapping the person without a pre-existing intent, but substantially more scope in the case of the person who has a pre-existing intent.[162] The test should reflect that the propriety of police conduct will vary from case to case depending on the crime charged and the accused's prior intent to engage in the activity.

Drafting such a test would not be easy. As with the concepts of causation and the *actus reus* for an attempt, a simple formulation would be preferable to an elaborate set of provisions which attempts to make too many fine distinctions. It would be better to leave the decision to the trier of fact and, because of the extraordinary nature of the defence, to place the burden of persuasion on the accused.[163] The issue would not get to the jury if the trial judge did not think there was sufficient evidence to permit

---

161 Canada Evidence Act, R.S.C. 1970, c. E-10, s. 12.

162 See Park, *supra* note 86 at p. 213.

163 Would such a provision violate s. 2(*f*) of the Canadian Bill of Rights ("presumed innocent until proved guilty") or s. 11(*d*) of the Canadian Charter of Rights and Freedoms? Probably not, just as s. 16, the insanity section, which places the onus of proof on the accused, probably does not.

the jury to consider the matter. One suggested test is that the jury should acquit the accused if they are satisfied that the police or their agent's conduct in instigating the crime has gone substantially beyond what is reasonable, having regard to all the circumstances, including, in particular, the accused's pre-existing intent.

Another, but less satisfactory, possibility, which follows Judge Bazelon's suggested test on the equally difficult insanity issue,[164] would leave it to the jury to acquit the accused if they were satisfied that all the circumstances, including, in particular, the police conduct and the accused's pre-existing intent make it *unjust* to register a conviction.

9. LIABILITY OF THE ENTRAPPER

Another method of controlling improper entrapment is to impose liability, civil or criminal, on the instigator.

It would be difficult to succeed in a civil action against the instigator if entrapment did not also create a defence to the criminal action. If an action were brought, the courts would probably invoke the analogy of malicious prosecution which involves an abuse of legal procedure, and in which the criminal action must have ended in the plaintiff's favour before a civil action can succeed.[165] But even if civil liability were a possibility it would not be particularly effective because the damages would no doubt be very low.

Criminal liability against the instigator offers greater possibilities than civil liability.[166] There are a number of judicial statements indicating that the police officer is not immune from prosecution. For example, in *Kirzner*, Laskin C.J. stated that "[t]he police, or the *agent provocateur* or the informer or the decoy used by the police do not have immunity if their conduct in the encouragement of a commission of a crime by another is itself criminal."[167] But this does not answer the question whether the "conduct . . . is itself criminal."[168]

---

164 *U.S. v. Brawner* (1972), 471 F. 2d. 969, at 1032 (Dist. Col. C.A.): "Our instruction to the jury should provide that a defendant is not responsible if at the time of his unlawful conduct his mental or emotional processes or behaviour controls were impaired to such an extent that he cannot justly be held responsible for his act."

165 See Winfield, *The Present Law of Abuse of Legal Procedure* (1921), at pp. 174 *et seq.*

166 See Smith and Hogan, *Criminal Law* (4th ed. 1978), at pp. 138-40; Williams *Textbook of Criminal Law* (1978), at pp. 310 and 566; *Report of the Canadian Committee on Corrections* (1969), at p. 78; Paterson, "Towards a defence of entrapment" (1979) 17 Osgoode Hall L.J. 261 at pp. 271 *et seq.*

167 (1977), 38 C.C.C. (2d) 131 at 134 (S.C.C.). See also *Brannan v. Peek*, [1948] 1 K.B. 68 (Div. Ct.).

168 See also Report No. 83 of the English Law Commission, *Report on Defences of General Application* (1977), at p. 50, which starts with the firm statement "Wherever a person, for the purpose of entrapping another, himself commits a criminal offence he can, of course,

The dicta in some of the cases are vague. In the *Sang* case the Court of Appeal simply stated that "[a] police officer who goes too far may himself be prosecuted for the crime which he has committed or for inciting another to commit a crime."[169] The judgments in the House of Lords in *Sang* are unhelpful on this question. Lord Salmon did not try to determine where the line should be drawn, but gave as an example a case crying out for prosecution; he referred to "the unusual case, in which a dishonest policeman, anxious to improve his detection record, tries very hard with the help of an agent provocateur to induce a young man with no criminal tendencies to commit a serious crime; and ultimately the young man reluctantly succumbs to the inducement . . . The policeman and the informer who had acted together in inciting him to commit the crime should . . . both be prosecuted and suitably punished."[170] In Canada the officer in such a case could be charged with "counselling or procuring" under section 22 of the Code.

It is not likely that the courts would convict a police informer who played a minor role in the execution of a crime in order to frustrate the crime. At the other extreme, they would convict an informer who played a major part in a serious crime, whatever his purpose. But few such cases will ever reach the courts and so the law will necessarily remain uncertain.

One Canadian case did reach the courts, however. An early liquor case in Alberta[171] held that the police-sergeant who purchased liquor in order to trap a suspected liquor violator was guilty of an offence. There was special provincial legislation exempting the police from prosecution, and it may be that the fact that the legislation did not cover the facts of this case was decisive in the view of the Alberta Court of Appeal in reversing the acquittal by the magistrate. The case, in my opinion, goes too far and would not likely be followed today in other cases of purchase, or at least the case would be distinguished as one depending on specific legislation. There are no recent cases where a police officer or a police informer has been convicted, although there are Canadian cases where persons who have at some stage acted for the police, but were not doing so at the time of the offence, have been convicted.[172]

---

be prosecuted for that offence." On the following page, however, they say, "[I]t is by no means clear that in all cases the trapper would be guilty."

169 [1979] 2 W.L.R. 439 at 456 (C.A.).

170 [1979] 3 W.L.R. 263 at 278. Lord Diplock (at 267) may not have been directing his mind to this question when he stated: "The fact that the counsellor and procurer is a policeman or a police informer . . . cannot affect the guilt of the principal offender", see also Lord Scarman (at 285) who also probably was not dealing with the point at issue here.

171 *R. v. Petheran* (1936), 65 C.C.C. 151 (Alta. C.A.).

172 See *Kirzner v. R.* (1977), 38 C.C.C. (2d) 131 (S.C.C.); *R. v. Ormerod*, [1969] 4 C.C.C. 3 (Ont. C.A.).

If society considers that it is a legitimate police practice for an undercover officer or agent to attempt to purchase a narcotic, then the courts should not convict the officer of possession.[173] The officer cannot be expected to arrest the accused before taking possession of the drug: if he did, the evidence of trafficking would be less certain and the officer might in the circumstances be incurring risk to himself. Similarly, if it is legitimate for an undercover officer to infiltrate a drug ring and he plays a minor role in the organization for a brief period, then it would be wrong to convict the officer of aiding and abetting in trafficking. Further, if it is legitimate for an undercover officer to infiltrate an espionage ring, he should not be convicted of committing an offence if he breaches a provincial law by registering in a hotel under a false name. It is not that the police should be exempt from the law, but that the law should not make such conduct criminal.

On what basis should these acts not be offences? The law of necessity, in the light of *Morgentaler*,[174] does not seem to be applicable. And superior orders should not by itself be a valid reason for illegal conduct.[175] Lack of *mens rea* is certainly a possible defence in some, if not most, cases, including aiding and abetting which requires "purpose,"[176] but will not help in those cases where no *mens rea* is required. Section 25 of the Criminal Code, which provides that "[e]veryone who is required or authorized by law to do anything in the administration or enforcement of the law . . . as a peace officer . . . is, if he acts on reasonable and probable grounds, justified in doing what he is required or authorized to do," has not been given a liberal interpretation by the Supreme Court of Canada.[177]

Once again it is difficult to find a concept which would prevent convictions in these cases. The courts would probably simply use section 7(3) of the Code to prevent a conviction when the officer is using legitimate and relatively harmless law enforcement techniques. In England the Divisional Court held[178] that it was proper for the police to instruct a

---

173 A regulation passed under the Narcotic Control Act, R.S.C. 1970, c. N-1, Regulation 3(1), permits a police officer "to have a narcotic in his possession where [he] has obtained the narcotic pursuant to these Regulations and . . . such possession is for the purpose of, and in connection with" his employment. It seems unlikely that the officer would fit the section because he would not have "obtained the narcotic pursuant to these Regulations."

174 *Morgentaler v. R.* (1975), 20 C.C.C. (2d) 449 (S.C.C.).

175 See Friedland *National Security: The Legal Dimensions* (1980), at pp. 104 *et seq.*

176 *R. v. Paquette* (1976), 30 C.C.C. (2d) 417. See also Williams *Textbook of Criminal Law* (1978), at p. 310.

177 See Friedland, *supra* note 175, at p. 100 *et seq.*; *Eccles v. Bourque* (1974), 19 C.C.C. (2d) 129 (S.C.C.).

178 *Johnson v. Phillips*, [1976] 1 W.L.R. 65 (Div. Ct.). See Williams, *supra* note 176, at p. 566.

person blocking an ambulance to go the wrong way on a one-way street. In Canada, in the area of arrest and search the Supreme Court has developed such doctrines. A police officer can search a suspect who has been arrested for carrying dangerous weapons;[179] and similarly police can go onto private property in making an arrest.[180]

Another approach would be to provide by legislation a specific statutory defence similar to section 25 to cover these cases. But it would be difficult to draft such a law. No doubt the police would prefer clarification by legislation, but it would be better to achieve clarification through administrative rules and then to rely on the good sense of the courts, if prosecutions are brought, not to frustrate legitimate police activity. Trying to set the guidelines by establishing criminal liability against the police is likely to establish the line at a level too favourable to the police.

It is for this reason that a new offence against the police, as recommended by the Law Commission,[181] while at first very attractive, is not a desirable approach. It would rarely be used, would be pitched to allow too much instigation, and would not serve to give the required guidance in this area.

In relation to provincial law, however, there is less danger in clarifying the law in advance. Provincial offences are less serious than Criminal Code offences. Moreover, many do not require *mens rea* and so the lack of *mens rea* defence is not open in many cases. New Brunswick has handled the problem legislatively by providing: "A member of the Royal Canadian Mounted Police or a member of a police force shall not be convicted of a violation of any Provincial statute if it is made to appear to the judge before whom the complaint is heard that the person charged with the offence committed the offence for the purpose of obtaining evidence or in carrying out his lawful duties."[182]

The federal government probably has constitutional power to pass a similar provision applicable to all summary conviction offences, federal and provincial. Would it be desirable to do so? In my opinion a statutory provision protecting police officers involved in undercover operations who "act reasonably in carrying out their lawful duties" from criminal liability for *minor* offences (for example, false registration in a hotel room) would assist the police without creating dangers of abuse. One objection might be that providing protection in certain cases would imply a lack of protection in others. However, it should be possible to draft language which would avoid such an inference.

---

179 *R. v. Brezack* (1949), 96 C.C.C. 97 (Ont. C.A.).

180 *Eccles v. Bourque* (1974), 19 C.C.C. (2d) 129 (S.C.C.).

181 Law Commission Report No. 83, *Report on Defences of General Application* (1977), at pp. 51-52.

182 New Brunswick Police Act, S.N.B. 1977, c. P-9.2, s. 3(4).

The protection could — and, in my opinion, should — be linked to the existence of published rules or, preferably, regulations relating to the conduct. The use of regulations would require that the rules be scrutinized by a parliamentary committee.

10. RULE-MAKING AND DISCIPLINARY ACTION

In England and the United States there have been publicly announced guidelines relating to informers and instigation designed to assist the police. There have been no such guidelines in Canada.

The Home Office in England issued general guidelines in 1969,[183] and in 1976 the U.S. attorney general issued detailed rules to guide the FBI.[184] In Canada the solicitor general could issue guidelines to cover federal forces, and provincial attorneys general could do the same for provincial forces.

Breach of the guidelines could, as apparently is now the case with respect to the FBI in the United States,[185] lead to disciplinary action. This is not the place to examine the difficult question of the type of machinery which could best deal with disciplinary problems. There have been a number of commissions and committees in Canada that have looked into the matter. It should, of course, be noted that disciplinary action cannot apply to non-police informers, although guidelines can attempt to give them guidance and can use the threat of prosecution as a sanction.[186]

What would the rules contain? They could, for example, include a simple rule, such as in England, that "[n]o member of a police force, and no police informant, should counsel, incite or procure the commission of a crime."[187] They could require approval for each operation at a senior level within the force. They could prohibit any acts of "violence"[188] in the course of an infiltration. They could require that the officer have reasonable grounds to "believe" or, at least, to "suspect" that the person instigated had been engaged in similar conduct in the past. The guidelines cannot, however, be too specific, or else criminals would be able to test confederates to try to ensure that they were not involved with the police. But they could set out what is thought to be necessary for proper and effective policing.

---

183 Set out in appendix 4 to the Law Commission's Report No. 83, *Report on Defences of General Application* (1977).

184 Memo from Edward H. Levi, attorney general, to Clarence Kelley, director, F.B.I., dated 15 December, 1976.

185 See Wilson, *The Investigators* (1978), at p. 84.

186 See the memo from Edward H. Levi, *supra* note 184.

187 *Home Office Consolidated Circular to the Police on Crime and Criminal Matters*, paragraph 92(a), set out in Appendix 4 to the Law Commission Report No. 83.

188 See the memo from Edward H. Levi, *supra* note 184.

11. CONCLUSION

A number of techniques to control improper instigation are needed.

1. Some guidelines, as in England and the United States, should be developed in Canada, leading to disciplinary action if they are breached.

2. A limited defence should be available to the accused if the guidelines are breached by the police or their agent. The courts could develop the defence under section 7(3) of the code or, possibly, through the concept of "abuse of process." A legislative solution would, however, be able to shape the defence better than a judicial one and so would be preferable. The test could be that proposed by the Ouimet Committee, which looks at whether the accused had a pre-existing intention to breach the law. A better approach is to combine the objective and subjective tests.

3. Exclusion of evidence to control entrapment is not a desirable way of dealing with the problem.

4. Whether or not a defence is permitted, the courts should continue to take entrapment into account in sentencing, including the possibility of granting an absolute discharge. The Canadian Criminal Code should be amended to eliminate the present restriction preventing the granting of a discharge in certain cases where the possible penalty is fourteen years or more.

5. The police should be protected by legislation from prosecution for breaching summary conviction offences when they act reasonably in carrying out lawful duties specifically permitted by rules relating to infiltration. Protection for the police for more serious breaches of the law should be left to judicial interpretation.

12. ADDENDUM

The McDonald Commission devoted considerable attention to what it called "undercover operatives",[189] and concluded that "there can be no doubt about the continued need to use undercover operatives both for criminal investigation and security intelligence work."[190] The Commission did not recommend that judicial approval be required for undercover operations, but did recommend[191] "that the R.C.M.P. establish administrative guidelines concerning the use of undercover operatives in criminal investigations" and that the guidelines "be approved by

---

189   See the Second Report, *Freedom and Security under the Law* (Ottawa, 1981) at pp. 295 *et seq.*, 536 *et seq.*, 1030-1033, and 1047 *et seq.*

190   *Ibid.* at p. 328.

191   *Ibid.* at p. 1032.

the Solicitor General" and be "publicly disclosed" by him. With respect to entrapment, the Commission recommended[192] that the Criminal Code be amended to include the following defence (similar to the one advocated in this paper):

> The accused should be acquitted if it is established that the conduct of a member or agent of a police force in instigating the crime has gone substantially beyond what is justifiable having regard to all the circumstances, including the nature of the crime, whether the accused had a pre-existing intent, and the nature and extent of the involvement of the police.

The Government's response to the McDonald Report, Bill C-157, the Canadian Security Intelligence Service Act, introduced on May 18, 1983, does not deal specifically with the issue of informers.[193] The Bill does, however, provide protection to employees of the service engaged, among other activities, in undercover operations. This protection goes far beyond — much *too* far beyond — the limited protection suggested in this paper or the even more limited protection which would be afforded by the McDonald Commission.[194] Section 21(1) of Bill C-157 provides that "The Director and employees are justified in taking such reasonable actions as are reasonably necessary to enable them to perform the duties and functions of the Service under this Act." Legislative protection should, at the most, be limited to summary conviction offences.

After the publication of the McDonald Commission Report, the Supreme Court of Canada delivered its judgment in *Amato v. The Queen*.[195] Amato had been convicted of trafficking in cocaine, and his appeal had been dismissed by the British Columbia Court of Appeal.[196] He had admitted sales to an R.C.M.P. undercover agent, but said he was entrapped because of the persistent pestering and pressure to sell the cocaine by an informer acting on behalf of the police. The Supreme Court of Canada dismissed Amato's appeal. The Court was divided. Four members of the Court, dissenting, in a comprehensive judgment by Estey J. (with whom Laskin C.J.C., McIntyre and Lamer JJ. concurred) held that Amato's "defence" should have succeeded through section 7(3) of the Code

---

192   *Ibid.* at p. 1053.

193   See the writer's criticism of this aspect of the Bill in his submission of September 12, 1983 to the Special Committee of the Senate on the Canadian Security Intelligence Service, established June 29, 1983 and chaired by Senator Michael Pitfield. The Pitfield Report (November, 1983) recommended at pp. 23-26 that the protection afforded security service personnel be no greater than that granted peace officers. At the time of writing, a new revised Bill has not yet been introduced, but it is almost certain to limit the protection given under Bill C-157.

194   *Supra* note 189 at pp. 541 *et seq.*

195   (1982), 69 C.C.C. (2d) 31. See Stuart, "Amato: Watersheds in Entrapment and Abuse of Process" 29 C.R. (3d) 54.

196   (1979), 51 C.C.C. (2d) 401.

as an abuse of the process of the court. Estey J. proposed the following test: "the scheme so perpetrated must in all the circumstances be so shocking and outrageous *as to bring the administration of justice into disrepute.*"[197] This test, it will be noted, is similar to the test for the exclusion of evidence now found in section 24(2) of the Canadian Charter of Rights and Freedoms. Four other members of the Court, in a short judgment by Dickson J. (with whom Martland, Beetz and Chouinard JJ. concurred) stated in part that "on the facts of this case the defence of entrapment, assuming it to be available under Canadian law, does not arise."[198] Dickson J. expressed the view that because the British Columbia judges who considered the issue were unanimous in concluding that, on the facts, the defence of entrapment did not arise, it did not "fall to this court to retry the case and arrive at different findings." So they left the issue undecided. The ninth judgment was delivered by Ritchie J. He accepted that there could be a defence of entrapment, but held that it did not arise on these facts. Ritchie J. tied the possibility of a defence to a lack of *mens rea*, stating that the defence might succeed because "the essential element of *mens rea* would be absent." Unfortunately, Ritchie J.'s reasoning would mean that an entrapment defence would rarely, if ever, succeed, because in almost all cases the accused would have the requisite *mens rea*.

So, what is the result? The majority of the Supreme Court (Ritchie J. plus the four dissenters) held that a "defence" of entrapment is part of Canadian law, but they do not all place the operation of the defence on a realistic basis. So we will have to wait for another Supreme Court case to clarify the law. Nevertheless, the handwriting is on the wall. The four dissenters will surely pick up one or more members of the Court in a judgment clearly holding that "abuse of process" is part of Canadian law and that it is applicable in a case of improper entrapment.

The Supreme Court will again have the opportunity to deal with the issue of entrapment on an appeal from the British Columbia Court of Appeal decision of *Jewitt.*[199] The trial Judge had left the issue of entrapment to the jury, ruling that it was for the Crown to prove beyond a reasonable doubt that there was no entrapment. The jury found entrapment and the judge entered a stay of proceedings. The Crown's appeal to the British Columbia Court of Appeal was dismissed on the basis that a stay is not the equivalent of an acquittal and so no appeal was possible.[200]

---

197 *Supra* note 195 at 62.

198 *Ibid.* at 40.

199 *R. v. Jewitt* (1983), 34 C.R. (3d) 193.

200 *Per* Lambert and Seaton JJ.A. Anderson J. held that the Crown had a right of appeal, but the trial judge did not err in holding that the onus was on the Crown to establish beyond a reasonable doubt that there was no unlawful entrapment. The entrapment issue, said Anderson J.A., should have been dealt with by the judge, not the jury, but in the circumstances it would not be just to have Jewitt face a second trial. *Cf. R. v. Mack* (1983),

The Supreme Court granted leave to appeal on June 21, 1983. The Court will therefore again have an opportunity to rule directly on the question whether entrapment is part of Canadian law, and whether it is to be handled by a stay of proceedings, whether an appeal lies from a stay, whether the issue of entrapment is one for the judge or jury and who has the burden of proof. It may be that these issues will all be clarified. On the other hand, it seems more likely, as argued above, that a legislative solution would be able to shape the defence better than a judicial one.

---

34 C.R. (3d) 228 (B.C. Co. Ct.) holding that the issue is for the jury, but that the onus is on the accused to prove entrapment on a balance of probabilities.

7

CRIMINAL JUSTICE AND THE CHARTER*

1. INTRODUCTION

One clear conclusion a year and a half after the passage of the Canadian Charter of Rights and Freedoms[1] is the important role of the Charter in the development of the criminal law. It has certainly been extensively argued by counsel and cited by the judiciary. In the first five volumes of the 1983 Canadian Criminal cases, for example, there were over a hundred cases in which the Charter was discussed in the reasons for judgment. This is over 25 percent of the reported cases in those volumes.

In the year and a half since the Charter was enacted there have been over 125 Charter cases reported in the Canadian Criminal Cases. In contrast, within a year and half after the Bill of Rights was enacted in 1960 there were only about a dozen cases on the Bill of Rights reported in the Canadian Criminal Cases. There has been, therefore, a ten-fold increase in reported decisions on the Charter in contrast with the Bill of Rights. If the number of cases citing the Charter starts dropping off in the next year and a half the Charter industry will be revived by the introduction of section 15 dealing with equality rights, which comes into effect on April 17, 1985.

Another clear conclusion is that the introduction of the Charter has brought us closer to American law. One can see this in the increasingly frequent citation of American authorities. When Chief Justice Laskin delivered the Hamlyn Lectures in 1969 he showed that the number of reported cases that cited American cases in the Dominion Law Reports in 1948, 1958 and 1968 was very low.[2] In the six volumes for the year 1968, for example, only 21 out of 575 reported cases cited U.S. authorities. Just

---

* An earlier version of this paper was delivered at the Annual Conference of the Canadian Institute for the Administration of Justice held in Winnipeg, Manitoba, October 12-15, 1983 and is to be published in (1984), 14 Man. L.J. It, in turn, drew on an earlier paper prepared for a seminar for Supreme Court of Ontario judges at Kempenfelt Bay, Barrie, and published in (1982) 24 Crim. L.Q. 430. I am grateful to Gordon Cameron, a recent graduate of the Faculty of Law, for his able assistance. I would also like to thank Peter Hogg, Peter Russell, Robert Sharpe and Stephen Waddams for their very helpful comments on an earlier draft of the paper.

1 Set out in Part I of the Constitution Act, 1982, as enacted by the Canada Act 1982 (U.K.), c. 11.

2 B. Laskin, *The British Tradition in Canadian Law* (London, 1969) at p. 104.

prior to the introduction of the Charter the figure continued to be low — in fact, proportionately lower than in 1968. In the thirteen volumes of the D.L.R.s published in 1981 only 36 out of 1,276 cases cited American authorities.

In contrast, in the first eight volumes of the D.L.R.s published so far in 1983 there have been 59 cases citing U.S. authorities out of 791 cases. The percentage has therefore increased from 2.8% to 7.5%. The increase in the Canadian Criminal Cases would no doubt be even higher because of the larger number of criminal cases reported. Even if one looks only at the non-charter cases the number has increased significantly, so there is a major spillover effect of the Charter. This trend will, no doubt, continue in light of the fact that the Supreme Court of Canada cited U.S. cases in seven of its judgments reported so far in the 1983 D.L.R.s.[3] Moreover, Mr. Justice Dickson, in an extrajudicial statement, has stated that "the United States has a body of jurisprudence accumulated over some 200 years from which we can learn not only positive points but also of the errors which have been made".[4]

Although most courts have been willing to cite U.S. authorities, some have shown a reluctance to do so. In the Saskatchewan Court of Appeal case, *Regina v. Therens*,[5] Tallis J.A. stated for the majority of the Court at the very end of his judgment:

> I would also observe that counsel did not refer to any American authorities on the hearing of this appeal. While in some cases, decisions of American courts may be persuasive references, I agree with learned counsel for the appellant that, in interpreting the Charter, we should strive to develop our own jurisprudence in response to cases that arise in our own country.

It seems unlikely that such a restrictive view will be applied by the courts, although there may be considerable sympathy with that position in the area of search and seizure, where there is an overwhelming abundance of U.S. case-law interpreting the comparable section, a section with a different history. So, it is likely that the increasing use of U.S. cases will continue. English cases will continue to become less important in the criminal law area. As England moves towards the Continent, economically and legally, Canada moves towards the United States.

---

3 See *Multiple Access Ltd. v. McCutcheon* (1982), 138 D.L.R. (3d) 1; *Atco Ltd. v. Calgary Power Ltd.* (1982), 140 D.L.R. (3d) 193; *Amato v. R.* (1982), 140 D.L.R. (3d) 405; *R. v. Gardiner* (1982), 140 D.L.R. (3d) 612; *Basarabas v. R.* (1982), 144 D.L.R. (3d) 115; *Nowegijick v. R.* (1983), 144 D.L.R. (3d) 193; *Naken v. Gen. Motors of Can. Ltd.* (1983), 144 D.L.R. (3d) 385. Dickson J. delivered four of the judgments and Estey J. the other three. A case has been included if the U.S. case is significant enough to have been noted in the list of cases following the headnote.

4 Address to the Canadian Association of Provincial Court Judges, Saskatoon, September, 1982, appended to *R. v. Hayden* (1983), 33 C.R. (3d) 363 (Man. Prov. Ct.).

5 (1983), 33 C.R. (3d) 204 at 227 (Sask. C.A.). Leave to appeal to S.C.C. granted 5 C.C.C. (3d) 409n.

Relatively few Charter cases in the past year and a half have cited the United Nations International Covenant on Civil and Political Rights[6] or the European Convention for the Protection of Human Rights and Fundamental Freedoms.[7] This is surprising, because many of the provisions in the Charter have been drawn directly from the U.N. Covenant, which came into force in 1966 and to which Canada became a signatory in 1976.[8] (Other provisions were drawn directly from the 1960 Bill of Rights,[9] which had itself drawn on the United States Constitution and the United Nations Universal Declaration of Human Rights.[10]) One of the reasons for enacting the Charter was to fulfil Canada's international obligations under the Covenant. Article 2.2 of the Covenant obligates each signatory state "to adopt such legislative or other measures as may be necessary to give effect to the rights recognized in the present Covenant." Perhaps in future cases the Covenant will be used to help interpret the Charter so that, if possible, Canadian law is in line with Canada's international obligations, just as the English courts have used the European Convention to interpret English legislation.[11]

I have examined all the provincial court of appeal decisions reported

6   Annex to G.A. Res. 2200, 21 GAOR, Supp. 16, U.N. Doc. A/6316, at 52 (1966).

7   213 U.N.T.S. 221, E.T.S.5, signed at Rome, November 4, 1950, entered into force on September 3, 1953. References to the International Covenant and the European Convention can be found in D.C. McDonald, *Legal Rights in the Canadian Charter of Rights and Freedoms: Manual of Issues and Sources* (Carswell, 1982).

8   Accession in force August 19, 1976: see O/C P.C. 1976-1156 of May 18, 1976, and Fischer, "The Human Rights Covenants and Canadian Law" [1977] Can. Yearbook Int'l Law 42, which deals with the problems of implementing the Covenant.

9   The Canadian Bill of Rights, R.S.C. 1970, Appendix III. The Act has not been repealed. It applies only to federal law, whereas the Charter applies to federal and provincial law. There are some differences between it and the Charter: *e.g.* the Charter does not deal with "property" in s. 7, whereas the Bill of Rights in s. 1(*a*) includes "the right of the individual to life, liberty, security of the person and enjoyment of property". Further, "Equality Rights" in the Charter do not come into operation for three years, but are in the meantime applicable under s. 1(*b*) of the Bill of Rights.

10   G.A. Res. 217, 3 GAOR, U.N. Doc. 1/777 (1948).

11   See, *e.g.*, Lord Denning M.R. in *R. v. Chief Immigration Officer, Heathrow Airport, ex p. Salamat Bibi*, [1976] 3 All E.R. 843 (C.A.); see also Lord Wilberforce in *Minister of Home Affairs v. Fisher*, [1980] A.C. 319 (P.C.); Warbrick, "European Convention on Human Rights and English Law" (1980) 130 New L.J. 852; Bayefsky, "The Impact of the European Convention on Human Rights in the United Kingdom: Implications for Canada" (1981) 13 Ottawa L. Rev. 507; and Cohen and Bayefsky, "The Canadian Charter of Rights and Freedoms and Public International Law" (1983) 61 Can. Bar Rev. 265. Note, however, that the Federal Court of Appeal held in *Re A.G. Can. and Stuart* (1982), 137 D.L.R. (3d) 740 that a Convention which Canada had signed could not be used in interpreting domestic legislation. But note the reliance on the International Covenant by the Ontario Court of Appeal in *Re Federal Republic of Germany and Rauca* (1983) 4 C.C.C. (3d) 385 at 402. And see the thorough canvass of the question in *Mitchell v. A.G. Ont.* (1983), 35 C.R. (3d) 225 (Ont. H.C.) *per* Linden J.

in the law reports or noted in one of the periodic bulletins prior to the commencement of the Supreme Court of Canada sittings in mid-September, 1983 — well over 50 cases. Although I have also looked at many lower court decisions, for the most part, this chapter will be confined to the court of appeal cases.

The current Supreme Court of Canada sitting that started in mid-September, 1983, is hearing many of the more than 20 Charter cases which have been appealed to the Supreme Court of Canada.[12] Those decisions will, of course, indicate how the Charter will be used by the courts. Some tentative conclusions can, however, be drawn from the decisions of the courts of appeal.

The first is that there appear to be very few surprises in the cases. Mr. Justice Zuber's statement in *Regina v. Altseimer*[13] that "the Charter does not intend a transformation of our legal system or the paralysis of law enforcement" is certainly the view of all the provincial appeal courts. The changes made by the courts, changes that have taken some of the harshness out of some laws and further individualized the criminal justice system, have been of a marginal nature. In the long run — and even for the most part in the short run — the Charter will block rather than promote change. It will prevent Parliament, provincial legislatures and municipalities from departing too far from the present criminal justice system. The Charter will help protect us from tyranny, but will not replace Parliament as the body to develop the criminal law. It is suggested that this is the proper use of the Charter. Although in the United States the Supreme Court has been forced to play an important role in imposing minimum standards on state institutions, in Canada, because criminal law is a federal responsibility, such standards can be imposed by federal legislation directly. Parliament and provincial legislatures will, however, be obliged to scrutinize proposed legislation to ensure that it will not breach the Charter, and we can expect amendments to existing provincial and federal Acts to make them conform to Charter requirements.

Not only should the Charter not replace Parliament in the development of the criminal law, it should not infringe on the normal role of the courts in developing the law. There is a danger in constitutionalizing the ordinary criminal law. The danger is, of course, that a constitutional decision is difficult to change; Parliament cannot change a constitutional decision unless it exercises its power of override,[14] which for political reasons it is reluctant to do, or unless there is a constitutional

---

12 See the address by Dickson J. to the Canadian Bar Association, Globe and Mail, Aug. 31, 1983.

13 (1982), 1 C.C.C. (3d) 7 (Ont. C.A.).

14 Charter s. 33.

amendment,[15] which would be difficult to achieve. It would be preferable to continue to develop ordinary criminal law concepts, such as "abuse of process",[16] and to save the constitution for cases where it is actually needed, such as to strike down legislation. If the courts do turn a matter into a constitutional doctrine they should be careful to avoid tying the hands of the legislature to such an extent that the legislature would be prevented from developing alternative techniques. The constitutional decision should be a guide to the legislature — by imposing, for example, minimum standards[17] — rather than a detailed elaboration of an area of law.

2. "PRINCIPLES OF FUNDAMENTAL JUSTICE"

The only surprising court of appeal case interpreting legal rights encountered so far by the author was the British Columbia case, *Reference Re S. 94(2) of the Motor Vehicle Act of B. C.*[18] In that case the Court struck down provincial legislation which made driving while prohibited or suspended an offence of absolute liability and provided a minimum seven day jail term. The Court stated that section 7 of the Charter is not restricted to procedural matters:[19]

> The Constitution Act, in our opinion, has added a new dimension to the role of the courts; the courts have been given constitutional jurisdiction to look at not only the *vires* of the legislation and whether the procedural safeguards required by natural justice are present but to go further and consider the content of the legislation.

Then, referring specifically to section 7, which provides that "Everyone has the right to life, liberty and security of the person and the right not to

---

15 *Ibid.* s. 38.

16 See *Connelly v. D.P.P.,* [1964] A.C. 1254 (H.L.) at 1280; *cf. R. v. Osborn* (1970), 1 C.C.C. (2d) 482 (S.C.C.); *Rourke v. R.* (1977), 35 C.C.C. (2d) 129 (S.C.C.); *Amato v. R.* (1982), 69 C.C.C. (2d) 31 (S.C.C.).

17 See, *e.g., Miranda v. Arizona* (1966), 384 U.S. 436.

18 (1983) 4 C.C.C. (3d) 243 (B.C.C.A.). See to the same effect *R. v. Hayden* (1983), 33 C.R. (3d) 363 (Man. Prov. Ct.). The Manitoba Court of Appeal took a different view of s. 7 in *R. v. Hayden* (1983), 36 C.R. (3d) 187. Hall J.A. stated (at 189) that "the phrase 'principles of fundamental justice' in the context of section 7 and the Charter as a whole, does not go beyond the requirement of fair procedure and was not intended to cover substantive requirements as to the policy of the law in question." The Court distinguished the B.C.C.A. case, stating that it dealt with "lack of guilty intent" and not with the policy of the law. The Manitoba Court of Appeal held in the accused's favour, however, holding that the section of the Indian Act making it an offence to be intoxicated on a reserve contravened "equality before the law" in s. 1(b) of the Canadian Bill of Rights. Whether the Court would have reached that conclusion before the enactment of the Charter is uncertain. Leave to appeal to the Supreme Court of Canada was refused (1983), 8 C.C.C. (3d) 33. With respect to remedies, *R. v. Therens* (1983), 33 C.R. (3d) 204 (Sask. C.A.) is a surprise.

19 *Ibid.* at 246.

be deprived thereof except in accordance with the principles of fundamental justice", the court said:

> the meaning to be given to the phrase "principles of fundamental justice" is that it is not restricted to matters of procedure but extends to substantive law and . . . the courts are therefore called upon, in construing the provisions of s. 7 of the Charter, to have regard to the content of legislation."

A similar issue arose in the Ontario Court of Appeal in *Regina v. Stevens*[20] where the accused challenged his conviction for having sexual intercourse with a female under 14 on the basis that the provision making his belief as to her age irrelevant was contrary to "fundamental justice". The court stated:

> Assuming, without in any way deciding the question, that s. 7 of the Charter permits judicial review of the substantive content of legislation, we are all of the view that, insofar as this case is concerned, s. 7 does not have the effect of invalidating s. 146(1) of the Criminal Code and preventing Parliament from creating the crime of having sexual intercourse with a girl under 14 years of age excluding mistake as to the age of the girl as a defence therefrom.

The B.C. case as well as the Ontario *Stevens* case are going to be heard by the Supreme Court of Canada. They are important ones to watch because, if the Supreme Court upholds the B.C. Court of Appeal, it will have a potentially wide-ranging effect in other areas of the law, such as abortion.

Should fundamental justice be limited to procedural justice? No doubt some of the drafters of the Charter thought so,[21] but there are not specific words to this effect in the Charter. Section 7 is similar to the "due process" clause of the 5th and 14th Amendments to the United States Constitution.[22] "Due process" in the United States has been used to encompass so-called "substantive" as well as "procedural" due process,[23] although many disagree with this approach. The drafters may well have used the words "fundamental justice" to avoid the "substantive due process" issue. Another possible reason was to avoid the extremely

---

20 (1983), 3 C.C.C. (3d) 198.

21 See Tarnopolsky, "The New Canadian Charter of Rights and Freedoms as Compared and Contrasted with the American Bill of Rights" (1983) 5 Human Rights Quarterly 227 at p. 235.

22 The 14th Amendment, added in 1868 after the Civil War, includes the words "nor shall any State deprive any person of life, liberty, or property, without due process of law." In the 1960's the Warren Court, starting with the landmark case of *Mapp v. Ohio* (1961), 367 U.S. 643, used the 14th Amendment to impose on the States some of the criminal law standards found in the earlier amendments that had been applicable only to the federal government.

23 For a recent application of the "discredited" *Lochner* principle *(Lochner v. New York* (1905), 198 U.S. 45) see *Roe v. Wade* (1973), 93 S.Ct. 705; *cf.* Ely. "The Wages of Crying Wolf: A Comment on *Roe v. Wade*" (1973) Yale L.J. 920.

narrow interpretation given to the phrase by some members of the Supreme Court of Canada. In *Curr v. The Queen*[24] Ritchie J. had stated that the phrase "due process of law" as used in the Bill of Rights is to be construed as meaning "according to the legal processes recognized by Parliament and the courts in Canada." So the words "fundamental justice" were probably used to encourage the courts to give a broader meaning to the concept than they had given to "due process", yet to discourage the courts from encompassing "substantive justice". Whatever the Supreme Court does with the issue of "substantive justice", section 7 will continue to offer the greatest potential scope of all the sections for challenging legislative and government action.[25] Thus far, however, the B.C. case is the only reported court of appeal decision applying section 7 in the accused's favour, although it has been raised in a number of cases. The Ontario Court of Appeal in *Regina v. Diotte*[26] held that "fundamental justice" did not require full disclosure at a preliminary hearing and the Manitoba Court of Appeal in *Regina v. Stolar*[27] held that there was no necessity to provide an opportunity for an accused to make submissions to the Attorney-General before a direct indictment was preferred. The Ontario Court of Appeal in *Regina v. Carter*[28] refused to exclude evidence of blood samples taken by hospital personnel and later seized by the police with a search warrant; and the same court held in *Regina v. Potma*[29] that it was not a breach of section 7 for the police to fail to produce the ampoules used in a breathalyzer test. The Ontario Court of Appeal in *Re Cadeddu*[30] was about to deal with a significant case on appeal from a judgment of Potts J. who held in the Ontario Supreme Court[31] that a person whose parole was revoked was entitled to an in-person hearing, but Caddedu died the day after the hearing of the appeal and before judgment, and the Court of Appeal refused to deal with a moot issue. The Quebec Court of Appeal in

24 (1972), 7 C.C.C. (2d) 181 at p. 185 (S.C.C.). See also *Hogan v. R.* (1974), 18 C.C.C. (2d) 65 (S.C.C.).

25 As to the application of s. 7 to "property" see *Elliott v. Director of Social Services* (1982), 17 Man. R. (2d) 350 (C.A.); *Re Estabrooks Pontiac Buick Ltd.; N.B. v. Estabrooks Pontiac Buick Ltd.; Re Fisherman's Wharf Ltd.* (1982), 44 N.B.R. (2d) 201 (C.A.); *Re Seaway Trust Co. and Ont.* (1983), 41 O.R. (2d) 532 (C.A.).

26 May 4, 1983.

27 (1983), 4 C.C.C. (3d) 333. Leave to appeal to S.C.C. refused 21 Man. R. (2d) 240.

28 (1982), 2 C.C.C. (3d) 412.

29 (1983), 2 C.C.C. (3d) 383 (Ont. C.A.).

30 (1983) 4 C.C.C. (3d) 112.

31 (1982) 4 C.C.C. (3d) 97. See also *Re Conroy and R.* (1983), 42 O.R. (2d) 342 (H.C.) *per* Craig J. Note *Soenen v. Director of Edmonton Remand Centre* (1983), 35 C.R. (3d) 206 (Alta. Q.B.), in which McDonald J. stated (at 222): "The principles of natural justice, and those of fundamental justice, do not impose procedural standards upon a director of an institution, in which pretrial or post conviction prisoners are held, when, pursuant to his statutory authority, he decides what the rules governing the institution shall be."

Regina v. Vermette[32] has agreed to hear an appeal from another significant case in which Greenberg J. stayed a prosecution under section 7 because of improper remarks by the Quebec Premier in the National Assembly which were given widespread publicity.[33] And, of course, the non-criminal Cruise missile case, in which section 7 is relied on by those opposed to the testing of the missile, has now been heard and reserved by the Supreme Court of Canada.

What is the relationship between section 7 and sections 8 to 14 inclusive? Certainly section 7 is wider than the specific sections that follow it. What if a matter is specifically dealt with under one of the specific sections; is it then excluded from section 7? In *Curr v. The Queen*,[34] Laskin J., as he then was, stated in a concurring opinion dealing with self-incrimination under the Bill of Rights that "due process" was not wider than the specific section dealing with self-incrimination. "I am concerned", he wrote, "with a submission that although self-crimination is expressly dealt with in one provision of the statute, this court should find another expression thereof in another provision of the same statute where it is not expressly mentioned." It is suggested that a similar approach will not be taken by the Supreme Court to the Charter. In the Bill of Rights the specific provisions were introduced by the words "in particular", showing, therefore, that they were meant to be applications of the general. But the scheme of the Charter is different, and the specific sections are not so related to section 7. So, for example, it would not be at all surprising for the courts to use section 7 in cases of delay before the accused is charged, assuming that delay in section 11(*b*) is limited to delay after the charge.

"Fundamental justice" has not been restricted to the trial itself. This had been done under the Bill of Rights[35] where the words "fundamental justice" were directly linked to the hearing. (Section 2(*e*) of the Bill of Rights refers to "a fair hearing in accordance with the principles of fundamental justice.") Under the Charter, courts of appeal have not, for example, objected to the potential application of section 7 to the preliminary hearing.[36]

---

32 (1982), 3 C.C.C. (3d) 36.

33 *R. v. Vermette (No. 4)* (1982), 1 C.C.C. (3d) 477. See also *Randall and Weir v. The Queen*, Nova Scotia Court of Appeal, June 29, 1983, where the accused unsuccessfully argued that it was contrary to the "principles of fundamental justice" to "apply the same minimum seven-year sentence to both 'hard drugs' such as heroin and 'soft drugs' such as marijuana."

34 (1972), 7 C.C.C. (2d) 181 at 202-3 (S.C.C.).

35 See *Duke v. R.* (1972), 7 C.C.C. (2d) 474 at 479 (S.C.C.).

36 See *R. v. Diotte*, May 4, 1983 (Ont. C.A.). See also *Stolar v. R.* (1983), 32 C.R. (3d) 342 (Man. C.A.); *R. v. Hislop et al.* (1983), 43 O.R. (2d) 208 (C.A.). Leave to appeal to S.C.C. refused 1 D.L.R. (4th) 424*.

3. "REASONABLE LIMITS PRESCRIBED BY LAW"

Not only will it be important to watch what the Supreme Court of Canada does with section 7, it will be equally important to see what the Court does with section 1, which states that the rights and freedoms set out in the Charter are "subject only to such reasonable limits prescribed by law as can be demonstrably justified in a free and democratic society." Section 1 was raised in about one third of the Court of Appeal cases I examined, although rejected in over half of the cases in which it was raised.[37]

It does appear that perhaps there has been too much reliance on section 1. Courts have taken the rather lawyer-like route of finding that there has been a prima facie breach of a named provision, and then testing whether the legislation or action can be upheld under section 1. Judges seem to like making their decisions within the comfortable confines of section 1. This gives the section greater prominence than it probably should have. Surely it would be better for the courts to concentrate on interpreting the named provision as they would have been forced to do if there *was* no section 1. There is no comparable section in the American Bill of Rights, and the so-called "limitation" clauses in the U.N. Covenant and in the European Convention are limited to emergency situations.[38]

Following is a discussion of some of the specific Charter provisions. I have not dealt with s. 8, the search and seizure section, in this chapter.

4. "ARBITRARILY DETAINED"

Section 9 provides: "Everyone has the right not to be arbitrarily detained or imprisoned." No court of appeal case has yet given a detailed exposition of the section. There is a similar provision in the Bill of Rights: "no law of Canada shall be construed or applied so as to . . . authorize or effect the arbitrary detention, imprisonment or exile of any person." No doubt a court interpreting the Charter would adopt the meaning that Arnup J.A. gave to the word "arbitrary" when dealing with the validity of writs of assistance under the Bill of Rights:[39] "To be 'arbitrary' in this context means to be unreasonable or capricious."

The question of what constitutes a "detention" has been the subject

---

37 Section 1 was relied on by the courts in *R. v. Altseimer* (1982), 1 C.C.C. (3d) 7 (Ont. C.A.); *Re Skapinker and Law Society of Upper Can.* (1983), 3 C.C.C. (3d) 213 (Ont. C.A.); *R. v. Carroll* (1983), 4 C.C.C. (3d) 131 (P.E.I.C.A.); *Re Federal Republic of Germany and Rauca* (1983), 41 O.R. (2d) 225 (C.A.); *Reference Re S. 94(2) of the Motor Vehicle Act of B.C.* (1983), 4 C.C.C. (3d) 243 (B.C.C.A.); *R. v. Holmes* (1983), 4 C.C.C. (3d) 440 (Ont. C.A.); *R. v. Carson* (1983), 4 C.C.C. (3d) 476 (Ont. C.A.).

38 See Article 21 of the International Covenant and Article 15 of the European Convention.

39 *Levitz v. Ryan* (1972), 9 C.C.C. (2d) 182 at 189 (Ont. C.A.).

of a number of court of appeal cases. Section 10(*b*) of the Charter provides: "Everyone has the right on arrest or detention . . . to retain and instruct counsel without delay and to be informed of that right." Must a person suspected of impaired driving who has been stopped for a roadside-screening test or who accompanies a police officer to a police station for a breathalyzer test be informed that he has the right to counsel? In the Supreme Court of Canada case of *Chromiak v. The Queen*[40] under the Bill of Rights the court said that a person stopped for a roadside test was not detained. That decision was followed by the Ontario Court of Appeal in *Altseimer*.[41]

The more difficult question is whether *Chromiak* should apply to a person who voluntarily accompanies an officer to a police station for a breathalyzer test. There are observations in *Chromiak* which would cover the breathalyzer situation and a number of courts of appeal have so applied it in Charter cases.[42] The Nova Scotia Court of Appeal in *Regina v. Currie* took the position[43] that "had the British Parliament intended to create a more substantial right by s. 10 of the Charter than that guaranteed by s. 2(*c*) of the Canadian Bill of Rights, it would have used different terminology." This may be the high-water mark of imputed parliamentary intention, considering that if the British Parliament intended anything it was to get rid of the whole question as quickly as reasonably possible. In contrast, the majority of the Saskatchewan Court of Appeal held in *Regina v. Therens*[44] that accompanying an officer to a station was a detention. *Chromiak* was of interpretative assistance, but did not bind a court under what was described as a "living" Charter. The court recognized that different considerations may apply to a roadside screening. My guess is that the Supreme Court of Canada will say that both the *Altseimer* and *Therens* decisions are correct, that an accused need not be told before a roadside screening test that he has the right to counsel, but must be told this before a breathalyzer test.[45]

5. RIGHT TO COUNSEL

The requirement that the accused must be told that he has the right to counsel differs from the previous law, one of the few major express changes in the legal rights from the existing law. (Perhaps the only other

---

40 (1979), 49 C.C.C. (2d) 257 at 262 (S.C.C.).

41 *Supra* note 37. See also *R. v. Simmonds, Globe, & Mail,* April 13, 1984 (Ont. C.A.), upholding airport strip searches without the necessity of informing the person of the right to counsel.

42 See *R. v. Currie* (1983), 33 C.R. (3d) 227 (N.S.C.A.); *R. v. Trask* (1983), 6 C.C.C. (3d) 132. Leave to appeal to S.C.C. granted 6 C.C.C. (3d) 132*n*.

43 *Ibid.* at 234.

44 (1983), 33 C.R. (3d) 204.

45 *Therens* and *Trask* are to be heard by the Supreme Court of Canada.

express change in legal rights is in section 13, the self-incrimination section, which we will come to later. Section 24, the remedies section, is also new.) The prior law was expressed as follows by MacKay J.A. in *Regina v. DeClercq*:[46] "I am not aware that there is any legal duty imposed on police officers, unless they are asked, to tell people they question when investigating complaints or before they take statements, that they are entitled to counsel." An accused now has to be informed of his right to counsel on arrest — as in the United States under the *Miranda* ruling[47] — and failure to do so will mean in most cases that a statement obtained will be excluded under section 24. Whether the courts will require the police to say that the accused does not have to make a statement, as in *Miranda*, remains to be seen.

Because the provision is new, the courts have understandably held that the Charter is not retroactive before April 17, 1982. The Saskatchewan Court of Appeal so held in *Regina v. Lee*[48] and this was followed by the Ontario Court of Appeal in *Regina v. Longtin*.[49] In the earlier Ontario Court of Appeal case of *Regina v. Potma*[50] the Ontario Court of Appeal avoided the issue on other grounds stating[51] that "It is better left for determination in a case where, unlike this one, the Charter has the effect of changing existing law and the issue is thus of practical consequence". No doubt, the Supreme Court of Canada will follow *Lee* and *Longtin*. It is possible that the Supreme Court, assuming such a case is tested in the Supreme Court, will apply section 24, the remedies section, to conduct which was illegal before the Charter came into effect, but which was tested after the Charter came into operation,[52] and they will surely not ignore conduct occurring before the Charter, such as delay and "cruel and unusual" punishment, which continued past the date of the implementation of the Charter. The Ontario Court of Appeal held in *Regina v. Antoine*[53] that pre-trial delay could be taken into account, although Martin J.A. stated for the Court that "delay antecedent to the Charter does not have the same weight as delay subsequent to the Charter."[54]

---

46 [1966] 2 C.C.C. 190 at 192 (Ont. C.A.), affirmed [1968] S.C.R. 902.

47 *Miranda v. Arizona* (1966), 384 U.S. 436.

48 (1982), 142 D.L.R. (3d) 574.

49 (1983), 41 O.R. (2d) 545 (C.A.).

50 (1983), 2 C.C.C. (3d) 383.

51 *Ibid.* at 393.

52 See also *R. v. Antoine* (1983), 41 O.R. (2d) 607 (C.A.), holding that s. 24 can, of course, apply to trials commenced before the Charter came into operation if there is a breach of a right secured by the Charter which occurred after the operation of the Charter.

53 *Ibid.* at 613. See also *R. v. Beason* (1983), 43 O.R. (2d) 65 (C.A.).

54 The issue of retroactivity was raised in the Ontario Court of Appeal decision of *Diotte*, May 4, 1983, from which leave to appeal to the Supreme Court of Canada was refused, Oct. 13, 1983.

One question not specifically dealt with in the Charter is whether the state has an obligation, as in the United States,[55] to supply legal aid to an arrested person who cannot afford counsel. Nor is any mention made in the Charter of an obligation to provide legal assistance at trial. This question had been raised under the Bill of Rights in the *Ewing* case,[56] where two members of the British Columbia Court of Appeal held that there was no obligation to supply counsel to an indigent person charged with possession of narcotics; two other members of the court said that fairness demanded that counsel be supplied; and the fifth member of the court said that, in any event, this was not a case where it was unfair not to provide counsel. Although the right to counsel at trial is not mentioned in the Charter, and there are as yet no appeal court decisions on the question, it is safe to assume that it will come under the concept of a "fair . . . hearing" in section 11. In certain cases legal assistance for the indigent will be considered essential to a "fair hearing". Article 14(3)(*d*) of the U.N. Covenant, which provides that a person "to be tried" has the right "to have legal assistance assigned to him, in any case where the interests of justice so require, and without payment by him in any . . . case if he does not have sufficient means to pay for it", might be used to flesh out some of the bare bones of the concept of a "fair hearing". The courts will probably also look to the American cases to determine when "the interests of justice" require counsel. In *Argersinger v. Hamlin*[57] the United States Supreme Court limited *Gideon v. Wainwright*[58] to cases where the accused receives a jail sentence. In other words, if he does not have counsel because he is indigent he cannot be sentenced to jail.

6. "PERSON CHARGED WITH AN OFFENCE"

Section 11 provides that "any person charged with an offence" has certain specified rights. The definition of these opening words are important because they determine to whom the rights apply. Is a corporation a person?

The British Columbia Court of Appeal held in *Re P. P. G. Industries and Attorney General of Canada*[59] that a corporation was not a person to which the right to a jury trial applied, and so a corporation was not entitled to trial by jury under the Combines Investigation Act. The Supreme Court of Canada has granted leave to appeal in this case, and so we may get guidance on the issue and the related question whether a corporation is

---

55 *Miranda v. Arizona, supra* note 47.

56 *Re Ewing and Kearney and R.* (1974), 18 C.C.C. (2d) 356 (B.C.C.A.).

57 (1972), 407 U.S. 25.

58 (1963), 372 U.S. 335.

59 (1983), 3 C.C.C. (3d) 97. Leave to appeal to S.C.C. granted 3 C.C.C. (3d) 97*.

covered by the search and seizure sections, as a number of trial judges have held.[60]

The author is not aware of a court of appeal judgment on the words "charged with," but trial judges have used those words to prevent the right to a jury trial applying to a summary application for contempt of court[61] and to a declaration as a dangerous offender.[62] Nor have I seen any court of appeal cases on the word "offence". A number of trial courts have, however, dealt with the question. A trial judge in British Columbia has held that a professional disciplinary proceeding is not dealing with an "offence", such that a person subject to discipline cannot be compelled to be a witness under s. 11(c),[63] and another British Columbia judge has held that an internal prison disciplinary proceeding is not an offence which will bar a subsequent criminal charge under s. 11(h) of the Charter.[64] In the Ontario Court of Appeal case, *Regina v. Carson*[65] the court assumed that the simplified procedure under the Provincial Offences Act came within section 11, but upheld the legislation under s. 1 of the Charter; and an Ontario trial judge has held that municipal parking infractions are "offences" within section 11 of the Charter.[66] One wonders whether the word "offence" should be given such a broad meaning. Note that the marginal designation, which has on occasion been looked to by courts in the past,[67] says "Proceedings in criminal and penal matters," which may be used to limit the application of the provision.

7. "TRIED WITHIN A REASONABLE TIME"

There have been a reasonably large number of trial judgments in which section 11(b), "to be tried within a reasonable time" has been argued. There are now several court of appeal cases. A Manitoba Court of Appeal case has held that a delay of eight months from an order

---

60   *Southam Inc. v. Hunter* (1982), 68 C.C.C. (2d) 356 (Alta. Q.B.) *per* Cavanagh J., affirmed (1982), 65 C.P.R. (2d) 116. Leave to appeal to S.C.C. granted 147 D.L.R. (3d) 420; *Re Balderstone et al. and R.* (1982), 2 C.C.C. (3d) 37 (Man. Q.B.) *per* Scollin J. Affirmed 8 C.C.C. (3d) 532 (Man. C.A.). Leave to appeal to S.C.C. refused 8 C.C.C. (3d) 532n.

61   *A.G. Que. v. Laurendeau* (1982), 3 C.C.C. (3d) 250 (Que. S.C.) *per* Rothman J. A further motion to the Quebec Court of Appeal was dismissed: *Laurendeau v. A.G. Que.* (1983), 33 C.R. (3d) 350.

62   *R. v. Simon (No. 2)* (1982), 141 D.L.R. (3d) 374 (N.W.T.S.C.) *per* de Weerdt J.

63   *Re James and Law Society of B.C.* (1982), 143 D.L.R. (3d) 379 (B.C.S.C.) *per* Murray J. See also *Re Rasenbaum and Law Society of Man.* (1983), 6 C.C.C. (3d) 472 (Man. Q.B.) *per* Scollin J., affirmed 8 C.C.C. (3d) 256 (Man. C.A.).

64   *R. v. Mingo* (1982), 2 C.C.C. (3d) 23 (B.C.S.C.) *per* Toy J.

65   (1983), 4 C.C.C. (3d) 476.

66   *McCutcheon v. City of Toronto* (1983), 41 O.R. (2d) 652 (H.C.). *per* Linden J.

67   See *Wright, McDermott and Feeley v. R.*, [1963] 3 C.C.C. 201 (S.C.C.).

transferring a juvenile to an ordinary court was not unreasonable[68] and the same court held that six months was not unreasonable.[69] In contrast, the Nova Scotia Court of Appeal in *Regina v. Corkum Construction*[70] — a case on which leave to appeal was recently refused by the Supreme Court of Canada — held that the magistrate did not err in ruling that a 3½ month delay between the serving of a summons and the trial was unreasonable in the light of a number of factors such as the nature of the charge, the length of the limitation period, the delay in serving the information and the possibility of prejudice to the accused. The Ontario Court of Appeal in *Regina v. Antoine*[71] held that a 26 month delay did not breach the Charter, but some of that period was delay before the Charter came into effect and, as we have already seen, the Court took the view that delay prior to the Charter is not entitled to the same weight as delay occurring after the Charter came into force.

In the United States the comparable "speedy trial" provision has been interpreted to mean a reasonable time from the charge; the pre-indictment period does not matter, although it can be argued that undue delay before a charge is a denial of "due process".[72] In *Corkum*, however, the Nova Scotia Court of Appeal ruled that it was proper to take into account the period of time prior to the laying of an information. The Ontario Court of Appeal in *Antoine*[73] implicitly accepted that section 11(b) related to delay between the initial information and the trial, but the possibility of a wider interpretation was not argued. It will be interesting to see what the Supreme Court of Canada says on this question, and whether the Court attempts to spell out a test for "unreasonable delay". The Court has granted leave to appeal from the Ontario Court of Appeal decision of *Regina v. Mills*,[74] which (unlike some of the other Ontario Court of Appeal decisions) dealt in a cursory manner with the issue of delay. The test used by the U.S. Supreme Court in *Barker v. Wingo*[75] is, in the words of the Court, "a balancing test, in which the conduct of both the prosecution and the defendant are weighed." In the U.S., crowded dockets do not constitute an excuse for delay, although deliberate delay will count for

---

68 *R. v. Belton* (1982), 3 C.C.C. (3d) 427 (Man. C.A.). Leave to appeal to S.C.C. refused 20 Man. R. (2d) 179 (S.C.C.).

69 *R. v. Burrows* (1983), 6 C.C.C. (3d) 54 (Man. C.A.).

70 (1983), 5 C.C.C. (3d) 575 (N.S.C.A.). Leave to appeal to S.C.C. refused 60 N.S.R. (2d) 270n (S.C.C.).

71 (1983), 41 O.R. (2d) 607.

72 *U.S. v. Lovasco* (1977), 431 U.S. 783.

73 *Supra* note 71.

74 Leave to appeal to S.C.C. granted (1983), 43 O.R. (2d) 632n from the decision of the Ontario Court of Appeal's eleven line judgment 43 O.R. (2d) 631, dismissing an appeal from Osborne J.'s judgment: (1983), 2 C.C.C. (3d) 444.

75 (1972), 407 U.S. 514 at 530.

more than delay because of crowded dockets. Mr. Justice Martin in *Antoine*[76] described *Barker v. Wingo* as an "illuminating judgment" and found it "both persuasive and helpful in determining the similar question whether an accused's right to be tried within a reasonable time . . . has been contravened." Mr. Justice Martin's judgment is itself illuminating. His approach requires a careful investigation of the reasons for delay. "Although the failure of the accused to object to delay", Martin J.A. states, "is a factor to which considerable weight must be given . . . there might be some delays by the prosecution that, in the circumstances, are so shocking that a court would be warranted in holding that an accused's right under section 11(b) to be tried within a reasonable time had been infringed, despite his apparent acquiescence in those delays." Martin J.A., for the Ontario Court of Appeal, also found "shocking" delay in the later case of *Regina v. Beason*[77] where there was a delay of more than four years in bringing the accused to trial on a "simple charge of theft". The court held that objections by the accused and a finding of prejudice were not necessary conditions for a breach of the Charter provision and concluded that in these circumstances "the only appropriate remedy is the dismissal of the charge."

A number of courts of appeal have dealt with the issue of whether an appeal lies from a refusal to hold that the delay was reasonable and have held that no direct appeal lies[78] and that a prerogative writ should not be used to split up the proceedings.[79] If there is one issue that appeal courts seem to be agreed on it is that trials should not be fragmented by prerogative proceedings and appeals during the course of the trial.[80] Of course, if the trial judge stays a proceeding based on unreasonable delay, one would expect an appeal court to hear an appeal and in the Manitoba Court of Appeal case of *Regina v. Belton*[81] the Court held that a stay under such circumstances was tantamount to a verdict of acquittal.

8. "PRESUMED INNOCENT"

The subsection which wins the prize for the greatest number of appeal cases is 11(*d*): "to be presumed innocent until proven guilty

---

76 *Supra* note 71 at 617 and 621.

77 *Supra* note 53. *Cf. Kott and R., Re* (1983), 7 C.C.C. (3d) 317 (Que. C.A.); leave to appeal to S.C.C. refused 7 C.C.C. (3d) 317 (S.C.C.).

78 *R. v. Cameron* (1982), 3 C.C.C. (3d) 496 (Alta. C.A.).

79 See *e.g. Re Krakowski and R.* (1983), 4 C.C.C. (3d) 188 (Ont. C.A.).

80 See also *Re Kendall and R.* (1982), 2 C.C.C. (3d) 224 (Alta. C.A.); *Re Anson and R.* (1983), 4 C.C.C. (3d) 119 (B.C.C.A.); *Laurendeau v. A.G. Que., supra* note 61; *Re Seaway Trust Co. et al. and Ont.* (1983), 41 O.R. (2d) 532 (C.A.). Leave to appeal to S.C.C. refused 37 C.P.C. 8 (S.C.C.).

81 (1982), 3 C.C.C. (3d) 427, leave to appeal to the Supreme Court of Canada refused 3 C.C.C. (3d) 427. See also *R. v. Holmes* (1983), 41 O.R. (2d) 250 (C.A.).

according to law in a fair and public hearing by an independent and impartial tribunal." Indeed, the first part of the subsection dealing with the presumption of innocence simply in relation to section 8 of the Narcotic Control Act could carry off the prize by itself.

The appeal courts have so far been unanimous in declaring that the reverse onus section found in section 8 of the Narcotic Control Act violates section 11(d) of the Charter. As is well known, section 8 provides that if an accused is proved to be in possession of a narcotic he must establish that the possession was not for the purpose of trafficking. The first appeal court judgment to decide the issue was a five-member Ontario Court of Appeal in *Regina v. Oakes*[82]. Once again, Mr. Justice Martin delivered a thorough and penetrating judgment for the Court, and once again carefully canvassed the American authorities. The court held that section 8 did reverse the onus and then quickly shifted attention to section 1, holding that the reverse onus could not be "demonstrably justified in a free and democratic society" under section 1 of the Charter. Earlier Supreme Court of Canada cases had dealt with the comparable section in the Bill of Rights. In the *Shelley* case,[83] Chief Justice Laskin stated that the comparable Bill of Rights clause does not violate the presumption of innocence if it "goes no farther than to require an accused to prove an essential fact upon a balance of probabilities", and if the essential fact is "one which is rationally open to the accused to prove or disprove." Martin J.A. held that these were not the exclusive considerations and added a further test: "a reverse onus clause which is unreasonable or arbitrary because there is no rational connection between the proved fact and the presumed fact offends against the fundamental principle that an accused has the right to be presumed innocent" under the Bill of Rights and, it would follow, under the Charter. Martin J.A. seemed somewhat nervous about this extension of *Shelley* and quickly shifted to section 1, applying the same test to that section: "a reverse onus provision . . . cannot be justified as a reasonable limitation of the right to be presumed innocent under s. 1 of the Charter in the absence of a rational connection between the proved fact and the presumed fact. In the absence of such a connection the presumption created is purely arbitrary." The Court more or less invited Parliament to redraft the section by suggesting that "Parliament, if it had wished to do so, might have decided that possession of a specified quantity of a certain drug was more consistent with trafficking than possession for pesonal use, and could have made the possession of the specified quantity presumptive evidence that the drug was possessed for the purpose of trafficking."

Other appeal courts have reached the same result with respect to

---

82 (1983), 2 C.C.C. (3d) 339. Leave to appeal to S.C.C. granted 2 C.C.C. (3d) 339.

83 *R. v. Shelley* (1981), 59 C.C.C. (2d) 292 at 295 (S.C.C.).

section 8: See Prince Edward Island,[84] British Columbia,[85] Nova Scotia,[86] New Brunswick,[87] Alberta[88] and Quebec.[89] Every court was unanimous on this issue, with the exception of the Alberta court, where Mr. Justice Mclung delivered a strong dissent stating that "there is a rational, fair and manageable onus within s. 8". "The Canadian Charter of Rights and Freedoms grants us no mandate," he states, "to strike down valid parliamentary expressions on the ground that their rational underpinning might be assailed in notional cases." Mclung J.A. even referred to Hansard[90] to show that the Minister of Justice at the time of the introduction of section 8 was of the view that the section did not conflict with the Bill of Rights.

The *Oakes* case is to be heard by the Supreme Court of Canada and it will be interesting to see what their approach will be. Most observers predict that they will strike down section 8. This is probable, but it is likely that they will build Martin J.A.'s "rational connection" test into section 11(*d*) and not force reliance on section 1.

There have been other challenges to legislation based on the "presumption of innocence." In *Regina v. Holmes*,[91] the Ontario Court of Appeal held — and this was subsequently followed by the Manitoba Court of Appeal in *Regina v. Kowalczuk*[92] — that Code section 309 placing the onus on the accused to prove a lawful excuse for possession of instruments suitable for housebreaking when found in possession under circumstances giving rise to a reasonable inference that the instrument was intended to be used for housebreaking, did not shift the onus of proof. Even if it did, the court said, it was not unreasonable under section 1, following *Oakes*, "by reason of the rational connection between the presumption and the facts required to be proved." Further, in *Regina v. Russell*[93] the Nova Scotia Court of Appeal held that the doctrine of recent

84 *R. v. Carroll* (1983), 4 C.C.C. (3d) 131 (P.E.I. C.A.).

85 *Re Anson and R.* (1983), 4 C.C.C. (3d) 119 (B.C.C.A.).

86 *Cook v. R.* (1983), 4 C.C.C. (3d) 419 (N.S. C.A.).

87 *R. v. O'Day* (1983), 5 C.C.C. (3d) 227 (N.B. C.A.).

88 *R. v. Stanger*, [1983] 5 W.W.R. 331 (Alta. C.A.).

89 *Landry v. R.* (1983), 7 C.C.C. (3d) 555 (Que. C.A.). L'Heureux-Dubé J. dissented on the basis that the facts warranted a finding of trafficking. The conviction was before the Charter came into operation, but the Court applied *Oakes* to the comparable section of the Bill of Rights, s. 2(*f*) — another illustration of the Charter giving new life to the Bill of Rights.

90 See also the reference to Hansard in *Re Federal Republic of Germany and Rauca* (1983), 4 C.C.C. (3d) 385 (Ont. C.A.) at 404-5.

91 (1983), 41 O.R. (2d) 250. The Supreme Court of Canada has granted leave to appeal from a similar decision of the Ontario Court of Appeal, *R. v. Pearce*, March 15, 1983.

92 [1983] 3 W.W.R. 694 (Man. C.A.).

93 (1983), 32 C.R. (3d) 307.

possession created only an evidential burden on the accused and not a persuasive burden, and so did not contravene section 11(d). The Ontario Court of Appeal in *Re Boyle and the Queen*[94] applied the reasoning in *Oakes* to section 312(2) of the Criminal Code, holding that the presumption that a motor vehicle which had its identification number obliterated had been obtained by crime was reasonable and therefore constitutionally valid, but the presumption that the accused had guilty knowledge of this fact was not. Note that the Court applied section 11(d) to a statute which placed an onus on the accused to adduce evidence of a reasonable doubt.

One issue that has not come before the Courts is whether the onus placed on the accused by the Supreme Court of Canada in *Regina v. Sault Ste. Marie*[95] to prove that he exercised due diligence in strict liability cases meets the Charter. One can be sure that the Supreme Court of Canada will find that it is valid. To strike it down might ultimately detract from the rights of the accused, by encouraging the legislature to create more absolute liability offences. A difficult question to sort out is how the Charter can permit the Ontario Court of Appeal in *Oakes* to strike down a reverse onus clause, and yet permit the same court two days earlier in *Regina v. Stevens*[96] to hold that Parliament can completely eliminate an otherwise essential element — in that case, knowledge of a girl's age. Maybe, in spite of its surprising decision, the B.C. Court of Appeal is on the right track.

9. "REASONABLE BAIL"

Two days after the *Oakes* case was released the Ontario Court of Appeal released *Regina v. Bray*,[97] again a unanimous judgment delivered by Martin J.A. The issue was the validity of the section of the Code (section 457.7(2)(f)) which places the onus on an accused charged with murder to show cause why he should be released from custody pending trial. No mention was made in the judgment of the presumption of innocence or the *Oakes* case; rather, it was section 11(e) which was analyzed: "not to be denied reasonable bail without just cause." The Court held that section 11(e) was not breached, and even if it was breached, the provision was a "reasonable limitation" under section 1. The Court also, in an obiter statement, took the view that detention to prevent the commission of offences would "clearly constitute 'just cause,'" an issue which is a contentious one in the United States.

The Ontario Court in *Bray* disagreed with the Nova Scotia Court of Appeal case, *Regina v. Pugsley*[98] which struck down the reverse onus bail

94 (1983), 41 O.R. (2d) 713.
95 (1978), 40 C.C.C. (2d) 353 (S.C.C.).
96 (1983), 3 C.C.C. (3d) 198.
97 (1983), 2 C.C.C. (3d) 325.
98 (1982), 2 C.C.C. (3d) 266.

section, again without reliance on the presumption of innocence subsection. "Under the Charter", the Court stated, "it seems clear . . . that a person who is charged with an offence is entitled to reasonable bail unless the Crown can show just cause for a continuance of his detention."

10. "FAIR AND PUBLIC HEARING BY AN INDEPENDENT AND IMPARTIAL TRIBUNAL"

Returning again to section 11(d), there is room for discussion and division on the words "fair", "public hearing", and "independent and impartial tribunal."

The word "fair" has been the subject of only one Court of Appeal decision. In *Regina v. Sophonow*[99] an accused who was appealing his conviction asked the Manitoba Court of Appeal for a ban on extra-judicial comment respecting his guilt or innocence until after his appeal was concluded, on the ground that his rights under section 11(d) of the Charter were infringed. The Court denied his application, not wanting to act as a censor, and keeping in mind the "freedom of the press" provision in s. 2. In the Quebec case of *Regina v. Vermette (No. 4)*[100] the trial judge stayed a charge because the Premier of Quebec made certain improper comments about the accused that were given widespread publicity. The Quebec Court of Appeal ruled[101] that an appeal can be taken from the stayed proceedings, but as yet there are no indications that a decision has been reached by the appeal court. The section may in the long run prove to be a very important one because of the elasticity of the word "fair". Perhaps Article 14 of the U.N. Covenant will be used to put flesh on the word. It provides some concrete cases of fairness not otherwise dealt with in the Charter. For example, Article 14(3) states in part that an accused is entitled "to have adequate time and facilities for the preparation of his defence"; "to be tried in his presence"; and "to examine or have examined, the witnesses against him and to obtain the attendance and examination of witnesses on his behalf under the same conditions as witnesses against him."

Section 11(d) refers to a "public hearing by an independent and impartial tribunal." The Ontario Court of Appeal in *Re Southam Inc. and The Queen (No. 1)*[102] held that the provision in the present Juvenile Delinquents Act that trials should be *in camera* was inconsistent with the Charter. Note, however, that it was section 2(b) relating to "freedom of the press" that was relied on by the court, not section 11(d), because the ap-

99 (1983), 21 Man. R. (2d) 110.

100 (1982), 1 C.C.C. (3d) 477 (Que. S.C.) *per* Greenberg J.

101 (1982), 3 C.C.C. (3d) 36 (Que. C.A.).

102 (1983), 3 C.C.C. (3d) 515.

plication for an open hearing was not made by the accused but by a newspaper. As in the *Oakes* case, the court invited Parliament to introduce a section individualizing the decision respecting barring the public: "An amendment giving jurisdiction to the court to exclude the public from juvenile court proceedings where it concludes, under the circumstances, that it is in the best interests of the child or others concerned or in the best interests of the administration of justice to do so would meet any residual concern arising from the striking down of the section." As in *Oakes*, the court was not willing to "rewrite the statute," but was willing to give guidance to the legislative draftsman. The net result will be, assuming new legislation is enacted, that the decision will be individualized on a case-by-case basis — the traditional judicial method of trying to achieve justice.

The words "independent tribunal" were analyzed in *Regina v. Valente (No. 2)*[103] where the Ontario Court of Appeal held that the Ontario Provincial Court Judges were "independent" within the meaning of the Charter. The case is to be heard by the Supreme Court of Canada. The test set out by Howland C.J.O. for a five-member court is "whether a reasonable person, who was informed of the relevant statutory provisions, their historical background and the traditions surrounding them, after viewing the matter realistically and practically would conclude that a provincial court judge . . . was a tribunal which could make an independent and impartial adjudication." The court held that there was not a "reasonable apprehension" that the judge was not able "to make an independent and impartial adjudication." Other cases will, no doubt, arise in the future. The Supreme Court of Canada held in *MacKay v. The Queen*[104] under a comparable provision in the Bill of Rights, that court martial proceedings were valid. This may be tested under the Charter, but undoubtedly the same result will be reached. Assuming that a professional disciplinary hearing comes within section 11, it would seem, therefore, that the tribunal would be considered "independent and impartial", even if composed of members of the same professional organization.

11. "TRIAL BY JURY"

Section 11(*f*) gives the right to a jury trial in any case "where the maximum punishment for the offence is imprisonment for five years." We have already seen that lower courts have found ways to hold that contempt proceedings and dangerous offender declarations do not require jury trials. Similarly, in *R. v. S.B.*[105] the B.C. Court of Appeal held

---

103 (1983), 2 C.C.C. (3d) 417. Leave to appeal to S.C.C. granted 2 C.C.C. (3d) 417*.
104 (1980), 54 C.C.C. (2d) 129.
105 (1983), 3 C.C.C. (3d) 390.

that a juvenile committed to an industrial school for more than five years did not have the right to a jury trial because the Juvenile Delinquents Act "does not contemplate punishment." Further, the Alberta Court of Appeal held in *Crate v. The Queen*[106] that a deemed reelection to be tried by a judge without a jury under section 526.1 of the Code is valid. Section 11(*f*) excepts from its operation "an offence under military law tried before a military tribunal." There are two relevant and interesting decisions of the Court Martial Appeal Court of Canada under the Charter. In *MacDonald v. The Queen*[107] the court held that the off-duty sale of marijuana by a serviceman had what is described as "a real military *nexus*" to the service because of the clear "connection between drug use and the user's performance of his or her military duties." Therefore, the accused was properly subject to military discipline and was not entitled to a jury trial. In a later case, *Rutherford v. The Queen*,[108] the court held that similar off-duty conduct by a serviceman who had subsequently left the service was not subject to military discipline under the National Defence Act and so could not be tried without a jury. According to the court, he would be denied his rights under section 15 of the Charter of "equality before the law enjoyed by other civilians", a rather interesting analysis considering that section 15 does not come into operation until 1985.[109] Section 1 was not applicable because it could not be demonstrated, stated the court, "that his escape from punishment, total or partial, will adversely affect 'the general standard of discipline and efficiency of the Service.'"

Some further issues may arise in the future. Will six-person juries, as now exist in the Yukon and Northwest Territories,[110] be permitted to continue? The Supreme Court of the United States in *Williams v. Florida*[111] upheld six-member state juries, as, no doubt, would our courts. What about non-unanimous majority verdicts, which now exist in England[112] and in some American states? It does not appear likely that majority verdicts will be proposed in Canada in the near future, in view of the Law Reform Commission of Canada's position[113] arguing against the practice. But assume that legislation were introduced. The United States Supreme

---

106 (1983), 7 C.C.C. (3d) 127.

107 June 1, 1983.

108 June 24, 1983.

109 The Court could have relied on — and perhaps intended to rely on — s. 1(*b*) of the Bill of Rights, "equality before the law".

110 Criminal Code, s. 561.

111 (1970), 399 U.S. 78.

112 Criminal Justice Act, 1967 (U.K.), c. 80, s. 13.

113 Working Paper No. 27, The Jury in Criminal Trials (Ottawa, 1980), at p. 19; Report No. 16, The Jury (Ottawa, 1982), at p. 77.

Court held in *Apodaca v. Oregon*[114] in 1972 that legislation providing for ten out of twelve jurors was constitutional and in *Johnson v. Louisiana*[115] in the same year that nine out of twelve was permissible. One should not conclude, however, that majority verdicts are therefore constitutional in the United States in all cases. These were state prosecutions which were subject to the "due process" clause of the 14th Amendment. They do not necessarily determine the issue for federal law which is governed by the right to an "impartial jury" in the sixth Amendment. Indeed, a majority of the Supreme Court in the two cases mentioned above held that majority verdicts were not permitted in federal prosecutions. So, when looking at American cases one must be careful to distinguish 14th Amendment cases from constitutional cases involving the amendments applicable to the federal government. To complete the picture on this issue in the United States, the Supreme Court held that the right to a jury trial is breached if the jury consists of fewer than six jurors[116] and in another case[117] did not permit majority verdicts in the case of six-person juries.

12. "SELF-CRIMINATION"

Self-incrimination — or as it is described in a marginal note, "self-crimination" — is discussed in two provisions of the Charter. Section 11(c) states that a person charged has the right "not to be compelled to be a witness in proceedings against that person in respect of that offence", and section 13 states that "a witness who testifies in any proceedings has the right not to have any incriminating evidence so given used to incriminate that witness in any other proceedings except in a prosecution for perjury or for the giving of contradictory evidence." In *Altseimer*[118] the Ontario Court of Appeal held that the breathalyzer provisions did not breach the Charter, stating that "it is plain that the protection continues to be protection against testimonial compulsion and nothing else."

Section 13 goes beyond the existing law, however, in that now a witness does not have to object to answering a question in order to prevent its use in a subsequent proceeding. Under Section 5(1) of the Canada Evidence Act an objection was necessary.[119] A minor change is that the Charter allows a later prosecution for giving contradictory evidence[120] as well as for perjury; the change was necessary because the Canada Evidence

---

114 (1972), 406 U.S. 404.

115 (1972), 406 U.S. 356.

116 *Ballew v. Georgia* (1978), 435 U.S. 223.

117 *Burch v. Louisiana* (1979), 441 U.S. 130.

118 (1982), 1 C.C.C. (3d) 7.

119 *Ibid.* at 12.

120 Criminal Code, s. 124.

Act had been interpreted[121] as not encompassing a contradictory evidence charge within the word "perjury".

In *Re Crooks and the Queen*[122] the Ontario Court of Appeal approved of a judgment by O'Driscoll J. holding that a separately charged accused could be compelled to give evidence at the trial of another person charged with the same offence. This case, for which leave to appeal has been granted by the Supreme Court of Canada, was followed by the British Columbia Court of Appeal.[123] Other questions will come up in the future. Will the courts allow an accused who has not yet been charged to be called before a coroner's inquest, as apparently happens in Quebec?[124] Would it violate the Charter if the Evidence Act was changed to allow the judge to comment on the accused's failure to testify, as in England,[125] and as in the Law Reform Commission of Canada's proposed Evidence Code?[126] As a trial judge in Ontario recently held,[127] does the section prevent a judge or jury or appeal court taking into account the fact that the accused did not testify?

13. DOUBLE JEOPARDY

The double jeopardy provision (section 11(h)) is a very narrow one: "if finally acquitted of the offence, not to be tried or punished for it again and, if finally found guilty and punished for the offence, not to be tried for it again." The language of the provision will not, without stretching the natural meaning of the words, cover the rule against multiple convictions,[128] the rule against unreasonably splitting a case,[129] issue estoppel,[130] termination before a final verdict, or even prosecutions for similar, although not identical, offences. It does not even cover all of the ambit of the traditional special pleas of *autrefois acquit* or *convict* which in addition prohibit subsequent prosecutions in certain cases for more serious

---

121 See *R. v. Chaperon* (1979), 52 C.C.C. (2d) 85 (Ont. C.A.).

122 (1982), 2 C.C.C. (3d) 57 at 64n. Leave to appeal to S.C.C. granted 2 C.C.C. (3d) 57 at 64n.

123 See *R. v. Walters* (1982), 2 C.C.C. (3d) 512.

124 See E. Ratushny, "The Role of the Accused in the Criminal Process" in W. S. Tarnopolsky and G. A. Beaudoin, *The Canadian Charter of Rights and Freedoms: Commentary* (Toronto, Carswell Co. Ltd., 1982).

125 See R. Cross, *Evidence*, 5th ed., (London, Butterworth's, 1979) at p. 413.

126 *Report on Evidence* (Ottawa, 1975), s. 56.

127 Killeen J. in *R. v. Pelley* (1983), 34 C.R. (3d) 385 (Ont. Co. Ct.).

128 See *Kienapple v. R.* (1974), 15 C.C.C. (2d) 524 (S.C.C.).

129 See cases listed in note 16, *supra*.

130 See *Gushue v. R.* (1979), 50 C.C.C. (2d) 417 (S.C.C.).

offences.[131] I say the above with some hesitation, however, because Dickson J., in an extrajudicial statement, indicated that section 11(h) would have a wider impact. "The *Kienapple* principle", he said,[132] "now has constitutional status under section 11(h) of the Charter." One of the two appeal court decisions which dealt with double jeopardy was the Manitoba Court of Appeal decision in *Regina v. Burrows*[133] in which the court held that a stay of proceedings was not a final acquittal within the meaning of the section. The second was an Ontario Court of Appeal decision, *Regina v. Krug*,[134] which simply adopted the trial judge's view that multiple convictions are permissible for theft and for an offence under section 83, using a firearm in the commission of an offence. This case is to be heard by the Supreme Court of Canada and so Dickson J. will, in fact, have the final say on the application of the *Kienapple* principle. I predict that the clause will continue to be narrowly construed. The word "finally" in the Charter provision makes it clear that new trials can be ordered following an appeal from a conviction and reasonably clear that, unlike the situation in England or the United States, appeals from an acquittal are permitted in certain cases.

There is a danger that the constitutional provision will stultify the development of non-constitutional criminal law rules by appearing to codify the double jeopardy principles. Of course the Charter does no such thing: section 26 clearly states that the Charter should not be "construed as denying the existence of any other rights or freedoms that exist in Canada".

Section 11(i) provides: "if found guilty of the offence and if the punishment for the offence has been varied between the time of commission and the time of sentencing, to the benefit of the lesser punishment." This is a relatively unimportant provision to be in a Constitution. The Interpretation Act[135] already makes this a rule of interpretation. Not surprisingly, there are as yet no court of appeal cases on the section. No doubt this provision was introduced into the Charter because of Article 15 of the U.N. Covenant which states: "Nor shall a heavier penalty be imposed than the one that was applicable at the time when the criminal offence was committed. If, subsequent to the commission of the

---

131 Section 538 of the Criminal Code. See generally, Friedland, *Double Jeopardy* (Oxford, Clarendon Press, 1969). These other aspects of double jeopardy could, however, come within s. 7 or 11(d).

132 Address to the Canadian Association of Provincial Judges, Saskatoon, September, 1982, appended to *R. v. Hayden* (1983), 33 C.R. (3d) 363 (Man. Q.B.).

133 (1983), 22 Man. R. (2d) 241 (C.A.). Leave to appeal to S.C.C. granted 22 Man. R. (2d) 240 (S.C.C.).

134 (1983), 7 C.C.C. (3d) 324 at 337 (Ont. C.A.). Leave to appeal to S.C.C. granted 7 C.C.C. (3d) 324 at 337n.

135 R.S.C. 1970, c. I-23, s. 36(e).

offence, provision is made by law for the imposition of a lighter penalty, the offender shall benefit thereby". Note, however, that not all of the U.N. Covenant Articles are covered in the Charter. For example, the Covenant specifies a "right to his conviction and sentence being reviewed by a higher tribunal according to law",[136] and for "compensation" in certain cases when there has been a miscarriage of justice,[137] but these are not contained in the Charter. One of the provisions in the U.N. Covenant, understandably not reproduced in the Charter, is a section which clearly dates the Covenant to a period before the decline of the "rehabilitative ideal" which started in about the mid-60s. The Covenant, which was adopted by the U.N. General Assembly in 1966 states (Article 10(3)): "The penitentiary system shall comprise treatment of prisoners the essential aim of which shall be their reformation and social rehabilitation". One rarely hears talk about rehabilitation in a prison setting today.

14. "CRUEL AND UNUSUAL TREATMENT OR PUNISHMENT"

The final provision I will deal with is section 12, "cruel and unusual treatment or punishment": "Everyone has the right not to be subjected to any cruel and unusual treatment or punishment." A similar provision is found in the Bill of Rights, where the words have been given effect in only one case; in *McCann*[138] the section was used to declare that the form of solitary confinement used in a British Columbia penitentiary was cruel and unusual.

Thus far, I have found only one court of appeal case which has discussed the section under the Charter. In *Regina v. Randall and Weir*[139] the accused argued that her seven-year minimum sentence for importing marijuana into Canada breached section 12. The case was argued without the assistance of counsel and the Court rejected the argument, saying simply that "The sentence cannot be considered 'cruel and unusual treatment or punishment'." The Ontario Court of Appeal in *Regina v. Shand*[140] had reached the same result in a pre-Charter Bill of Rights case. Will it maintain that position under the Charter? The words "cruel and unusual" were the subject of analysis in the 1976 case of *Regina v. Miller and Cockriel*[141] where the Supreme Court of Canada unanimously held that the

---

136 U.N. Covenant, s. 14(5).

137 *Ibid.* s. 14(6).

138 *McCann v. R.* (1975), 29 C.C.C. (2d) 337 (F.C.T.D.); *cf. R. v. Bruce, Wilson and Lucas* (1977), 36 C.C.C. (2d) 158 (B.C.S.C.). See also Michael Jackson, *Prisons of Isolation: An Analysis of Solitary Confinement in the Canadian Penitentiary* (Toronto, U. of T. Press, 1983).

139 (1983), 58 N.S.R. (2d) 234 (C.A.).

140 (1976), 30 C.C.C. (2d) 23. Leave to appeal an 8-year importing sentence was granted by the S.C.C. in a B.C. case, *R. v. Smith* on April 24, 1984.

141 (1976), 31 C.C.C. (2d) 177.

imposition of capital punishment was not cruel and unusual punishment. It seems likely that under the Charter Laskin C.J.C.'s concurring opinion that the words "cruel and unusual" are "interacting expressions colouring each other, so to speak, and hence, to be considered together as a compendious expression of a norm" will be preferred over the majority's view that the conduct must be both cruel and unusual.[142]

Several trial judges have dealt with the section in relation to prison conditions, both before and after conviction. Although the courts show a reluctance to interfere with prison administration, there are indications that they would be prepared to interfere in a proper case. A Federal Court judge, Dubé J., in *Collin v. Kaplan*[143] held that, on the facts presented, "double-celling" of convicted persons did not breach the section, noting that the situation was to be temporary. A Saskatchewan judge, Sirois J., examined pretrial incarceration in Saskatchewan[144] and held that the various concerns complained of were reasonable restrictions under section 1, stating: "The institution may and certainly must place restrictions and limitations on the rights of the applicants so that sufficient security will ensure that they will remain in custody and will not pose a danger to themselves or to other inmates or staff." So, for example, the court did not condemn the practice of transporting the prisoners "with their hands handcuffed behind their back and their legs in shackles". The court warned, however, that "if there were no valid reasons for using handcuffs and shackles on a particular case, and these were in fact used then that would or could constitute cruel and unusual treatment or punishment." The court also upheld the prison rules respecting visitation as well as strip searches after visits. All the procedures were upheld, with the exception of denial of the right to vote which the court held violated section 3 of the Charter. Mr. Justice McDonald in Alberta arrived at a similar result,[145] agreeing with the Saskatchewan judge that "Courts do not sit to superintend the administration of the jail and penitentiary systems." McDonald J. upheld a directive limiting contact visits to monthly visits as well as such other practices as visual strip searches (even "in the absence of reasonable and probable cause to believe that the

---

142 Laskin C.J.C.'s approach was adopted by Linden J. in *Mitchell and R., Re* (1983), 42 O.R. (2d) 481 (H.C.) and by Mahoney J. in *Re Gittens and R.* (1982), 68 C.C.C. (2d) 438 (Fed. Ct. T.D.).

143 (1982), 1 C.C.C. (3d) 309 (Fed. Ct. T.D.).

144 *Re Maltby et al. and A.G. Sask.* (1982), 2 C.C.C. (3d) 153 (Sask. Q.B.).

145 *Soenen v. Director of Edmonton Remand Centre* (1983), 35 C.R. (3d) 206 (Alta. Q.B.). McDonald J. points out that the comparable American provision speaks of "cruel and unusual punishment" whereas ours speaks of "treatment or punishment" and "treatment" is a more general word than "punishment". He warns of the danger, therefore, of relying too heavily on American cases.

prisoner being searched has concealed an object in his body-cavity") and the use of pesticides.

15. CONCLUSION

The courts have clearly interpreted the Charter more liberally than the similar provisions in the Bill of Rights. There is no ambiguity in the Charter as to the power to strike down legislation or to grant an appropriate remedy for breach of the Charter as there is in the Bill of Rights. Many courts have pointed out that the Charter is now part of the Constitution and not just a statute, or even a "quasi-constitutional" document, as Laskin C.J.C. called the Bill of Rights in *Hogan v. The Queen*[146] and *Regina v. Miller and Cockriell.*[147]

Parliamentarians, the legal profession, and the public expect the courts to be more involved in policy issues than in the past — and, to a considerable extent, the Courts have attempted to meet these expectations. The courts seem prepared to travel beyond the "frozen concepts" doctrine which has characterized the interpretation of the Bill of Rights[148] and onto the more fertile plain of Lord Sankey's "living tree"[149] concept, in which the Canadian Constitution is "capable of growth and expansion within its natural limits." As stated earlier, the changes that have been made by the courts have been of a marginal nature; still, the changes have been important, taking some of the harshness out of some laws and further individualizing the criminal justice system. In the pre-Charter case, *Attorney General of Quebec v. Blaikie,*[150] dealing with language rights under the Constitution Act, the Supreme Court, in a unanimous judgment, stated that the court should avoid "overly technical" interpretations of constitutional guarantees so as to give them "a broad interpretation attuned to changing circumstances". A broad, but careful, approach has been given by the appeal courts so far, and undoubtedly a similar approach will be taken by the Supreme Court to the Canadian Charter of Rights and Freedoms.

---

146 (1974), 18 C.C.C. (2d) 65 at 81 (S.C.C.).

147 (1976), 31 C.C.C. (2d) 177 at 184 (S.C.C.).

148 See generally, Tarnopolsky, "The Historical and Constitutional Context of the Proposed Canadian Charter of Rights and Freedoms" (1981) 44 Law and Contemporary Problems 169.

149 *Edwards v. A.G. Can.*, [1930] A.C. 124 at 136 (P.C.).

150 (1979), 49 C.C.C. (2d) 359 at 368. See also *Minister of Home Affairs v. Fisher,* [1980] A.C. 319 at 328, in which Lord Wilberforce stated for the Privy Council that the Bermuda Constitution should be given "a generous interpretation avoiding what has been called 'the austerity of tabulated legalism'."

8

A CENTURY OF CRIMINAL JUSTICE*

In order to show the changes in Canadian criminal law and procedure over the past century I will analyze a number of murder trials which took place in Ontario exactly 100 years ago and consider how similar trials would be conducted today.

1. INTRODUCTION

First, let me say how the cases were selected. The Public Archives of Canada contains very full records of capital cases for which the Minister of Justice had to decide whether to recommend to the Governor General that a reprieve be granted.[1] Murder and, of course, treason[2] were the only capital offences at the time. In 1882 there were only eight murder convictions in all of Canada, including the West, which certainly confirms the view of historians that Canada was a more peaceable and law-abiding country than our neighbour to the south. And it still is: the per capita murder rate in the United States is four times the Canadian rate. Out of the eight Canadian cases in 1882, five occurred in Ontario and I have selected three of these for discussion in this paper.[3]

Murder cases may not be typical of other offences, but they do illustrate how major criminal trials were conducted. Moreover, transcripts for non-murder cases are not available for trials that took place 100 years ago because there were then no appeals in criminal cases and so transcripts were not prepared. They were prepared in capital cases, for the use of the Minister of Justice, and contain a vast reservoir of information for legal historians.

---

* This paper was prepared for the Annual Meeting of the Royal Society of Canada held in Ottawa, June, 1982, celebrating the 100th anniversary of the founding of the Society and was published in (1982) 20 Transactions of the Royal Society of Canada, 285, reprinted in (1982) 16 Law Society of Upper Canada Gazette 336. I am indebted to Justices John Arnup and G. Arthur Martin of the Ontario Court of Appeal and to Professors John Beattie, Department of History, and R.C.B. Risk, Faculty of Law, University of Toronto, for reading and commenting on an earlier version of this paper.

1 RG 13 c-1, vol. 1419. In addition, the Ontario Archives has Assize Records (RG 22) for each county, which contain additional, although sketchy, information on the cases. Further, the *Globe* and, of course, local papers contain very full coverage of all the trials.

2 The only treason case close to 1882 was the trial of Louis Riel in 1885.

3 The non-Ontario cases do not contain trial transcripts and so are less useful. The file of one of the Ontario cases is missing and another case (dealing with insanity) is similar to one of the cases selected.

The three trials took place in Napanee, Milton, and Toronto. After studying these cases, and looking at other cases around that time, I am struck by the fact that the trial of serious criminal cases has not changed as much in the past 100 years as almost all other areas of the law and, indeed, of society. There have been changes of course — many of them very significant. Still, the present-day lawyer would feel very much at home in courtroom 100 years ago, and the lawyers of that time would be surprised at how little change has occurred over the course of the century.

The judge then and now would be a Supreme Court of Ontario judge travelling on circuit from Toronto. There are, of course, many more Ontario High Court trial judges today: about forty-five compared to nine 100 years ago, but this is not much greater than the fourfold growth in the population and far less than in other areas of the criminal justice system, such as the spectacular growth in the number of police officers, from under 1,500 in 1882 for all of Canada to over 60,000 in 1982 — a forty-fold increase.[4] Counsel and the judge would be dressed in much the same gowns now as then. In some cases the same courtroom would be used. The Napanee courthouse is still in use (the fluorescent fixtures are new, of course) and the Milton courthouse was used until a few years ago.[5] The Toronto Courthouse of 1882 is now, appropriately, the Adelaide Court Theatre. Counsel from the past would no doubt be surprised at the number of women lawyers today — now about one-third of the graduating class. Women were not admitted to the bar until the 1890s in Ontario, the first jurisdiction in the British Empire to admit female lawyers[6] Counsel from the past would certainly be surprised at the large number of Queen's Counsel practising in Ontario. The present-day lawyer might, perhaps, be surprised at the number of Irishmen practising law 100 years ago. There were four times as many persons with Irish backgrounds entering the legal profession in Ontario in the middle of the last century than persons with English backgrounds.[7] In general, though, the various participants in the trial, including the accused, would be much the same today as 100 years ago.

The locale of murders change over time, reflecting changes in society. One of the three murders took place on a farm, and another in a stable. And the weapons have changed: two of the three murders were committed

---

4 See the Government of Canada policy paper, *The Criminal Law in Canadian Society* (Ottawa, 1982).

5 Early Ontario courthouses are described in M. MacRae and A. Adamson, *Cornerstones of Order: Courthouses and Town Halls of Ontario 1783-1914* (Toronto, Clarke Irwin, 1983).

6 See Wright, "Admission of Women to the Bar: An Historical Note" (1982), 16 Law Society Gazette 42.

7 See G. B. Baker, "Legal Education in Upper Canada 1785-1889" in D. H. Flaherty, ed., *Essays in the History of Canadian Law*, Vol. II (Toronto; University of Toronto Press, 1983).

with an axe, a weapon which is rarely used today. The motives, however, have not changed over the years — jealousy, anger, and revenge will be with us for some time.

Before turning to the individual cases, I want to point out that there was no Canadian Criminal Code in 1882. (Indirectly, this lack of codification may, in part, be traced to the influence of the English Royal Society.) Today, the criminal law is contained in the Criminal Code, a statute first passed by Parliament in 1892.[8] In 1882, however, the criminal law of Canada was contained in various statutes and in the judge-made common law. The law of murder was found solely in the common law. England still does not have a Criminal Code. One of the main reasons why there has always been strong resistance to codification in common-law jurisdictions, but widespread acceptance of the concept in continental law, may be because of the close identification of legal and scientific thought in England in the seventeenth century.[9] One of the most famous scientists of the time, Sir Francis Bacon, was also one of the most famous jurists, and lawyers were actively involved in the work of the Royal Society, which was founded in London in 1662. The English Royal Society was, in fact, begun in a lawyer's chamber in the Middle Temple, and some of the earliest presidents of the Society were lawyers. Lawyers were part of the intellectual community and were influenced by and, in turn, influenced scientific ideas. The Chief Justice of England, Sir Matthew Hale, like Lord Chancellor Bacon, was both a lawyer and a scientist, and believed in the inductive approach to knowledge. In 1677, for example, he published *Observations touching the Principles of Natural Motions, and especially touching Rarefaction and Condensation.* He was also a great jurist and the first major writer on the criminal law in England. I see a close relationship, therefore, between the Baconian method of scientific empiricism and the common law case-by-case method of building general principles from specific instances. Both use the inductive approach. Similarly, one can see a close relationship between the continental Cartesian method of deductive analysis and the concept of codification, which necessarily goes from general principles to specific applications. But I am getting out of my depth and, like a good common-law lawyer, I will return to specific cases.

2. THE HIGH PARK CASE

The first murder case took place in High Park in Toronto during the summer of 1882. Part of High Park had been given to the city by the archi-

---

8 The Criminal Code, 1892, c. 29.

9 See the fine article, Shapiro, "Law and Science in Seventeenth-Century England" (1969). 21 Stanford L. Rev. 727 on which I have relied for much of the factual material in this paragraph.

tect John Howard in 1873 in exchange for a yearly pension.[10] The southern part of what is now High Park, including Grenadier Pond, was kept by Howard as his private property and was only to become city property at his death. Not only did the city give John Howard a pension, but they provided him with a constable, John Albert, to keep trespassers off his property. Albert was kept very busy that summer, at the urging of John Howard, trying to keep the nearby Parkdale children from using Grenadier Pond.

On Sunday, 23 July 1882, just before noon, a seventeen-year-old boy, Andrew Young, was boating on the pond with some of his friends. Constable Albert went to the pond, fired a warning shot in the air, and when the boat landed on the shore ran after Young. Constable Albert's gun went off and the bullet went through Young's head, causing his almost immediate death. A witness had heard Albert shout "Stop or I'll shoot." The Crown Attorney charged Albert with murder, claiming the shooting was intentional.

The trial took place at the next assizes, on 12 October 1882, within three months of the killing. Aemilius Irving, Q.C., later the Treasurer of the Law Society of Upper Canada for a remarkable twenty-year span, prosecuted; Nicholas Murphy defended. The Milton trial also took place at the next assizes, also within three months of the killing. The Napanee case took a little over six months before it was tried, but, as we will see, it was complicated by psychiatric evidence. Today, of course, it takes considerably longer before a case is heard. Not only does it take longer before the case is tried, but the trial lasts much longer today. While preparing this section I called the Crown Attorney's offices in Napanee and Milton to get some comparative figures. The Napanee Crown Attorney was not in; his secretary told me that he was then on the third week of a murder case. I did speak to the assistant Crown Attorney for Milton just before he was to enter court for the fourth week of the murder case he was then prosecuting.

In contrast, the High Park case took one day to try, the Milton case two days, and the Napanee case three days. Some of the reasons for the lengthening of trials over the years will become apparent as we examine each case. One reason for delay before trial today is that some of those accused of murder are released on bail pending their trial, thus decreasing the pressure for an early hearing. None of the three accused in 1882 was released before trial. Four out of the six persons tried for murder in Milton over the past year were released on bail.

The issue in the Albert case was a simple one. Did the gun go off by accident, or did Albert intentionally shoot the lad? Albert was convicted of

---

10 See *Dictionary of Canadian Biography* (Toronto, University of Toronto Press, 1982), Volume XI, at pp. 426-8.

murder by the jury, with a strong recommendation for mercy, and was sentenced to be hanged. I must say that after reading the file and the transcript I probably would have acquitted Albert of murder. The evidence indicated that Albert was right-handed but was holding the gun, with which he was unfamiliar, in his left hand.

Would Albert be convicted today? Although the law is essentially the same today as it was then, there are two major differences in procedure which might affect the outcome. The first is that 100 years ago the accused was not permitted to give evidence at his trial. The reason was that he was disqualified because of his interest in the outcome — not a particularly persuasive reason for excluding him. In 1893[11] the rule was changed in Canada, and in 1898[12] in England. Indeed, in 1882[13] some of the judges in England, and in the late 1880's[14] some in Canada, permitted the accused to give unsworn evidence from the dock. But in 1882 this was not yet permitted in Canada and so the jury in the Albert case never heard Albert give his version of the story. Today he would almost certainly go into the witness box.

Another crucial change over the last 100 years is that the presumption of innocence is now more solidly a part of our law than it was then. The change came about because of the House of Lords' case of *Woolmington v. D.P.P.*[15] in 1935. Until 1935 — and in the Albert case the trial judge would have so told the jury — the onus was on the Crown to show that the accused committed the physical act but on the *accused* to satisfy the jury that the shooting was accidental. After *Woolmington* the onus of showing that it was *not* an accident was on the Crown, and the Crown had to show this *beyond a reasonable doubt*. So Constable Albert today probably would not have been convicted of murder, although he may well have been convicted of manslaughter because of his recklessness.

Albert was sentenced to be hanged on 10 November 1882. The focus then shifted to the Minister of Justice in Ottawa. There was then no right of appeal on matters of law or fact in criminal cases. Appeals would delay the desired deterrent effect of a hanging. Appeals in criminal cases were not introduced in Canada until 1892[16] and not until 1907[17] in England. In the Albert case, petitions to commute the sentence were sent to the Minister of Justice by all twelve jurymen, by the major and aldermen of Toronto, by the three Toronto M.P.'s, by many of the police officers in Toronto, and by a large

11 Canada Evidence Act, 1893, c. 31.

12 Criminal Evidence Act, 1898, 61 & 62 Vict., c. 36.

13 See R. v. Shimmin (1882), 15 Cox C.C. 122 per Cave J.

14 See R. v. Rogers (1888), 1 B.C.L.R. (part 2) 119 per Crease J.

15 [1935] A.C. 462.

16 Canadian Criminal Code, S.C. 1892, c. 29, s. 742.

17 Criminal Appeal Act 1907, 7 Edw. 7, c. 23.

number of influential citizens. The Chief Constable of York pointed out that Albert's "obnoxious . . . vigilant conduct" in the park over the years may have influenced the jury. The Minister (actually the Governor General on the recommendation of the Cabinet) commuted the sentence to twenty years in the penitentiary, which at that time meant Kingston penitentiary. There was then only one class of penitentiary, maximum security, with a harsh regimen.

What would happen in a similar case today? Capital punishment was officially abolished in Canada in 1976[18] and Albert would today have been sentenced to life imprisonment. There are now two classes of murder, first- and second-degree murder. Albert's case would today be classified as second-degree murder because it would not be considered "planned and deliberate," one of the categories of first-degree murder.[19] After the Albert jury had been out about three hours they returned and asked whether the required "intent" or, as it was then called, "malice," had to be present more than two minutes before the shooting. The trial Judge told them that "if the malice exists at the time the act is done which caused death, that is sufficient." Fifteen minutes later the jury returned the verdict of guilty. So the result today, assuming the jury found Albert guilty of murder, would be life imprisonment, without eligibility for parole for ten years.[20] Note that the decision to release today is made by the Parole Board acting under the Parole Act.[21] This is a relatively new institution, having been introduced in Canada in its present form only in 1959.[22] Before that, the release was under what was called the Ticket of Leave Act enacted in 1899.[23] In 1882 release was through the Governor General's Royal prerogative of mercy on the recommendation of the Minister of Justice.[24]

The parole system and the Ticket of Leave Act were part of the renewed quest for the rehabilitation of offenders in a prison setting. Deterrence and retribution, the principal objectives of the penal system in 1882, were replaced by rehabilitation. The influential Archambault Royal Commission on the Penal System of Canada,[25] for example, reported in 1938 that "it is admitted by all the foremost students of penology that the revengeful or retributive character of punishment should be completely

---

18 Criminal Law Amendment Act (No. 2), 1976, c. 105.

19 S. 214 of the Criminal Code.

20 *Ibid.*, s. 669.

21 R.S.C. 1970, c. P-2.

22 See the Report of the Canadian Committee on Corrections (the Ouimet Report) (Ottawa, 1969) at p. 333.

23 C. 49.

24 Ouimet Report at p. 332.

25 Report of the Royal Commission to Investigate the Penal System of Canada (Ottawa, 1938), at p. 9.

eliminated, and that the deterrent effect of punishment alone . . . is practically valueless . . ." The Commission recommended that "the task of the prison should be . . . the *transformation* of reformable criminals into law abiding citizens."[26] In the 1960s, however, a revolution occurred in penal philosophy and the quest for the "rehabilitative ideal" was jettisoned by many influential writers[27] — in my opinion jettisoned a little too vigorously. A number of American states have now eliminated parole and introduced fixed sentences. Normally change comes slowly and gradually in the law; the abandonment of rehabilitation through the penal system may be one of the very few revolutions in thought (as the concept is used by Thomas Kuhn)[28] in the law. So we have come almost full circle in the last century on the central issue of penal policy.

A great effort was made over the years to have Albert released, but without success. Many of the letters stressed the hardship faced by Albert's wife, who had to raise six children herself. There is a poignant letter in the file to the Minister of Justice from Mrs. Albert in 1890 where she says: "My health is now failing me, and our three younger children are still unable to support themselves." These were the days before public welfare, and the family of the convict suffered greatly. But so did the family of the deceased. There was then no scheme, as there is now, for compensating victims of crime. The deceased boy's sister wrote to the papers stating: "I hope the public will not forget the cruel way in which he deprived my mother of a son and an honest support." Perhaps the main reason why Albert was not released was because the trial judge was against it. Mr. Justice Armour took an extremely harsh position, reporting several years later that "If ever there was a case of murder this was one and deserved the extreme penalty of the law."

3. THE MILTON CASE

The second murder, in this case a double murder, of eighty-five-year old Edward Maher and his thirty-five-year-old daughter Bridget, occurred in a farmhouse near Hamilton. The trial took place at the Milton Assizes. Michael O'Rourke, the accused, had worked on the farm cutting wood. On the evening of the murders in January 1882, he appeared at a neighbour's farmhouse and told of quitting his job that morning, drinking in town, and then returning to the Mahers later that night to pay a visit. The farmer's daughter, O'Rourke said, was sitting on his knee with

---

26 *Ibid.*

27 Perhaps the most influential legal article was Francis Allen, "Criminal Justice, Legal Values and the Rehabilitative Ideal" (1959), 50 J. Crim. L.C. & P.S. 226. An earlier important article by a non-lawyer was C.S. Lewis, 'The Humanitarian Theory of Punishment' (1953), 6 Res Judicatae 224.

28 T.A. Kuhn, *The Structure of Scientific Revolutions* 2nd ed. (Chicago, University of Chicago Press, 1970).

her arms around his neck when her brother appeared and was so infuriated that he killed her and their father and wounded him, O'Rourke. The next morning the police set out to arrest the brother, but did not do so because that morning O'Rourke made a confession of guilt.

An officer staying with the injured O'Rourke suggested that Bridget Maher had been "violated" by O'Rourke, and O'Rourke is alleged to have said: "I neither ravished her before I killed her or after." When the officer asked whom he killed first, O'Rourke replied: "The old man first; now you have it." O'Rourke later gave a fuller confession which was taken down in writing and acknowledged with O'Rourke's mark.

The crucial issue in the case, as in so many murder cases today, was the admissibility of the confession. In the nineteenth century the judges were more inclined to exclude a confession than they are today.[29] Today, the underlying question is simply: "Is the statement freely and voluntarily made?"[30] One hundred years ago there was a far better chance of having the statement excluded on a technicality. In 1881 Lord Coleridge, the Chief Justice of England, had adopted the view that "a confession, in order to be admissible, must be free and voluntary: that is, must not be extracted by any sort of threats or violence, nor obtained by any direct or implied promises, *however slight*, nor by the exertion of any improper influence."[31] I stress the words "however slight." The defence concentrated on trying to show that the police officer had improperly questioned O'Rourke. A witness claimed to have heard the officer say: "You are guilty, Michael, and you had better confess at once; it will be better for you." The officer denied making the statement. The transcript does not contain counsel's argument, but no doubt defence counsel also argued that the liquor the police gave O'Rourke that morning was an improper inducement. The Judge, Mr. Justice Cameron, ruled that the confession was admissible. The almost inevitable result was that O'Rourke was found guilty of murder and was sentenced to be hanged.

It came as a surprise to me to note that the evidence respecting the admissibility of the confession was heard in the presence of the jury. Today, the evidence would be heard in what is referred to as a *voir dire*, that is, a trial within a trial, in the absence of the jury.[32] The reason for a *voir dire* is that a jury would not be able to disregard the prejudicial evidence if the trial judge excluded the confession. Today, if the confession is held to be admissible, the evidence is then presented before the jury. The present practice is certainly much fairer to the accused, but it necessarily results in

---

29   See *Wigmore on Evidence,* Volume III (Chadbourn Edition, Boston, Little, Brown, 1970) at pp. 297 *et seq.*

30   *Boudreau v. R.* (1949), 94 C.C.C. 1 at 8 (S.C.C.) *per* Rand J.

31   *R. v. Fennell* (1881), 7 Q.B.D. 147 at 151 (my italics).

32   See *e.g., R. v. Viau* (1898), 7 Que. Q.B. 362 (C.A.), appeal quashed 29 S.C.R. 90; *R. v. Sonyer* (1898), 2 C.C.C. 501 (B.C.C.A.); *R. v. De Mesquito* (1915), 24 C.C.C. 407 (B.C.C.A.).

a much lengthier trial because if the confession is admitted much of the evidence is heard twice.

Another factor in causing lengthier trials today is that legal aid is now available, but was not then. The defence counsel, Murphy, the same counsel who had lost the High Park case, took the case as an act of charity and later admitted that the conduct of the accused's defence was not as good as it might have been. Indeed, he used this as a reason why the Minister of Justice should commute the sentence: "The jury would have been justified on the evidence in finding a verdict of manslaughter and perhaps would have done so, had the case for the defence been marked up [i.e., with a fee] as capital cases usually are and not by counsel without funds at his command and who was only imported into the case as an act of charity towards the unfortunate O'Rourke." Crown counsel was B.B. Osler, Q.C.,[33] the brother of the famous doctor, and the person who successfully prosecuted Louis Riel for treason three years later. Osler, who, I might add, was the first professor of criminal law at the University of Toronto, was a partner in the seven man firm of McCarthy, Osler, Hoskin and Creelman. The firm split some years later, one part growing into the well-known firm of McCarthy & McCarthy, and the other half into the equally well-known firm of Osler, Hoskin & Harcourt, each of which now has well over 100 lawyers. So this aside tells us something about the growth of the legal profession in Ontario. As a further aside, I should note that the Osler, Hoskin firm does not handle murder cases today.

A striking difference between the O'Rourke case and a similar case today is the almost complete absence of scientific evidence then introduced by the Crown. Such evidence is now standard practice in similar cases. Today, scientists at the Centre of Forensic Sciences in Toronto would provide evidence dealing with blood types, fingerprints, possible semen stains, hair fibres, and many other pieces of circumstantial evidence. Much of this type of evidence was not available a century ago. Even when it was available, being circumstantial evidence, it was considered suspect and a special warning, now no longer strictly required,[34] had to be given to the jury. The growth in scientific evidence in criminal trials again causes trials today to be lengthier than in the past.

Murphy, the defence counsel, to his credit, did not abandon the case after the conviction. He obtained the Attorney General's consent to appeal the conviction by way of Writ of Error, a very limited technical form of appeal. As I mentioned earlier, there was then no general right of appeal in criminal cases. A Writ of Error was used to attack convictions on formal

---

33 See Note, "B.B. Osler" (1968), 2 Law Society Gazette 27.
34 See *R. v. Cooper* (1977), 34 C.C.C. (2d) 18 (S.C.C.).

grounds,[35] and in this case Murphy repeated before the Queen's Bench Division of Ontario[36] the argument that he had made at the commencement of the trial: that the jury were improperly chosen (technically referred to as "challenging the array"). There were two grounds to his argument. The first was that all the members of the jury had been chosen from the same letter of the alphabet — apparently the letter "P"; the second was that the federal Parliament, which was responsible for criminal law and procedure under the British North America Act,[37] had improperly delegated the responsibility for determining the qualifications for jury service to the provinces. In December 1882, the Divisional Court dismissed the appeal[38] on both grounds; the Minister of Justice recommended that "the law be allowed to take its course", and on Friday, 5 January 1883, Michael O'Rourke was hanged in the Milton jail.

Would O'Rourke be convicted of murder today? There is little doubt that the confession would now also be admissible. But I believe that there would be a very good chance for a manslaughter verdict on the basis that drunkenness may have affected O'Rourke's mental state. One hundred years ago, to quote from another case in 1882,[39] "drunkenness in the slayer at the moment of causing death was no answer to the charge either in whole or in part."

4. THE NAPANEE CASE

The final case to be explored here is *The Queen v Michael Lee* involving a murder in the spring of 1882 in Napanee. The defence was insanity. Lee admitted killing eighteen-year-old Maggie Howie with an axe in the stable attached to the hotel where they both worked. They had been engaged, but the night before the murder she had given him back the engagement ring. Apparently she had discovered that he was keeping a mistress. The next morning when she went to the stable to milk the cow he struck her with the axe which he had hidden under his coat. The only question at the trial was whether he was insane at the time the act was committed. The case is still well known in eastern Ontario because of the folk-song "Maggie Howie," which starts with the words

I am an Irishman by birth, my name is Michael Lee.
I fell in love with a pretty girl, which proved my destiny.

---

35 See generally, M.L. Friedland, *Double Jeopardy* (Oxford, Clarendon Press, 1969) at pp. 238 *et seq.*

36 *R. v. O'Rourke* (1882), 1 O.R. 464. The trial judge had reserved the case at trial for hearing by the Common Pleas Division, but that Court held that it was not a proper case for reserving a point of law: see (1882), 32 C.P. 388.

37 S. 91(27).

38 *Supra*, note 36.

39 *R. v. Marcel* (1882), RG 13 c-1, Vol. 1419, No. 160.

It ends with the verse:

So it's now I am a prisoner in the town of Napanee,
It's there I'll stand my trial and the judge will sentence me.
For I know that I am guilty and I do deserve to die
For the murder of my own true love upon the gallows high.

The folk-song contains no mention of the insanity defence.

The case has a particularly modern flavour because cases today still result in the same clash of psychiatrists and there continues to be controversy over the proper test for insanity. There was evidence that Lee had had delusions in the past: he believed persons were trying to poison him and were shooting symbolic arrows at him. Moreover, he saw special signs in ordinary conduct. A number of his cousins had already been committed to mental institutions.

Two highly respected psychiatrists, at the request of the Crown, examined Lee shortly before the trial: Dr W. G. Metcalfe, the medical head of the 400-bed Kingston Asylum for the Insane, and Dr Daniel Clark, the medical superintendent of the 700-bed Queen Street Lunatic Asylum in Toronto. Clark was the predecessor at the Asylum of Dr C. K. Clarke, after whom the Clarke Institute of Psychiatry is named, although they were not related. It is worth noting that the number of beds in the Queen Street Mental Health Centre is under 600 today, compared to 700 a century ago, and of the 600, less than 100 persons at any one time are compulsorily confined. One hundred years ago everyone in the institution was held compulsorily. Science has produced drugs to control mental instability, but not criminal activity.

Clark and Metcalfe were not called by the Crown. Their evidence strongly supported insanity, and so they were called by the defence. Clark (Metcalfe's evidence was similar) testified that Lee was suffering from "acute dementia" and should not be considered responsible for his act. Was Lee faking? Clark was sure he was not: Q: "You have no doubt in your mind at all?" A: "No doubt in my own mind at all." A few years later Clark was one of the principal defence witnesses in the treason trial of Louis Riel, but on that occasion he was much more cautious in his testimony, stating, 'I assume. . . that not only the evidence given is correct, but that he was not a deceiver.' Some writers consider that Clark's weak "assumption" rather than a positive "belief" may have been responsible for the failure of Riel's insanity defence.[40]

Clark disagreed with the legal view of insanity derived from the well-

40   See G.F.G. Stanley, *Louis Riel* (Toronto, McGraw-Hill Ryerson, 1963) at p. 353; Verdun-Jones, "The Evolution of the Defences of Insanity and Automatism in Canada from 1843 to 1979: A Saga of Judicial Reluctance to Sever the Umbilical Cord to the Mother Country?" (1979), 14 U.B.C.L. Rev. 1 at p. 9.

known M'Naghten Rules of 1843,[41] still the basis of the test in Canada[42] M'Naghten's case had decided that an accused is insane if "at the time of the committing of the act the party accused was labouring under such a defect of reason, from disease of the mind, as not to know the nature and quality of the act he was doing, or, if he did know it, that he did not know he was doing what was wrong." Clark testified: "I say right and wrong is no test of insanity." Moreover, he disagreed with the view that a person could have delusions but be in other respects sane: "I don't believe at all in partial insanity." One interesting question asked by the Crown in cross-examination dates the trial: "What do you say about the general appearance and formation of the person's head?" I like Clark's reply: "There is nothing in that. Most of us would not like to be judged by the shape of our head."

The trial judge's charge to the jury left them little choice other than to reject insanity. Chief Justice Wilson did not agree with Clark's idea about the unity of the mind:

> It does not it seems to me follow that if a mind is deranged on one subject it is deranged altogether. Dr. Clark and the other gentleman both admitted that that was the view entertained by many professional men and I venture to say it is the view entertained by most professional men and by most people who are not professional men and it is the view which the law lays down to be the correct view; that a person may have a delusion upon some particular subject and not upon another at all.

But even if the accused was medically insane, that was not enough. Insanity is a legal test: the accused must not know the difference between right and wrong, that is, according to Chief Justice Wilson's charge to the jury, whether the act was contrary to law or not. The evidence, the Chief Justice said, showed that Lee knew the act was contrary to law. The issue whether the word "wrong" means "contrary to law" or "wrong in a moral sense" is still a live issue in Canada. A few years ago the Supreme Court of Canada in *Schwartz v. R.,*[43] a five to four decision, held that it meant "contrary" to law." The decision has been much criticized, however, and many think that the Supreme Court of Canada will reverse the decision at some future time.

The jury in the Lee case retired at 3:30 and returned at 6:00 stating that Lee was guilty and "did know the difference between right and wrong." It is likely that a jury today in the light of the *Schwartz* case, and

---

41 M'Naghten's Case (1843), 10 Cl. & Fin. 200, 8 E.R. 718.

42 S. 16(2) of the present Criminal Code states that "a person is insane when he . . . has disease of the mind to an extent that renders him incapable of appreciating the nature and quality of an act or omission or of knowing that an act or omission is wrong." The principal difference between the M'Naghten test and s. 16 is the wide meaning given by Canadian courts to the word "appreciate" in contrast to the narrow meaning given in England to the word "know": see *R. v. Cooper* (1979), 51 C.C.C. (2d) 129 (S.C.C.).

43 (1976), 29 C.C.C. (2d) 1.

assuming the Crown did not agree to accept a plea of guilty of manslaughter, would find a similar verdict. Lee was sentenced to be hanged.

Lee did not hang. His mental condition became progressively worse. The Minister of Justice commuted the sentence after further representations by a number of doctors including Dr Metcalfe, who put it quite bluntly: "I do not see what will be gained by hanging a lunatic." Even the trial judge, who was of the view in his Report to the Minister that Lee "did the act by design, knowing well the difference between right and wrong," suggested that "It may . . . be that his excellency the Governor General may not enforce a greater penalty than imprisonment for life." Lee was sent to Kingston Penitentiary where for the rest of his life he was kept in the new ward for the insane.[44]

5. CONCLUSION

The analysis of the three cases illustrates, I believe, that in the main the criminal law and the trial process have not changed much in the past 100 years. The same key arguments regarding the accused's mental state in the High Park case, the question of the admissibility of the confession in the O'Rourke case, and the issue of insanity of the accused in the Lee case could all have taken place in a courtroom today.

There have, of course, been changes, but most have taken place outside the formal structure of the trial. Techniques of police and scientific investigation have changed; legal aid is available in all serious cases; bail is more readily granted; plea bargaining is now widespread; capital punishment has been abolished; and a parole system has been brought in. Within the trial process itself perhaps the most significant changes in the past 100 years have been the placing of the onus of proof on the prosecution, giving the accused the right to give evidence on his own behalf, and the lengthening of the trial. But, in general, the criminal process has not been subject to radical change, nor is it likely to undergo such change in the future, as many of the procedures have now been included in the Charter of Rights and thus entrenched in the Constitution. So a present-day lawyer would also likely feel at home in a major criminal case a century from now.

---

44 Such a ward was kept at Kingston Penitentiary until 1915 when arrangements were made to transfer insane prisoners to provincial mental institutions: see the *Archambault Report* (1938) at p. 150. The ward, constructed in 1881, is described in Calder, "Convict Life in Canadian Federal Penitentiaries, 1867-1900" in L.A. Knafla, *Crime and Criminal Justice in Europe and Canada* (Waterloo, Wilfred Laurier University Press, 1981) at p. 308.